America:
Exploration and Travel

America:
Exploration and Travel

Steven E. Kagle
Editor

Bowling Green State University Popular Press
Bowling Green, Ohio 43403
1979

Cover design by Victoria Heninger

CONTENTS

Exploration Studies and Popular Culture

Ray B. Browne

The popular culture movement broke upon the academic scene in 1970 with something of the enthusiasm and hope that must have sustained Cortés in his drive to explore Mexico to find the much-rumored gold there or Ponce de Leon in his search for the Fountain of Youth, for the proponents of this area in academic studies realized that great riches and vitalities of youth lay for the finding. Although some of the earliest movements in popular culture studies may have resembled to some people the pioneer's slash and burn policy, those individuals seriously interested in these studies realized that exploring popular culture meant discovering new materials—and this would be of immense importance and potential—but also in using the study of these new areas to probe for new meanings and new significances for the world at large and for the individual in particular.

In a way this new study was the classic Westward movement all over again, a thrust into uncharted lands seeking whatever treasures could be found. But, contrary to the physical pioneer, the student of popular culture recognized that as much as a venture into terra incognita this new movement was also a settling down in familiar land, an exploration rather than a march through an area, an investigation of a land covered with highways and television antennas with a newer and wider lens than had conventionally be used in the past. It was indeed a recharting of old and familiar lands.

Ten years after the beginning of formal popular culture studies, the enthusiasm of the scholars is by no means diminished; they still face the West and dream new dreams. They realize that there are still many lands that need to be explored or re-explored, and the riches reaped and understood. No area is too far from or to close to home, too seemingly insignificant, too esoteric. Academics owe it to themselves and to the humanities at large to explore all possibilities. But it is also a journey over well-traveled roads, a look homeward, a stirring of old ashes.

For those reasons the study of exploration and travel is of utmost importance at this time, both in its own right and as another probe into the larger field of popular culture. It is only logical that today as we complain that there are no new horizons for us to conquer, no new challenges, we realize that the challenge is in fact right under our noses, or our feet, and that is the understanding of where we have been and where we are—in other words the challenge of exploration and understanding rather of travel. Travel gets us from one place to another—often with wonderful attendant enjoyment—but exploration makes us understand our travel, the places we travel to—and ourselves.

The essays in this collection constitute a major step toward this understanding. They open up new areas for concern and draw many valuable insights and conclusions. But most important, perhaps, they demonstrate the viability of the study of these materials. Many more studies should follow this one.

Introduction

Unaccustomed Earth:
The Movement of Americans from Travel to Exploration

Steven Kagle

In his poem "The Gift Outright," Robert Frost wrote:

> The land was ours before we were the land's,
> She was our land more than a hundred years
> Before we were her people, She was ours
> In Massachusetts, in Virginia
> But we were England's, still colonials
> Possessing what we were still unpossessed by.

In these lines and those that followed them, Frost asserted that the colonists lacked more than the name "American" to belong, that we lacked an identification with the land that could only be achieved through struggle. Frost's poem not only argues for such things as the "Declaration," the battles of the Revolution, and the new political and social order set forth by the "Constitution" and the "Bill of Rights"; he argues that we needed to give ourselves "to the land vaguely realizing westward."[1] What was necessary was a shift in the direction of attention from East to West, a shift that involved a change from travel to exploration.

Of course the colonists had moved steadily westward as individuals, but as a society their eyes were still directed eastward. One possible reason for this eastward vision was the early colonists' dependence on Europe for supplies, but their behavior seems less conditioned by such physical concerns than by intangible attitudes.[2] In their consideration of the physical world these early colonists seemed to consider where they were going to be less important than where they had been. As a result though they bordered a wilderness, they were travelers before they were explorers.

There were men who explored the frontier during the colonial period, but most of these explorers were Europeans. As Turner points out, the Atlantic coastal frontier "was the frontier of

3

Europe." It was only later as the frontier moved west that it "became more and more American."[3] The early explorers came questing to the New World but returned to the Old. When examining the diaries and autobiographies of those who were born or who settled in America during the seventeenth and eighteenth centuries, one finds that they are far richer in accounts of travel than in those of true exploration. The colonists "traveled," visiting and writing about the known world—Europe and the coastal areas already settled. Geographical and political barriers were partly responsible for this situation, but they do not adequately explain the situation especially during the two decades after the Revolution. One can find works like those of Knight and Woolman after the eighteenth century, but one rarely finds ones like those of Pike and Parkman before the nineteenth.

One example of the colonial attitude can be seen in John Winthrop's "A Modell of Christian Charity." Here Winthrop declares that New England shall be a "City on a Hill," a model for Europe to follow. Thus rather than turning their backs on their native England, these colonists kept it as a major concern and were less attentive to the frontier than they might have been. As Perry Miller pointed out in his "Errand in the Wilderness," this attitude contributed to the failure of the Puritans' experiment, because their European audience neglected them, while the frontier they devalued caused economic and cultural changes which threatened their traditional social order.

The period of the Enlightenment saw Americans remain more interested in travel than in exploration. This era was still intellectually conservative accepting changes and even a revolution as long as that change was in the direction of the eternally consistent ideal that the society believed in. As the wild frontier was further from that ideal, it had little to offer. Consequently, the end desired and expected was the imposition of civilization on the frontier.

This attitude is still apparent in the journals kept by Lewis and Clark (1804-1806). While conveying a sense of the power and immensity of the western wilderness, these journals show the explorers imposing the order of civilization on their observations. The hours and minutes of a lunar eclipse are totaled in neat columns; new plants are placed in categories and described in appropriate botanical terms; the animals are skinned or caged for further study; and, when Lewis and Clark encounter an Indian tribe that believes a certain hill is the residence of devils, the explorers march directly to it and exorcize its demons by recording the hill's size, form and location in their notebooks.

However, while Jefferson sent Lewis and Clark out as scouts for the Age of Reason, they actually helped to open America to the romantic force of the West. Their writing was literature of exploration that helped to further the consideration of exploration in American literature. For example, in his novel *Mardi* (1849) Melville could announce the mystical force of the west that had so captured the attention of his society:

West, West! West west! Witherward point Hope and prophet fingers; Witherward at sunset kneel all worshipers of fire...witherward lie heaven and hell! West, west! Witherward mankind and empires—flocks, caravans, armies, navies—worlds, suns, and stars all went! West, west! Oh, boundless boundary! eternal goal.... Beacon by which the universe is steered! Like the north star, attracting all needles! Unattainable forever, but forever leading to great things this side thyself.[4]

Significantly in the chapter in which this passage appears Melville's protagonists sailing westward reach the orient. But as in the case of many of the writers of America during this period, Melville is more concerned with direction than location.[5]

This development is expressed in "Walking"; here Thoreau states his belief "that there is a subtle magnetism in Nature, which if we unconsciously yield to it, will direct us aright. It is not indifferent to us which way we walk. There is a right way." For him that way is west, for he feels that "the future lies that way." Thoreau reverses the assumptions of the previous age in America by declaring that wildness and not civilization "is the preservation of the world." Thoreau explains: "We go eastward to realize history and study the works of art and literature, retracing the steps of the race; we go westward as into the future, with a spirit of enterprise and adventure." He exhorts his fellow Americans to be explorers rather than travelers by considering that even if only symbolically eastward migration is "retrograde movement."[6]

Hawthorne in his "Custom-House" preface to *The Scarlet Letter* writes about the effect of his family's two and a quarter century residence in Salem, Massachusetts:

This long connection of a family with one spot, as its place of birth and burial creates a kindred between the human being and the locality, quite independent of any charm in the scenery or moral circumstances that surround him. It is not love, but instinct. The new inhabitant—who came himself from some foreign land, or whose father or grandfather came— has little claim to be called a Salemite; he has no conception of the oyster-like tenacity with which the old settler, over whom his third century is creeping, clings to the spot where his successive generations have been imbedded. It is no matter that the place is joyless for him; that he is weary of the old wooded house, the mud and dust.... The spell survives, and just as powerfully as if the native spot were an earthly paradise. So it has been in my case.... This connection, which is an unhealthy one, should at last be severed. Human nature will not flourish any more than a potato, if it be planted and replanted, for too long a series of generations, in the same worn out soil. My children have had other birthplaces, and so far as their fortunes may be within my control, shall strike their roots into unaccustomed earth.[7]

It is unlikely that a similar attitude could have been expressed by Hawthorne's Puritan ancestors for whom this "unaccustomed earth" was an adversary, not a source of hybrid vigor. They, like Hawthorne's Goodman Brown, were likely to enter the forest fearing "a devilish Indian behind every tree" and "the devil himself" right beside them.[8] Their salvation, they believed, lay in travel eastward toward Jerusalem, the known, the orthodox; exploration westward toward the unknown forest was heresy. These ancestors studied the Bible and might well, as Hawthorne suggests, have considered it "quite a sufficient retribution" for their own transgressions to have a descendant who was "A writer of story-books!"[9]

Although for Hawthorne the frontier was potentially dangerous, stagnation was a surer evil; therefore, exploration, even if only intellectual exploration, was essential. As traditional as Hawthorne may seem to the modern reader, he is still liberal in his acceptance of change. He is willing to experiment and to reject unsuccessful attempts.

Significantly, when Melville, Thoreau and Hawthorne wrote the passages quoted above, each author was living within a short distance of the Atlantic coast and from the Boston that had once been John Winthrop's. Clearly a change in the focus of attention, an acceptance of the "idea" of exploration, was more significant for them than a change in location. But whatever its type, exploration is still vital to the American identity. Americans have walked on the moon and, through the eyes of television cameras, explored the surface of Mars. Such events are possible, because the American identity includes the impetus to explore. As we examine exploration as fact and idea, so we become better able to understand the American identity. This situation offers one of the most important justifications for the continuing study of exploration and travel.

The original version of this paper and other papers in this book were part of a conference on America; Exploration and Travel held at Illinois State University in 1976. That conference was sponsored by *Exploration,* a journal of the literature of travel and exploration and by the Illinois State University Bicentennial Committee.

NOTES

[1]Robert Frost, "The Gift Outright," *Collected Poems of Robert Frost* (Garden City: Halcyon House, 1942), p. 445.

[2]Walter Allen, *Urgent West* (New York: E.P. Dutton & Co. Inc., 1969), p. 49.

[3]Frederick J. Turner, "The Significance of the Frontier in American History," Annual Report of the American Historical Association for the Year 1893, facsimile reprint (Readex Microprint, 1966), p. 201.

[4]Herman Melville, *Mardi* (Evanston: Northwestern University Press, 1970), p. 551.

[5]Edwin Russell, *Frontier: American Literature and the American West* (Princeton: Princeton University Press, 1965), pp. 175-191.

[6]Henry David Thoreau, "Walking," in *Excursions* (Boston: Houghton Mifflin & Co., 1863), pp. 176-185.

[7]Nathaniel Hawthorne, "The Custom-House," preface to *The Scarlet Letter* (Columbus: Ohio State University Press, 1962), pp. 11-12.

[8]Nathaniel Hawthorne, "Young Goodman Brown," in *Mosses From An Old Manse* (Columbus: Ohio State University Press, 1974), p. 75.

[9]Hawthorne, "Custom-House," p. 10.

Travel
and the American Identity

The Idea of National Character: Inspiration or Fallacy?

Lynn Altenbernd

It took many generations to trim and comb and perfume the first boat-load of Norse pirates into royal highnesses and most noble Knights of the Garter; but every sparkle of ornament dates back to the Norse boat. There will be time enough to mellow this strength into civility and religion....

The mildness of the following ages has not quite effaced these traits of Odin;...The nation has a tough, acrid, animal nature, which centuries of churching and civilizing have not been able to sweeten.

That's Ralph Waldo Emerson in *English Traits,* published in 1847. Like most responsible travelers of his century, Emerson assumed that his duty was to record the national character of the people he visited. That assumption may well have been conscious; more likely unconscious—unquestioned because unquestionable—was the assumption that every nationality has an ascertainable national character. The idea was endemic in the nineteenth century, though it was not invented in that otherwise fertile age. It appears in the world's oldest literature, and may well have had its origins in preliterate times. In the rivalries between tribes and city-states and ultimately nations, every people who have left a record of themselves appear to have elaborated collective character portraits of their enemies, their friends and themselves. We hear of supersubtle Venetians, of perfidious Albion, of lascivious Frenchman, and a thousand other national types and stereotypes that populate the pages of the world's history books—and literature. Lest we smile too smugly at the naivete of more primitive generations, let's not forget the latest Polish joke.

Let me attempt a definition of the idea of national character as I propose to use the term: The idea of national character is the assertion that the citizens of a nation share widely a set of relatively stable traits of physique and personality, patterns of behavior, and attitudes. This apparently innocent idea went unchallenged so long as everyone knew what qualities characterize a nation. A nation has a shared ancestry; a common

9

history; a generally accepted tradition, including a religion, a myth and a literature; a national language; allegiance to a state; occupation of a territory; and—climactically—a national consciousness reflecting the joint possession of a national genius, soul or character. Well, a nation has at least some of these qualities, and the trouble really started when the world began to wonder whether a large, diverse and widely scattered people like the Americans of the early republic could in fact be a nation. They could claim only a dominant language, allegiance to a state, and a territory. They were acquiring a history at a great rate and presumably a culture would follow. But whatever the current rate of accumulation, they didn't really have very much history behind them, and they were diverse in tribal origins, religion and tradition. Under such adverse circumstances, did they already possess, or were they evolving, a national character?

A flat affirmative was given by Hector St. John de Crevecoeur in his *Letters from an American Farmer* of 1782. In the third letter he asked his famous question: "What then is the American, this new man?" This new man, he replied, "acts upon new principles; he must therefore entertain new ideas, and form new opinions." Crevecoeur's American is, in general, an individualist, an egalitarian and a practical idealist. Crevecoeur's description became and remained the dominant image of the national character; the assertion of Alexis de Tocqueville in *Democracy in America* of 1835 that the American is a conformist and a materialist ran a poor second in the generalization sweepstakes. But these two French observers and a host of other visiting and resident commentators agreed that there is an American national character, whatever its components. Hence the idea of national character had survived its sternest trial in the emergence of a new national type under the eyes of a watching world. The concept became an unquestioned commonplace of the writers of travel essays and of international fiction throughout the nineteenth century and on into our time. Let me offer a few examples drawn from novels, travel books, letters and journals.

Many of you will remember that in the first scene of *The Scarlet Letter*, Hawthorne characterizes the English-born women of seventeenth-century Boston as more robust and bold than their descendants were to be. Dealing with the contemporary generation in *Our Old Home* of 1863, Hawthorne still depicted the English woman as a fit spouse for John Bull:

It strikes me that the English woman of fifty is apt to become a creature less refined and delicate, so far as her physique goes, than anything that we Western people class under the name of woman. She has an awful ponderosity of frame, not pulpy, like the loose development of our few fat women, but massive with solid beef and streaky tallow; so that...you inevitably think of her as made up of steaks and sirloins.

In *A Chance Acquaintance* (1873) Willliam Dean Howells makes some remarkably fine distinctions in national physical types when he describes a Canadian girl:

The young girl was redeemed by her New World birth from the English heaviness; a more delicate bloom lighted her cheeks; a softer grace dwelt in her movement; yet she was round and full and she was in the perfect flower of youth. She was not so ethereal in her loveliness as an American girl, but she was not so nervous and had none of the painful fragility of the latter.

In *A Woman's Reason* (1883) Howells says of a young American male, "He was the sort of young American whom you might pronounce an Italian before you had seen the American look in his grey eyes."

Henry Adams had special reasons to dislike the English during his term as confidential secretary to his father in the American legation in London during the Civil War, but during the remainder of his life and despite close friendships with a number of English women and men, he never really repudiated the view of English attitudes which he expressed in a letter to *The New York Times* in December, 1861: "The phlegmatic and dogmatic Englishman...is seldom well informed on any but English subjects looked at from a national point of view; he is often sullen, dogged, and unsocial."

Howells's generalizations about the Italians in *Venetian Life* (1866) are rather more affectionate, but still tinctured with condescension. While he corrected his countrymen's misconceptions by denying that Italians display the carefree gaiety attributed to them, he did speak of their "passionate nature" and "their large, natural capacity for enjoyment." He found them childlike and simple in many ways, indolent or at best inefficiently industrious, and naturally dignified but willing to beg or cheat. Later in the same volume, Howells offers an explanation for the characteristic moral composition of the Italians:

There is that equality in Italian fibre which I believe fits the nation for democratic institutions better than any other, and which is perhaps partly the result of their ancient civilization. At any rate, it fascinates a stranger to see people so mutually gentle and deferential; and must often be a matter of surprise to the Anglo-Saxon, in whose race, reclaimed from barbarism more recently, the native wild beast is still so strong as to inform the manner. The uneducated Anglo-Saxon is a savage; the Italian, though born to utter ignorance, poverty, and depravity, is a civilized man. I do not say that his civilization is of a high order, or that the civilization is at all comparable to that of a gentleman among ourselves. The Italian's education, however profound, has left his passion undisciplined, while it has carefully polished his manner; he yields lightly to temptation, he loses his self-control, he blasphemes habitually; his gentleness is conventional, his civilization not individual. With us the education of a gentleman (I do not mean a person born to wealth or station, but any man who has trained himself in morals or religion, in letters, and in the world) disciplines the impulses, and leaves the good manner to grow naturally out of habits of self-command and consequent habitual self-respect.

The Italian possesses manners, form; the Anglo-Saxon, though self-taught and lacking in form, exhibits the essence of morality and civilization.

Finally, to bring in the French and to illustrate the high intellectual level on which the debate was sometimes conducted, let me recall an exchange between Mark Twain and the French novelist Paul Bourget. In his *Outre-Mer* of 1897, Bourget marveled over the great freedom allowed to unmarried young women in the United States. Similarly he was puzzled at the infrequency of attempts to seduce young married women; he supposed that the lingering effect of Puritan laws providing the death penalty for adultery and the ease of divorce accounted for this phenomenon. Mark Twain retorted that it had never occurred to the Frenchman that the young people were moral—that they were pure in their hearts. And Mark Twain topped this stunner by recalling Napoleon's slur on a democratic people notorious for their interest in discovering illustrious ancestors. If an American is ever without a pastime, Napoleon had said, he can occupy himself trying to find out who his grandfather was. A Frenchman, Mark Twain replied, can always put in his time trying to find out who his father was.

The idea of national character was never without its critics. Even Mark Twain, who was jingoistic and cosmically humane by turns, denied that it was possible to sum up so vast a nation as the United States in a single work. But the most serious assault on the concept grew out of the Nazi promulgation of the Aryan superiority lie during the thirties and forties of this century. Some critics sought to modify the idea into defensible form; others mounted an argument that there simply isn't any such thing as national character. An example of the latter tactic is Hamilton Fyfe's *The Illusion of National Character* of 1940. The argument of this English writer is impassioned and in many ways persuasive. On the theoretical side he contends that generalization about the charactistics of a large and diverse population is simply not possible; all nations are racially mixed, and the qualities of occupations, sexes, classes and other subcommunities are at least as important as national traits. On the practical side Fyfe argues that the idea of national character irresistibly becomes an idea of national superiority and eventually leads to international conflict instead of harmony.

Fyfe's book is in large part a rejoinder to a work of Sir Ernest Barker, first published in 1927, *National Character and the Factors in Its Formation*. Barker was not driven from the field, however; indeed, he revised his book shortly after the close of World War II and reiterated and strengthened his original insistence on the importance of national character. According to Barker, the factors in the formation of national character are these: race; territory and climate; population and occupation;

politics, law and government; religion; language, literature and thought; and ideas and systems of education. Barker's work is a curious mixture of almost mystical British patriotism and scrupulous scholarship; it too is in many ways a persuasive document.

Meanwhile on this side of the ocean the concept similarly went into eclipse during the Nazi period and gradually recovered respectability in a modified form after the War. The social scientists were perhaps more prominent than the humanists in this development. Ruth Benedict's *Patterns of Culture* (1934) and Margaret Mead's *And Keep Your Powder Dry: An Anthropologist Looks at America* (1943) were significant works in tribal and national characterization. After the War, Mead revised her book without fundamentally altering its position on national character. *The Lonely Crowd: A Study of the Changing American Character* by David Riesman, Reuel Denney and Nathan Glazer (1950), David M. Potter's *People of Plenty: Economic Abundance and the American Character* (1954), and Max Lerner's *America as a Civilization* (1957) were only the most prominent works in a substantial body of writing dealing with our subject.

These American essays considered the attacks on the idea of national character and responded with a modification and a defense. An important modification was accomplished by eliminating race as a source of national character. Max Lerner put the matter succinctly in *America as a Civilization*: "Much of the chauvinist and racist treachery of the term can be avoided if it is remembered that national character is a doctrine not of blood but of culture." In addition, David Potter found it necessary to offer an addendum to *People of Plenty* eight years after the book was published. In an article entitled "American Women and the American Character," he observed that most delineations of the supposed national character were really best applicable to adult white males. Rather than abandoning the enterprise, Potter proposed more meticulous attention to the diversity of the population.

The defense was curiously negative in its logic, though not necessarily false for that reason. Character is a product of culture, the social scientist argues; cultures are demonstrably different from one another; hence national characters must differ. One might properly add, I think, that a persistent and powerful subjective sense of national difference, felt by virtually all who travel abroad, has persuaded behavioral scientists and humanists alike to persist in efforts toward an acceptable and defensible theory of national character.

In effect, the social scientists have put in a claim to hegemony in the study of national character, and particularly American character. The case is effectively summed up in an excellent book of readings, Michael McGiffert's *The Character of Americans,* first published in 1964 and reissued in a revised edition in 1970. Anthropologists, sociologists and psychologists, McGiffert wrote in his foreword to the first edition, "have held up a mirror to America and, over the last two decades, have developed a formal theory for the analysis of national character as an enterprise of the behavioral sciences." The foreword to the revised edition speaks of "deepening misgivings about the applicability of the formulas of culture and personality to the explanation of large, complex, modern national societies," and the revision adds essays on sexual, racial, and regional varieties of American character.

If the humanists have been less articulate about theory and methodology than the behavioral scientists, they have nevertheless made significant contributions to the study of the American character. As early as 1931 Constance Rourke gave us *American Humor: A Study in the National Character.* In 1941 F.O. Matthissen's *American Renaissance* gave new vigor and a new direction to the study of American literature. R.W.B. Lewis jarred us awake once more in 1955 with *The American Adam; Innocence, Tragedy, and Tradition in the Nineteenth Century.* Leo Marx's *The Machine in the Garden: Technology and the Pastoral Ideal in America,* of 1964, added further momentum to the study. I note finally, though there are other titles that deserve mention, Roderick Nash, *Wilderness and the American Mind* of 1967, revised in 1973. Two objections can be brought against this list: Each of these works is more or less beside the mark; none of these authors—not even Rourke and Nash, who come closest— deals directly and explicitly with the issue of national character.

Secondly, these authors are concerned with myth as well as actuality. The first of these objections seems to me wholly valid: We should have more studies from humanists dealing with instances of national characterization, both American and other, and with theoretical analysis of the concept as it appears in literature. The second objection, that the authors listed have studied myth, represents an opportunity rather than a disqualification. Few phenomena are more important to a culture than its mythology, and the interplay of myth and actuality, where they diverge, is a fascinating and revealing study of human motivation and aspiration. The study should not be left to anthropologists alone.

Literature offers a concreteness, specificity and vividness that can usefully supplement the sometimes sweeping and abstract generalizations of the behavioral scientists. The latter are likely to object to literary works, and to the work of critics and historians of literature as well, that their evidence is "impressionistic" and "anecdotal." So it is; we might take courage from Max Lerner, who writes of Emerson's *English Traits* as "witness that literary insight may be worth more than all the paraphernalia of recent social science." We need more and more studies that demonstrate the value, if not the validity in the strictest scientific sense, of studies like those I named a few moments ago.

In thus seeking to hearten and challenge students of literature, I am not suggesting that we try to snatch the initiative from our colleagues in the social sciences and show their work to be deficient, but rather that we join forces with them, each group studying its chosen body of material through its distinctive methods, so that together we can carry forward the unfinished work. We need to collect many more citations than have yet been gathered, and we must face up to a number of issues: What are the sources of national character? Does it alter with time? How is national character influenced by the traits of subcommunities within a nation? What is the character of Americans and of other groups? Finally, it seems to me still an open question whether there is such a thing as national character. Certainly the idea of national character is an actuality worthy of study, whether the alleged phenomenon exists or not. And what a lot of travel such research will justify!

Speaking and Touching:
The Problem of Inexpressibility in American Travel Books

Wayne Franklin

Columbus and those who followed him to the Americas before 1600 often complain, in their narratives of travel and exploration, about the tendency of their *literary* precursors to use language not merely inaccurately but even with malice. Columbus himself rails at casual travelers who indulge their private fantasies at the cost of blinding themselves and their audiences to the public truth; and, though he has fantasies of his own regarding the presence of Paradise near the Orinoco, his criticisms of older travelers do reflect a sincere effort on his part to approach the discovered lands with a fresh eye, subordinating as much as possible in his age the preconceived to the literally seen. Yet perception alone is not the issue, in his case or in that of other travelers. His critique underscores the peculiar relation between word and thing which one often discovers in travel books; it accuses his predecessors, in effect, of constituting things by naming them—which is to say, of dealing in words rather than in those facts (whether fantastic or mundane) which it was the traveler's task to address and convey. As a man who had full knowledge of the intractable nature of reality—perhaps only as a sea captain in his age could know such things—Columbus apparently was irked by the ease with which imaginary or imaginative travelers could regard the world.[1]

One might pursue this opening distinction in many directions: as Columbus makes it, for instance, it points toward the growing rift between science and the imagination, and toward the debate over style which was to affect Francis Bacon, and which was to surface, later in the seventeenth century, as an issue of large dimensions for the British Royal Society. Then again, one might see in the distinction a certain obtuseness on the part of Columbus and others—an insensitivity to the creative nature of any act of writing, whether the text produced concerns "scientific" facts, "real" events, or deeds utterly within the writer's mind. Aware as he is of the need for close seeing and

attentive writing, Columbus seems curiously dead to the
difficulties of exposition; one wonders, as a result, if he ever found
himself struggling with that other intractability—the one
discovered when words and things fall asunder.

It is this question which I wish to pursue. One need not go
very far, even in Columbus, before finding ample evidence that
the struggle did take place. That, by his own account, he heard
nightingales singing in the Caribbean provides a nice indication
of the problem.[2] Are we to take this remark as a reflection of his
lack of perceptivity? or, perhaps, as a mark that species names
were not as rigid in his age as they have become in ours? or,
finally, as a fundamental sign of the New World traveler's
accommodating spirit when faced with a flora and a fauna (and a
human world) for much of which few immediate resemblances
could be found in European experience? Is this a case of
misnaming through inattention, or of approximate naming
motivated by a sharp attention to the abundance of unknown
details?

All these explanations, and others, can throw light on the
problem, but this last one will prove most fruitful here. Wherever
they went, New World travelers were agreed about the
inexpressibile quality of their visual, social, and—as I hope to
show later—their spiritual life on this side of the Atlantic. Things,
people and experiences all taxed the lexical equipment of these
travelers, and they reacted to the challenge thus given them in
similar, and highly interesting, ways. Hernán Cortés, almost
literally rapt by the sounds, sights and human events of the
Mexican world he was to destroy in his weirdly ritualistic
conquest—perhaps the shock of newness itself recoiled at the
natives in his own violence—Cortés writes to Charles V time and
again about the beggarly power of his language in the face of this
apparitional world. Montezuma's palace is "so marvelous that it
seems to me impossible," Cortés writes, "to describe its excellence
and grandeur. Therefore, I shall not attempt to describe it at all,
save to say that in Spain there is nothing to compare it with."[3] Or,
again, he relates how rich the native marketplaces are in
appearance and in the goods exchanged in them; after listing a
great many items regularly sold there—"lime, hewn and unhewn

stone, adobe bricks, tiles, and cut and uncut woods of various kinds," runs one catalogue; "onions, leeks, garlic, common cress and watercress, borage, sorrel, teasels and artichokes," runs another one (*Letters,* pp. 103-104)—Cortés finds even this particularized vocabulary failing him, rich as it is in its own way: "Finally, besides those things which I have already mentioned," he concludes, "they sell in the market everything else to be found in this land, but they are so many and so varied that because of their number and because I cannot remember many of them nor do I know what they are called I shall not mention them" (p. 104).

There are rhetorical principles behind these passages, and the many others like them, to be sure: the need to convince Charles of his own purity, for one thing, forces Cortés quite obviously into a hyperbolic mood—for his legal standing as the subordinate of the Cuban governor, a man whom he had disobeyed pointedly at the start of his expedition, left him with the large burden of washing his spotted linen in the golden streams of the continent, and in the equally golden language of a man almost too fully overwhelmed by the territory he had discovered by what was, after all, an accident. Screw invention to its utmost stop, and the scurrilous becomes laudable. There is another rhetorical principle involved here, as well, what Faulkner might have called the *reducto parvum*: the conveying of a large field of objects or people or events by rendering a few in high detail and then suggesting how partial this recovered list is, how vast the unending list never quite encompassed by words.

But Cortés will not let us off with rhetoric alone: his sense of inexpressibility is real, even devastating at times—indeed, a source of embarrassment before the distant eyes of Charles, not of reconciliation. "Because I do not know the names of things," he admits to the Emperor, "I cannot express them."[4] Here is a European man, not highly educated perhaps, but able nonetheless, a man voluminous in his prose renderings of American experience; and yet a man up against the blank wall of what remains unnameable and hence unknown, incapable of the symbolic transit back to Europe through language. He is a little naked in Mexico, "unaccommodated" in King Lear's terms. Eager of eye and ear, he is confronted with a limit beyond which his curiosity cannot pass, and that outer limit rebounds against his own inner failures. Beneath the rhetorical flourishes, the traces of courtly politics which pervade his accounts and those of many other early Spanish explorers, one finds the bedrock of a nagging recognition that surpasses all merely European concerns. And that recognition, altered as it may become by later centuries of "converting" the American scene through word and deed—strewing the names and institutions of Europe over it—that recognition continues to exist at the center of the American travel book. It typifies the psychological shock of Westward discovery, and this points ahead to that sense of alienation which Octavio Paz has described in *The Labyrinth of Solitude,* and for which Philip Slater has provided Northern analogues in *The Pursuit of Loneliness.*

But I started with language, and I want to return to it. If the apparent failure of his language helps us to hear in Cortés the early rumblings of later cultural themes, the same failure points with even greater intensity toward later *literary* situations. The programmatic impulse in his own *Letters*—the desire to filligree the outer edges of a vacuum which itself remains unfilled—abides through the course of all subsequent American literatures, and this impulse takes (in Melville's *Moby-Dick,* for instance, as in the writings of Cortés) a markedly linguistic direction. Melville shares with the Spanish conquistador, as does Whitman, the deeply felt urge to fill empty space with a torrent of words, to name and codify reality as a means of self-expression and self-knowledge.

We must begin here with lexical concerns, and then move on to grammatical ones. The first level of literary reaction to what I have called the "inexpressibility" of America is diffident. Random items must be named, either with utterly new terms—as when John Winthrop dubs one Massachusetts hill "Cheese Rock" after he and his fellow explorers discover that they have only cheese for summer, "(the governor's man forgetting, for haste, to put up some bread)"—or with terms imported directly or by analogy from the Old World.[5] In cases where fortuitous events or imported words would not work, recourse was had to native terms, or, less frequently in the early years, to pure invention.

Columbus supplied, even from the voyage of 1492, a surprisingly
large number of native borrowings, some of which—like *canoa*—
entered quite quickly into the major European tongues. Such acts
of linguistic accommodation have more than a lexical interest,
however. They point, to be sure, toward lexical needs, and toward
that larger need for bridging New World experiences and Old
World audiences which forms the rhetorical core of American
travel accounts. But to take over Indian terms, and to do so for
lexical convenience, is to raise a further problem: the puzzling
fact of a language existing already in the land, of a linguistic field
causing almost as many problems as it solves—and problems
analogous to those voiced by Cortés in his attempt to describe the
indescribable artifacts or natural products or institutions of the
culture with which he had contact. Far from enjoying the simple
position of an eyewitness, the traveler becomes an interpreter as
well; and as his roles diversify, his task as a writer becomes more
difficult. Added to the failures of close observation are the failures
of cultural misunderstanding. More "foreign" at times than
American objects, the native words which describe them may
interpose another barrier between self and world.

The nature of native American languages excited much
speculation among early travelers and among the proto-
anthropologists to whom their reports gave such impetus. In the
debate over the supposed origins of the American tribes which
Lee E. Huddleston has recreated, for instance, the nature of
native languages (or even their presumed absence in some cases)
was regarded as a key piece of evidence, and the diversity of
spoken tongues clearly seemed, to European minds accustomed to
a relatively unified linguistic world, a piece of accidental or even
intentional deviltry. Gregorio García, who along with Joseph de
Acosta was the most influential theorist of Indian origins in the
early period, blamed Satan outrightly for the diversity of
languages: as the New England Puritans regarded America as
the devil's final refuge, so Garcia saw as a primary weapon in
Satan's fight against God the invention of new tongues faster
than the missionaries could learn them. The latters' spreading of
the Word thus was frustrated by the devil's spreading of countless
words, and systems of words, among the infidels.[6]

One has, on the opposite side of such fantasies, the theory of Fernando de Montesinos, who referred to the New World as "Hamerica," for he apparently believed that its name did not stem from Amerigo Vespucci, but rather from an anagram of "Hec Maria" ("Behold Mary, Mother of God")—so clearly had God indicated, against the schemes of Satan, the true destiny of European efforts in the West. For this writer, one solitary word uttered in the Old World, and simply reordered for the New, contains a complete solution to the vexing problem of American "Newness." Or, to put the idea another way, the making sacred of America's name can make sacred, and thus consoling, all that it embraces.[7]

Broaching the topic of native tongues, even as modestly as Columbus and other explorers did, thus opened up between the would-be travel writer and his chosen subject a further perspective which increased rather than diminished the vexations caused by unworded terrain. Most writers could retreat from this new threat, and from the danger of linguistic alienation which it posed if one pursued native resources too far, by exploiting adeptly the analogies and comparisons which I have noted already. Even Cortés, confronted with the palace of Montezuma, would pursue this route if he could, but no ready analogue from his Spanish experience occurred to him. Hence he left that object undescribed, mentioned in his text only for the sake of being dismissed. Other writers were more ingenious: Magellan, for example, rendered the bananas which he saw as "figs a foot long"—certainly a rather curious instance of the practice.[8] And beyond such botanical or zoological analogies, one has, even into the nineteenth century—and in places far removed from one another, though sharing a great literal and cultural distance from Europe and from European America—more puzzling and potentially more dangerous instances of analogical naming. Captain James Cook, an astute observer and a highly scientific voyager, as well as a systematic tester of older, more fantastic hypotheses, labored under a cultural burden which forced him to seek out "kings" among the Pacific islands, and thus misled his perceptions about native political and cultural structure.[9] In this sense, his observations were warped by the "words" of his own origin; the limit placed on his understanding of native cultures did not come from his lack of Pacific experience—for Cook was enormously experienced in that ocean, more so than any European before him—but rather from the linguistic biases of his past, and from the values which those biases in part formed and in part reflected. The "things" of Europe, freighted in his mind as surely as the trade objects he carried were freighted in his ships, provided him with a lexicon which subtly caused him to misperceive, and to misrender, the "things" of Pacific culture. Closer to home, one may point to the persistent failure of white Americans, even to this day, to understand the roles and powers of those native figures whom *we* call "chiefs." Even adopting native terms, such as the Spanish "*cacique,*" first used in December, 1492, by Columbus, was no protection against lexical misunderstandings.[10] The root of many subsequent tragedies in American history lies in language misappropriated or misapplied; and the root of such misapplications and misappropriations lies less in wilful or lazy habits of seeing and listening than in the strong desire to codify American sights and sounds as quickly as possible in written language.

Much more could be said about these lexical problems, about their origins, about their cultural and literary consequences. But we must turn now to the second level of linguistic reaction to the problem of inexpressibility—away from lexical and toward grammatical solutions. The first, and simplest, such solution has been demonstrated already in the case of Cortés: for the catalogues which one finds throughout his prose are not merely lexical lists, but rather rudimentary attempts to organize events and objects into groups—that is, to form "sentences" which do not just name, but put into relation whatever they contain. Most of these sentences do not have verbs, to be sure; like the simple act of naming, they seek to freeze whatever they point to. But once the shift away from naming has been made, once the possibility of more complex kinds of statement has been discovered, action and the words which suggest it are bound to follow. The progression I shall outline now thus moves from isolated words and phrases toward collections of terms, and finally toward something like a "native" form of narrative. This development is a logical one, not a historical one; it is found in a number of books from a variety of literary periods, and no one stage of it ever is lost from the tradition.

Perhaps the best list or catalogue which Cortés gives us is appended to the first letter. An inventory of objects sent to the Emperor, the list describes fifty-two separate items, or groups of items, with admirable attention to detail. "First," it begins, "a large gold wheel with a design of monsters on it and worked all over with foliage"; then it goes on to featherwork fans, a jewelled mirror, a gold alligator's head, scepters, miters, "imitation" birds (made of "thread and feather work," with gold quills and claws and eyes and beaks).[11] It is a virtual abstract of the exotic cultures already seen by Cortés, or soon to be discovered, a linguistic model not merely of the things sent to the Emperor, but also of that larger collection of peoples and objects of which the things conveyed to Spain themselves are a tangible abstract. If one can picture the loading of these objects onto the ship, the image thus evoked provides a perfect expression of the linguistic act performed in his letter by Cortés. Sending word and thing alike to the Old World, Cortés gives one an early example of those "cabinets of curiosities" which Margaret Hodgen has described in her book on early anthropology, and which often contained substantial numbers of American artifacts or natural products.[12] If the attempt to name single items elsewhere in the writings of Cortés may be likened to the fine New World paintings of John White (to those which treat natural objects, not those which are concerned with native life), or to the finer paintings of Jacopo Ligozzi, based on that Italian's experience of animals and plants in European collections, then such lists as the one referred to here find their own analogues in the kind of illustration exemplified in the early seventeenth-century engraving of Ole Worm's "Museum" in Copenhagen.[13] In place of merely giving us a single object, or term, against the background of a blank page or an artist's blank ground, the cataloguers and the collectors begin to create a grammar, principles of subordination and coordination, or of relation and difference. The aesthetic principle of composition does not enter into the former acts of rendering, while it is crucial to the latter.

As a guide to scientific understanding, the catalogue predates New World exploration—Aristotle's *Parts of Animals,* or even Pliny's *Natural History* clearly employ the device, for instance, and one may speculate that language itself rests in large part on the human need to catalogue, and thereby to understand, the myriad objects of human curiosity. Yet in the case of New World travel books the general principle becomes of acute significance: for one must see such books against the background of a long period of relative stability in European culture, and hence as literary attempts to catch up with the sudden loss of that stability in the face of rapid physical expansion. Certainly the word always lags behind the thing, but this principle is exemplified with particular force in the two centuries following the discovery of America. In strictly linguistic terms, to be sure, Europe had had a good deal of experience during the late medieval period with the entrance of new words and new ideas from the Arabic world; but that world never had been so completely unknown as the American landmasses were, and if a certain exoticism attached itself to the former exchange, and hence a certain inexpressibility arose in it, both these traits entered much more crucially into the Western excursion of European in the sixteenth and following centuries. Never before, in its relation to other peoples, had Europe relied so heavily on the word alone, or on those few objects which, like the shipment sent by Cortés in 1520, made their way to the Old World. As Hodgen argues, for instance, the connections of Europe with the Near and even the Far East relied on commercial contacts built up over a long period of time; its connections with the West, however, began quite suddenly, and this sudden rise of another, radically different perspective accounts for many of the differences between the *Letters* of Cortés and, say, the *Travels* of Marco Polo.[14] At its outer reaches, to be sure—as Columbus complains— Polo's book touches on worlds quite as exotic as those described by Cortés some two centuries later. But Polo's *Travels* remains, on a grander scale, the medieval version of Gilbert White's *Natural History of Selbourne*—a close account of the known— whereas the *Letters* of Cortés stands in the line which leads finally to the radical "travels" of Darwin in South America and among the Galapagos Islands. Venerable as the catalogue tradition was when the first American travelers turned toward it; established as the form of the travel account was by that time; aware as Europe had been of regions far severed from itself—yet the essential and abiding newness of the Americas made all these hackneyed facts and themes into something equally new. The catalogue was not merely a convenient form of expression: it bore, for Cortés and for other New World travelers, a crucial importance as a means of knowing the unknown, and as a means of impressing upon it—and upon the traveler's psyche—the gridwork of old and comforting assumptions.

To list details becomes, in these works, a way of domesticating them, and of giving to them an order that is both linguistic and more broadly intellectual. As one discovers it in John Lawson's *A New Voyage to Carolina* (published in 1709), for instance, the catalogue aspires toward a full anatomy of the landscape, of flora and fauna, of social life among white settlers and among the Indians. After giving the "Journal" of his own travels in the Carolinas, Lawson goes on to discourse minutely on the landforms and the rivers, the trees and wild animals, the birds and the fish, the domestic animals and crops and finally on the customs and beliefs of the native inhabitants. Both his "Journal" and the later sections of his book report on the same body of experience—the former organizing it by means of space and time, the latter, by means of logical categories. The catalogues thus become an attempt to go back through the undigested events and sights described earlier, and to lift them above the level of merely private (and hence arbitrary) life in the New World—to insert between the traveler's mind and his experience a series of reassuringly general frameworks. Starting with the bald statement of his travels, Lawson moves toward a higher plane of description and analysis, and thus is able to escape from the limits of actual space and time both as conditions of life and as grounds of expression. His initial grammar is narrative; his second means of relation, however, pushes away from action and toward contemplation. It is a movement from feet to head, from touching the region to speaking about it in increasingly abstract ways.

Lawson's catalogues serve, by this movement, a definitely scientific purpose, as well as a mildly propagandistic one. The need for generalization springs, in other words, from public as well as private considerations. The balance between such differing drives can be assessed by comparing Lawson's work with another one inspired by it,[15] the promotional tract written by Samuel Jenner, Swiss agent for William Byrd II, as an inducement to emigration. *Neu-gefundenes Eden* (1737) uses Lawson's natural history less as a way of organizing the American scenes which it describes than as a way of inciting action within those scenes—its catalogues *imply* a journey in the future rather than build on one from the past. Contemplation yields to motivation; the organization of detail points toward the feet, not toward the head. Though Lawson himself is not adverse to adding succulent details to his own lists, or to inserting the facts of his personal experience into the description of any animal or plant or locale, he adheres generally to an aesthetic which limits such intrusions. Jenner's book, on the other hand, is almost pornographic in its aesthetic: it resembles a harangue delivered to a hungry army of emigrants about to pounce on the plenty which he salaciously describes. "*Herring* are not as large as the European ones," he writes, "but better and more delicious." Lawson says of this fish: "The Herrings in *Carolina* are not so large as in *Europe*. They spawn there in *March* and *April*, running up the fresh Rivers and small fresh Runs of Water in great shoals, where they are taken. They become red if salted; and, drest with Vinegar and Oil, resemble an Anchovy very much; for they are far beyond an *English* Herring, when pickled."[16] Jenner embroiders on this description in his own prose, for he continues: "After being salted they become red. If one prepares them with vinegar and olive oil, they then taste like anchovies or sardines, since they are far better in salt than the English or European herring. When they spawn, all streams and waters are completely filled with them, and one might believe, when he sees such terrible amounts of them, that there was as great a supply of herrings as there is water. In a word," he concludes, though he uses three words, "it is unbelievable, indeed, indescribable, as also incomprehensible, what quantity is found

there. One must behold [the sight] oneself."[17] Lawson is not blind
to the culinary uses of his catalogue, or of the items it describes;
but he evinces much more balance than Jenner, more distance
and objectivity. The Swiss writer transforms the catalogue
technique from its function in the *Voyage* as an anatomizing
device into a less intellectual, more tangible—and yet not naively
tangible—vehicle. It is as if his words are virtually one with the
things they describe, and hence as if reading his book is an act of
consumption. In one sense, of course, this transformation rests on
Lawson's own usage, and thus points to a practice common
among travel writers. Hard and clear in its details, a catalogue
conveys the sense of a world touched, and a world inviting our
own touch in return. Yet the kinds of experience which can be
rendered by the catalogue are severely limited. One never "feels"
the scenes described as complete landscapes, multi-dimensional
and complex, but rather as a collection of objects to which one's
relation remains simple. That relation is one-way: traveler and
reader alike are in control of the objects, never at *their* mercy—the
author and his audience possess a fund of verbs which determines
the grammar of New World action. One can discover, to be sure,
catalogues of "discommodities" (as in the account of Frobisher's
second voyage by Dionise Settle, found in Hakluyt)—and one can
discover, as in Just Girard's *Adventures of a French Captain*
(American translation, 1876), the touching description of a Texas
river "as wide as the Seine, but full of alligators."[18] Yet the
cataloguer remains, despite these subversions of his form, a man
whose attributions to the world he describes appear to have the
warrant of the land's own "text," and whose prose elides
wherever possible the suggestion that this given text may include
distressing passages—objects beyond the control of *our* language
and hence of our selves. His basic pretense is that he "gives voice"
to the country, not that he lays his words over its surface.

The catalogue device thus becomes a form of insidious
predication which extends the acts of naming into newer, more
evaluative fields. The nature of New World items remains of
interest to the cataloguer; but far more important is their
potential meaning, defined most usually through the listing of
their uses. Grammatically, this shift involves the addition of

implied or uttered verbs of the sort already mentioned. To the nouns of the namer are added the terms of the possessor, terms which bridge the gap between mere economic interest and vaguely emotional satisfactions. Whereas Cortés, despite his own economic drives, and his need to possess Mexican things by word and deed, rests most typically at the level of enumeration, promotional writers like Jenner transform the inventory into a true bill of lading—one which, unlike that supplied by Cortés at the end of his first letter, has more to do with worldly gain than with exotic delight. Under the pressure of this sort of language, the traveler's New World becomes a vast storehouse of goods on which every act of writing resembles a requisition. Though Jenner himself protests about the "unbelievable, indeed, indescribable, as also incomprehensible"nature of American herring, he is in fact unmoved by the naive sense of inexpressibility which keeps even Cortés slightly innocent. His lists of commodities—as well as his redundant section on "What one generally eats and drinks in Virginia"—become a frenzied means of ignoring silence, of filling it with the greedy words of a mind less stated by the bombardment of details than deranged by the possibility that any one detail might prove intractable—or, God forbid, inedible. That his America is so fully worded proves how attuned this man who never came to the New World is to the abiding mystery of a region beyond the power of received language. Jenner's predications aim, like the simpler lists of Cortés, or the single words of other travelers, at lining in a canvas all-too-blank.

Those predications were heard, and responded to, by a group of Swiss citizens who set sail for Byrd's supposed Eden, only to die in shipwreck off the American coast, or to survive that disaster only to encounter failure on the land. Responding to a world constituted by Jenner's language, these men and women were testing, in effect, the supposed congruence of word and thing in America—or, more precisely, the relation of European word and American thing. Experience in the New World often has become such a test, an act of practical criticism which compares some invented text with the hard text of reality. One may say that the "anatomy" as a New World form of writing has helped us to imagine a static universe, and then has caused us to enter—and to touch—the field of an actual universe which requires rather a physiological than an anatomical imagination. The failure of the catalogue as a linguistic (and a cultural) device springs from its limitation of relations—its tendency to suggest that the most important bearing of any rendered detail is that which it has on us, rather than on other details existing in its own natural environment. As a grammer, it is woefully inadequate (its inadequacy accounts, perversely enough, for its ready acceptance by writers); it allows for subordination only along a single axis, and for action only in one direction. American things are named in the catalogue merely as objects for our own desire, as passive subjects yielding all to their imported beneficiaries. Almost never do the objects interact with each other; even less rarely do they acquire the power of aggressive action over those who have named them and have set out to appropriate their virtues.

Yet that power is sensed even within the catalogue, is, in fact, the reason for the great popularity of this static means of rendering the New World scene. The movement in Lawson's book away from the narrative approach—the presentation of experience within the spatial and temporal terms in which it actually occurs—and toward more categorical forms of language, reflects something other than his scientific bent, reflects as well the abiding pressure in American travel books to discover alternate means of organization. There is in human experience here, as in the abundance of sights and sounds encountered in that experience, something inexpressible: some sense of alienation and displacement, and the traveler often retreats from this fact, as from the unnameable objects around him, by adopting a language which minimizes such evanescent and yet potentially frightening things. Lawson, accomplished traveler and sage observer, was captured by the Tuscaroras in 1711— never mind his marginal comment in the *Voyage*, "Natives are docile," or his assertion later in that book that Carolina is "not a frontier"—and he died in the hands of his captors, while, ironically enough, his fellow captive and colonial promoter, Christopher de Graffenried, escaped by his powers of persuasion.[19] At the crucial moment of his life, Lawson's language failed him: prescient as his *Voyage* might have been, inclusive as it sought to be, there is no place in the linguistic universe of his book for the experiences he later endured, or rather failed to endure. His language in the book acts as a barrier to such events, in fact; nowhere do we sense the possibility that the "observer" may be swallowed in the world he is naming and ordering—even though we may sense that his rage for giving name and shape to the American objects or places he has seen springs indeed from a subliminal awareness of just this chance.

This sort of inexpressibility I have in mind finally, then, is like that which Conrad's Mistah Kurtz manages to indicate in that vaguest of last words—"The horror! the horror!" I am thinking, too, of all the lost travelers, and all the rumors and legends concerning them. The roster begins with the natives borne back to Spain by Columbus—most substantial of New World "objects," brought back as if no words imaginable can convey their meaning home as well as their own flesh can—and it goes on, through the alienation of Columbus himself ("in spiritual things," he writes in reporting the fourth voyage, "I have ceased here in the Indies from observing the prescribed forms of religion.... Weep for me, whoever has charity, truth, and justice!"); through the marooning of those Spanish sailors one begins to hear about in the conquistadors' records, some of them happy in their isolation, others lost in spirit as in body, forgetting their native tongues; on through the countless lost settlers (the Roanoke people, first among the English, rumored to be off with the Indians for twenty years after John White the painter, governor of the colony and grandfather of the famous, and lost, child, Virginia Dare, sought for them, and failing to find them—finding in fact only their ruined dwellings, their scattered possessions, and three large letters carved on a tree, "C R O," suggesting the settlers' departure for the island of Croatoan— renounced all his interest in the New World, his last words on it extracted only by the insistent curiosity of Hakluyt); on, too, through the list of explorers lost at sea (most touching among the English, the case of Sir Humphrey Gilbert, whose small ship disappeared at night after he had spent the day before sitting on its deck quoting vaguely from More's *Utopia,* book in hand, "We are as neere to heaven by sea as by land"; and lost with him, too, the Hungarian humanist and poet Stephanus Parmenius, who had gone along with the Newfoundland voyage to capture the New World in his verse); on, finally, through the senseless destruction of native cultures in all parts of the Americas, the temples destroyed and the memories effaced in the South, whole tribes extirpated in the North with nagging but false sadness; and on through the present crisis of extinction and exhaustion with which we have visited the land—so efficiently that we have lost the things, and keep now only the words for them, and we must make catalogues of our depredations. Once more we may say, as the chronicler of Gilbert's end did, that we can "not observe the hundreth part of creatures" here; but we cannot mean by this, as he did, that the abundance of life forms outruns our attention—rather, that we have cursed that abundance by applying to it too insistently the consumptive terms of our cultural, and our linguistic, traditions.[20]

Oblivion, forced or freely coming, has been one of the constant muses of America, and in its face all lesser inexpressibilities seem trivial. As a single example of this theme, and of the place of language in it, I would point to *La Relacion* of Alvar Núñez Cabeza de Vaca, first published in 1542, and telling an incredible story of almost eight years of wandering in the American South from Florida to Mexico. Cabeza de Vaca was second in command to Pamfilo de Narvaez on an expedition sent out to conquer Florida—Narváez, whom the Cuban governor had sent to arrest Cortés years before, but whom Cortés put in jail—and his commander's incapacity quickly brought the party of four hundred men to ruin. Forging inland in search of a golden city, Narváez left his ships coasting North, but failed to find them again when his men reached the panhandle region. Building makeshift vessels, Narváez and the rest embarked on the Gulf; a storm soon separated them, however, and the commander himself never was seen or heard from again. Cabeza de Vaca and the others were wrecked off the Texas coast late in 1528, and it is from that point that their overland journey, ending finally in Mexico City in July, 1536, began. They survived famine and storm, slavery among the natives, loneliness and extreme psychological stress (at one point, for instance, Cabeza de Vaca himself performed a risky operation on an Indian, removing an arrowhead from his chest and then patching him up successfully, knowing the probable result of failure all the time); and yet the tale which Cabeza de Vaca tells shifts its attention, and ours, away from such surface details, harrowing as they are, and points instead toward precisely that more ample grammar missing from Lawson or Jenner or Cortés, a way of arranging facts and feelings which preserves their complex relations, which does not remove the empty spaces of America from our consideration, but rather makes of them (and of their cultural analogues) the prime subject of inquiry and expression. It is in such books that a truly native form of language first emerges, a language responsive to the strange amplitude of emotion and experience in the vast reaches of the New World, a language which does not minimize but stresses this amplitude; and which draws us into it as readers, forcing us to see how inadequate any mere formulas, of feeling or of words, must be in a true attempt to render the traveler's life in America. More fully than any of his contemporaries, Cabeza de Vaca touched America, and was touched by it. *La Relación* records the shifts of viewpoint which resulted. Its central theme is the wilful embrace of "nakedness," both literal and cultural, and the development in this state of nakedness of new ways of seeing and feeling. When Cabeza de Vaca adopts Indian dress; when he begins to render time according to the native sense, rather than the European; when he emerges at the end of the book as an advocate for Indian rights against Spanish corruption and mistreatment—we find, at last, a traveler who has entered the American world fully, and who has responded to that world on its own terms. At the end of his wanderings, we see him *within* the Indian circle, dressed as his hosts dress, sharing in their customs and even their beliefs. And we thus can see in him the threat which he posed for the Spanish overlords whom he accuses, in his final pages, of gross cruelties: the threat of complete alienation from imported ways, and that chance for personal and communal growth which that threat carried with it. It is highly appropriate, almost ritualistic, that the Spaniards on whom Cabeza de Vaca stumbled in upper Mexico

should regard him with a horror to match Mistah Kurtz's, with a
sense of imminent dread generated by his endurance. Seeing
Spanish artifacts among one tribe, Cabeza de Vaca is
enthusiastic; but when he finds those who have left them there, he
is taken by them as an enemy, is put in chains by the countrymen
from whom his own separation has been such a long trial. Even
though he later is freed and exonerated, other troubles intercede:
appointed governor in Paraguay, he leads an expedition in search
of the golden city of Manoa—one begins to wonder how much he
had learned, after all, on the Narváez expedition, but these doubts
evaporate as one learns more, learns, for example, that his
attempt to enforce humane policies toward the natives in the
South causes the settlers to rise up against him as an enemy to
their own interest, to depose him and send him home to Spain in
disgrace. After eight years of exile in Africa, he is pardoned and
given a judicial position. He was not a man untouched by
delusions, but he remains in the catalogue of American travelers
as a permanent reminder of the challenge to an open bearing on
New World experience, a bearing unencumbered by the typical
anxieties and false ideas—as well as the false words—which
hampered so many of his contemporaries. Unlike most of those
others, except for the fully lost, he touched the continent, and the
act of touching it gives his prose, as it gave his mind, a life beyond
the formulas imported so greedily from Europe. Perhaps no one is
equal to the challenge—even Cabeza de Vaca, one must be
amused to learn, forced his men to carry a fine camp bed for him
from stage to stage during his delusive South American
odyssey—but much more than most, this Spaniard found in the
terms of his confinement and shipwreck resources of emotion and
of tongue that bring back to us even today, across multiple
barriers, sharp words from what remained for so many others not
only inexpressible but also unsensed. In the fifty years which
separate his narrative from the first voyage of Columbus, a
tremendous flexibility has been wrung from countless bitter lives
and the tales which record or fail to record them—a flexibility of
vast consequences for the future of American narrative art. All
the stages in the development which I have sketched here
survive—one finds, on the first page of Gabriel García Márquez's

One Hundred Years of Solitude, for instance, the following rune freshly rendered for our own century: "The world was so recent," he writes, "that many things lacked names, and in order to indicate them it was necessary to point."[21] Such survivals provide continually rich resources for the New World writer, whether the book to be written is actually a work of travel or not. A good many of the best American novels employ the typical devices of the traveler, in fact—much more so than do the contemporaneous novels of English authors—and the same may be said of such American classics in other forms of Crèvecoeur's *Letters from an American Farmer,* Thoreau's *Walden,* or Aldo Leopold's *Sand County Almanac.* In such works, as in our novels, one continually finds runes like those exhibited in *One Hundred Years of Solitude,* old snatches of language and idea first developed in the contact of American scene and European words. But the example of Cabeza de Vaca is not simply a local or particularized one: the gift which he and other, similar writers bequeathed to later American literature entails much more than single terms or even single linguistic strategies. It is the "mixed" nature of his art that matters—the invention of a language suitable to a world of wonders and things unknown, of events and sufferings and delights beyond imagination, a language which thrives on the destruction of older forms and older awarenesses, which reaches out like Melville's prose or Whitman's poetry not simply to catalogue but to engage a universe particolored in its appearance and bewildering in its sense and its implication. American travel books, and the literary forms to which they have given so much, have been created out of the clash of a language like a palisade, a form of blindness rather than sight—and a language as expansive as the New World scene, as open and rich as the possibilities of life, and of death, beyond the pale. Of this latter language no one provides a better example than Cabeza de Vaca when he tells, near the end, of the efforts of his "rescuer," Diego de Alcaraz, to convince the native Mexicans that the wanderers and he himself are men of the same race, and that *he* is a man of greater importance than any of the castaways. "Alcaraz bade his interpreter tell the Indians," Cabeza de Vaca writes, "that we were members of his race who had been long lost; that his group were the lords of the land who must be obeyed and served, while we were inconsequential. The Indians paid no attention to this. Conferring among themselves, they replied that the Christians lied: We had come from the sunrise, they from the sunset; we healed the sick, they killed the sound; we came naked and barefoot, they clothed, horsed, and lanced; we coveted nothing but gave whatever we were given, while they robbed whomever they found and bestowed nothing on anyone." Cabeza de Vaca himself is anxious for the natives to understand this linkage—or says he is—but his full reporting of the native response, as well as his own adoption, as a term for the other Spaniards, of the derogatory word "Christians," shows how deeply into his mind, and into its language, the burden of his long experience in the wilderness has impressed itself. Neither native nor colonizer, he occupies as a man and as a writer a mediate position which remains for us a challenge to full perception and matured belief. And his prose remains as an allied challenge—a call upon us to abandon categorical language, and to respond to the amplitude of life in what still is a New World if we only have the power of sight, and of word, required for its imagination.[22]

NOTES

[1]The issue of Columbus as an "observer" is a complex one: whereas, in the account of his first voyage which he prepared in Lisbon during March, 1493, he boldly contrasts his own attentiveness with the fantasies of earlier travelers to the "East" (surely he is thinking of Marco Polo here), he evinces in the full record of all four voyages a growing mysticism born partly of his failures but partly also of his own imaginative biases. In terms of language, this tension becomes most interesting when, in the "History" of his third voyage which he wrote in Hispaniola and sent to Ferdinand and Isabella, he subtly shifts away from verbs of "discovery" and employs in their place verbs of speculation—shifts away, in other words, from a language of experience and toward a language of thought, supposition, and deduction. (See *Select Letters of Christopher Columbus,* ed. R.H. Major, and published in London by the Hakluyt Society in 1847, esp. pp.127-146).

[2]Major, p.5.

[3]Hernán Cortés, *Letters from Mexico,* trans. and ed. A.R. Pagden (New York: Grossman, 1971), p.109.

[4]This confession is quoted, without citation, by Jean Franco, *An Introduction to Spanish-American Literature* (London: Cambridge Univ. Press, 1969), p.viii.

[5]*Winthrop's Journal,* ed. James Kendall Hosmer (New York: Scribner's 1908),

I, 74. Three helpful articles on the problems of language in America can be found in *First Images of America: The Impact of the New World on the Old,* ed. Fredi Chiappelli (Berkeley: Univ. of California Press, 1976), II, 561-611 (Stephen J. Greenblatt, "Learning to Curse: Aspects of Linguistic Colonialism in the Sixteenth Century"; Yakov Malkiel, "Changes in the European Languages under a New Set of Sociolinguistic Circumstances"; and Edward F. Tuttle, "Borrowing versus Semantic Shift: New World Nomenclature in Europe").

[6]Lee Eldridge Huddleston, *Origins of the American Indians: European Concepts, 1492-1729* (Austin: Univ. of Texas Press, 1967), p.66. Margaret T. Hodgen, *Early Anthropology in the Sixteenth and Seventeenth Centuries* (Philadelphia: Univ. of Pennsylvania Press, 1964), also deals with the problem of native languages.

[7]Huddleston, p.82.

[8]J.C. Beaglehole, *The Exploration of the Pacific,* 3rd ed. (Stanford: Stanford Univ. Press, 1966), p.32.

[9]Beaglehole, *The Life of Captain James Cook* (Stanford: Stanford Univ. Press, 1974), *passim.* Beaglehole's humorous account of the naming practices of Samuel Wallis and Philip Carteret *(Exploration,* pp.200-21) is also worthy of consideration here. Wallis began his voyage in the Pacific by seeding the ocean with names derived from members of the Royal Family; exhausting this supply, "he was obliged to fall back on the royal navy" (p.206).

[10]Tuttle, *First Images,* II, 596, lists such terms.

[11]Cortés, *Letters,* pp.40-46.

[12]Hodgen, *Early Anthropology,* pp.111-206.

[13]Hugh Honour reproduces the Worm engraving, many John White works, and several of Ligozzi's, in *The New Golden Land: European Images of America from the Discoveries to the Present Time* (New York: Patheon, 1975), *passim.*

[14]Hodgen, pp.80-81.

[15]Percy G. Adams, *Travelers and Travel Liars, 1600-1800* (Berkeley: Univ. of California Press, 1962), pp.144-57, discusses Lawson, Jenner, and Byrd. He provides convincing proof that Jenner relied heavily on Lawson's work.

[16]John Lawson, *A New Voyage to Carolina* (London: 1709), p.158.

[17]*William Byrd's Natural History of Virginia or The Newly Discovered Eden,* ed. and trans. Richmond C. Beatty and William J. Mulloy (Richmond: Dietz Press, 1940), pp.78-79.

[19]*New Voyage,* pp.84, 88; see *DAB* for Lawson's fate.

[20]Major, p.203; John White, *Hakluyt* (London: Everyman's Library, 1907), VI, 211-27; Gilbert's death, described by Edward Haies, *Hakluyt,* VI, 35; More's *Utopia* is identified by S.E. Morison, *The European Discovery of America* (New York: Oxford Univ. Press, 1971-74), I, 577; Haies on the creatures, *Hakluyt,* VI, 23.

[21]I quote from the translation of Gregory Rabassa (New York: Avon, 1971), p.11.

[22]*Adventures in the Unknown Interior of America,* trans. by Cyclone Covey (New York: Collier, 1961), p.128.

Originally published in *Exploration,* IV:1, December 1976. Reprinted with the permission of the editor and the author.

Foreign Travelers in America

Exploration and Creativity: Chateaubriand's *Travels in America*

Frans C. Amelinckx

From the time of its discovery, America has excited the European imagination. To some, it has appeared as a Utopian dream, with its promises of freedom and opportunity; to others a land of unexplored frontiers, and natural, unspoiled man.

All of these aspects attracted a young French officer whose career in the army had been frustrated by the political upheaval. Francois-Rene de Chateaubriand wanted to leave his mark on the world around him. Young and ambitious, he sought to acquire fame by becoming an explorer. He had been enthralled by Cook's voyages and the search for the Northwest passage. He hoped to find the passage by exploring the region by land. His plan was to cross the North-American continent, staying close to the Great Lakes, going down the Mississippi valley to the fortieth parallel and from there to go west. Upon reaching the Gulf of California, he planned to go north following the coast to a river discovered by Cook and from there up to Copper River near the seventy-second parallel west. If his search for the Northwest Passage proved unsuccessful, Chateaubriand planned to return to the United States through Hudson Bay and Labrador.[1]

The young man's enthusiasm was fueled by Malesherbes, the scholarly secretary of the court of Louis the sixteenth, and the grandfather of Chateaubriand's sister-in-law. Malesherbes, member of the French Academy and the Academy of Sciences and Letters, had a passion for natural history and travels. His personal library, which had an exceptional collection of travel books dealing with the New World, became a resource center for Chateaubriand. In his *Memoirs,* he recalls fondly the time spent in conversations and in making plans: "M. de Malesherbes excited me on the subject of this voyage. I went to see him in the mornings: we sat, with our noses glued to maps, we compared the different plans of the Artic Circle; we calculated the distances between Behring's Straits and the furthermost part of Hudson Bay; we read the different narratives of the travellers and navigators, English, Dutch, French, Russian, Swedish, Danish; we enquired into the roads to be followed on land to reach the shores of the Polar Sea; we discussed the difficulties to be overcome, the precautions to be taken against the rigors of the climate, the attacks of wild animals, the scarcity of food."[2] Apparently Malesherbe's encouragement was not purely scientific. According to an article by George Colas, Malesherbes, in conjunction with Chateaubriand's family, wanted to get the young man away from the nefarious indolence of Parisian life.[3]

Chateaubriand left for America in April, 1791, arriving in Baltimore on the 11th day of July. His stay in the New World was rather short, as he returned to France at the end of November in the same year.

His grandiose project, conceived in the comfortable surroundings of Malesherbes's library, came to naught in America. In Buffalo, the young man contacted a fur trader, named Swift, who, upon hearing of the project, simply laughed it off. He recommended that the young Frenchman prepare for his undertaking by acquainting himself with life in the American wilderness while learning several Indian languages and spending time with some of the Hudson Bay agents. Swift further suggested that after a training period of about 4 or 5 years, with the financial backing of the French government, he might be ready to begin his search for the Northwest Passage. This very wise advice did not set well with the impatient young man. He had wanted to go to the North Pole as one would go from Paris to Pontoise.[4] Later, he mentioned in his *Historical Essay* that his trip to the United States was to have been purely exploratory.[5] He had planned to submit a more definite project to Malesherbes who would in turn have requested governmental subsidies for its undertaking. Of course, this too was never realized because of the political turmoil in France and Malesherbes's execution under the Reign of Terror.

Although the exploration was never realized and his stay in the United States was very short, the American experience was for Chateaubriand a lasting one in terms of creativity. Rene Bazin in *Chateaubriand et l'Amerique* notes that for Chateaubriand it was the journey par excellence, one which exerted on his sensibilities and on his genius the most decisive influence and which made him one of the giants of literature.[6] And certainly this is true, for the American experience in one form or another, apeared in Chateaubriand's writing from his first work—*Historical Essay*—in 1797, to his last—*Memoirs from Beyond the Grave*—published in 1848.

Generally the American influence is considered in terms of descriptive poetry such as the beautiful settings of Chateaubriand's novels. Even more, perhaps, his own experience of life. My contention is that the American travels influenced the writer in terms of his vision of the world expressed through the main themes of his writings: Conflict between cultures and glorification of the past. In terms of Chateaubriand's creativity, his American experience opened him to the possibility of transforming reality and disillusion into poetic beauty, and taught him that imagination is the mainspring of human experience and literature. As Richard Switzer in his introduction to Chateaubriand's *Travels in America* comments, "America, as Chateaubriand portrayed it, was much more a product of his reading and his imagination than of his actual visit."[7]

The first result of Chateaubriand's reading and imagination was the itinerary of his travels. So intertwined was reality and imagination that it has been a subject of debate since 1827.[8] Most scholars agree on two itineraries, one factual, the other fictional. The former appears less exotic than the latter, and it reveals the fact that the young traveller remained mostly in the Northeastern part of the United States. He visited Baltimore, Philadelphia, and New York, probably Boston, and Lexington, then Albany, following the Mohawk Trail to Niagara Falls. After the Falls his itinerary is uncertain. He claimed visits to Pittsburgh and on the warpath. Since Chateaubriand makes no mention of the Indian troubles nor of the French settlement of Scioto, which at that time had received much publicity in France, it appears that he did not actually visit that region. We may presume that he spent most of his time around Niagara Falls.

The fictional itinerary covers the whole length of the United States. According to Chateaubriand, after his visit to Niagara Falls, he went down to Pittsburgh, then down the Ohio and the

Mississippi, visited the Natchez, making a side trip to Florida. After visiting the Southern part of the United States, he returned to Ohio. While there he read about the flight of Louis the sixteenth and decided to return to France. This itinerary was obviously the product of Chateaubriand's imagination; during his brief stay in America, he could not possibly have travelled so extensively, even under the best of circumstances and certainly not when there were Indian troubles in the Ohio valley. In fact, the fictional itinerary developed only after the publication of *Atala and Rene* ten years after the actual visit.

In his *Historical Essay,* published in 1797, the only reference made to his American voyage is with regard to the Northeastern part of United States. In describing what he did not really see, Chateaubriand followed the tradition of early travel literature. Great travellers, aware that their travel narratives could not be checked on, added an element of fantasy and imagination—a poetic veneer to their narratives. Chateaubriand himself mentioned that in America the poet overcame the traveller and promised to poetry what had been lost for science.[9]

The transformation of reality by the use of imagination is a particular characteristic of Chateaubriand. We find it again in another travel narrative, the *Itinerary from Paris to Jerusalem.* In this narrative of Chateaubriand's journey to the Middle East, the factor of disillusion with reality is one of the processes of creativity.

In his *Travels in America,* Chateaubriand shares with his readers his experiences in America. He had been overwhelmed by the scenic beauty and had experienced an exhilarating feeling of complete freedom in the wilderness, but was disappointed by the American cities, the people and his first meeting with Indians. He described Philadelphia in these terms: "The aspect of Philadelphia is cold and monotonous. In general the cities in the United States are lacking in monuments, especially old monuments...almost nothing at Philadelphia, New York, Boston, rises above the mass of walls and roofs. The eye is saddened by this level appearance."[10] As for the people, he had imagined them as being the new Romans, full of virtue and probity: "A man landing as I did in the United States, full of enthusiasm for the ancients, a Cato seeking everywhere for the rigidity of early Roman manners, is necessarily shocked to find everywhere the elegance of dress, the luxury of carriages, the frivolity of conversations, the disproportion of fortunes, the immorality of banks and gaming houses, the noise of dancehalls and theaters" (15). And his long-awaited introduction to the "noble savage" might well be termed one of the greatest disappointments he had ever felt. He described it in great detail: "In the midst of a forest, there could be seen a kind of barn; I found in this barn a score of savages, men and women, daubed like sorcerers, their bodies half naked, their ears slit, raven's feathers on their heads and rings in their noses. A little Frenchman, powdered and curled as in the old days, with an apple-green coat, brocaded jacket, muslin frill and cuffs, was scraping on a miniature violin, having these Iroquois dance Madelon Friquet..."(22). The writer concludes sadly "it was a rather strange thing for a disciple of Rousseau to be introduced to primitive life with a ball given for Iroquois by a former kitchen boy of General Rochambeau" (23). The Indians no longer conformed to the image of the natural man which Chateaubriand had envisioned before his departure. The traveller sadly notes: "I inquired into their usages [those of the Indians]; in return for small presents, I was given representation of their former customs, for the customs themselves no longer exist" (230).

The mental image which Chateaubrand had formed in Europe of the American people and of the Indians was rapidly dispelled when he came in contact with reality. The disenchantment which resulted from it led to a creative process of reconstruction of the former glory of the Indian nations, of a return to the past through imagination.

Chateaubriand, in his contacts with the American Indians, was greatly impressed by the decadence he saw within the tribes. As a disciple of Rousseau at the time of his travels, he had sought the natural man only to find him corrupted by civilization. The following remark shows clearly that the decay was already in progress: "The Indian has become perfidious, selfish, lying and dissolute; his cabin is a receptacle for filth and dirt. When he was nude or covered with animal skins, there was something proud and great about him; today European rags, without covering his nudity, merely attest to his misery: he is a beggar at the door of the trading post; he no longer is a savage in his forest" (182).

In his analysis of the causes of the decay of the Indian nations, Chateaubriand very carefully points out that, contrary to what many colonists believed, the Indians were not savages but had already attained a highly sophisticated level of culture which was incompatible with that of the Europeans: "...the European civilzation did not act on the pure state of nature; it acted on the rising American civilization; if it had found nothing, it would have created something; but it found manners and destroyed them because it was stronger and did not consider it should mix with those manners" (178).

Several factors combined to speed up the annihilation of the Indians: religious, political, economic, psychological and sexual. As Chateaubriand sees it, the native religious traditions have become confused, through the mixing of foreign ideas with those of the Indians. However, he feels that the Catholic religion is more appropriate than Protestantism to the education of the Indians, and praises his native countrymen—the early French missionary priests—for their exemplary lives and generosity to the Indians, while criticizing the Protestant governments for having been more interested in trading with the Indians than in caring about them as human beings.

In the area of politics, Chateaubriand feels that the delicate political structures of the Indian tribes were subverted by the European presence. He adds that "our presents, our vices, and our arms bought, corrupted, or killed the individuals who made up the several powers" (180-181).

Economics between Indians and Europeans was weighted heavily in favor of the latter. The fur traders were responsiblefor a subtly corrupting influence: "Pursued by the European avidity and by the corruption of civilized people even in the depths of their forests, the Indians exchange at these trading posts rich furs for objects of little value but which have become for them objects of prime necessity" (181-182).

The psychological cause for the decadence was even more subtle, for it attacked the dignity of man and put to question the

intrinsic worth of the Indians. The commanders of American and
English military posts assumed that they had authority over the
Indians and treated them as minors with no rights to the land
they occupied. Thus "the savage ends up believing he is not the
real possessor of the land disposed of without his being consulted;
he becomes accustomed to look upon himself as a species inferior
to the white; he consents to receive orders, to hunt, to fight for
masters" (181).

The final reason for the slow destruction of the Indian
nations was the sexual contacts between white adventurers and
Indian women. Chateaubriand felt that the half-breeds possessed
the vices of both parent races. They were the businessmen and the
brokers between the tribes and the fur-trading companies. For
Chateaubriand, they had no past and no culture and they were
the incarnation of the economic and political evils. He describes
them thus: "These bastards of civilized nature and savage nature
sell themselves now to the Americans, now to the English, to
deliver to them the monopoly of the pelts..." (182).

If reality and the present are so disappointing, and the
Indian culture has become decadent, there remains the
possibility of returning to the past. Chateaubriand casts himself
in the role of the spokesman for the Indians, as their historian:
"the roll of the indigenous peoples of that part of the New World
has not been called: I shall do it. Many men, many tribes will fail
to answer: a last historian of these peoples, I shall open their
death register" (174). This desire which corresponds so well to
Chateaubriand's personality and character, stems in part from
his own concept of the past and of literature. Its function is to
preserve the past and to set it against the devalued present, to
contrast glory and decay. The idea of preserving the past as a
living monument to former grandeur can only be accomplished
through literature. The Indians, because of their culture have
only an oral tradition which can disappear under the impact of
cultural strife. For Chateaubriand, the written word has the
power to keep and to preserve: "Civilized people have monuments
of letters and arts to preserve the memories of their homeland;
they have cities, palaces, towers, columns, obelisks; they have the
furrows in the field they have cultivated; their names are

engraved on bronze and marble; their actions are preserved in chronicles. The savages have nothing of all that: their names are not written on the trees of the forests; their hut, built in a few hours, perishes in a few moments; their simple plowing stick, which has only grazed the earth, has not even been able to raise a furrow; their traditional songs vanish with the memory that retains them, with the last voice that repeats them" (231).

Thus in recalling the religion, the political institutions, the mores and customs of the Indian nations, Chateaubriand preserves their past glory. In every instance the writer's purpose is to show that the Indian culture was not inferior to that of the Europeans, it was simply different and that, in fact, it had many traits of the ancient culture of Greece and Rome. At the same time, he attempts to make a balanced presentation. He notes that there are two ways of portraying the native population, neither of them correct: "one is to speak only of their laws and their manners, without entering into the details of their bizarre customs and their habits which are often disgusting to civilized men. Then all you will see will be Greeks and Romans... the other way consists in representing only the habits and customs of the savages, without mentioning their laws and their manners; then you will see only the smoky, filthy cabins to which retires a kind of monkey endowed with human speech" (81).

Chateaubriand also attempts to give a complete picture of the Indian culture as it had once been, including marriage customs, education of children, funerals, feasts, dances and games, medicine, languages, hunting, war, religion and political institutions. The presentation is made not by a trained anthropologist, but by a poet who finds grace and poetry in the Indian customs. Consequently, he points out the intrinsic value of these customs and makes it clear that the people called savages were indeed very much advanced in the art of languages and the combination of ideas. In other instances, he refers to the similarities between Indian customs and those of Europeans. He feels there is even a superiority in some of their customs, such as those of the Muskogees who have slaves but with whom slavery is not hereditary. Chateaubriand remarks on this subject: "the misfortune of the parents is not passed on to their posterity; the

Muskogees did not want servitude to be hereditary: a fine lesson that savages have given to civilized man" (164).

The task of the historian ends with the recording for posterity of what constitutes the grandeur of natural man. The Indian nations are no longer: "pushed by the European population toward the Northwest of North America; the savage population comes by a singular destiny to expire on the very shore on which they landed in unknown centuries to take possession of America. In the Iroquois language the Indians give themselves the name of 'men of forever'—*Ongoueonoue*. The 'men of forever' are gone, and the foreigner will soon leave to these legitimate heirs to a whole world, only the earth of their tombs" (178). The saga of the Indian nations ends in death.

But for Chateaubriand, death can be conquered. For him it is a literary theme which sustains his inspiration. By the power of the written word he has succeeded in creating a world where his "natural man" can live and remain forever free from the contamination of civilization. And, in the building of this new world, he has at the same time erected a kind of monument, not only to the Indian nations, but to his own creative genius as well.

Notes

[1] The project is first mentioned in the *Essai historique sur les revolutions anciennes et modernes,* published in London in 1797, and reprinted in the *Oeuvres completes* in 1826. It also appeared in the preface of *Atala* published in 1801, and in *Travels in America,* trans. by Richard Switzer (Lexington: University of Kentucky Press, 1969), p. 6.

[2] *Memoires of Francois Rene Vicomte de Chateaubriand,* trans. by Alexander Teixeiros de Mattos (London: Freemantle, 1902), I, p. 180.

[3] Georges Colas, 'L'Embanquement de Chateaubriand pour l'Americaque," *Nouvelle Revue de Britagne,* No. 2 (1947), p. 129.

[4] *Memoirs,* p. 218.

[5] *Essai sur les revolutions, Oeuvres completes* (Paris: Furne, Jouvet et Cie, 1880), vol. I, pp. 304-305.

[6] Rene Bazin, *Chateaubriand et l'Amerique* (Paris: La Table Ronde, 1969), p. 39.

[7] Switzer, p. xvi.

[8] cf. Richard Switzer, edition critique du *Voyage en Amerique* (Paris: Didier, 1964), pp. xxvi-xxxi.

[9]R.-R. de Chateaubriand, *Memories d'Outre-Tombe,* edition du Centenaire (Paris: Flammarion, 1948), I, pp. 287-288, 328.

[10]F.-R. de Chateaubriand, *Travels in America,* trans. by Richard Switzer (Lexington: University of Kentucky Press, 1969), p. 14. Subsequent references will be indicated in the text.

Originally published in *Exploration,* IV:1, December 1976. Reprinted with the permission of the editor and the author.

Travel Narratives of D.F. Sarmiento:
A Seminal Frontier Thesis

Cathryn A. Ducey

Until the relatively recent (1970) publication of Michael Rockland's translations of Domingo Faustino Sarmiento's *Travels,* interest in the Argentianian theorist and statesman has been practically nonexistent. Although some writers mention him as an advocate of public and progressive education in South America, and some economic and political studies deal with him as a liberal Latin-American President, Sarmiento's interest in the frontier development in Argentina are largely ignored. His *El Facundo* is read by some undergraduate and graduate students, with an emphasis upon the attacks, political and personal, on Rosas and other of the "barbarous" dictators.[1] Neglected, overlooked aspects of *Facundo* must be examined, along with his *Travels,* as presaging the frontier thesis of Frederick Jackson Turner, for Sarmiento theorized, generalized and applied concepts of the frontier based upon travels and observation.

Faustino Valentin Sarmiento was born February 15, 1811, in the Argentinian frontier town of San Juan de la Frontera. Located between the Andes and the Pampas, it had a population in 1811 of about 3,000. His family was poor, as were most of the inhabitants of San Juan. Early in life the young man took the name of his patron saint and became known as Domingo Faustino Sarmiento. He attended the first established school in the frontier province of San Juan; in 1825 he left school to become apprenticed to a French engineer; he next accepted the offer of his priest-uncle, Jose de Oro, to travel far outside the province and to study; in 1827 Sarmiento returned home to San Juan and began work as a shopkeeper in his aunt's store.

Somehow copies of Benjamin Franklin's *Autobiography* and of some works by Thomas Paine came into his hands. These books led him to decide that a "rationally ordered and understandable universe should exist."[2] Yet he saw no evidence of it on the Argentine frontier. Instead he saw only poverty, ignorance and a chaotic political situation. *Caudillo* (strongman) leaders like Manuel Rosas and Juan Facundo Quiroga were unconcerned about organized programs to combat poverty, illiteracy and uncertain political conditions.

As civil dissension became widespread, Argentinians were forced to choose between bending to the will and whip of the caudillos or following revolutionaries in the hopes of bringing reform to the government of Argentina. Sarmiento fought the caudillos and was forced into exile during the years 1828 to 1832.

While in self-imposed exile in Chile he began writing for newspapers, expressing his bitter disgust for the Federalists who were raping his country and undertaking what was to become a life-long role: teacher and advocate of public education.

He learned English, became caught up with the fever of the Chilian silver rush, became a mine worker and then a foreman. Such work must not have been fully satisfying, even if physically tiring, for he also gave English lessons, wrote assiduously, and began to develop his first full reform work—a program to colonize the Colorado River Valley.

From 1832 to 1839, while political equilibrium in Argentina was shakily maintained, Sarmiento zealously applied himself to personal development and to reforming some of the conditions in San Juan. The soldier-miner-fledgling teacher phases of his life were over. While earning a sketchy living as a journalist, he also founded a literary society and edited reform newspapers. Sarmiento set out to become a European in education, a North American in politics and a South American in loyalty.

Sarmiento began his best known work, *Civilization and Barbarism: the Life of Juan Facundo Quiroga* (popularly known in South America as *El Facundo* and in the United States as *Life in the Argentine Republic*), during the 1840s. This pseudo-biography was a vehicle for his attack on caudillo government and an analysis of the social and political causes of Argentina's problems. Primarily for this work Sarmiento is considered the major reformer of South America and the "Father of Spanish-American sociology."[3]

With the exception of particular passages dealing solely with the tyrant Juan Facundo Quiroga most of Sarmiento's *El Facundo* presages in tone, style and content both Mark Twain's

Roughing It and Turner's thesis. Sarmiento granted that he was not writing an unbiassed history of Argentina; he intended, rather, a study of "national antecedents, the features of the soil, in the popular customs and traditions."[4]

It is difficult to tell that it is Sarmiento writing of Argentina rather than Turner of the United States in the following passage from the end of *El Facundo:*

...Our future destiny is foretold in our numerous rivers, the boundless pasturage of our plains, our immense forests, and a climate favorable to the production of the whole world. If we lack an intelligent population, let the people of Europe once feel that there is permanent peace and freedom in our country, and multitudes of emigrants would find their way to a land where success is sure.[5]

A strong faith in Argentina's future is clear throughout *El Facundo.* The primary concerns trace the geographical and political conditions which transformed Argentina and describe individuals, both specific and archetypal, who influenced change.

Of the fourteen provinces in Argentina all except San Juan and Mendoza were pastoral; the city-dwellers of Buenos Aires were Europeanized and civilized, while the plains-frontier people recognized only the brutishness in life:

supremacy of the strongest, the absolute and irresponsible authority of rulers, the administration of justice without formalities or discussion.

Rule by force, whether by the leaders of cattle trains and caravans or by local gauchos (cowboys), is accepted and respected, as it was in the American West. Emigrants to the plains, enduring long journeys by caravan, learned to

acquire the habit of living far from society, of struggling, single-handed with nature, of disregarding privation, and of depending for protection against the dangers ever imminent upon no other resources than personal strength and skill.

Although Sarmiento continues to emphasize the self-sufficiency of the pampas pioneer/frontiersman, he finds the frontier traits only half-admirable. He contends, unlike Turner, that the lack of a stable, unified government, the isolation of "self-concentrated feudal" families, the roving nature of the gaucho, the lack of public schools and lack of tolerance for religious differences, and the "dearth of all amenities of life induces all the externals leading to barbarism."

The continual struggle of "isolated man with untamed nature," the constant "defying and subduing of nature," develops the "consciousness of individual consequence and superior prowess," but for Sarmiento it does not foster those principles of concern for the common good and progress which he believed so necessary for the development of a republic.

Life and customs on the pastoral pampas contrasted sharply with life in the commercial, water-based cities:

distinct, rival and incompatible forms of society, two differing kinds of civilization existed in the Argentine Republic: one being Spanish, European, and cultivated, the other barbarous, American, and almost wholly of native growth. The revolution which occurred in the cities acted only as the cause, the impulse, which set these two distinct forms of national existence face to face, and gave occasion for a contest between them, to be ended, after lasting many years, by the absorption of one into the other.

Sarmiento saw the struggle between Hispanic European civilization and native barbarism as a struggle between "mind and matter" quite different from anything else in the world.

Sarmiento's thesis is that the way of life on the pampas, the individualism, independence and anti-European traits of the gaucho, and the isolation from centers of culture, led directly to a confrontation of values culminating in the revolution.

It is important to note that the same traits which Turner cites as leading to democracy on the American frontier, as supportive to the principles of liberty and responsibility, are pointed to by Sarmiento as leading to precisely opposite goals and conditions. Just as these traits strengthened the North American Union they fractured Argentina.

Embarking on a fateful trip to the United States in 1847, arranged as a public relations gesture by his government, Sarmiento began a series of letters which later were published as his *Viajes,* translated as *Travels in the United States in 1847.*[6] Always perceptive and inquisitive, Sarmiento's discussions of and observations on American life in mid-century anticipate the personalistic reportorial genre of Mark Twain's *Roughing It* and *Life on the Mississippi.* Rambling, sympathetic, humorous, often disconnected, descriptions are recorded with the intention of suggesting some insights to the American character.

On his initial trip he visited twenty-one states and was impressed by the technology, the industrial growth of cities, and by the order resulting from a federal republic based upon allegiance to ideals.

On the other side of the Alleghenies, the New World begins.... In the west, Yankee genius has more room to move about and expand to try new things that would seem impossible in the older states. In the West they try things which are superhuman, inconceivable, seemingly absurd.[7]

In his *Travels* the various stages in frontier development which he describes in *Facundo* are re-established and a model of the frontier is expanded. On the American frontier, he says, the first pioneer is the "Indian Hater" who persecutes the native inhabitants of the lands so that they will desert them. Then come the Squatters, "who are misanthropes looking for solitude in which to dwell, danger for excitement, and the work of felling trees...." The real pioneers come next, "opening the forests, sowing the earth, and spreading themselves over a great area." Once they are established, the "capitalist impresarios" follow, nearly on their heels, along with immigrant laborers and fortune-hunting youth. Finally are established the proprietary class, the cities, and the commercial routes.[8]

Sarmiento suggests that the availability of free and open land partially contributes to the prospering western development of the United States. But he asks, "...then why in South America, where it is just as easy if not easier to take up new land, are population and wealth not increasing?"[9] There, with a greater amount of virgin land than in the United States "have the backwardness, poverty and ...ignorance" continued unabated. The reason why the mere existence of free land cannot be accepted as the major impetus for prosperity is clear:

> The American is a man with a home or the certainty of having one, a man beyond the clutch of hunger or desperation, a man with hopes for the future as bright as the imagination can invent, a man with political sentiments and needs. He is, in short, master of himself with a spirit elevated by education and a sense of his own dignity.[10]

These are attributes the Hispano-American lacks, and until they can be developed through education the free land of the Pampas will remain uncultivated, the masses of people will remain in poverty, and the nation of Argentina will not prosper. "...Being a new country does not mean anything if action is wanting."[11]

Americans, in contrast, are "free men and not disciplined prisoners whose lives are administered," and they are energetic and active.[12]

The North American frontier land belongs to the Union and is sold for a dollar an acre to any man; while in Argentina, says Sarmiento, the system of land distribution is different. There land concessions are granted first to the conquistadors

> ...who established earldoms for themselves, while soldiers, fathers of the sharecropper, that worker without land who multiplies without increasing the number of his buildings, sheltered themselves in the shade of their improvised roofs. The passion to occupy lands in the name of the king drove men to dominion over entire districts, which put great distances between landowners so that after three centuries the intervening land still has not been cleared. The city, for this reason, has been suppressed in the vast design, and the few villages which have been created since the conquest have been *decreed* by presidents."[13]

On the other hand, the American takes possession of his lands "in the name of the kings of the world: Work and Good Will."[14]

Sarmiento's view of the American seeking to tame the wilderness is admittedly romantic. He sees the Yankee as "a born proprietor," dreaming of conquering the forests. The western wilderness is tamed by "American Alexanders, who wander through the wilds looking for points that a profound study of the future indicates will be centers of commerce. The Yankee, an inventor of cities, professes a speculative science which leads him by deduction to the divination of a site where a future city must flourish."[15] Unhampered by the stigmas of ignorance or poverty and unimpeded by governmental regulations he accepts the land as his. His is a free "colonizing spirit," untrammelled by outside forces. Thus do

Americans cross six hundred leagues of wilderness for an ideal....They sacrifice themselves for the future of the nation....These people carry with them, like a political conscience, certain constitutive principles of association. Political science becomes moral sentiment, perfecting the man, the people, even the mob. The municipality is converted into a phenomenon dependent upon spontaneous association. There is liberty of conscience and of thought. There is trial by jury.[16]

How different are the Americans from the Argentinians of any class, who are unable to conceive of voluntary association for the common good, unable to consider a political system based upon the principle of liberty, unable to forget the strictures of both religion and class. For they, their revolution not withstanding, assume that government exists because of the necessity to regulate the actions of individuals according to a predetermined code. And, says Sarmiento, without a system of universal education, the Argentine Republic will not be able to provide man with the means to develop fully his moral and political conscience.

    In his *Travels* Sarmiento is concerned with actions and attitudes and customs of people throughout the United States, although his recurring emphasis is upon the westward movement and progress. Various customs are a source of both interest and amusement. Lack of attention paid to leisurely eating is somewhat disconcerting to the fastidious Sarmiento: "The American has two minutes set aside for lunch, five for dinner, ten for a smoke or to chew tobacco....The Yankee *pur sang* eats all his food, desserts, and fruit from the same plate, one at a time or all together."[17]

Lack of respect for privacy is rife in America: "In the reading rooms [of large hotels] four or five parasites support themselves heavily on your shoulders to read the same tiny bit of print you are reading....If you are tranquilly smoking your cigar, a passerby will take it out of your mouth in order to light his own."[18] If certain niceties of manners are not observed as they are in Europe or in South America it is perhaps because the trappings of civilization are unimportant in a burgeoning, apparently classless society. More to the point, for Sarmiento, is the acceptance by the American of man by man, whatever he may be lacking in the social graces.

Tolerance for men, and for their vagaries and differences, impresses the Argentinian visitor. As a Hispano-Catholic, reared with the rigid authority of the Spanish church ubiquitous in his country, Sarmiento is amazed by the American acceptance of the number and variety of religious sects. Although some of the frenetic, enthusiastic, or faith healing sects are both strange and unusual, he is impressed by the tolerance among the people he meets of and for religious differences.

Related to the tolerance of religious attitudes and practices is the American development and support of philanthropic and improvement organizations, an interest unheard of among South Americans. That individuals would give away capital to help their fellow man, that others would crusade against drunkenness, that anyone would freely donate money to establish institutions for the sick, the insane, or for the education of orphans—these are aspects of the uniquely North American way of life which so intrigues Sarmiento, and of which he approves. Groups and individuals seeking the improvement of society, with nothing to gain personally, he believes are a reflection and product of the American's overwhelming interest in mass education.[19]

Even if he sees much of the country and the lives of its inhabitants through the proverbial rose-colored classes, even if he can believe that all the mill girls in Lowell are "educated...conscientious and devoted to their work."[20] one comes to understand that such seemingly naive conclusions and his almost child-like acceptance of anything American are understandable. He reaches conclusions because he almost desperately wants to believe that somewhere in the world an ideal state for all men could exist.

Such was his dream for his homeland. If the North American model could be imposed upon, or accepted by, Argentina then there was reason to hope and dream that his country could one day be as settled, as prosperous, its lands as cultivated, its people as free as in the United States.

The United States progressed rapidly because Old World values were cast off, because Americans continually searched for ways of improving the land and society. Thus, Sarmiento reflects bitterly about South America. In his own country he deplores what the Spaniards had not done in three centuries compared to what had been acomplished in less time in the United States.

Sarmiento remains optimistic that there will be a change, for he believes that in the expansion and "mixing and juxtaposition" of peoples that someday all America will be "homogenous." He firmly accepts the idea of the "melting pot," although slavery was a jarring note.

Sarmiento sees slaves as unassimilated and suppressed, describing slavery in the United States as "the deep ulcer and the incurable fistula which threatens to corrupt the robust body of the Union!"[21] He believes that the Founding Fathers made a "fatal error" in allowing the injustice of man's subjugation to man to exist in a country founded on diametrically opposed principles. He astutely remarks that had slavery been abolished with the Declaration of Independence or the Constitution at a time when the number of slaves was relatively few that it would have been a much more acceptable act then than in the nineteenth century. He suggests that a "racial war within a century" will take place, for he sees the division between slave and free states and the increasing numbers of Negroes as portents for a dire future.[22] He is concerned that slavery is a blight upon a fruitful democratic nation.

In spite of such weaknesses in the North American system, by and large Sarmiento sees only good. As a thoroughly curious traveller he remarks upon the many freedoms that Americans have. Among these is the freedom to travel at will. "Since everyone travels, there is no impossible or unprofitable enterprise in the field of transportation.... The great number of travellers makes for cheap rates, and cheap rates in turn tempt those who have no precise object in mind to go somewhere."[23] Even in 1847 Sarmiento was aware that the peripatetic American was unique in the world.

As he moves about the country, Sarmiento observes that in this dynamic society "the hotels will be more important than any other kind of public construction." Not only do the hotels which accommodate the increasing number of travellers impress him with public and private appointments, but so also do other buildings, such as banks and municipal edifices. The eclectic attitude of the American architects suggests: "If the Americans have not, then, created a new kind of architecture, they have at least developed national applications, forms, and a character influenced by their political and social institutions."[24]

The "melting pot," adaptability, and ingenuity in architecture, manners, and customs contrast with differences in his own country. In the Argentinian population centers public and private architecture was solely Spanish-inspired, modified only by availability of materials. Country adobe huts were crude, built from available materials. Hispanic class and national attitudes were reflected in architecture. In the United States, however, the buildings reflect pride in monuments, a penchant for echoing styles of past, republican, ages, and general experimental uses of forms and materials.

As population moved restlessly the need for railroads and varieties of internal communication and transport systems developed. The westward movement and attendant growth of industrial cities Sarmiento attributes, partially, to "the infallible Yankee instinct for sensing places which will produce wealth...."[25]

Sarmiento judged the adaptability of the new westerners to be important, but recognized that even as emigrants from the East Coast and immigrants from Europe and the Orient adapted to new conditions so also

the land soon puts its stamp upon them.... So the fragments of old societies are coming together in the flood of immigrants, mixing and forming the newest, the youngest, and the most daring republic on the face of the earth.[26]

The words foreshadow Turner's assertion that the land makes an impression on the people who set out, initially, to conquer it; "Americanization" takes place.

Portents for success on the frontier include, says Sarmiento, not only the adaptability of the new westerners and their inherent native ingenuity, but also the development of towns. Sarmiento describes "the village, which is the center of political life, just as the family is the center of domestic life...the essence of the United States is to be found in its small towns. This cannot be said of any other country."[27]

Even in the poorest of villages, he notes, North Americans repect and use manufactured items (locks, kitchen utensils, plows, axes) rather than local, crudely crafted items. Amenities lacking in South American villages (signposts, hotels, newspapers, banks, churches, post office, streets) are omnipresent in even the newest of American villages. What he sees as a basic difference between life in semi-isolated areas on the two continents is "widespread distribution of civilized ways in the towns as well as in the cities and among men of all classes."[28]

Sarmiento is quick to accept, however, that the signs of "civilized ways" do diminish the further west one moves.

"Westward, where civilization diminishes," he writes, "and in the FAR WEST, where it is almost non-existent because of the sparseness of the population, things are, of course, different. Comfort is reduced to what is strictly necessary....But even in these remote plantations there is an appearance of perfect equality among the population in their dress, in their manners, and even in their intelligence. The merchant, the doctor, the SHERIFF, the farmer—all look the same....Americans do not wear jackets or ponchos, but have a dress common to all and a universal roughness of manner which gives an impression of equality in education."[29]

How different are these views, of dress and attitudes, from appearances on the Argentinian frontier! There class differences in clothing and manner are readily apparent. The peon would be recognized by poncho and hand woven garments, the cleric by black robes, and if perchance a wealthy merchant or doctor travelled through a farm region the European cut in jackets, trousers and imported linens would be signs of wealth.

Beyond the superficial similitude in clothing and roughness of manner what Sarmiento finds most characteristic of Americans

Is their ability to appropriate for their own use, generalize, popularize, conserve, and perfect all the practices, tools, methods, and aids which the most advanced civilization has put in the hands of men. In this the United States is unique on earth. There are no unconquerable habits that retard for centuries the adoption of an obvious improvement, and , on the other hand, there is a predisposition to try anything. . . . You would have to wait a century for something like this to happen in Spain, or in France, or in our own part of America.[30]

In his continuation of a seminal "frontier thesis" Sarmiento says that civilization is comprised of "moral and physical perfection or the abilities which a civilized man develops in order to subject nature to his desires."[31] Such perfection and abilities exist on only one frontier in the world and only among the men who forge their way through that frontier. Only the American is able to adapt to conditions easily, accept man as man, believe in his own ability to conquer nature, to use technology, to rely on his own native gifts of intuition and intelligence not only to survive in the wilderness, but to succeed. The ability and the willingness to try new things, new ways, new lands, is intrinsic to the American: ". . . If you want to know if a machine, an invention, or a social doctrine is useful and can be applied or developed in the near future, you must test it on the touchstone of Yankee knowhow."[32] The pragmatic and utilitarian and ingenious American "far from barbarizing, as we have, the elements which European civilization handed him when he came as a settler, has worked to perfect them and even improve upon them."[33]

With the attributes Sarmiento describes he finds it understandable that American inventions, products, and business forms rapidly displace those of Europe. But America's greatest potential for development lies in the citizen's "possession of the land which will be the nursery of his new family,"[34] in the small free-hold system.

Again and again Sarmiento recalls the points first made in *El Facundo:* that an inevitable confrontation occurs when civilization and barbarism meet and that the outcome decides the future of a nation. At the beginning of *El Facundo* he writes:

If any form of national literature should appear in these new American societies, it must result from the description of the mighty scenes of nature, and still more from the illustration of the struggle between European civilization and native barbarism, between mind and matter— a struggle of imposing magnitude in South America....[35]

In North America only Cooper, Sarmiento suggests, was able to capture the sense of the struggle:

by removing the scene of the events he described from the settled portion of the country to the border land between civilized life and that of the savage, the theatre of war for the possession of the soil waged against each other, by the native tribes and the saxon race.[36]

As he pursues these points as journalist and statesman he repeatedly affirms his frontier thesis.

Although the cultural historian Henry Nash Smith asserts Turner's

most important debt to his intellectual tradition is the idea of savagery and civilization that he uses to define his central factor. His frontier is explicitly 'the meeting point between savagery and civilization.'[37]

Clearly Sarmiento's location of the scene of man's struggle as "the border land between civilized life and that of the savage" and his emphasis upon the battle between "European civilization and native barbarism," nearly fifty years before Turner, is equally, if not more, important to the intellectual tradition.

What makes Sarmiento unique is the background from which he writes. He was neither a semi-trained political theorist as was a de Tocqueville, nor was he a transplanted—but seemingly thoroughly adapted "American" as a de Crevecouer. Nor was he a native-born, self-made, thoroughly new-world, North American as was Franklin. Although he could assess and accept the vagaries of American frontier life, he was not the native satirist, or the "adaptable" American that was a Mark Twain. Nor, indeed, was he a Ph.D. trained historian, a product of the West, of the East, of universities, of the Germanic "school" of analysis as Turner was. He was not the interesting romantic novelist, as Cooper was, nor an intellectual like Emerson, nor a politician-statesman like T.R. Roosevelt. He was none of these and yet all of them.

Sarmiento is examined, although rarely at length, by historians who concern themselves with developments in Latin and South American history and political theory. He, Echeverria and Mitre and Rivadavia, as Argentine political theorists and presidents, belong in histories and analyses of South American development. But only Sarmiento can be considered as an instigator of changes in Argentina based upon analyses of a North American model. For it is he alone who could look at his own country and decide that he needed to assess analogues before he could set forth possible changes. He alone looked to a North American model as a total possibility for a means to develop a free and prosperous Argentina.

Beyond and above all else, it is the traveller-statesman D.F.V.Sarmiento of Argentina who formulates a thesis concerning the American Frontier as coherent and complete—if not more complete—as that of Frederick Jackson Turner of the United States.

Many contemporary historians have dismissed Turner's thesis for its generalizations, its roots in a romantic view of the American West, and its over-emphasis upon individualism. Others have questioned his lack of emphasis upon economic changes and his over-emphasis of the frontier as a decisive factor in shaping American life and thought. Few argue, however, about his definition of the frontier as a meeting point between civilization and savagery as being uniquely American. And historians credit Turner with being the first commentator to approach the concept of the American frontier from an analytic viewpoint. It seems almost futile to dismiss his "Frontier Thesis" as unimportant in analyses of American culture. If nothing else, he precipitated arguments about the nature of American development, and thus prompted other historians to delve into reasons for what shaped "the American Character."

Turner wrote, primarily, in the late nineteenth century, and he is especially important for: 1) precipitating historiographical inquiry based on New World, not Old World, models; and, 2) attempting a definition of New World development unlike any previously recognized by the North American academic world. He wrote within a context; he was a westerner, a man brought up on the frontier past—its realities and myths. His was an "insider's" interpretation.

Turner was nurtured on generalizations about the American frontier. It was the "safety-valve," a place where Huck Finns could "light out," to, if necessary, to build a new life. Frontier life produced archetypal political characters in Daniel Boone and Andrew Jackson. Controversy over slavery was promoted because of the Territories. Travellers continually commented about the New American produced on the frontier. Many of the frontier aspects celebrated by Turner existed in a Tidewater Virginia or a Puritan Massachusetts; de Tocqueville and de Crevecouer described many of the same concepts of the American Character as "foreigners" observing life in the New World. Turner wrote out of his understandings and experience about frontier attributes psychologically accepted by most nineteenth century Americans. He solidified concepts, myths and psychological viewpoints.

In contrast, D.F. Sarmiento's interpretation of the frontier arises from a different set of experiences and background. He is the "outsider," a Hispanic-American, self-educated, relatively uninformed about North America. His knowledge was very limited when he finished *Facundo* in 1845. Yet from that limited knowledge he expresses in *Facundo* and later in the *Viajes* some startling insights: 1) a redefinition of the frontier as a meeting place between barbarism and civilization; 2) a celebration of individuality as it develops away from the cities; and, 3) an elaboration of the several phases of frontier social development.

Sarmiento, like Turner, sees the frontier as a step in the development of a nation and a national character. From a totally different psychological, social and educational background he arrives at similar definitions. His travels in the United States solidified his impressions and interpretations, but did not create them.

Notes

[1] *El Facundo* is best known in the English translation by Mary Peabody Mann, *Life in the Argentine Republic in the Days of the Tyrants; or, Civilization and Barbarism.* (New York: 1960). All quotations from *El Facundo* will be referenced hereinafter as *Life in the Argentine Republic....*

[2] Allison Williams Bunkley, *The Life of Sarmiento* (Princeton: 1952), p. 63.

[3] Bunkley, pp. 179-80.

[4] *Life in the Argentine Republic,* p. 4.

[5] *Life in the Argentine Republic,* p. 247. Unless otherwise noted all successive quotations from Sarmiento are from this source.

[6] Michael Aaron Rockland, Sarmiento's *"Travels in the United States."* (Princeton: 1970).

[7] Quoted by Rockland, pp. 64-5, from "Hacia el Oeste."

[8] Rockland, p. 190.

[9] Rockland, p. 153.

[10] Rockland, p. 153.

[11] Rockland, p. 155.

[12] Rockland, p. 158.

[13] Rockland, p. 165.

[14] Rockland, p. 165.

[15] Rockland, p. 166.

[16] Rockland, p. 171.

[17] Rockland, pp. 147-8.

[18] Rockland, p. 148.

[19] Rockland, p. 244, and elsewhere in text.

[20] Rockland, p. 246.

[21] Rockland, p. 304.

[22] Rockland, p. 305.

[23] Rockland, pp. 133-4.

[24] Rockland, p. 145.

[25] Rockland, p. 123.

[26] Rockland, p. 124.

[27] Rockland, pp. 126-7.

[28] Rockland, p. 131.

[29] Rockland, pp. 131-2.

[30]Rockland, pp. 132-3.

[31]Rockland, p. 133.

[32]Rockland, p. 144.

[33]Rockland, pp. 162-3.

[34]Quoted in Edmundo Correas, *Sarmiento and the United States* (Gainesville: 1961), p. 19.

[35]*Life in the Argentine Republic,* p. 25.

[36]*Life in the Argentine Republic,* p. 25.

[37] Smith, p. 293.

American Travelers Abroad

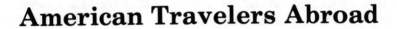

Americans Abroad:
The Popular Art of Travel Writing in the Nineteenth Century

Ahmed M. Metwalli

Almost every prominent American literary figure of the nineteenth century has written one type or another of travel book or based some of his literary output on his experiences of travel in foreign lands. And yet the travel literature of the century has not been adequately studied and, so far, books of travel have never been universally accepted as a literary genre. More than twenty years ago, Thomas H. Johnson underscored the undeserved neglect that was and still is the lot of this genre: "And discussion of the literature written to interpret foreign countries," said Johnson, "must at present be very incomplete, for few investigations of the subject have been undertaken."[1] Yet the value of this literature in interpreting the Old World to America in the nineteenth century, especially on the level of popular interest, the vital role it played in mass culture,[2] and the impact it had on some cultural trends of the century cannot be overestimated.

The "cultural" orientation of the age was responsible for the increased production and dissemination of books of travel. During the nineteenth century, almost every literate and zealous traveler managed to avail himself of one or more, and sometimes all, public media, to excite, entertain, or instruct the masses with his own experiences in foreign lands. Public lectures in the increasingly popular Lyceums, serialized travel letters, serialized articles, and books were available organs of expression. The romantic adventurer, the explorer, the missionary, the merchant or mercantile agent, the diplomatic and military envoy, as well as the man of letters, were all able to reach and influence the public in one way or another.

The interest and avidity of a reading public aware of its deficiency in knowledge and information encouraged this kind of composition. The cultural milieu was certainly ripe. Moreover, since it was the fashionable thing to do and also the most lucrative financially, almost every individual who left home—

even for a hike in the mountains—committed his impressions and experiences to paper and inflicted them on the reading public. Most of these producers of travel yarns lacked what Matthew Arnold calls "the power of the man," which, combined with "the power of the moment," produces a work of literary merit. The very few nineteenth-century travelers who possessed this "power" and who concern us here, were submerged in an interminable sea of mediocrity. And though their travel books were instrumental in the ultimate shaping and vitality of their literary artistic lives, these books were engulfed in oblivion—the oblivion which is almost always the destiny of whatever is written for the level of popular rather than intellectual interest—by the indiscriminate and uncritical taste of the contemporary reading public which made an instant success of almost every travel book.

All kinds of books of travel, a large number of which were mere hasty collections of unedited letters or article serials, sold by the tens of thousands. Many ran into tens of reprints and were in constant demand for decades after their first publication. Because they almost always succeeded in satisfying the immediate cultural and nationalistic needs of the reading public, they were among the best sellers of the day. Publishers encouraged authors to write accounts of their travel experiences at home and abroad; they knew well that travel narratives needed very little promotion and almost no puffing.[3] Six editions of Bayard Taylor's first book of travels, *Views Afoot,* plublished in 1846 when he was barely twenty years old, were sold in the first year; and in less than a decade twenty editions were printed.[4] His royalties from *Journey to Central Africa* (August, 1854) and *The Lands of the Saracens* (October, 1858), had mounted to $2,650 by the first of the new year.[5] He must have anticipated the success of his volumes of travel and the sums that would accrue from their immediate sale. Attuned to the needs and demands of the reading public, Taylor, in a casual and business-like manner, stated in the preface to the first edition of his second volume of travel, *Journey to Central Africa,* that his "reasons for offering this volume to the public are, simply, that there is room for it." Indeed, there was "room" enough not only for his personal accounts, but for a *Cyclopedia of Modern Travel* and a whole *Illustrated Library of*

Travel, both of which he edited.

Nor was this instant success and popular favor Bayard Taylor's lot alone. The travel books of other literary figures were similarly, if not as spectacularly, blessed. The first edition of 2,500 copies of George William Curtis's book, *Nile Notes of Howadji* (1851) was exhausted within six months.[6] His second book, *Howadji in Syria* (1852), met with the same success. Significantly, the sale of Melville's books declined as he moved away from the domain of popular travel literature which he had considered at the onset of his career to be his literary field. The first edition of some 3,000 copies of *Omoo* (1847), which is a melange of fact and fiction based on Melville's travel adventures in the South Seas, was selling out so rapidly in its first week of publication that a new printing was immediately planned. On the other hand, the more intellectual and subtle *Moby Dick* (1851) sold only 2,500 copies in its first five years, and only 2,965 in its first twenty.[7]

Emerson was also graced by this same popular favor. The first printing of 3,000 copies of his *English Traits* (1856), which is actually more an essay in cultural anthropology dealing with ideas and institutions than a travel book of intinerant wanderings and recorded experiences, sold immediately. Within a month, a second edition of 2,000 copies was printed. Mark Twain's *The Innocents Abroad* (1869) established his fame as a popular author. A little over thirty thousand copies were sold during the first five months after publication, and by the end of the first year 67,000 copies were bought at $3.50 each.[8]

The demand for travel literature was not restricted to the printed word. Lyceums and the popular lectures which grew out of the Lyceum system were other media used by travelers to entertain, instruct and satisfy the curiosity of the public about ancient and faraway places. Enterprising lecture booking-agents, such as James Redpath and his successor, James B. Pond, guided and catered to the needs and tastes of the new national audience; and travelers and travel writers were their most profitable assets. Much could be learned about the popularity of travel literature from the fact that while Emerson could earn as much as $2,000 for a season of lecturing after a considerable effort, Bayard Taylor often made $5,000 from his travel lectures.[9] These travel lectures were derived mostly from the lecturer's own travel journal or book; sometimes, the lecture room functioned as a useful proving ground for materials intended for publication. In either case, the lecture podium was utilized by the travelers to promote their already available or forthcoming travel books, augmenting their sales considerably.

These figures provide us with ample evidence of the phenomenal popularity of travel literature. But the question that needs to be answered is why were nineteenth-century books of travel the best sellers of their time?

Geared for the masses, popular literature in all its infinite variety—and American popular literature included such diverse types as travel books, tall tales of the Near and Far East and the American West, sea-lore adventures, popular journals and magazines, almanacs, dime or best-selling novels—mirrors the intellectual complex of an age, reflecting its ideas, activities, and motivations to action; in short, it sums up its culture. It also reveals the "cultural dialects" which may exist side by side in the writings of representative men in any given period, and which may appear, especially if divested of their historical and intellectual contexts, as puzzling or paradoxical. Arthur E. Christy aptly described popular literature as the "weathercock which points the direction of all winds of opinion that blow."[10] An understanding of these "winds of opinion" is essential in comprehending the *raison d'etre* of the bulk and popularity of books of travel in the nineteenth century. It was the remarkable increase in the number of travel books as the century progressed that prompted James Grant Wilson to note in 1886 that "American books of Old World travel" were appearing in "battalions."[11] Stanley Williams pointed out the necessity of tracing the real roots of this pehnomenal growth and popularity of travel books, which rivaled those of history and fiction, when he observed:

To ascribe the increase of travel books, expanding from a rivulet at the beginning of the century to a gigantic river at its close, to the growing number of travelers and these to the enlarged facilities of transportation is too simple a logic.[12]

The not too simple logic behind the phenomenal growth and popularity of travel books could be traced to two seemingly opposed traits in the American temperament, which were markedly reflected in the American literary scene. The one was the conscious need for a past with its established values, institutional continuity, and stable traditions. The other was a similarly strong conscious need for national identity and the establishment of the definable American "Self," the creation of the "New Adam" entirely based on the exclusively American vistas of democratic experience. The pull of the past and the push of the present formed the nucleus of this double consciousness, and most travel books of the nineteenth century did indeed embody it.

Culturally, America was still an unhistorical land, a land which had neither a childhood replete with romantically lovable experiences nor a youth confirmed in exemplary patterns. The short historical past that the Americans possessed was not yet crystallized in terms of popular "traditions" or "myths," which are needed psychologically for man's sense of stability. A large number of Americans who were entering upon the life of the mind for the first time during the first half of the nineteenth century had a strong romantic bent. This bent expressed itself in a serious interest in the past, in faraway places, and in the vast treasures of knowledge that they contained. The strong obsession with the past was partially, yet vehemently, stirred by the public's acute consciousness of the wide chasm that separated it from old stable traditions. A large segment of the new reading public was aware of what it lacked and also was concerned about the danger of both intellectual and cultural insularity that 3,000 miles of ocean could lead to.[13] The measure of the awareness and concern of this new class evinced itself in the response of the literary figures. American men of letters were obliged to satisfy the needs of increasing millions of new readers. Lacking a past, the literary figures in the United States had to look to the other side of the Atlantic and more often than not cross the Atlantic itself in their endeavor to meet their obligations. Inevitably, the development and growth of an indigenous literature were hampered in proportion to the success of the literary figures in their attempts to satisfy these needs; for the outcome was largely a derivative literature.

The strong need for national identity and the desire to trace and establish an identifiable American "Self" was the other facet of this double consciousness. It had its roots in the political experiment of the new nation, which demanded a break with the past and an assertion of the sovereignty of the present. Such sentiment was forcibly conveyed in the declamation of the *Democratic Review* in 1839: "Our national birth was the beginning of a new history...which separates us from the past and connects us with the future only."[14] Declamations like this had their repercussions in the literary scene; and as R.W.B. Lewis has pointed out, such "a manifesto of liberation from the past" meant a more vigorous demand "for an independent literature to communicate the novelty of experience in the New World."[15]

Furthermore, since the beginning of the century, the question of a native literature was constantly confused with the issue of patriotism; and patriotism was rampant in a nation that had won its political independence only a few decades earlier, and whose viability was further tested in the War of 1812. In the eighteen twenties and early thirties the British reviews, the *Quarterly* and *Blackwood's*, carried on a campaign of invective in which they "decried and insulted America as a barbarous land," intending, as Van Wyck Brooks remarked, to "discourage emigration and arouse a republicanism in the rising English masses."[16] Accounts written by English travelers who visited America in the eighteen thirties and forties contributed to igniting the patriotic zeal of Americans, for a goodly number of these accounts depicted the new nation as uncouth and vulgar. Americans were hypersensitive to criticisms leveled against them in such books as Mrs. Frances Trollope's *Domestic Manners of the Americans* (1832), Harriet Martineau's *Society in America* (1837), Captain Marryat's *A Diary in America* (1837), and, the unkindest of them all, Charles Dickens' *American Notes* (1842). These and various other accounts of travelers nurtured what Washington Irving termed "the literary animosity daily growing up between

England and America." To him, as to most of his contemporaries, these accounts seemed "intended to diffuse error rather than knowledge."[17] Such unfair treatment of the new nation by the British reviews and travelers confirmed patriotic Americans in their detestation of the imitative quality of their literature, and in their rejection of what they regarded as toadying to the Old World, and especially to England.

But despite Emerson's teachings, particularly in "The American Scholar," and the zeal of such representative Americans as Bryant, Thoreau and Whitman, most men of letters persisted in relying on European ideas, literary traditions and intellectual habits as sources of inspiration.[18] They realized that the total American experience had no rich local accumulation of character, legend or lore, sufficient to ignite originality or sustain the creative imagination. To be sure, such figures as Irving, Cooper and Hawthorne were indubitably successful in their determination to grasp the "usable truth" defined by F.L. Matthiessen as "the actual meaning of civilization as it had existed in America";[19] yet they were nonetheless aware of the scantiness of native sources and frequently voiced their concern.[20]

Nineteenth-century authors' awareness of the lack in America of what Henry James called "the items of high civilization"[21] was rendered much more acute by their sense of obligation to satisfy the need of the growing reading public for knowledge and for a romantic past with all its traditions. Since the past could not be invented, most of the authors persisted in facing eastward, in borrowing and recreating. Similarly, since "items of civilization" could not be imported, most men of letters crossed the Atlantic to plunder the riches of old-world cultures.

Almost all of the well-known American authors of the nineteenth century traveled extensively: Irving, Bryant, Cooper, Hawthorne, Dana, Melville, Emerson, Longfellow, Howells, DeForest, Lowell, Mark Twain, Bret Harte, Henry Adams, James, Crane—and this is only a partial list of major writers. It does not include authors who were well known and influential during their lifetime but who are regarded now as minor: N.P. Willis, John Lloyd Stephens, George William Curtis, Bayard

Taylor, Charles Dudley Warner, Charles Warren Stoddard—to mention only a few. As travelers they were all in a sense pilgrims on a quest—a quest for both knowledge and experience.

However, there was the other facet of the double consciousness that characterized the American temperament throughout the century, namely, the patriotic, the conscious need for national identity and the assertion of the rising American "Self," which paradoxically enough regarded dependence on Europe and the Old World as sycophantic and unpatriotic, and demanded dispensing with the past and all that it connoted. The American men of letters found themselves caught in a dilemma. On the intellectual and literary level the dilemma emanated from this double consciousness could not be resolved. Despite the growing utilization of native materials, literary traditions and forms remained largely foreign. It was on the popular level and most notably in the multifarious forms of the travel book that the American author was able to resolve the dilemma. No other literary genre was as successful as the travel book in providing the author with a medium by means of which he could fulfill some of his literary and personal aspirations, and, most importantly, the conflicting demands of this double consciousness.

Written chiefly for those who, in Bayard Taylor's words, "can only travel by their fireside"[22]—and most Americans, especially in the years before and during the Civil War, were unable to enjoy the pleasure of foreign travel—the travel book, in its fluid, undefined shape enabled its author to give the growing reading masses what they needed, when they needed it. Everything that was old enchanted Americans. They shared this romantic bent with their European counterparts of the first half of the nineteenth century; yet the enchantment of Americans was more poignant and lasted longer because their country was all so new. They cherished the relics of the European past, the memories and culture of their "Old Home."[23] The newness of their country was an underlying factor in the persistence, almost permanence, of an important ingredient of the romantic movement throughout the century, namely the craving for remoteness both in space and time. The hunger of the reading public for every crumb of knowledge about the lands of the oldest civilizations was

satisfied by the vicarious tours of these lands. To the average
American the words of the travelers who had beheld with their
own eyes the ancient sites of London, Paris, Rome,
Constantinople, the Holy Land or Cairo were more authentic
than the words of the poets, historians or translators which were
secondhand and remote. And as Willard Thorp has pointed out,
even amateur travelers "often returned home better instructed
than the scholars and critics whose profession it was to interpret
European civilization."[24]

The authentic element in books of foreign travel was largely
engendered from the desire to convey information and
communicate firsthand personal experiences and impressions.
This authenticity was further enhanced by the personal
approach employed by most travel writers in the retelling of their
experiences. The reader is almost always addressed in the second
person. He is often called upon to join the traveler in touring a
famous monument or exploring an ancient site. Nonetheless,
when carried to an extreme, this personal approach rendered the
travel writer more of a tourist guide in the modern sense of the
term; and his account can be legitimately described as not written
but told. Moreover, the emphasis on authenticity caused most of
these travel accounts to become anecdotal rather than analytical,
and hence not very demanding intellectually. They were easy
reading material for the new literate class. Dry information,
whether historical, geographical, cultural or statistical, was often
made alive and palatable by the inclusion of vignettes of native
exoticism. The fact that they conveyed information of various
kinds in an entertaining context gave travel books much
prominence and popularity in an age which was not only thirsty
for knowledge but intent on disseminating it.

Travel books also satisfied vicariously the general readers'
craving for the romantic associations of adventure. Some of the
actual experiences of the travelers were exaggerated in the
retelling to make them assume the dimensions of real adventure.
Even the sophisticated travelers who criticized this bent among
some of their predecessors and made fun of the anticipated
adventure that never came did not tone down accounts of
incidents involving encounters with danger. A touch of

adventure, factual or fanciful, gave the vicarious experience of the general reader an added measure of charm.

Similarly, the reading public found in books of foreign travel a gratification of their patriotic zeal, and an assertion of their national identity. In spite of all the interest in the Old World and its culture, many Americans still considered the vogue of foreign travel unpatriotic. Traveling abroad was declared unhealthy for all young men. It was even thought that travel corrupted them and weakened their patriotism; that the experience of visiting or staying in foreign countries made Americans worse instead of better, for it led them not only to praise but to adopt some foreign manners and habits. Washington Irving, for instance, was frequently chided for his long sojourns abroad. Howells, in later years, spoke contemptuously of those American romancers who tried to be "little Londoners."[25] For this reason, many authors did not spare the chance when it offered itself on the pages of their accounts of travel to reveal to their readers the great value of foreign travel to the American national character. They constantly reassured their countrymen that their stay abroad had increased their faith in their country, and strengthened rather than weakened their patriotism and loyalty to America.[26] They demonstrated that in addition to the acquisition of the knowledge and culture which the Old World offered them—and which were essential to the gradual education of the American masses themselves—they were also able to gain new insights into the traditions and institutions of the Old World. By contrasting the traditions and institutions of the Old World societies with those of the New, the travelers contributed significantly toward fulfilling the need for national as well as cultural identity. They exhibited and interpreted the American way, its republicanism and the virtue of its free institutions in the light of European and Eastern history. In this juxtaposition the readers were made to perceive the intrinsic values of the democratic traditions of their nation and the salutary effects they had on the ultimate betterment and happiness of the individual. It was repeatedly pointed out in books of foreign travel that if the Old World excelled in the cultural and historical riches of the past, America had a better present and certainly a more promising future.

The appeal to the patriotic and national impulses of the reading public was often sentimental and in some instances verged on the chauvinistic. The sight of the Stars and Stripes flying from the tallest of poles in some remote corner of the world was always declared to be a source of unexpected delight to the traveler. On learning that Bayard Taylor was ready to leave the town of Berber in the Sudan, the Governor sent word to him that he would bring a company of his soldiers down to the banks of the Nile and salute his flag; and, Taylor wrote,

Truly enough, when we were all embarked and I had given the Stars and Stripes of the Ethiopian winds, a company of about fifty soldiers ranged themselves on the high bank, and saluted the flag with a dozen rattling volleys.[27]

The flag was much more than a mere symbol in books of travel. There was always the satisfaction of identifying with it. Physically, its presence was an assertion of the eminent place the young nation occupied in the world community and an evidence that other peoples recognized and respected that place. Psychologically, the flag was a source of inner security; the American's sense of his personal value and importance was largely derived from his feeling of belonging to America, the favored land, rather than from an inner conviction of his worth as a well-rounded individual. He was acutely conscious of what he lacked: culture, experience, and cosmopolitanism—the qualities that his European counterparts possessed. He could not vie with them on those grounds. But by posing as a representative of America, which he believed to be morally and politically superior to the Old World, he could bolster his own ego and extract a deep sense of pride in his identity. Simultaneously, the loyalty of the traveler was assured; and the reader, by experiencing the vicarious thrill, could identify with the writer and share his feelings.

In the same patriotic vein, the travel book was frequently used as a weapon of retaliation. American authors found in books of travel a conveniently fitted platform for rebutting the criticisms and misrepresentations of European, especially

English, travelers in the United States. (Cooper's *Notions of the Americans* [1828] is a good case in point.) The virtue of American traditions and free institutions was reiterated vis-a-vis the current evils and injustice inherent in the European and Eastern societies. Patriotic Americans who were incensed by the condescending attitude of European and English observers read with great approbation the pages of the travel books that vindicated their country. Some American authors went so far as to give European and English travelers a taste of their own medicine. Usually assuming an air of superiority, they singled out and conspicuously framed the vulgarities of the European and English travelers, especially those who made claims to nobility, whom they encountered on neutral grounds—for example, in the Levant. With a streak of sarcastic glee, in *My Winter on the Nile* (1876) Charles Dudley Warner gibed:

I hear the natives complain that almost all the English men of rank who came to Egypt, beg, or shall we say accept? substantial favors of the Khedive. The nobility appear to have a new rendering of *noblesse oblige.* This is rather humiliating to us Americans, who are, after all, almost blood-relations of the English; and besides, we are often taken for *Inglese,* in villages where few strangers go.

Inwardly, readers must have revelled in sharing Warner's conscious snobbery, and relished the connotations of such words as "complain," "beg" and "substantial favors"; and the more so because these words were used in direct reference to English nobility—the standard-bearers of tradition with all their civilized embellishments—in an attempt to mark a low ebb in their values and codes of moral behavior. Self-righteously and with an added degree of pride, they must also have winced at being often branded in faraway lands as *"Inglese"* and thus suffering what they considered an undeserved humiliation.

Significantly then, the travel book gave the growing reading masses all they needed when they needed it. The two poles of nineteenth-century American temperament, the conscious need of the public for knowledge, specifically that of its ancestral heritage and of the stable traditions and institutions of old civilizations, and its conscious need for national identity, inspiring confidence and pride in being American, were reconciled in books of foreign travel. Knowledge of European and Eastern civilizations was disseminated in America to satisfy the insatiable appetite of the reading public. Yet the travelers never portrayed the Old World as the exemplary or redeemed society to the American Man. This Old World was seen and criticized from a peculiarly American point of view. Furthermore, by seeing in juxtaposition the structures and textures of both the Old and the New societies, the American reader was able to perceive the intrinsic value and virtues of the democratic traditions and free institutions of his society. This was ultimately the logic behind the phenomenal growth and popularity of travel books in the nineteenth century. They were triumphantly American, written by Americans exclusively for Americans.

Notes

[1] *The Literary History of the United States,* third revised edition, ed. Robert E. Spiller, Willard Thorp, Thomas H. Johnson and Henry S. Canby (New York: The Macmillan Co., 1963), III, 356. Johnson's list of the American writers who traveled abroad and "whose works have literary merit" is incomplete. It is beyond the scope of this article to list all books of travel or books based on travel experience that were written by the literary figures of the nineteenth century. For such a list to be adequately complete it should begin with Washington Irving and end with Henry James, and should embrace almost every major writer of the century. However, for the sake of emphasis we should mention that the "international novel," exemplified in Hawthorne's *The Marble Faun* (1860) and later perfected by Henry James in his novels that deal with Americans abroad and the confrontation between the Old and New, is an important offshoot of travel literature.

[2] The word "culture" is used here to mean, according to Webster's *Third New International Dictionary,* the act of developing the intellectual and moral faculties especially by education. This was largely what the word "culture" meant to the nineteenth-century reading public.

[3] Why books of foreign travel were particularly successful and needed little publicity campaigning on the part of the publishers will be shown later in some detail. For an excellent discussion of the tradition of puffing in the mid-nineteenth century see *The Profession of Authorship in America, 1800-1870: The Papers of William Charvat,* ed. Matthew J. Bruccoli (Columbus: Ohio State University Press, 1968), particularly chapter ten, "James T. Fields and the beginning of Book

Promotion, 1840-1855." Hereafter cited as *The Papers of William Charvat.*

[4]Albert H. Smyth, *Bayard Taylor,* American Men of Letters (Boston and New York: Houghton, Mifflin & Co., 1896), p. 51.

[5]Richard C. Beatty, *Bayard Taylor, Laureate of the Gilded Age* (Norman: University of Oklahoma Press, 1936), p. 180.

[6]Edward Cary, *George William Curtis,* American Men of Letters (Boston and New York: Houghton, Mifflin & Co., 1894), pp. 59-60.

[7]*The Papers of William Charvat,* pp. 240-241.

[8]James D. Hart, *The Popular Book: A History of America's Literary Taste* (Berkeley: University of California Press, 1963), p. 147. In 1869 one edition often contained over 20,000 copies as contrasted to smaller editions of 3,000 or so each, more than a decade earlier. The increase in number of copies in each edition should be considered here also as indicative of the concomitant increase in the number of the reading public.

[9]*The Papers of Willliam Charvat,* p. 306. Taylor's dashing figure was partly responsible for his popularity as a lecturer. He was given to a certain degree of exhibitionism and frequently appeared on the podium in Arab garb. In contrast, Melville, who also delivered some lectures based on his travels, was not an exciting figure. He was considered a dull lecturer.

[10]*The Asian Legacy and American Life,* ed. Arthur E. Christy (New York: The John Day Co., 1945), p. 51.

[11]James G. Wilson, *Bryant and His Friends: Some Reminisences of the Knickerbocker Writers* (New York: Fords, Howards, & Hulbert, 1886), p. 235.

[12]Stanley T. Williams, *The Spanish Background of American Literature* (New Haven: Yale University Press, 1955), I, 51.

[13]This national trait is evinced in the overwhelming desire of many European immigrants, once they are comfortably established in the United States, to return to the old continent as American tourists.

[14]Quoted in R.W.B. Lewis, *The American Adam: Innocence, Tragedy, and Tradition in the Nineteenth Century* (Chicago: The University of Chicago Press, 1965), p. 5.

[15] Ibid., p. 20.

[16]Van Wyck Brooks, *The World of Washington Irving* (Philadelphia: The Blakiston Co., 1945), pp. 248-249.

[17]Washington Irving, *The Sketch Book* (Philadelphia: David McKay, Publishers, 1893), p. 62.

[18]For the battle of words that raged on the New York literary stage "in the era of Poe and Melville" between those who advocated the importance of the past and of continuity and those who preached the gospel of national identity and the sovereignty of the present, see Perry Miller, *The Raven and the Whale* (New York: Harcourt, Brace & World, Inc., 1956).

[19]F.O. Matthiessen, *American Renaissance* (New York: Oxford University Press, 1964), p. 235.

[220]Cooper complained of what he called "the baldness of American life" in *Notions of the Americans Picked Up By a Travelling Bachelor* (New York, 1863),

II, 108. Irving who, like Cooper and Hawthorne, did his share in creating an American *mythus,* wrote on August 1, 1841, to his niece, Sarah Storrow, then in Paris: "Good Lord, deliver me from the all pervading commonplace which is the curse of our country," (quoted in *The American Writer and the European Tradition,* ed. Margaret Denny and William Gilman [New York: McGraw & Hill Book Co., 1964], p. 45).

[21] Henry James, *Hawthorne* (New York: Doubleday and Co., 1879), p. 43.

[22] Bayard Taylor, *The Land of the Saracens; or, Pictures of Palestine, Asia Minor, Sicily and Spain* (New York: G.P. Putnam & Co., 1856), p. vi.

[23] Until recently Americans made little effort to preserve their old cultural shrines as objects of veneration belonging to times past. If America is not privileged enough to have a Stratford-on-Avon, it still has a Concord; if it does not have "Abbotsford" or "Dryburgh Abbey," it has "Sunnyside," and "Idlewild." Therefore, how important it would have been for the cultural history and heritage of America if a native or a foreign visitor had been able to tour the house where Melville lived on Market Street in Albany, N.Y! That is but one example, and is as culturally and historically valuable as sites of Battlefields, Forts and old Warships! No small wonder that some Americans feel that they have no alternative other than to worship at the cultural shrines of the Old World.

[24] Willard Thorp, "Pilgrims' Return," in *Literary History of the United States,* ed. Robert E. Spiller, *et. al.* revised edition in one volume (New York: The Macmillan Co., 1955), p. 830.

[25] *Literary History of the United States,* p.621.

[26] From Frankfort Bayard Taylor wrote his relative Hannah M. Taylor: "The more we see of other lands the more we love our own." In another letter to the same relative he wrote: "I must say that with us (he was traveling with his cousin), as with all Americans who go abroad, everyday but proves that the free States are far, far beyond any other nation in the world, though it is foolish to suppose we can learn nothing from others." (*The Unpublished Letters of Bayard Taylor,* ed. John R. Schultz, *The Huntington Library Publications* [San Marino, California, 1937], pp. 9-11).

[27] Bayard Taylor, *A Journey to Central Africa; or, Life and Landscapes from Egypt to the Negro Kingdoms of the White Nile* (New York: G.P. Putnam & Sons, 1866), p. 218.

[28] Charles Dudley Warner, *My Winter on the Nile* (Boston: Houghton, Mifflin Co., 1904), pp. 389-390. *Inglese* (Ingliz) is the Arabic word (pl.) for British. It was used by the populace generally to refer to foreigners who spoke English.

Originally published in *Exploration,* IV:1, December 1976. Reprinted with the permission of the editor and the author.

The Traveller as Antihero :
Richard Smith Elliott in the Mexican War

Nicholas T. Joost

Six years ago, in a long essay on Keemle and Fields's newspaper the St. Louis *Weekly Reveille,* I wrote about a young Pennsylvania lawyer named Richard Smith Elliott and his part in the war between Mexico and the United States of America. My purpose here is not so much to recapitulate what was said six years ago but to expand those remarks with a brief sketch of Elliott's character as a traveler through regions then as exotic and dangerous as they were little known

Fortunately Elliott wrote a memoir, *Notes Taken in Sixty Years,* which he published himself in 1883 in St. Louis, and which usefully supplements his letters and other writings in the *Reveille.* Thus we learn that he was born in Lewistown, Pennsylvania, on 10 July 1817, that like millions of other Americans young Elliott started for the West at the age of twenty, "going to Texas" to join the "Texian campaign," that he abandoned that scheme in Louisville, where he briefly essayed acting and dutifully repaid his enlistment fee of six dollars, and that he returned home to Pennsylvania, where he helped run once again his father's rural paper and engaged himself as a "jour. printer" and then as an editor to sundry employers. Elliott married a local girl in 1838 and read for and was admitted to the bar. Also he dabbled in Whig party politics with the result that he received through the help of President John Tyler, early in 1843, from his "old friend, Mr. Potts, chief clerk of the Indian Bureau...'a little sub-agency' at Council Bluffs, $750 Salary." Mr. Potts kindly explained the difference between an agency and a subagency: the latter was an "agency except in title, salary, and mode of appointment. Same duties as those of an Agent, who gets $1,500. The Council Bluffs sub-agency is east of the Missouri river, and disburses over $40,000 a year. The bond is $20,000. The Secretary of War appoints the sub-agents—the President appoints the agents." Because the prospective subagency might lead to something, Elliott decided, for the second time, to go West:

"I had a vague idea that something might come of it."

There proved to be several things. Because he was in law, Elliott dabbled in politics, for which he had little heart, however; but by an osmotic process, because he was in politics, he became interested in the future of the American railroad system, then just entering its golden age of expansion and rapacity. And since he was interested in the railroads and the law and politics, Elliott became interested in land speculation, and where else but in the West? As early as 1838, he dabbled—the *Notes* become imprecise here—in the building of a "continuous railroad to the city of St. Louis," from Pennsylvania.

When he went West in 1843, St.Louis was still the center of the American fur trade and accordingly was the major entrepot for that great enterprise as well as the American-Mexican trade across the Sante Fe trail and on to Chihuahua; St. Louis merchants also took the lead in outfitting emigrants then beginning to settle the lands west of the Mississippi. Eventually Elliot would settle in St. Louis; the title page of his *Notes* would describe him as "Richard Smith Elliott of St. Louis, Missouri, U.S.A."

When he first arrived in St. Louis on 13 May 1843, Elliott found himself in a city of "probably 25,000 people," which had been, he avers, a town of merely 2,000 in 1822. Elliott did not tarry, apparently. He took his younger brother Joe with him and they walked and rode to what is now Council Bluffs, Iowa, to attend to the affairs of the Indian subagency and to raise corn on a plot where the brothers built of cottonwood logs the first house ever erected in the city of Council Bluffs by a white man not connected with Indians (p. 171). For 1843 and 1844, the reader of Elliott's *Notes* must work his way through some addled chronology: Elliott now has an infant son; back in St. Louis, Judge Bryan Mullanphy grants him a license to practice law after a few casually put questions; the three Elliotts journey *en famille* to the farm and subagency at Council Bluffs; Mrs. Elliott and "little John D." go back to Pennsylvania, whence she returns with John D. and "his wee sister," plus an aunt, this event occurring not until the spring of 1845.

During the months that he lived alone in his log cabin,

Elliott's "greatest enjoyment was vocal and instrumental music," and he began to read—at any rate, as regularly as the frontier mails permitted—the St. Louis *Weekly Reveille*. In return, the *Reveille* printed his first contribution in its issue for 12 August 1844. We now have a second source for getting to know Richard Smith Elliott. The grandfather of 1883, the white-haired and full-bearded old gentleman peering wistfully into the unimaginable distances of 1976, whose memory of the past is precise for one occasion and vague for another, contrasts to the ebullient young frontiersman, with his gift for doggerel and playacting and for the casual, easygoing cameraderie of the great western waters.

Elliott's first contribution to the *Reveille* was a letter that he signed as "John Brown"; the pseudonym was a common device of the day, whether in journalism or in less ephemeral writing. The *Reveille* was also a vehicle for the new American humor of the frontier, and "John Brown" was an exponent of that humor. Under the title of "What's in a Name?" "John Brown" wrote that

At the present writing, I have not seen *The Reveille*. I may never see it. I am only mortal, like its editors (the paper, too, perhaps!) and may die, as others have done. But I am assured by good authority, that *The Reveille* is seen and felt every morning, Sundays not excepted, by the good people of St. Louis, and that its rub-a-dubs are directed by good *Field* officers. Seen and felt! *Reveille!* But there's no telling what will come next, as the old lady said when told of the new way to hatch eggs by steam. "Dear me," says she, 'I suppose the next thing"—and here she muttered something— "but for my part, I would prefer the old way!"

"John Brown" added a postscript to the effect that if editors thought his letter worth a place in their columns—"your name is so military that I can't keep war-like thoughts down"—they should "place it among the *rank* and *file*. Just *say* if you please, it is very humorous and good, or your readers may not discover its merits." Elliott's writing for the *Reveille* is characterized largely by the quizzical, pawky tone of that first letter, whether in the verse he published in the paper—with which I am not concerned here—or in his travel letters and news dispatches.

For Elliott, 1845 was largely taken up with various negotiations in Washington, for the Potawatomies, and he was away from Council Bluffs and St. Louis part of the year. He continued, nevertheless, to report back to the paper, whether an account of his activity as subagent for the Otoes, Pawnees, and Potawatomies or an entry from his "Hibernian Log-Book—A Trip to Galena."

Early in 1846, Elliott left his subagency and moved himself and his family to St. Louis, where he set himself up as an attorney-at-law, in an office on the second floor of a building opposite what he called the "old Court House." Shortly thereafter, however, his legal career ended for the duration of the war with Mexico. During May and June of 1846, after President Polk declared war on Mexico, the "decisive call on Missouri" came, and, as Elliott remarked ironically in his *Notes,* "the air was full of patriotism." Another St. Louis attorney, Thomas B. Hudson, began to organize a company, with Elliott acting as first lieutenant. The hundred men of the company rapidly enlisted, as cavalry soldiers, calling themselves the "Laclede Rangers." The Laclede Rangers formed part of the Regiment of Missouri Mounted Volunteers in June 1846 and elected William Alexander Doniphan as their Colonel. Unofficially but vitally for our topic, Elliott was their most important reporter; there were other men in Doniphan's regiment who wrote accounts for the *Reveille* as well as other newspapers printed in St. Louis; Elliott, however, is by all odds the most important reporter of the group, sending back upwards of seventy dispatches printed in the *Reveille* between June 1846 and July 1847, when he returned to St. Louis at the disbanding of the Regiment of Mounted Volunteers.

As I have mentioned elsewhere in some detail these dispatches by Elliott that were printed in the *Reveille,* I need not dwell here on their content. What is of further interest is that Elliott's *Notes* contain a complementary account of his experience as a horse soldier in 1846 and 1847. The obvious value of the dispatches is their freshness, their immediacy, their careful regard for fact, and their omission of jingoist propaganda. The value of Elliott's complementary account in Chapters 32 through 37 (pp.214-257) of his *Notes* lies in their being a retrospective account, a story matured and composed and mulled over for many years. These chapters are the most vivid pages of an uncommonly entertaining and kindhearted autobiography. They show, morever, how sharply one's youthful enthusiasms may differ from one's elderly qualifications regarding the very experience about which as a young man he had been so enthusiastic.

That the war with Mexico was a bitterly divisive war—as indeed have been the majority of the conflicts our nation has waged—remains part of the historical record. Every student of American culture recalls the energy with which such men as Emerson and Thoreau inveighed against what they regarded as the enormity of our collective action. But what most of us fail to recall is that, by and large, divisive though the war may have been, it was one of our more popular wars. Emerson and Thoreau were disgruntled intellectuals. The slave-owning group that still dominated the Congress, adventurers on the make, such as Fremont, his father-in-law Senator Benton, the incumbent president, Polk, bankers, railroad magnates, manufacturing interests outside Massachusetts (which has traditionally been isolationist)—all these were in an expansionist mood, and they carried the great mass of Americans with them. The youthful Richard Smith Elliott cheerfully allowed himself to be carried along, too. After all, he helped organize a company of cavalry, all of them volunteers.

The elderly Richard Smith Elliott held rather different opinions regarding that youthful experience riding through the deserts and mountains of the Southwest. He admits as much in his *Notes*:

Not the least animosity had I felt towards the Mexicans, nor did I wish to kill anybody; but as the war seemed to be taking so much of the Government's attention. . . and as, by volunteering I would acquire a sort of right to talk against war in the future—I had decided that I might as well be one of the 'Army of the West,' which I had a notion would be recalled before we should get half way to Sante Fe. The narrow strip of country between the Nueces and the Rio Grande, which Texas had only conquered constructively, did not appear to be worth fighting for; and I supposed the Governmeent would occupy it with large armies, and then negotiate, as the cheapest way of acquiring title. I even imagined the St.

Louis Legion marching up and down along the Rio Grande, scaring away any Mexican troops that might want to come over.

But President Polk, who declared in his message that war existed 'by the act of Mexico,' had views differing from mine, as I had not risen above plain common sense, and he had got up to statesmanship. The upshot was, that before the dispute was settled, millions on millions of wealth were wasted, thousands of good lives were sacrificed, unutterable distress brought to many homes, and a crop of veterans left to solicit in vain for pensions. Mr. Polk's policy, thanks to the soldiers, added to the national domain nearly all of what are now Colorado, Utah, New Mexico, Arizona, and California. We took them as 'indemnity for the past and security for the future'; and then, in the Gadsden Purchase, we bought a strip to straighten our southern boundary, just as we might have bought the land between the Nueces and Rio Grande, and had no war at all. But the general sentiment was, that the Mexicans were a half-barbarous set anyway, and had no business to send their greasy and ragged soldiers over the Rio Grande, into a territory always owned by them but constructively conquered by the Texans, who were the advanced guard of our superior civilization; and we taught the successors of Montezuma the infallible maxim that justice and right are always on the side of the strongest armies. Abraham Lincoln, Thomas Corwin, and a few others in Congress regarded the war as cruel and unjust, but once begun it had to go on.

I find this passage (p. 218) a curious mixture of disingenuity and sincere feeling. There is an unpleasant cynicism about the admission that "by vounteering I would acquire a sort of right to talk against war in the future"—and it simply does not square with Elliott's known course of action at the time, as we learn of it from his dispatches in the *Reveille* as well as from the *Notes* themselves. Missouri at the time of the war with Mexico was at least nominally one of the "Southern" states dominated by the slave-owners and their representatives. Missouri, in addition, was one of the states that were strongly in favor of westward expansion; many of the so-called "Texans"—an identity appropriated by the Americans of dominantly Anglo-Saxon culture (ironically, many of them were Celtic in their origins) who settled in Texas early in the nineteenth century—had migrated from Missouri. Richard Smith Elliott went along with the tide of

public opinion and in fact even helped to channel it in a particular
direction.

Both Elliott's dispatches and his *Notes* emphasize certain
aspects of the war peculiar to New Mexico. Curiously, he does not
emphasize the remarkable nature of Doniphan's expedition as
half travel, half exploration. Rather, Elliott discusses at length
the turning over of New Mexico and its capital of Santa Fe to the
Americans and the consequent intrusion and dominance of novel
concepts of law, governance, and social conduct. He has many an
anecdote illustrating local Latin-American manners and
working habits, and it is pleasant to note that Elliott seems not to
have had in his make-up the racial snobbery that still
characterizes the North American relationship with Latin
America. It is true, however, that Elliott commented often and
invariably unfavorably on the technology of the Mexican
inhabitants of the newly conquered territory, as when he alluded
in passing to "the miserable little axes now used by the Mexicans,
which resemble in shape and size the wedges used by our farmers
for splitting rails." His relations to several New Mexican
families, on the other hand, were of a socially friendly nature, and
he describes with evident approval how the officers of the
occupying force regularly attended the nightly *fandangos* or
dances, some of them accompanied by local *senoritas*.

The occupation of Santa Fe had been bloodless, but relations
with both the Navajos and the Pueblo Indians (i.e., those Indians
dwelling in their own villages) were eventful. At length a treaty
with the Navajos was concluded, but the Indians of one of the
villages in the valley of Taos began rioting over the jailing of
three of their number who were "notorious thieves" (p.247), and
several Americans were massacred, including the territorial
governor, Bent. In the spring of 1847, matters came to a head
because of the many outrages "committed by Indians on the
plains, and even on the borders of New Mexico" (p. 251). Elliott
was one of a force of seventy-five men sent out "to hunt Indians,
and if possible recover stolen animals" (p. 252). At one point the
Indians cleverly ambushed the soldiers in a deep canyon of the
Canadian River. In an engagement lasting four or five hours,
several men were wounded and one "man from Callaway

County" was killed—as Elliott wrote in italics: *"The Indians were charging after us."* At nightfall the Americans dispiritedly bivouacked and reached their camp the next day. Their haversacks of provisions and some other property had been lost in the melee, and even though reinforcements arrived, with a small howitzer, the nine officers leading the group decided to hold "a council of war on a proposal to go back to the canyon." The passage here is one of the most revealing in Elliott's *Notes*:

...four ayes and five noes. I voted no. We had neither provisions nor ammunition to continue the campaign. Besides, I had been in the canyon, and, on reflection, did not like it. I did not want to hear any more bullets singing. It was afterwards ascertained that the Indians had left the same night and gone a long march in another direction. They had greatly outnumbered us, and their loss was estimated at forty killed.

The most wonderful thing to me in the fight was, the entire absence of fear. In crossing the creek, a possible bullet in my back suggested the thought, that after my body should be found people might impugn my courage; but there was no other dread of that possible bullet. But at the council next day the scare that I ought naturally to have felt in the fight came on, and I was not at all sorry that with over two hundred men, no provisions, and no ammunition, my negative vote was a matter of duty as well as inclination. I have never been in a fight since, but have held bravery during battle in low estimation. If a man with a big bump of caution could be as cool and self-possessed as I was during our Indian fight, those with little bumps may easily be heroes. To deliberately go into battle requires courage; but once in, excitement seems to swallow up fear.

And with that comment Elliott proceeds abruptly to the sentence in which he tells his readers that he and the Rangers in his command were honorably discharged from the service of the United States and "on 13th June we started for 'home'." Despite a couple of alarms, the return journey was peaceful, even though the Santa Fe trail, Elliott reports, was always dangerous for travelers until "private capital had put a railroad in the Arkansas Valley! It seemed that there never was capacity in the government to deal with the wild Indian question" (p. 255).

So, as Elliott tells us, he "quietly subsided to private life." It is a remarkable story, whether read in *Notes Taken in Sixty Years* or in the discontinuous dispatches printed in the St. Louis *Weekly Reveille*. Not the least remarkable aspect is its having been lived and recounted by a man who explicitly considered himself an antihero. Here is a man who volunteered to go on one of the most reckless adventures in American military history, a feat that, as Senator Benton first told Doniphan himself, exceeded that of the Ten Thousand; yet when Elliott could have been elected Major in the Regiment of Missouri Mounted Volunteers,he decided to stand and in 1883 was still moaning, "The bump of 'Caution' lost me the rank of Major" (P.221). Elliott deliberately adopted the nearly anonymous name and attitude of "John Brown," the pawky frontiersman, in an age of gaudy flamboyance and grandiloquent oration. In Santa Fe he became so ill that he nearly died and his attending physician saved his life, says Elliott, only by giving him a massive dose of sixty grains of calomel. He had hoped to go with the body of Doniphan's regiment to take part in the major battles down in Mexico, and to report them back to the *Reveille*; instead he was relegated by his illness to the life of a soldier in an army of occupation. Gambling at *monte* alternated with evenings of quadrilles and waltzes. His one brush with violent death seems to have been rather disappointing, for the experience taught him to "hold bravery during battle in low estimation." The mystery to me is why this remarkable man firmly resolved to relate his life, both in youth and in age, in terms of the antihero "John Brown" with the bump of caution, cracking his mild jokes in the mildest of tones. It is as though a John Wayne Western thriller were being filmed in tones of grey and mauve!

Science in the Exploration Narratives Authored by U.S. Naval Officers

V. Ponko, Jr.

At the end of the nineteenth century there were few areas of the world yet to be explored. Humboldt had completed his travels in South America and, in North America, Mackenzie had journeyed from the St. Lawrence River to the Pacific coast. In Africa, Mungo Park had gotten to the Niger River while Bruce returned to the sources of the Blue Nile. Further east, the modern exploration of Arabia had begun with the work of Niebuhr and the foundations of the Indian surveys had been established by Rennel. In Australia, the nineteenth century witnessed the first settlements and the first inaland exploration expeditions; in the latter part of the century, exploration was particularly vigorous in Central Asia, Central Africa, Central Australia, the East Indies, New Guinea and the Arctic. Although it was not until the twentieth century that such prized objectives as the North Pole and the South Pole were reached, it is reasonable to agree with J.N.L. Baker that the nineteenth century had left relatively little in the way of discovery for the twentieth century to accomplish.[1]

In this work of filling in the last unknowns, the navies and naval officers of many nations were active participants. The Navy of the United States, for instance, in the years before the Civil War, conducted major exploring expeditions in at least eleven, sometimes overlapping but yet distinct, areas of the world. These forays were purposely planned and aimed not only at surveying, charting and, in general, increasing the world's geographical knowledge, but also at the advancement of other aspects of scientific inquiry and discovery. After the Civil War, the intensity and scope of the Navy's role in exploration was not as great, but it did not die. Officers of the U.S. Navy, for example, explored South America, Africa, the Arctic and other areas of the globe.

In addition to the reports, charts, maps and other items such as natural history specimens which were deposited with various governmental agencies, this activity also resulted in the production of books through which the exploits of the explorers and the results of their expeditions became known to the general public.

Science, both in relation to its general meaning of knowledge gained by study, as well as in its more restricted connotation as knowledge acquired by the study of natural and technical matters, constitutes an integral part of these presentations. In them scientific inquiry and the results of such investigations range from the study of music in the Samoas to the dissection of the ocean floor; from the examination of Penguin habits in the Antarctic to the life of whales in the Arctic. The areas and topics studied are broad and, one is tempted to say, almost all encompassing.

To substantiate this assertion one need only read such works of general circulation as Herndon, William Lewis, and Gibbon, Lardner, *Exploration of the Valley of the Amazon, Made Under Direction of the Navy Department* 2 vols (1854); Kane, Elisha Kent, *The U.S. Grinnell Expedition in Search of Sir John Franklin, A Personal Narrative* (1853) and *Arctic Explorations; The Second Grinnell Expedition in Search of Sir John Franklin in 1853, '54, and '55* 2 vols (1856); Lynch, William F. *Narrative of the United States Expedition to the River Jordan and the Dead Sea* (1849); Page,Thomas J. *La Plata, The Argentine Confederation and Paraguay* (1859); Wilkes, Charles, *Narrative of the United States Exploring Expedition During the Years 1838, 1839, 1840, 1841, 1842,* 5 vols (1845).[2]

Agreeing that the books noted above contain words about science vital to their purpose and structure is not, however, the point at which one should leave any discussion about science in the exploration narratives authored by United States Naval Officers. One might, for instance, ask how these officers evaluated science as an activity in their narratives, what sort of style they used in writing it, and how they viewed the knowledge gained through their efforts in relation to the climate of opinion in their eras. However, I am not a literary critic and I do not want to venture into the field of literary criticism under false colors. Neither do I intend to give a full assessment of the scientific achievements of these expeditions about which these naval officers wrote.[3] I think it worthy of note that the narratives under consideration were tales not only of heroic individual and team efforts at survival and recognition from a personal point of view, but also of heroic endeavors for the advancement of science in an impersonal way made all the more detached by deft touches of humor. These works associate knowledge and seekers of knowledge, i.e., science and scientists, as worthy of being considered heroic not only in terms of a particular problem, but also in a manner speaking of an eternal and universal justification independent of the local situation being described. As an example one might cite the following passages from Elisha Kent Kane's *Arctic Exploration in the Years 1853, 1854, 1855* on the subject of gathering magnetic data in the far north:

March 7, Tuesday.—I have said very little in this business journal about our daily Arctic life. I have had no time to draw pictures.

But we have some trials which might make up a day's adventures. Our Arctic observatory is cold beyond any of its class, Kesan, Pulkowa, Toronto, or even its shifting predecessors, Bossetop and Melville Island. Imagine it a term-day, a magnetic term-day.

The observer, if he were only at home, would be the "observed of all observers." He is clad in a pair of seal-skin pants, a dog-skin cap, a reindeer jumper, and walrus boots. He sits upon a box that once held a transit instrument. A stove, glowing with at least a bucketful of anthracite, represents pictorially a heating apparatus, and reduces the thermometer as near as may be to ten degrees below zero. One hand holds a chronometer, and is left bare to warm it; the other luxuriates in a fox-skin mitten. The right hand and the left take it "watch and watch about." As one burns with cold, the chronometer shifts to the other, and the mitten takes its place.

Perched on a pedestal of frozen gravel is a magnetometer; stretching out from it, a telescope: and, bending down to this, an abject human eye. Every six minutes, said eye takes cognizance of a finely-divided arc, and notes the result in a cold memorandum-book. This process continues for twenty-four hours, two sets of eyes taking it by turns; and, when twenty-four hours are over, term-day is over too.

We have such frolics every week. I have just been relieved from one, and after a few hours am to be called out of bed in the night to watch and dot again. I have been engaged in this way when the thermomenter gave 20 degrees above zero at the instrument, 20 degrees below at two feet above the floor, and 43 degrees below at the floor itself: on my person, away from the stove, 10 degrees above zero. "A grateful country" will of course appreciate the value of these labors, and, as it cons over hereafter the four hundred and eighty results which go to make up our record for each week, will never think of asking, "*Cui bono* all this?"

But this is no adventure. The adventure is the travel to and fro. We have night *now* only half the time; and half the time can go and come with eyes to help us. It was not so a little while since.[4]

In this passage the uncomfortableness of the local situation, the surmounting of which is heroic in itself, acts as the foil to the depiction of a process which, for all its aggravations, is given as one to be followed as a matter of course. Here science is depicted as exacting but heroic in relation to its demands; the person gathering the data suborinates his comforts to a large universal purpose and, in this respect, is a hero.

This presentation of science as a process independent of man's whims and desires, but at the same time as a laudatory enterprise demanding uplifting sacrifices of an heroic kind of advantage to the indivduals concerned, may be found in many of the other exploration and travel narratives authored by U.S. Naval Officers in the nineteenth century. Moreover, it was a popular theme as far as the general public was concerned and in most instances it was presented as a section of readable, sometimes exciting prose, which gave it even greater appeal. Consider, for example, the following passage from William Herndon's *Exploration of the Valley of the Amazon*:

Though not yet sixty miles from the sea, we had crossed the great "divide" which separates the waters of the Atlantic from those of the Pacific. The last steps of our mules had made a striking change in our geographical relations; so suddenly and so quickly had we been cut off from all connexion with the Pacific, and placed upon waters that rippled and sparkled joyously as they danced by our feet to join the glad waves of the ocean that washes the shores of our own dear land. They whispered to me of home, and my heart went along with them. I thought of Maury, with his researches concerning the currents of the sea; and, recollecting the close physical connexion pointed out by him as existing between these—the waters of the Amazon and those of our own majestic

Mississippi—I musingly dropped a bit of green moss, plucked from the hill-side, upon the bosom of the place lake of Morococha, and as it floated along I followed it, in imagination, down through the luxurious climes, the beautiful skies, and enchanting scenery of the tropics, to the mouth of the great river; thence across the Caribbean sea, through the Yucatan pass, into the Gulf of Mexico; thence along the Gulf-stream; and so out upon the ocean, off the shores of the "Land of Flowers." Here I fancied it might meet with the silent little messengers cast by the hands of sympathizing friends and countrymen high upon the head-waters of the Mississippi, or away in the "Far West," upon the distant fountains of the Missouri.

It was, indeed, but a bit of moss floating on the water; but as I mused, fancy, awakened and stimulated by surrounding circumstances, had already converted it into a skiff manned by Fairies, and bound upon a mission of high import, bearing messages of peace and good-will, telling of commerce and navigation, of settlement and civilization, of religious and political liberty, from the "King of Rivers" to the "Father of Waters"; and, possibly, meeting in the Florida pass, and "speaking" through a trumpet louder than the tempest spirits sent down by the Naiads of Lake Itaska, with greetings to Morococha.

I was now, for the first time, fairly in the field of my operations. I had been sent to explore the Valley of the Amazon, to sound its streams, and to report as to their navigability. I was commanded to examine its fields, its forest, and its rivers, that I might gauge their capabilities, active and dormant, for trade and commerce with the states of Christendom, and make known to the spirit and enterprise of the age the resources which lie in concealment there, waiting for the touch of civilization and the breath of the steam engine to give them animation, life and palpable existence.[5]

Passages such as the foregoing made Herndon's *Exploration of the Valley of the Amazon* a very popular book. Even Mark Twain read it and there is some indication also that it influenced him in the preparation of his Huckleberry Finn stories.[6]

In the midst of general acceptance, however, there were critics. Some British periodicals claimed that Herndon had not contributed anything new to geographical knowledge about the region. The *Spectator,* for instance, pointed out that Herndon followed generally the route taken in 1834 by Lieutenant William Smyth of the Royal Navy.[7]

Lack of originality in the selection of routes was not the only criticism leveled at the exploration efforts of the United States Naval Officers. Lynch's *Narrative of the United States' Expedition to the River Jordan and the Dead Sea* was criticized particularly with regard to its style. Fairly early in his presentation, for example, Lynch described two metallic boats used by the expedition in the following way: "The boats 'Fanny Mason' and 'Fanny Skinner,' of nearly equal dimensions, were named after two young and blooming children, whose hearts are spotless as their parentage is pure. Their prayers, like guardian spirits, would shield us in the hour of peril; and I trusted that, whether threading the rapids of the Jordan or floating on the wondrous sea of death, the 'Two Fannies' would not disgrace the gentle and artless beings whose names they proudly bore." This passage the *Boston Post* called well-meant but "fudge-like."

Also, in the first chapter of his book, Lynch writes about sickness which had afflicted one of his officers and he noted that the man "must naturally have longed to exchange his hard and narrow berth, and the stifling atmosphere of a ship, soon to be tossed about, the sport of the elements, for a softer and more spacious couch, a more airy apartment, and, above all, the quiet and the better attendance of the shore." The *Boston Post* characterized this observation as "one of the clearest examples of bathos, common-place and downright twattle extant." In the end, however, the *Boston Post* evaluated Lynch's product as being:

...really interesting and instructive, and is really and obviously the work of an able, well-educated man. How such silly defects of style should coexist with the more essential merits of the text is almost unintelligible, and, indeed, were we upon oath for our opinion at this moment, we should say that one man must have written the twattle, the triteness, the bad grammar and the bad taste, while another furnished the learning and narrated the facts.[8]

The somewhat harsh literary criticism of Lynch's work must be considered in relation to the fact that Lynch, as well as other officer authors, was writing for at least three audiences. Not only were these authors interested in winning acceptane from the general reader, they hoped for a favorable reception from their official superiors, as well as recognition for their achievements from the scientific community. In Lynch's case, whatever disappointment he might have had with regard to criticism of his presentation, was compensated by the fact that the work of the Dead Sea expedition "became the foundation on which all subsequent knowledge of the river and its valley was built and until the 1930s remained the main source of technical information on both the Jordan and the Dead Sea."[9]

In bringing this short excursion to a close, I think it worthy to note that science in the travel and exploration narratives authored by U.S. Naval officers was, at least in the first half of the period, accompanied by a pride in the achievements of the United States and confidence in the future.

These officers who traversed unknown regions or foreign soil took pains to see that the Star Spangled Banner was carried appropriately while on the march or flew correctly while in camp. Lynch, for instance, entered Damascus with the flag of the United States at the head of his group:

Before entering the city, we were advised to furl our flag, with the assurance that no foreign one had ever been tolerated within the walls; that the British Consul's had been torn down on the first attempt to raise it, and that the appearance of ours would excite commotion, and perhaps lead to serious consequences. But we had carried it to every place we had visited, and, determining to take our chances with it, we kept it flying. Many angry comments were, I believe, made by the populace, but, as we did not understand what our toorgeman was too wary to interpret, we passed unmolested.[10]

Too much, however, should not be made of these displays of patriotism. They were, I believe, nationalistic rather than imperialistically chauvinistic and were spurs to scientific achievement rather than representations of warlike propensities or blatantly imperialistic ventures. Moreover, they did not prevent Lynch and other U.S. Naval Officers from sharing their knowledge with explorers from other countries that they met, so to speak, on the road, and giving full credit to the work of other explorers. (In at least one instance this generosity formed the basis of an attack by the person to whom it was extended against the scientific integrity of the U.S. Naval officer concerned.) Pride and confidence in the United States did not conflict with an appreciation of teamwork relative to increasing the world's stock of knowledge.

Science in the exploration and travel narratives authored by U.S. Naval officers in the nineteenth century is a laudable, perhaps even a romantic, activity. Even apart from the increase in knowledge it brings in its own right to the reader, science in the exploration and travel narratives authored by U.S. Naval officers acts as a spur and model for human conduct. From a military service based on precedent the reader is advised to engage in the pursuit of truth rather than lolly or languish in the mire of tradition. The U.S. Naval officers who wrote exploration and travel narratives in the nineteenth century believed, to paraphrase Steven Marcus,[11] that science encompassed problems to be solved and that solutions could be found through hard work and courage. From this point of view their attitude toward science is both Victorian and modern. Their books can—and are— recommended to be read from these different but similar viewpoints. They have a lot to offer the contemporary reader. They should be edited and reprinted.

NOTES

[1]J.N.L. Baker, *A History of Geographical Discovery and Exploration,* New Edition Revised (New York: Cooper Square Publishers, Inc., 1967), p. 490.

[2]William Lewis Herndon and Lardner Gibbon, *Exploration of the Valley of the Amazon, Made Under Direction of the Navy Department,* 2 vols. (Vol. I, Herndon,Washington, D.C.: Taylor & Maury, 1854; Vol. II, Gibbon,Washington,D.C.: R. Armstrong, 1854); Elisha Kent Kane, *The U.S. Grinnell Expedition in Search of Sir John Franklin, A Personal Narrative* (New York: Harper & Bros., 1853); *Arctic Explorations, The Second Grinnell Expedition in Search of Sir John Franklin in 1853, '54, and '55* 2 Vols. (Philadelphia: Lea and Blanchard, 1849); Thomas J. Page, *La Plata, The Argentine Confederation and Paraguay* (New York: Harper & Bros., 1859); Charles Wilkes, *Narrative of the United States Exploring Expedition During the Years 1838, 1839, 1840, 1841, 1842,* 5 Vols. (Philadelphia: Lea and Blanchard, 1845).

[3]This topic deserves the attention of a full scale monograph.

[4]Kane, *Arctic Exploration in the Years 1853, 1854, 1855.*

[5]Herndon, *Exploration of the Valley of the Amazon,* p. 63.

[6]Charles Neider, ed., *The Autobiography of Mark Twain* (New York: Harper Brothers, 1959), p. 98.

[7]Smyth's account was published in 1836 as Frederick Lowe and William Smyth, *Narrative of a Journey from Lima to Para, Across the Andes and Down the Amazon: Undertaken with a View of Ascertaining the Practicability of a Navigable Communication with the Atlantic by the Rivers Pachitea, Ucayoli, and Amazon* (London: 1836).

[8]*Littell's Living Age,* Vol. XXII (July, August, Sepltember, 1849), 160.

[9]Robert St. John, *Roll Jordan Roll: The Life Story of a River and Its People* (New York: Doubleday and Co., Inc., 1963), p. 360.

[10]Lynch *Narrative,* pp. 147-48.

[11]Steven Marcus, *The Other Victorians, A Study of Sexuality and Pornography in Mid-Nineteenth Century England* (New York: Basic Books, Inc., c. 1966), p. 2.

Exploration
and the American Naturalists

John Muir's
My First Summer in the Sierra

Donez Xiques

John Muir is usually remembered for his accomplishments as an explorer and for his role as founder of the Sierra Club. However, his work as an author is less well-remembered. During his lifetime, John Muir published a number of books and articles relating to his experiences as a naturalist and conservationist; these and some posthumously published works fill ten volumes in the Sierra edition of his writings.[1]

Although the present ecological crisis provides good reason for a return to John Muir's books, his writing also invites attention because of its intrinsic merit. His prose reflects his incredible spirit of self-reliance and his great reverence for nature, qualities which serve to place him well within the tradition of nineteenth century American Romanticism. In addition, Muir's writing invites our attention because it often embodies features which are characteristic of exploration literature. This genre has been described by Jerome Rosenberg as follows: "Exploration literature depicts the discovery of self, of one's place in space and time, as one confronts the unknown, and as one confronts it under a particular set of personal, cultural, and historical contexts."[2]

A return to Muir as writer of exploration literature might well begin with *My First Summer in the Sierra,* a book he gleaned from notes made in 1869, but not published until 1911, more than forty years later. In this work Muir records in a series of chronological entries the impact of his first sojourn in the wilderness of the Sierra. He came to San Francisco by steamer in March 1868 and spent the summer of the following year in the Sierra earning a livelihood by overseeing some shepherds and a flock of more than two thousand sheep. During those months, Muir witnessed the ravages of unchecked grazing and the effects of man's domestication of the wild sheep.[3] That summer in the mountions of California was a turning point in his life. From that time onward he remained for almost twenty years amid the great outdoors: exploring the mountains, tracing the paths of ancient glaciers, and absorbing all in nature.

An interesting and appealing feature of *My First Summer in the Sierra* is the fact that Muir chooses to remain in the background. Even though his narrative is written in the first person, Muir is not anxious to tell what he has done, but rather what nature has done for him, an infinitely more important story.[4] Both the content of this book and its form reflect this focus. Nevertheless, the reader's interest is drawn to the narrator, John Muir, to his response to nature and the wilderness as it is revealed in this work: for in *My First Summer in the Sierra,* Muir really is describing his own awakening to his life's work.

Unlike some persons who set out in their explorations to conquer or subdue nature, Muir always endeavors to establish an harmonious relationship with nature. This is clear throughout *My First Summer in the Sierra.* He does not percive anything in nature merely as thing or object, but he ardently believes that everything that his senses apprehend is informed with life or spirit. He writes, "When we try to pick out anything by itself, we find it hitched to everything else in the universe. One fancies a heart like our own must be beating in every crystal and cell" (211). Elsewhere he notes, "the landscape beaming with consciousness like the face of a god" (113); and "the rocks, the air, everything speaking with audible voice or silent" (209).

The stylistic choices which Muir makes throughout *My First Summer* provide insight into the mind of this explorer. Rarely does the reader feel Muir strives to incorporate the artful phrase, finely balanced sentence or erudite allusion. On the contrary, one finds, for instance, abbreviated openings for sentences, such as the following: "Left camp soon after sunrise" (161); "Found a lovely lily" (22); "Have been sketching" (191). Other entries such as "Sundown, and I must to camp" (188) and "Saw a few Columbines Today" (52) lead one to feel that the published work retains the flavor and freshness of Muir's original jottings. In its own way this style is rather appealing. The reader is attracted by what sounds like an authentic voice. It is as if one is overhearing the dialogue of Muir with himself.

Over and over he remarks that the beauty of nature draws

him in some inexplicable way, "Beauty beyond thought everywhere, beneath, above, made and being made forever" (18). His delight in nature seems spontaneous and continuous. He can write, "Am delighted with this little bush" (44). The sunset can so excite him that he runs back to camp down slopes, across ridges and ravines, through avalanche gaps, firs, and chaparral (209). While treking along behind the herd of sheep, he sports a wild rose in the buttonhole of his jacket (26).

Amid those mountains Muir misses nothing. He observes the patterns made by the sunshine, writing, "How beautiful a rock is made by leaf shadows" (79). He is amazed even by the presence of the ordinary housefly (184) and in July, when the hemlock is in full bloom, he is not content simply to admire it; he climbs one of the trees to revel in the midst of the flowers (203).

Although the prose of a contemporary of Muir, the British naturalist Charles Darwin, also expresses wonder in the presence of nature, Darwin rarely displays the sense of exhilaration one finds in Muir's writings. That is a feature of his style which seems to be a consequence of his profound sense of God. For Muir, like Moses, was never quite the same after his journey to the mountain top. Those three months in the Sierra held a religious significance which he frequently alludes to and which colors his attitude toward his explorations. Lines such as the following are characteristic of *My First Summer:* "The place seemed holy, where one might hope to see God" (65); "A fruitful day, without measured beginning or ending. A terrestrial eternity. A gift of good God" (178). Muir is convinced that all in nature is part of the beneficient and wise handiwork of God. Nature, consequently, is something he respects, reverences, and seeks to understand. Product of God's thought and design it is not a threat to him. This attitude is apparent in *My First Summer* where his notes as naturalist indicate accuracy and attention to data, and also reflect his value judgments. Even when the weather is inclement or nasty, Muir avoids that sort of assessment. Writing on June 23, he simply says, "Our regular allowance of clouds and thunder" (82).The following month when there was an exceptionally heavy rain and thunder storm, he does not bemoan that, but is fascinated by it, commenting, "Now comes the rain with corresponding extravagant grandeur, covering the ground high and low with a sheet of flowing water, a transparent film fitted like a skin upon the rugged anatomy of the landscape" (166).

Muir would never concur with the Wordsworthian notion that nature teaches by a ministry of fear as well as beauty. In *My First Summer,* nature is never source or cause of fear. Even in its wild and unpredictable moments, Muir says, "We see that everything in Nature called destruction must be creation,—a change from beauty to beauty" (308). In an article on Yosemite he writes, "If among the agents that nature has employed in making these mountains there be one that above all others deserves the name of Destroyer, it is the glacier. But we quickly learn that destruction is creation."[5]

Muir's explorations, in fact, led him to conclude that then prevalent opinions were erroneous concerning the origins of the Drift (i.e., the vast layer of soil, sand gravel, and boulders derived from the far north which overlies eastern Canada and much of the United States to the 40th parallel). In the 1870's most American geologists were catastrophists who believed that a series of cataclysmic occurrences had caused the Drift. Muir rejects their theories, maintaining that the Drift is chiefly the result of gradual change, the action of glaciers, for example.

Although Muir believes change is constant in nature, he also believes that nothing is lost as a consequence of change. For him all that happens in nature is part of a larger harmony and unity. "How lavish is Nature," he writes, "building, pulling down, creating, destroying, chasing every material particle from form to form" (318-19).

This attitude that everything is in purposeful movement can be seen in *My First Summer.* By using verbs of motion as well as present participles, Muir conveys a sense of the vitality of all things and enables the reader to feel more like a participant and less like an observer. This effect is evident in the passages following: "Down over this ice-planed granite runs the glad young Tamarack Creek, rejoicing, exulting, chanting, dancing in white, glowing, irised falls and cascades on its way to the Merced Canon" (135). This emphasis on movement is characteristic of Muir's way of perceiving and relating his observations in *My*

First Summer in the Sierra. He speaks, for example, of shadows on rocks, "now gliding softly as if afraid of noise, now dancing, waltzing in swift, merry swirls, or jumping on and off sunny rocks in quick dashes" (79).

Although there is a sense here of vividness and immediacy, Muir's habit of personifying elements in nature tends to detract from the overall quality of some of his passages. When one reads of daisies "too small to fear" (177) and flowers leaning "confidingly" (35), it seems a bit too precious, at least for today's readers.

What does emerge very clearly, however, is the fact that amidst the mountains of California John Muir experiences a freedom of body and spirit that is exhilarating. At the end of his first month in the Sierra he writes: "This June seems the greatest of all the months of my life, the most truly, divinely free, boundless like eternity, immortal. Everything in it seems equally divine..." (90).

A passage such as that highlights the curious fact that while on the one hand both the style and content of *My First Summer* place Muir well in the background, on the other hand, the tone of the book brings him very clearly into focus. He expresses such an enthusiasm for all that he beholds that as he shares his reactions and appreciation of the Sierra, the reader becomes aware of a tone which is very much Muir's own.

When he tries to verbalize the impression made upon him by those wonderful months in the mountains, he declares that he can never adequately describe their impact. "It is easier," Muir says, "to feel than to realize, or in any way explain Yosemite grandeur" (175). "The whole body seems to feel beauty when exposed to it as it feels the camp-fire or sunshine, entering not by the eyes alone, but equally through all one's flesh like radiant heat" (175).

It is this conviction that the Sierra affects one's whole person and not simply the sense of sight or sound which prompts Muir, in my opinion, to work toward a prose style which will offer the reader a means of sharing with him the felt experience of the Sierra's grandeur. It is not surprising, therefore, to find that his diction appeals to the reader's senses through the use of concrete and particular words rather than ones which are abstract and generalized.

In *My First Summer in the Sierra* there are many passages in whch the imagery helps to re-create a scene or incident for the reader. Muir describes the Indians' way of walking, as "making themselves invisible like certain spiders I have been observing here" (71). When he spies some giant Sierra lilies, he remarks that some of their bells are "big enough for children's bonnets" (48). A bear is called a "broad rusty bundle of ungovernable wildness" (182). Occasionally his metaphors are mixed delightfully as in these two examples: "The dawn a glorious song of color" (317) and "The pines marshalled around the edge of the sky made a yet sweeter music to the eye" (29).

Although sight and sound imagery predominate in this book, there is also reference to the senses of touch and smell. In fact, throughout *My First Summer* the reader finds that all Muir's senses are engaged by the Sierra. He notices the varied sounds of nature, from a field humming with bees (112) to the "wind-tones in the great trees overhead" (118). He even likes to hear the "cheery tronk and crink" of the frogs (270). He often comments on the fragrance of the air (80, 116) and says after climbing a hemlock which was in full bloom, "How the touch of the flowers makes one's flesh tingle!" (203). When Muir tries to sum up the effect of the Sierra, he turns to images based on the sense of touch. "In the midst of such beauty, pierced with its rays, one's body is all one tingling palate" (206).

Some features of his style, however, are less memorable. Muir's adjectives, for example, are irritatingly trite. Phrases such as "nobly proportioned," "noblest view," "splashy brook" and "a worthy companion" are frequent and to us sound hollow. But Muir's similes are different. They often reflect his own unique way of perceiving and the reader can be engaged by the freshness of Muir's comparisons: "Saw a large black tailed deer, a buck with antlers like the upturned roots of a fallen pine" (273); "My fire squirmed and struggled as if ill at ease" (296); "A small brown partridge with a very long, slender, ornamental crest worn jauntily like a feather in a boy's cap" (234-5).

When Muir first ventured into the Sierra, he was a competent scientist. One might, therefore, expect his prose to be somewhat factual and uninteresting to the general reader. However, that is not the case. His scientific observations are couched in language which reflects Muir's continuing enthusiasm and zest for living amidst the mountains and which helps the reader experience the grandeur of Yosemite. There seems to be little that escapes Muir's attentive eye, and he is equally adept at describing both the small and great in nature.

In the valley of Yosemite, for example, the sights and sounds of the tremendous waterfalls are most impressive. How, one may ask, can a writer distinguish one waterfall from another for the reader? Here are passages from two scientists who attempt to do just that. The first quotation is by J.D. Whitney, a California state geologist, whom Muir knew:

The first fall reached in ascending the canon is the Vernal, a perpendicular sheet of water with a descent varying greatly with the season. Our measurements give all the way from 315 to 475 feet for the vertical height of the fall, between the months of June and October. The reason of these descrepencies [sic] seems to lie in the fact that the rock near the bottom is steeply inclined, so that a precise definition of the place where the perpendicular part ceases is very difficult amid the blinding spray and foam. As the body of water increases, the force of the fall is greater, and of course it is thrown farthest forward when the mass of water is greatest.[6]

When Muir describes the same waterfall, his language is much more specific, appealing to one's senses more directly than that of the Whitney passage. Such stylistic choices reflect accuracy and yet engage the reader more fully. Here is Muir's verbal sketch:

The Vernal, four hundred feet high and about seventy-five or eighty wide, drops smoothly over a round-lipped precipice and forms a superb apron of embroidery, green and white, slighly folded and fluted, maintaining this form nearly to the bottom, where it is suddenly veiled in quick-flying billows of spray and mist, in which the afternoon sunbeams play with ravishing beauty of rainbow colors (252).

It is not only such magnificent and grandiose features of

nature which attract Muir. He also has comments about nature's small creatures. In the following passage he combines precise observation with interesting description:

[The grasshopper] seemed brimful of glad hilarious energy, manifested by springing into the air to the height of twenty or thirty feet, then diving and springing up again and making a sharp musical rattle just as the lowest point in the descent was reached.... The curves he described in the air in diving and rattling resembled those made by cords hanging loosely and attached at the same height at the ends, the loops nearly covering each other.... How the sound is made I do not understand. When he was on the ground he made not the slightest noise, nor when he was simply flying from place to place, but only when diving in curves, the motion seeming to be required for the sound (185-7).

Here is another passage in which Muir vividly describes the bite of an ant:

I fancy that a bear or wolfbite is not to be compared with it. A quick electric flame of pain flashes along the outraged nerves, and you discover for the first time how great is the capacity for sensation you are possessed of. A shriek, a grab for the animal, and a bewildered stare follow this bite of bites as one comes back to consciousness from sudden eclipse (60-61).

In the foregoing selections the effectiveness of the imagery arises from its naturalness. The comparisons are apt and have a flavor all Muir's own. They arise from his experience and reveal a perceptive eye and keen imagination at work. The scenes and events encountered during those months exploring the Sierra have become transformed through Muir's prose style from personal autobiography to shared participation for the reader in a past event made present.

While Muir was in those mountains, he realized that the beauty and significance which he found in virtually everything surrounding him were not shared by everyone. He was appalled at the effects of careless mining in those mountains. "Wild streams dammed and tamed and turned out of their channels...like slaves...imprisoned in iron pipes to strike and wash away hills and miles of the skin of the mountain's face, riddling, stripping every gold gully and flat. These are the white man's marks" (73-4). Even Muir's companion during that first summer, Shepherd Billy, was unresponsive both to nature and to Muir himself. Once when the sheep were pastured within a mile of the Yosemite valley and the falls, he tried to persuade Billy to go off and have a look. Billy declined, "What," he said, "is Yosemite but a canon—a lot of rocks—a hole in the ground" (197). On another occasion Muir marvelled at a field where ferns more than seven feet tall were growing close together "overleaning and overlapping." When the shepherd was asked for his reaction, he merely replied, "Oh, they're only d[amne]d big brakes" (54-5).

It was a similar sort of obliviousness which Muir observed on other occasions when visitors came through Yosemite scarcely aware of their surroundings, "as if their eyes were bandaged and their ears stopped" (255). He has an amusing description of such visitors as they fished one day in Yosemite:

Yet respectable-looking, even wise-looking people were fixing bits of worms on bent pieces of wire to catch trout. Sport they called it. Should church-goers try to pass the time fishing in baptismal fonts while dull sermons are being preached, the so-called sport might not be bad; but to play in the Yosemite temple, seeking pleasure in the pain of fishes struggling for their lives, while God himself is preaching his sublimest water and stone sermons (255-6)!

Such early experiences with the indifference of others to the miracles which Muir himself constantly saw in nature were repeated throughout his lifetime. Later, when saving these unique natural areas from destruction and exploitation became urgent, he was able to write with people such as this in mind.

According to one recent author it is balanced tension in the account of any individual explorer, between the tendency to catalog or botanize, on the one hand, and the tendency to succumb to feeling or intuition on the other, which provides not only narrative characterization in the writing, but offers one means of distinguishing genuine literature of exploration from mere landscape description.[7] When such criteria are applied to *My First Summer,* it is clear that this book belongs among the volumes of authentic exploration literature. Clearly, Muir's work as an author flowed from his life as an explorer. And the pages of *My First Summer in the Sierra* not only describe the wonders of those mountains, but also disclose to the reader the mind of John Muir.

A glance at the years prior to 1869 shows Muir struggling to delineate his life's goals. It also shows a boyhood and adolescence filled with hardship and backbreaking labor. Perhaps that served to prepare him in some way for the rugged and solitary life of his adult years. The wonder is that he survived emotionally and physically, that his relationship with a stern father did not congeal the joy, curiosity and imagination which seem naturally to be part of him as a boy. It is known, for example, that on one occasion John's favorite horse died as a consequence of being ridden too hard by Muir senior as he dashed from one church meeting to another. Once John's father required the boy to dig a well ninety feet deep, eighty feet of which had to be chipped through limestone. Each day for weeks the elder Muir would lower John in a basket, haul him up for lunch at noon, then lower him into the hole where he chipped away at the rock until nightfall. One day the boy passed out from the noxious fumes, but after being brought to the surface, he was sent back down again by his father. This incident is recounted in *The Story of My Boyhood and Youth* with the comment, "constant dropping wears away stone. So does constant chipping, while at the same time wearing away the chipper. Father never spent an hour in that well."[8]

One can only guess the feeling of relief in adult years when John was away from the parental voice and no longer felt the threat of the rod. Yet he remained concerned about his father and family all his life, corresponded with them and saved enough money so that he could promise them that in an emergency he was ready to offer financial as well as personal assistance.

After such severity and grimness at home it is not surprising that Muir found a benevolence and joy in nature—though it need not have been so. In *My First Summer* he rarely comments about himself, but there seem to be unwritten volumes behind his entry written during his very first week in the Sierra: "We are now in the mountains and they are in us.... Our flesh-and-bone tabernacle seems transparent as glass to the beauty about us.... How glorious a conversion, so complete and wholesome it is, scarce memory enough of old bondage days left" (20-21).

The writing of John Muir, explorer, naturalist, humanist, deserves a revival. *My First Summer in the Sierra* is a good place to begin. In it, he speaks of gazing and sketching "without definite hope of every learning much, yet with the longing, unresting effort that lies at the door of hope...eager to offer self-denial and renunciation with eternal toil to learn any lesson in the divine manuscript" (175).

It seems clear that Muir succeeded in deciphering nature's hieroglyphics and in so doing revealed that his concern was not to flee from men into wilderness, but to seek to discover there the place of man in the world. A recent biographer offers this summary of Muir's significance: "It is his ability to convey a whole, living sense of wilderness—and to hold up the natural mirror to man—that mark his greatness."[9] This living sense of wilderness and keen understanding of man, Muir's gift to us, emerge clearly in *My First Summer in the Sierra*.

NOTES

[1]William Bade, ed. *The Sierra Club Edition of the Works of John Muir* (Boston: Houghton Mifflin Company, 1915-1924).

[2]Jerome H. Rosenberg, "Exploration Literature—A Distinguishable Genre," *Exploration,* III (December 1975), iv.

[3]John Muir, *My First Summer in the Sierra* (Boston & New York: Houghton Mifflin Company, 1911), pp. 28, 75, 343.

[4]Bade, II, 317.

[5]John Muir, "The Yosemite National Park," *Atlantic,* 84 (1899), 145-52.

[6]J.D. Whitney, *The Yellowstone Guide-Book* (Cambridge: University Press: Welch, Bigelow and Company, 1869), pp. 70-71.

[7]Charles D. Harrington, "Self-Definition in Literature of Exploration," *Exploration,* III (December 1975), 2.

[8]John Muir, *The Story of My Boyhood and Youth* (Boston: Houghton Mifflin Company, 1913), p. 186.

[9]Thomas Lyons, *John Muir* (Boise: Boise State College, Western Writers Series No 3, 1972), p. 15.

Originally published in *Exploration,* IV:2, July 1977. Reprinted with the permission of the editor and the author.

John Muir, Emerson, and the Book of Nature:
The Explorer as Prophet

John Tallmadge

We are accustomed to thinking of John Muir primarily as a naturalist and to reading his works as inspirational tracts from the wilderness preservation movement he helped found.But he was also an explorer, a gifted mountaineer and a shrewd observer of both wild and human nature. Geographically, his explorations were not the kind to make history. He discovered no new lands. Yet, during the years he lived in Yosemite Valley he travelled more extensively in the little-known High Sierra than anyone else. And in his four subsequent voyages to Alaska he discovered and named many glaciers, most of them in and around the uncharted Glacier Bay. His explorations were, in a word, intensive: they raised no geographical landmarks. Yet Muir always considered himself an explorer and assumed that stance in his writings. My purpose here will be to examine Muir's stance, chiefly with reference to his *Travels in Alaska*. I wish to suggest a way to read and appreciate him both in the tradition of American wilderness writing and in the larger context of literature of exploration. For the former tradition we must begin with Emerson, for of all the early nineteenth century American nature writers, he was the most articulate and influential. And he was one of the first to proclaim that natural science, religion and the search for a national identity should be considered parts of a single enterprise.

I

Several commentators have discussed the transcendentalist strain in Muir's writings,[1] and Muir's cordial relationship with Emerson is well known. In 1871 Emerson visited Yosemite Valley during his grand tour of the west. Muir was living there at the time and he had been alerted to Emerson's arrival by a mutual friend. The two men spent many hours together, scrambling about the feet of the great cliffs and admiring the flora and the

views. Emerson's east coast companions were somewhat
alarmed, as they considered Muir rustic and uncouth. But
Emerson returned to Boston convinced he had found another
representative man, a type of the devout naturalist whose
scientific investigations were carried out in a spirit of worship.
This was the figure he had called for thirty years earlier when he
wrote in *Nature:*

But when a faithful thinker, resolute to detach every object from personal
relations and see it in the light of thought, shall, at the same time, kindle
science with the fire of the holiest affections, then will God go forth anew
into the creation.[2]

When Emerson returned to Concord, he wrote Muir urging
him to come east and meet Louis Agassiz, Asa Gray and other
eminent scientists of the day. Muir demurred, saying he had more
field work to do. [But at the same time he confided to a friend,
"Imagine me giving up God's big show for a mere profship!"[3]]
This refusal did not dampen Muir's enthusiasm for Emerson,
however. He continued to write long exuberant letters from
Yosemite. But when he finally did visit Concord, thirty years
later, it was to lay flowers on his friend's grave.

During his excursions into the High Sierra, Muir often
carried a copy of Emerson's essays. This remarkable book, well-
thumbed, scuffed, and stained with pine pitch and charcoal, now
resides in the Beinecke Library at Yale. Its markings reveal much
about Muir's intellectual relationship with Emerson. Reading it
along with Muir's books, one senses how easy it was for Muir to
consider himself a disciple of Emerson. Yet one also notices clear
lines of divergence in both the pattern and the substance of their
thinking.

The metaphor of the Book of Nature offers a good example.
This ancient literary trope is one of Muir's favorite rhetorical
devices, and Emerson gives it a central place in *Nature* as well.[4]
In his chapter entitled "Language" Emerson develops the
metaphor according to a doctrine of correspondences he distilled
from Swedenborg and the German Idealists. Words, he asserts,
are signs of natural facts. But natural facts themselves are signs

of spiritual realities. By extension, therefore, all nature becomes an expression of the human psyche and its perfected form in the Divine Mind. "The world is emblematic," Emerson writes. "Parts of speech are metaphors, because the whole of nature is a metaphor of the human mind. The laws of moral nature answer to those of matter as face to face in a glass.... The axioms of physics translate the laws of ethics."[5] This being the case, the study of nature can become a moral discipline. Science ceases to be merely the servant of commodity and becomes instead a tool of religion. It reveals the manner in which man participates in the creation, or rather, the true basis for any "original relation" which he may choose to establish with any part of the creation. The real aim of science, says Emerson, ought to be to bring man's vision into line with the "axes of things." "All things with which we deal preach to us," he concludes.[6] Man's difficulties arise because he cannot see things in their right relations, to each other, to himself and to God. The proper study of nature is an ethical one, teaching both reverence and self-reliance. It is therefore the true foundation of both culture and character.

Emerson's call for an "original relation to the universe," then, is really a call for moral and social revitalization. Nature is the new book of prophecy and enlightenment for Americans in search of an identity. Emerson's ideal scholar is one who can read this book in a spirit of devotion and humility, whose vision can pierce the veil between the material fact and the moral essence. In his chapter "Idealism," Emerson makes clear that nature, for all her charm, must be surpassed in order to reach true enlightenment. Though he may expand and live in the warm day like corn and melons, Emerson seems finally less interested in the natural facts themselves than in the spiritual realities they represent. "If the reason be stimulated to more earnest vision," he says, "outlines and surfaces become transparant, and are no longer seen; causes and spirits are seen through them."[7] Natural facts become stairs the mind mounts up in contemplation until at last it has no need of them and stands in the naked presence of God.

The euphoric optimism with which Emerson concludes might obscure this shift in his attitude toward nature were it not for the consistence of his central metaphor. The conception of the Book of Nature with its doctrine of correspondences allows him to rank his various uses of nature one above the other while at the same time viewing each use in terms of all the others. Thus poetry becomes a higher form of science, science becomes worship, vision becomes action and experience becomes revelation. Emerson's poet-scientist is the type of man seeing, the one whose vision is in line with the axes of things. He reads the Book of Nature and what he finds there are essentially moral lessons. Nature is to man "the present expositor of the divine mind."[8] It is therefore, from Emerson's point of view, fundamentally didactic.

Now Muir shared many of Emerson's concerns, but he did not embrace Emerson's Idealism. Like many another reader, he found Emerson highly quotable, but the markings in his copy of *Nature* show just how far he was willing to follow. For example, he scored several passages in "Language" where Emerson asserts the immanence of spirit in natural facts, but he left unmarked those passages where Emerson speaks of the moral aspect of physical laws. On the other hand, he marked almost every sentence describing the beauty of nature or the exhilaration produced by contemplation of landscapes, flowers, or the heavens. And in his own writings the metaphor of the Book of Nature appears in a manner significantly different from Emerson's. Here is a passage from one of his Sierra journals:

Glacial records. Nothing goes unrecorded. Every word of leaf and snowflake and particle of dew, shimmering, fluttering, falling, as well as earthquake and avalanche, is written down in Nature's book....

Glaciers, avalanches, and torrents are the pens with which Nature produces written characters most like our own, and every canyon of the Sierra displays examples of this writing.[9]

Clearly, Muir and Emerson do not mean the same thing when they speak of nature as a divine language. They share the metaphor but not the interpretation. Elsewhere, Muir speaks of a horizon of pine trees as "definite symbols, divine hieroglyphics written with sunbeams."[10] And in the same work he calls Yosemite Valley "a grand page of mountain manuscript that I would gladly give my life to be able to read."[11]

There is no doctrine of correspondences at work here. The "divine hieroglyphics" Muir writes of are glacial striae, morainal deposits and the channels of stream erosion. Rather than pointing beyond nature to spiritual essences, they point backward in time to pre-existent physical realities. They never transcend nature. They do not comprise a philosophical code or spiritual allegory, but rather a kind of sacred history.

When the Book of Nature appears as a figure in Muir, it is usually embedded in an enthusiastic landscape description. When all is said and done, Muir seems motivated more by a simple love of natural beauty than by an Emersonian zeal for visionary perfection. To Muir, the Book of Nature is worth reading because it was written by God, the true fount of all beauty. If there are morals to be drawn from such work, they are not complex ones. Muir studies nature and learns the language of praise. He discovers the delight of celebration, the exuberance of all beings participating in the creation. This feeling uplifts and rejuvenates, and therefore it seems reason enough for him to seek out the wilderness.

This aesthetic outlook distinguishes Muir's use of the Book of Nature from Emerson's. To Emerson, beauty was one of the more obvious and thus ultimately inferior uses of nature. But Muir, it seems, was unwilling to follow him beyond that point and into the rarefied atmospheres of "Idealism." In that chapter Muir underlined passages dealing with science and the joys of the nature lover, but he seems to have ignored the argument's key paragraphs. He apparently saw no need to render the world transparent. Rather than surpass nature, he wanted to fling himself into it. He sought his God in things themselves and searched out His inscriptions in the wildest regions, where they would not be obscured by the refuse of human enterprise. And it was this search, finally, which led him beyond the Yosemite to Alaska.

II

To understand the lure of Alaska in John Muir's mind, we

must remember that his wilderness conscience was formed by ten years of exploration in the High Sierra. It is difficult to conceive how deep an impression the stupendous glaciated landscapes of Yosemite made on him. Throughout his life glaciers and their effects remained his preeminent concerns, overshadowing even the love of botany which had originally brought him to California. So ardent was his passion for glaciers that it sometimes appears comical in the accounts. Linnie Marsh Wolfe, Muir's biographer, describes a typical incident during one of his botanical trips to the Mt. Shasta country:

> One day they were footing over a barren volcanic plain when Muir discovered glacial striae upon the lava. "Hurry, run, see this wonderful thing!" he yelled at them. Mrs. Bidwell, panting along in the rear, breathing red dust, gasped out: "I can't hurry any faster than I am. I'm spitting blood now." But Muir had no mercy. "Oh,never mind that. Hurry. This is worth dying to see!"[12]

Muir was dead serious about glaciers. To him they were the instruments God used to create sublime landscapes. The scriptures in the rocks revealed that God had been at work. Interpreting these scriptures was an act of appreciation, as one might learn to appreciate a work of sculpture as both craft and art. But since the artist was divine, the act of appreciation became an act of worship. Gazing upon the distant peaks of the High Sierra, Muir wrote: "Some one worthy will go, able for the Godful work, yet as far as I can I must drift about these love-monument mountains, glad to be a servant of servants in so holy a wilderness."[13]

But the Sierran landscapes were created long ago, and Muir finds that the glaciers which formed them have all but vanished. The tools of the Craftsman have been withdrawn. Thus, Muir finds the relation between man and the Creator mediated by the passage of time. The books of the rocks can reveal the power and grace of the Creator, but only when they have been interpreted. And this interpretation consists in reconstructing the ancestral landscape from the extant inscriptions. The work of the naturalist is a struggle to look back in time, to glimpse the origin of that sublimity in the landscape which so dazzles and uplifts the beholder. But suppose one could watch a Yosemite being born. Then one might stand directly in the presence of the Creator, with no need to see through or beyond the creation itself.

Muir's *Travels in Alaska* is full of references to Yosemite. In fact, it is his most common comparison and it occurs always in the superlative degree. For Muir, Yosemite was the archetypal sublimity. Describing one glacial fiord he entered while sailing up the coast from Ft. Wrangell, he exclaims:

No words can convey anything like an adequate conception of its sublime grandeur—the noble simplicity and fineness of the sculpture of the walls; their magnificent proportions....
...This is a Yosemite Valley in process of formation, the modelling and sculpture of the walls nearly completed...(79-81).[14]

Elsewhere he speaks of Sum Dum Bay as a "wild, unfinished Yosemite" (275). Along the valley of one of the Stickeen Glaciers he observes that "all the wall rocks...are more or less yosemitic in form and color" (127). That this is sacred ground to Muir becomes clear at once, for in his Sierran writings he has referred repeatedly to Yosemite as a temple. Now he calls the splendid fiord a "glorious temple" and the awe it inspires in him and his companions is "only the natural effect of appreciable manifestations of the presence of God" (80).

Muir seems drawn to Alaska for two primary reasons. On the one hand he seeks confirmation of his interpretations of the Book of Nature. After a few days of scrambling over the Big Stickeen Glacier, for example, he discovers a place where he can crawl down and watch the ice pouring over a hard granite rib. "A most telling lesson in earth-sculpture," he exults, "confirming many I had already learned in the glacier basins of the High Sierra of California " (139).

On the other hand, Muir seeks unobstructed vision. He wants to see God at work in the world. He longs to be caught up in joyful contemplation of that work. Thus, he travels farther and wider from the human world, seeking ever the regions more northerly and more wild. And at the point farthest out he has his vision. At the head of Glacier Bay, surrounded by the most spectacular glaciation he has ever seen, Muir watches the dawn come up on the distant Fairweather Range:

Instead of vanishing as suddenly as it had appeared, it spread and spread until the whole range down to the level of the glaciers was filled with the celestial fire.... Beneath the frosty shadows of the fiord we stood hushed and awe-stricken, gazing at the holy vision.... The white, rayless light of morning, seen when I was alone amid the peaks of the California Sierra, had always seemed to me the most telling of all the terrestrial manifestations of God. But here the mountains themselves were made divine and declared His glory in terms still more impressive. How long we gazed I never knew (186-87).

This passage lies at the visionary core of Muir's book. Its location in the plan of the voyage, at the point farthest from the "civilized" world, determines the cosmographic scheme of his account. For the journey is also a spiritual one. Muir proceeds from the profane landscapes of civilization to the sacred landscape of Glacier Bay, encountering every gradation in between.

Muir's references to civilization are generally deprecatory. Ft. Wrangell appears "at first sight the most inhospitable place I had ever seen" (22), though the "disorder and squalor" (33) belie the healthful climate and comfortable life of the Indians. In contrast, the surrounding wilderness is a veritable paradise, abundant with fish and wild fruits of all kinds (37-8). And this impression of lushness and fertility is not diminished the farther Muir goes from the settlements. On the moraine of one of the Stickeen glaciers he finds a botanist's dream-garden. "In the gardens and forests of this wonderful moraine one might spend a whole joyful life," he cries (137). And the country he paddles through on the way to Glacier Bay seems a "foodful, kindly wilderness" (153).

Needless to say, the people he meets are measured by the degree to which they participate in this spiritual geography. Thus the Indians, who depend so intimately upon the land, are described with glowing affection. At Glacier Bay Muir talks with his guides about the stars and recalls how "their eager, childlike attention was refreshing to see as compared with the deathlike apathy of weary town-dwellers, in whom natural curiosity has been quenched in toil and care and poor shallow comfort" (191). Elsewhere Muir praises the Indians for their woodcraft, their kindness as parents, their dignity, reverence and desire to learn. He attributes these high moral qualities to the influence of the land in which they live. In contrast, the influences of the white man's world (with the notable exception of the missionaries) are perverse and destructive. Time and again, Muir deplores the corrosive effects of whisky. He sees the gold rush as a plague and the miners as poor misguided souls who seek the wrong kind of riches: "Just struggling blindly for gold enough to make them indefinitely rich to spend their lives in aimless affluence, honor and ease" (107). As for himself, he finds the wilderness treasure enough, and returns from the Stickeen "happy and rich without a particle of obscuring gold-dust care" (107).

In fact, Muir finds in the Alaskan wilderness three traditional attributes of the earthly paradise: an innocent race, an abundance of nourishing life, and the tangible presence of God.[15] Needless to say, this view sets him apart from the mass of his contemporaries bred to civilization, who, for the most part, thought of the wilderness as a howling waste peopled by devil-worshipping savages. All of Muir's writing could be seen as an effort to correct that mistaken idea. In his own forthright and exuberant manner, he is always trying to bring our own vision into line with the axis of things. This sense of duty combines with the spiritualized geography of his Alaskan voyages to determine his narrative stance: he is a prophet who goes to the wilderness in search of a vision.[16] He loves the wilderness, for that is where his vision abides. It is where he sees God. But the truth of the vision is always directed toward the human world and thus, for all his ascetic yearnings and love of the wilderness, the prophet is bound to return. It is his role to bear witness, so that the world may be changed.

Muir comments often enough on his own enterprise to make it clear that he takes the prophetic role seriously (though he is not above jesting about it from time to time). He feels as if he has literally been called by the mountains. For example, as he gazes at the Big Glacier of the Stickeen, he can exult, "So grand an invitation displayed in characters so telling was of course irresistible" (128). And when he answers the call, we find him depending to an almost superstitious extent on his own instincts and good luck. When Mr. Choquette, the keeper of Buck Station on the Stickeen, warns him about the dangers of the Big Glacier, adding that many have been killed on it, Muir replies breezily, "Never mind me. I am used to caring for myself" (130). And near the entrance to Glacier Bay, when the Indians are dismayed by the foul weather and dangerous ice conditions, Muir confidently assures them "that for ten years I had wandered alone among mountains and storms, and good luck had always followed me: that with me, therefore, they need fear nothing" (179). This is big talk for a man on his first visit to Alaska, yet it proves true. Nothing, it seems, can shake Muir's enthusiasm. Despite narrow escapes from clashing icebergs, labyrinthine crevasse fields or storms at sea, despite miserable nights in a leaky tent, hours of bashing through hideous Devil's Club thickets or dreary, bone-chilling days in an open canoe, he still writes with all the fervor of a true believer.

Both the lineaments and message of Muir's vision are easily grasped. He says: "The care-laden commercial lives we lead close our eyes to the operations of God as a workman, though openly carried on that all who will look may see" (282). Our lives in the human world seem impoverished to him. He means to restore them by rectifying our attitudes. First, we must learn to see the Creator manifested in His creation, to see that creation going on all around us. "One learns, " Muir writes, "that the world, though made, is yet being made; that this is still the morning of creation; that mountains long conceived are now being born..." (85). This awareness comes about through the discipline of voyaging itself, whereby "you may be truly independent and enter into partnership with Nature; to be carried with the winds and currents, accept the noble invitations offered all along your way..." (252). The result of this vision-cleansing will be a return to joy. "How delightful it is," Muir exclaims, "to get back into the reviving northland wilderness! How truly wild it is, and how joyously one's heart responds to the welcome it gives!.." (251).

Rejuvenation lies at our fingertips. In a sense, it is almost as though we had never left Paradise at all, but merely ceased to acknowledge its presence.

III

As a wilderness writer, Muir set out to answer Emerson's call for an original relation to the universe. He stands near the head of a tradition which includes Thoreau, Robert Marshall, Robinson Jeffers, Aldo Leopold, Theodore Roethke and Edward Abbey. As a voice crying out for wilderness he has few rivals, and few writers have had more impact on the nation's land-use policies. He embraced Emerson's desire to make the study of natural history a tool of religion, but beyond that his thinking diverged. His attention was always directed outward, toward the creatures and things of this world. He remained a passionate celebrant, concerned not to achieve union with God in the purest mystical sense, but always to behold Him at work in His creation. Thus, he did not choose to follow Emerson beyond nature. And he did not attempt in his writings to measure the mind of man, nor to account for the vicissitudes and turbidities of his own consciousness, as Emerson did, through the medium of a universal philosophy.

As an explorer, Muir belongs in that class for whom the expedition was always a solitary enterprise, undertaken for personal and largely private reasons. In this respect he resembles men like Thoreau, Joshua Slocum and Bertram Thomas. These explorers were all in a certain sense exiles. Estranged by circumstance or temperament from their native societies, they made their spiritual homelands elsewhere. In their writings, they lean heavily toward the confessional mode. If they succeed, it is because, while attempting to justify their ways to men, they present such a compelling alternative that our lives are enriched. They change our angle of vision.

Muir's enthusiasm is endearing and often infectious, though at times the reader may sympathize with Mrs. Bidwell running across the lava after him. Despite its extremism, his love for the wilderness is absolutely sincere, and this is finally what makes him such an engaging writer. Nowhere in Muir's scientific discussions is there any hint that he means to astound the academies. He seeks no breakthrough, only to improve his own knowledge. He lacks the self-conscious professionalism of a Darwin or a Whitney. And his descriptions of remarkable mountaineering feats, such as the rescue of Rev. Young on Glenora Peak or the terrible crossing of the Taylor Bay Glacier with the dog Stickeen, are all told in the frankest and least melodramatic fashion. Obviously, Muir took physical vigor, endurance and courage for granted. One does not find in his writings the athletic posturing of a Clarence King, nor the grim determination and rock-jawed nationalistic pride of a Shackleton or a Burton.

Perhaps Muir's most inspiring contribution, though, is the example he sets for exploration as a way of life. His Alaska travels are finally not so important to the geographer as they are to the literate adventurer. With him, the literature of exploration takes one more step away from geographic chronicle in the direction of self-conscious, universalized autobiography. He answered Emerson's call by establishing his own relation and then writing about it, exactly as Thoreau had done a generation before. With splendid sincerity, he tests the stance himself, and Thoreau, who had travelled much in Concord and read copiously in the literature of voyages, would certainly have approved.

NOTES

[1]See, for example, Herbert F. Smith, *John Muir,* N.Y. (Twayne Series), 1965; Thomas J. Lyon, *John Muir,* Boise, Idaho, 1972; Roderick Nash, *Wilderness and the American Mind,* New Haven, p.125-29.

[2]Emerson, *Nature,* in S.E. Whicher (ed.) *Selections from Ralph Waldo Emerson,* Boston, 1957, p.55.

[3]William Frederic Bade, *Life and Letters of John Muir,* Boston, 1923, vol. 2, p. 292.

[4]See, for example, E.R. Curtius, *European Literature and the Latin Middle Ages,* Princeton, 1953, pp. 319-26; also the discussion in Arthur O. Lovejoy, *The Great Chain of Being,* Cambridge, 1964, pp. 67-73; for an example of medieval

attempt to "read" the Book of Nature, see Pierre Bersuire, (1290-1362), *Morale Reductorium super Totam Bibliam,* Lyons, 1520. Emerson's use of the metaphor is actually closer to the medieval sense, which assumes that species are fixed and have been since the Creation. Emerson does not take the historical view of natural history which is so important to Muir. To Emerson, nature is more a museum than a process.

[5]Emerson, *Nature* (ed. cit.), p. 35.

[6]*Ibid.,* p. 39.

[7]*Ibid.,* p. 43.

[8]*Ibid.,* p. 50.

[9]*John of the Mountains: the Unpublished Journals of John Muir,* ed. Linnie Marshe Wolfe, Boston, 1938, p. 171.

[10]John Muir, *My First Summer in the Sierra,* Boston, 1911, p. 29.

[11]*Ibid., p. 135.*

[12]Linnie Marsh Wolfe, *Son of the Wilderness: The Life of John Muir,* New York, 1945, p. 195.

[13]*My First Summer in the Sierra,* p. 22.

[14]John Muir, *Travels in Alaska,* Boston, 1915. Page numbers in parentheses refer to this edition.

[15]For a summary of literary topoi associated with the earthly paradise, see A.B. Giamatti, *The Earthly Paradise and the Renaissance Epic,* Princeton, 1966, chapter 1.

[16]The scenario of the prophet's visionary sojourn in the wilderness is a commonplace in the Judeo-Christian tradition. For biblical examples, see Exodus 3:1-2, 18 (Moses), 1 Kings 19:4-15 (Elijah), Matthew 3:1-4 (John the Baptist), Luke 4: 1-15 (Jesus). See also the discussion and references in Nash, *op. cit.,* pp. 13-17.

Originally published in *Exploration,* IV:2, July 1977. Reprinted with the permission of the editor and the author.

Travel & Exploration
as a Theme
In American Literature

Hawthorne's "Foot-prints on the Sea-Shore" and the Literature of Walking

Roberta F. Weldon

Much of the American literature of the nineteenth century is a "literature of movement."[1] As in the English and German Romantic tradition, the central figure of the major novels is often a wanderer[2] who is in quest of himself and of some redemptive knowledge. Some of these questers, like Ishmael or Huck Finn, journey, with great explicitness, to some goal, while others, like Natty Bumppo, are driven to escape some inexorable force—call it progress or civilization. The strength of the fictional literature of travel in America is rightfully undisputed, but its unquestioned dominance has unfortunately tended to cast into the background another vital aspect of the literary tradition of this century—the non-fictional travel narrative.[3] This form shares many of the characteristics of the fictional literature of travel. At its best the essay will also use the metaphor of travel to provide the shape for an internal journey. Oftentimes, the movement of the journey will involve something more significant than a review of the landscape, for it traces the progress and growth in perceptive awareness of a sensitive persona as he encounters the world outself the self.

The characteristic American journey tends to be imagined in at least two common ways. The first, of course, is that the American journey moves westward, and the second, that the mode of conveyance which the traveler chooses probably depends upon how quickly it can bring him to the destination. The American mind is fascinated by speed—perhaps ever since some of the earliest explorers in seeking a faster passage to India happened upon this land. And yet, the most significant form of the travel essay in nineteenth century America is the essay which focuses on walking.

It is perhaps especially ironic that the generation that built the railroads and first gave shape to many of our ideas about the power of speed should also produce some of the finest writers in the tradition of the American literature of walking. It is ironic, but not inexplicable, for lying behind what a writer like Thoreau or Hawthorne says about walking as an imaginative and redemptive process is the spectre of "the steam fiend." In *Walden*, Thoreau sets the sounds of nature against the whistle of the locomotive. For him, the railroad with its velocity and direction is a symbol of the "restless world" which threatens to disrupt and eventually destroy the pastoral life. In Hawthorne's sketch "The Celestial Rail-road," the railroad symbolizes the too easy philosophy of Mr. Smooth-it-away that hinders a pilgrim's progress to the Celestial City. It becomes an almost diabolical presence in whose "horrible scream" is distinguishable "every kind of wailing woe, and bitter fierceness of wrath, all mixed up with the wild laughter of a devil or a madman." For both these romantic writers, the railroad not only cannot permit reflective progress but stands in opposition to closeness with nature or a true encounter with reality that walking encourages.

Admittedly, though, the essay on walking is not a new form that first appeared in the nineteenth century in response to the phenomenon of the railroad. To make this assertion would be, at best, to oversimplify and to overlook an entire British and American tradition of walking literature. Even during the seventeenth and eighteenth century works were published that describe walking excursions in this country. Most of these were written simply to acquaint the reader with locales inaccessible to him or to describe local history and points of interest. These works served a purpose by broadening the reader's knowledge of his new land and offering an access to experiences he often could not have hoped to enjoy. Still, the nineteenth century did perfect this form as imaginative art.

Washington Irving was among the first to extend the possibilities of the walking tour form in America. In *The Sketch Book* he adopts the stance of the gentleman or cultivated observer describing his surroundings both to enrich his own and his reader's experience and to provide a vehicle for his reflections on society, its manners and customs. Significantly, Irving chooses the British, not the American countryside for his walks because, as he says, he is not "merely a lover of fine scenery" but is more concerned with "the charms of storied and poetical associations."

When moving through the landscape Irving does not journey into the future of America's "youthful promise" but steps back into Europe's "shadowy grandeurs" of the past, reviewing the history of the landmarks he visits. Irving's walking tour essays, then, while among the first in the American creative essay tradition, are still close in their style and form to the British tradition of Addison and Steele. Irving's persona makes an excursion not to discover himself to achieve a greater understanding of human nature. Thus, he is concerned less with the intensity of his experiences than with "the range of his observations," accepting that the more he can experience and the more human types he can encounter, the more accurate will be his conclusions about the human condition.

In this respect he is very unlike Thoreau, who readily asserts that he has only "traveled widely in Concord." Thoreau's excursions are intense journeys of self discovery. When he describes himself as a saunterer in "Walking" he acquaints the reader with the etymology of the word, as if he were consciously attempting to distinguish his type of sauntering from Irving's in "An Author's Account of Himself." Thoreau's walking is an excursion to a holy land ("sainte terre"), a blessed region of introspection and oneness with nature, and bears little resemblance to Irving's rambling and poking about in the "nooks and corners and byplaces" of European society. While Irving journeys to the east, choosing to walk on trodden land retracing the progress of past ages, Thoreau walks westward to the future to embrace its wildness and newness.[4] Thus, Thoreau's walking seems to be a reflection of a more uniquely American experience.

Perhaps because Thoreau's position in the American essay tradition is so central, and his essays on walking so well known it is natural to assume that he was the first American romantic writer to develop the literature of walking. And yet, Hawthorne's essay "Foot-prints on the Sea-shore," which shares much of Thoreau's philosophy of walking, antedates by five years Thoreau's first published excursion, "A Winter Walk," written in 1843. This essay is so important because it reveals a matrix of ideas out of which developed much of the conception of walking common to the essay and even to fictional literature of travel.

Like so much of the literature of travel, "Foot-prints on the Sea-shore" is structured as a sensitive observer's account of an excursion through a landscape. It is impossible to read the sketch without recognizing that the author is attempting to structure a description of both an outward and inward journey. Its symbolic overtones are certainly as intense as any of Thoreau's early excursion essays, and the metaphor of self exploration at its core makes it clear that this essay belongs in the company of the romantic tradition of literature of the journey. Yet, unlike Thoreau, the narrator of the essay rejects the journey westward. Hawthorne tells the reader, almost apologetically, that, although the forest beckons him "I must wander many a mile, ere I could stand beneath the shadow of even one primeval tree."[5] Still, he does not choose to journey eastward, as Irving does, to the haunts of the past. He walks instead to the shore and makes his progress along the coast. In this way, he skirts the antipodal regions of Irving and Thoreau to stake his claim instead in a borderland world, that many American writers also choose, bridging the old and the new, Europe and America.

Hawthorne sounds uncommonly like the British neo-classical writers and their poetry of retirement when he admits at the beginning of "Foot-prints on the Sea-shore" that when his "health and vigor" (451) need to be restored he walks from town to exchange "the sultry sunshine of the world" for "the cool bath of solitude" (451). On the most immediate level, Hawthorne seems to understand his walk as little more than a ramble which affords the opportunity to retreat from the heat and dust of the arena of daily life. But it is soon apparent that the narrator's impressions and feelings about his solitary walk run much deeper and are more complex. When we explore the internal region of his walk, we find that it could stand in the company of some of the finest descriptions of travel in romantic literature. Like the "water gazers" in *Moby Dick*, Hawthorne is inevitably drawn to the sea by its primitive power. Walking along the coast almost necessitates introspection, for Hawthorne would agree with Melville's assertion that "Meditation and water are wedded for ever." Nevertheless, it is not simply the meditative aspect of the walk which signifies that this essay has more in common with a romantic, rather than a neo-classical, sensibility. What distinguishes Hawthorne's reflections on walking from those of a British essayist, like Addison and Steele, or any American writer like Irving is that the literal walk comes to objectify the quest for self-awareness and for some knowledge of life's meaning. In this respect, it seems especially significant that after Hawthorne walks down the coast he chooses to return and to retrace his steps. By describing his walk in this way, he presents a recognizable version of the circular journey, a journey in which the traveler ultimately returns to the place where he began but with a different and usually deeper awareness that is the result of the intervening period. Further, retracing his steps here anticipates a larger structural pattern which is realized at the conclusion of the sketch.

The design, then, of Hawthorne's internalized quest also points to his romantic vision. The action of retracing his steps allows him to step aside and reflect on experience. He can now contemplate his "mood" while in a sense distancing himself from his feelings about his seaside walk so that he is better able to understand it:

When we have paced the length of the beach, it is pleasant, and not unprofitable, to retrace our steps, and recall the whole mood and occupation of the mind during the former passage. (453-4)

The recollection of emotion in tranquillity helps him to reorder his experience, perhaps to shape it into the raw material of his art. But whether or not reflection is directed toward the creative act it is still important because "to track our own nature in its wayward course" will always "make us wiser" (454).

This personal wisdom is gained for Hawthorne, as it often is for the American romantic writer, by a movement into nature. Hawthorne chooses to take his walk along the shore, not in the city, because for him the self educative journey involves a wedding with nature. In the sketch, the meeting between the solitary walker and the ocean is described as "mutual"—his "homage" is repaid by the sea's "sweet breath" of blessing. What the narrator experiences is a transcendence of the self, or in

Emersonian terms, a merging or union of the me and the not-me. The walk frees his spirit to "leap forth and suddenly enlarge its sense of being to the full extent of the broad, blue, sunny deep" (452). The act of walking provides the immediacy or the concreteness, the Emersonian experience described in "Nature" of "standing on the bare ground," which can bring with it the uplift "into infinite space."

Hawthorne values this experience because it allows him to escape from himself, while paradoxically moving most deeply into himself. As a result, he is awakened to hear "the sea's unchanging voice" and lets "the infinite idea of eternity pervade his soul" (460). His walk into nature provides him with a way outside of life; he journeys to the only place where he can get in touch with the "unchanging" and the "idea of eternity." Consequently, on the solitary walks the artist is not upset that the ocean washes away his verses. The idea of his own death and the impermanence of his art no longer frightens him, for by his union with nature he is able to approach a knowledge of a constant in the flux. In an important episode in "Foot-prints on the Sea-shore," Hawthorne celebrates this new covenant with nature in "a recess in a line of cliffs, walled round by a rough, high precipice, which almost encircles and shuts in a little space of sand" (458). Within this circle of solitude the progress ends in an almost sacred or ritualistic way. Here he sups on a communion feast of biscuits and water and consecrates the day with a prayer of thanks to God.

Thus, Hawthorne's day ends with his lost integrity restored and with a renewed sense of what he must be and do. His walk circles back at the conclusion to the place from which it originated. But the circular pattern does not reflect an absurdist view of reality, as it will in *Ethan Brand,* where the journeyer travels a never ending circle and returns to the same spot exhausted and embittered. Instead, the shape defines the harmony and wholeness that the circularity of the walk brings to the traveler. Hawthorne reinforces the impression of unity, as Thoreau does in many of his walking essays, by consciously using the time interval of a single day's walk as an analogy for the whole of one's life. Hawthorne's ramble begins in the morning; he progresses through the zenith of the day and concludes his journey "as the sun sinks over the western wave" (461). In this way the cycle of renewal appears never ending, for there is always the implicit promise of a new day. The religious imagery—the walk is described as a pilgrimage; the traveler as a "holy hermit" consecrated with "vows"; the union with nature as a "soul's communion" (451)—supports his day's walk as a holy quest for a personal redemption. The circular walk becomes the way of the soul in quest of wholeness.

"Foot-prints on the Sea-shore" concludes with the narrator's reunion with society. The marriage of his mind with a reality outside the self prepared him for a reintegration with society. Putting aside his private meditations he joins with a group of people on the shore and seals a new covenant with society which brings to fulfillment his earlier covenant with nature. In a scene that neatly parallels the solitary communion repast, he now sups on fried fish and chowder with his new friends and acknowledges that "after all my solitary joys, that this is the sweetest moment of the Day by the Sea-Shore" (462). Thus, the literal walk reaches its fulfillment in return. As in the fictional journey of Ishmael and Thoreau's journeys to the woods in *Walden* and the excursion essays, the process involves departure *and* return.

Perhaps, though, the pattern implicit in "Foot-prints on the Sea-shore" is most fully realized in Hawthorne's major work, *The Scarlet Letter*. Hester considers but rejects the journey west, and, although she chooses to make the journey east to Europe, she eventually returns to live in the borderland world near the sea. The circular pattern of the romance operates against the play of these polarities, with the scafford scenes providing the continuity and unity. And still, related to the opposition between east and west are other contraries which sustain this pattern. These implicit polarities are also developed as journeys—for example, Hester's walk from the prison to the scaffold; Hester and Dimmesdale's journey to the woods; and Dimmesdale's progress from the Election Day pulpit to the scaffold. Thus in *The Scarlet Letter*, as in "Foot-prints on the Sea-shore," the organizing figure of the journey works on more than one level. The literal journey modulates into the symbolic journey. In addition, the departures and returns, which can be thought to exist on a linear plane, are eventually assimilated or resolved into the circular pattern.

Perhaps because of the implicit tension between the movement of departure and return and the circular pattern, the dynamic element in Hawthorne's walk is not lost. Instead, it operates to impress the reader that the restored unity that the narrator achieves at the conclusion of his walk is not the same as the original state of the departure but represents an advance. The journey pattern of "Foot-prints on the Sea-shore" as well as *The Scarlet Letter* and *The Marble Faun,* can be represented most accurately not by the circle but by a dominant romantic symbol, the ascending spiral,[6] for the journeyer has aspired toward a higher harmony and wholeness and has achieved it. He returns, like Wordsworth in *The Prelude* and the Ancient Mariner in Coleridge's poem, with a renewed sense of individuality. Still, in Hawthorne's account of the walk, the integrity of mind he achieves is justified not in itself but by what this mind can now contribute to society. Without the renewed sense of "individuality unviolated" (461), Hawthorne would be incapable of "affection" and "sympathy":

And when at noontide, I tread the crowded streets, the influence of this day will still be felt; so that I shall walk among men kindly and as a brother, with affection and sympathy....(461)

Wordsworth may state that "love of nature" leads to "love of man" but there is not a sense in this work, as there is in Hawthorne's, that individuality may somehow be a threat if it is not directed toward the good of the social whole. The emphasis on the return to the social order is simply more dominant in Hawthorne's journey than in that of the British romantic writer.

Undoubtedly, then, in structuring "Foot-prints on the Seashore," Hawthorne has created a remarkably developed work with a complex and detailed unity. Certainly, the pattern of the walk shares much with that of voyages in the British romantic tradition. Still, in subtle, yet important ways it becomes clear that Hawthorne is describing an American walk—one that looks ahead to Thoreau's excursion more than it does back to Irving's rambles; and one that has at its core a metaphor of travel which anticipates the romance accounts of the journey. The description of walking in "Foot-prints on the Sea-shore" is one example, and a strong one, indeed, of Hawthorne's ability to assimilate the traditions of past literature while breaking new ground for the American artist.

Notes

[1]Novalis, *Briefe und Werke* (3 vols.; Berlin, 1943); III, 173-4. As quoted in M.H. Abrams, *Natural Supernaturalism* (New York, 1971), p.186.

[2]Abrams, p.186.

[3]Two kinds of non-fictional travel narratives were popular during the nineteenth century. The first group includes descriptions by American writers of journeys in their native land. Within this group certain narratives concentrate on historical descriptions and record factual data; for example, Daniel Drake, *Natural and Statistical View, or Picture of Cincinnati and the Miami Country* in *Physician to the West* (1815; rpt. Lexington, 1970), pp. 66-125, and Amos Stoddard, *Sketches, Historical and Descriptive, of Louisiana* (1812). I am more interested in the travel narrative which, while it may primarily be an observer's record, may also give some evidence that the writer tried to create a more consciously artistic work; for example, the narrative may be architecturally shaped, or may include landscape descriptions that reveal some poetical as well as pictorial power. Some examples of this type are: John Bradbury, *Travels in the Interior of America* (1817; rpt. Ann Arbor, 1966); Timothy Flint, *Recollections of the Last Ten Years in the Valley of the Mississippi* (1826; rpt. New York, 1968); N. Parker Willis, *A L'Abri or The Tent Pitch'd*, 1839; Henry David Thoreau, "A Winter's Walk," 1843 and *A Week on the Prairie*, 1835; Margaret Fuller Ossoli, "Summer on the Lakes," 1844. A second group of travel narratives describe the excursions of Americans abroad. This genre was an extremely popular form in the middle of the nineteenth century and includes such well-known narratives as: Washington Irving, *The Sketch Book*, 1819-20 and *Bracebridge Hall*, 1820; N.P. Willis, *Pencillings By the Way*, 1835; Margaret Fuller Ossoli, "Things and Thoughts in Europe," in *At Home and Abroad* (1856; rpt. New York, 1971); James Russell Lowell, "Leaves of My Journal," 1854; Nathaniel Hawthorne, *Our Old Home*, 1863.

[4]Frederick Garber, "Unity and Diversity in 'Walking'," *Emerson Society Quarterly*, 56 (1969), 36.

[5]*Twice-told Tales*, ed William Charvat, et al. (Columbus, 1974), IX, 451. Citations in my text to "Foot-prints on the Sea-shore" are to this edition.

[6]Abrams, p. 184.

Expatriation and Exploration:
The Exiled Artists of the 1920s

Marjorie Smelstor

Expatriation is often a form of exploration, an exploration for new values, new insights, new experiences. This was especially true for many of the expatriated artists of the 1920s, for they left America, transplanted themselves on the Continent—usually in Paris—and appeared to have withdrawn in order to escape from the American way. Disillusioned by the War and discontented with the post-war atmosphere in the United States, these artists apparently were abandoning the nation in the hopes of finding a place more conducive to their artistic and personal drives. This typical interpretation of expatriation, however, is simplistic and reductionist. Expatriation was more complex than mere escape because it was, for the most part, withdrawal for the sake of clearer vision, better articulation, freer expression. The expatriates did not sever themselves from their origins, but rather altered their relationship with that source. They left America for negative reasons, and only temporarily, as one exile explained:

If we were sometimes called 'expatriates' the appellation had only a partial truth. We were really removing ourselves for a while from our business civilization, and from our middle-class families that counted fondly on our making our career in an advertising office or a bank.[1]

Paradoxically, they returned to America for positive reasons because they experienced, not an embittered cynicism, but a new sense of loyalty to their homeland, a loyalty which was characterized by a reflective, analytical and critical posture. In this respect, many expatriates were cultural nationalists of a special type, sharing the same concerns as the earlier, pre-War nationalists, such as Randolph Bourne and Van Wyck Brooks, as well as the post-War natioinalists who remained at home, and yet manifesting these concerns in new ways and from different geographical perspectives. These Americans who uprooted themselves from the United States remained faithful to their homeland, and their critical stance was the manifestation of their fidelity to and hope for their nation.

One of the best summaries of this expatriate criticism with its nationalistic basis is given by Warren Susman, who suggests that six concepts informed it: a concern with the aesthetic task; a rejection of current tools for cultural analysis that were prominent in America at the time; an awareness of the major problems connected with modern industrial capitalism, as well as an insight into the consequences of the machine; an understanding of the confusion left by the War and newer philosophical concepts; a desire to create a new and non-imitative American culture; and a belief in the American cult of optimism.[2] These concepts indicate that the expatriates, even at a distance from their nation, were concerned with the two questions that America as a whole was grappling with: What was the new America? What was American culture? Furthermore, these concepts suggest that the expatriates were not abandoning their country, but rather declaring their belief in it and in its future.

Gertrude Stein, one of the most vocal in the discussions of expatriation, offered several explanations for this physical withdrawal from America. For her, America was the "most important country in the world—but a parent's place is never the place to work in."[3] Furthermore, it was a good thing for a writer looking at his own civilization "to have the contrast of another culture before him."[4] Thus distance from the "parent" country and internationalism were two motivations for expatriation, which, in turn, led to a strengthened belief in America:

Paradoxically, one of the most important results of exile was a new faith in America and a desire to rediscover it.... The rediscovery of America was not, for these intellectuals, merely the assertion of values long since discarded; it was the beginning of a belief in the present and future potentialities of American culture and a belief that these possibilities could be realized by ending middle-class dominance of culture. The trip to Europe also revealed how profoundly American culture had influenced Europe, how important advertising, jazz, and the skyscraper had become to the avant-garde artists of the Continent.[5]

Furthermore, for most of the self-exiled artists, the process of expatriation revealed the mythic pattern of alienation and reintegration, of departure and return.[6] In this respect, their homecoming reminds one of Eliot's description:

> We shall not cease from exploration
> And the end of all our exploring
> Will be to arrive where we started
> And know the place for the first time.[7]

One way to examine this expatriate-as-explorer idea is to study three exiles who edited *Broom,* a little magazine of the 20s. Harold Loeb, Matthew Josephson and Malcolm Cowley—explorers who searched for new ways to express America's cultural identity after the War—published *Broom* from 1921-1924 in Rome, in Berlin, and then in New York City. *Broom's* history is an interesting one, with its colorful and often eccentric editors, its censorship problems, its difficulties with finances and editorial policies, its printing of significant works by artists like Ernest Hemingway, Gertrude Stein, e.e. cummings, Marianne Moore, Paul Strand and others, and its movement from the Continent to the United States.[8] *Broom* itself was an exploration, a search for the ways in which a little magazine could be an effective vehicle for artistic and national expression. More specifically, however, the major editors of *Broom*—Loeb, Josephson and Cowley—were explorers who deserve our attention, for these expatriates were leaders in the effort to see America from a new perspective and to praise the country which they were seeing in this new light. By examining each of these editors' views of America, views expressed both in their *Broom* articles published during the expatriate period and in their memoirs published after the exile experience, we can see that their expatriation was not simple alienation, but rather more complex exploration.

Harold Loeb's memoirs, *The Way It Was,* published in 1959, describe Loeb's motivation for both his expatriation and his founding of *Broom.* The son of a father who was a Wall Street broker and a mother who was a member of the famous Guggenheim family, Loeb enjoyed a privilege of the wealthy, the opportunity to test out all sorts of occupations.[9] For young Loeb, this included being a Princeton student, a day laborer, a building contractor and a purchasing agent. Probably his most important job was a partnership in the Sunwise Turn bookshop in New York City, for this position plunged him into the artistic world of the 1920s, the world of literature, literati and aesthetic movements. Because of his exposure to this milieu, Loeb developed definite literary convictions, and in 1921 he decided to found a new literary magazine, one that would be experimental and innovative. He decided to publish his magazine in Italy. In addition to the financial advantages and the good printing and paper available there, this location would give the magazine an international dimension since it would be an opportunity to communicate American culture to Europe. "As far as I knew," Loeb recounted, "no one had ever published America's young writers in old Europe, where it was supposed in certain circles that American literature had stopped with Edgar Allan Poe" (*Way*, p. 6).

Loeb needed editorial assistance for his publication, and he found it in Alfred Kreymborg, a writer who had edited his own little magazine, *Others*. When Loeb met Kreymborg during a poetry evening at the Sunwise Turn, Loeb realized that the two men were attracted to each other "by a congruity of tastes. Both of us prized the new, the different, and the experimental, and tended to underrate traditional expressions...we both deplored the obeisance to Europe prevalent among Americans who aspired to culture" (*Way*, pp. 7-8). These words suggest the way in which Loeb and Kreymborg reflected the combination of expatriation and American cultural nationalism which would permeate *Broom*. Loeb specifically justified his expatriation in cultural nationalist terms: "I was convinced that whatever priority Europe may have had in the past, the new world was taking shape in these United States. And I believed I could recognize America's significant aspects more easily by living abroad for a while and observing them from a distance" (*Way*, p.8).

In his memoirs, Loeb remembered how *Broom* began, how this exploring, American publication took its first steps:

...I continued to welcome the visitors who came singly and in groups with bulging briefcases and large portfolios. As much as the conventional and the steadfast, they constituted America's strength, breaking ground when the old ways faltered: men and women with hopes, faiths, and doubts, smiling and scowling, agreeing, sometimes snarling: riffs and raffs from farm and city, the maladjusted and the visionary, those with fixed ideas and those with no ideas but nonconformism; marginal America, roles for which their conditioning should have prepared them, individuals who preferred to ask questions and to seek more congenial solutions.

To this task, in the field of values, *Broom* was dedicated (*Way*, p. 15).

Loeb's various articles in *Broom* were tributes to this American strength and to these American values. For example, in the February number, he contributed an editorial comment which emphasized the importance of a non-imitative, indigenous culture for the new American popular culture: "The Kid" by Charlie Chaplin, popular novels, *Saturday Evening Post*, the American newspaper, American architecture, street planning and the football stadium. These aspects of American life were of the utmost value in Loeb's view, for they were both enjoyed by and representative of the majority of the nation's populace.[10] As his contemporary, Gilbert Seldes, would later write: "...entertainment of a high order existed in places not usually associated with Art."[11] Loeb concluded that this new American Art was especially significant, for it was a national experience which should help its audience to recognize the "intrinsic value" and "originality" of their culture (pp.378-379).

In "Foreign Exchange," published in May, 1922, Loeb considered the same subject by describing the effect Europe was having upon the exiled American writers. Originally, these American expatriates, these "artistic pioneers," had withdrawn for two reasons: first, faced with a choice between deadening hack work or flight, they chose the latter; and second, confronted with democracy's negative results—the curtailment of individual liberty such as the adoption of Prohibition—they opted for exile. Paradoxically, these expatriates, in Loeb's view, were coming to a new vision of technological America, however, because of the admiration of the French artists for industrialism. In addition, the French writers were exposing the young American artists to a meticulous attention to form. In Loeb's opinion, this was a most desirable combination, for it merged art and cultural nationalism, a nationalism which revered technological culture and communicated it to the rest of the world. This nationalism, unlike the version of critics like Waldo Frank and Van Wyck Brooks, was not skeptical about the machine's effects upon modern America; on the contrary, it championed this technological progress and its influence upon the cultural life of the United States.[12]

In the September, 1922 issue, Loeb's article entitled "The Mysticism of Money" also expressed this nationalistic bent. (In 1941, Loeb said that "The Mysticism of Money" was badly written;[13] thus readers should be prepared for the article's stylistic inadequacies.) Analyzing modern "religion" and its effects upon the new America, Loeb called this religion the "mysticism of money":

Money, because that which was originally but a medium of exchange and valuable metal, has become the measuring staff of all values and the goal and reward of all efforts conventionally accepted as proper.

Mystic because the validity of the money standard and the intrinsic merit of money making are accepted on faith, extra-intellectually....Reasons are superfluous when a belief is obviously true.[14]

Using this definition of American religion, Loeb explored the relationship between the new technological art and its "religious" motivation:

The art of forming objects in the round or in relief by chiselling, carving, modelling, casting, etc. has reached greater proportions to-day than possible ever in the past. Engines, forges, hearths, furnaces, turbines, kettles, motors, generators, dynamoes, automobiles, ships aeroplanes—the list has no end. The purpose of all these is the efficient performance of specific tasks, which tasks are required by the industrial organization brought into existence and urged ever onward by the Mysticism of Money. These forms are not static but, like the older art forms, continually evolve through the introductions of small variations, in the direction of greater efficiency. The result is simplification, elimination of inessentials, balanced beauty. As perfection is approached the designer becomes more and more conscious of the aesthetic possibilities so that in well developed forms, such as the automobile body, new variations are primarily justified aesthetically. Other things being equal, the more beautiful form has a higher selling value. Thus in the end the technical intent of the designer is aesthetic (p. 120).

In addition to its influence upon technology, the mysticism of money, in Loeb's view, had a direct effect upon American writing. Specifically, three areas were transformed by the new religon. First, a new language was evolving: "Vigorous, crude, expressive, alive with metaphors, Rabelaisian, resembling Elizabethan rather than Victorian English. Conceived on sidewalks and born over bars, it can be found comparatively anywhere on the sporting sheets of newspapers, on the funny pages, occasionally on advertisements and on the stage, quite frequently in short stories" (p.125). Secondly, a new narrative technique had emerged, a technique best seen in the Nick Carter stories. With speed as their essential ingredient, these stories eliminated the data which usually accounted for logical continuity and produced, instead, stories characterized by their shock value, emotional intensity and sensationalism. Finally, new human types were being created by the mysticism of money. Strong man, chaste young girl, villain—these were all formed by some aspect of money, that "measuring staff of all values and the goal and reward of all efforts conventionally accepted as proper" (pp. 126-27). This last seems to have been more of an innovation to Loeb than to other literary critics, but Loeb nevertheless saw it, without any apparent irony, as a curiously contemporary development.

In addition to his praise for Nick Carter, Loeb also championed other examples of American art which are now identified as popular culture: the high place of Charlie Chaplin in the artistic world; the influence of American advertising upon Marinetti, Wyndham Lewis' *Blast,* and the dadaists; the difference between jazz as a universal ("Its melodies come from everywhere, stolen, bought and invented...") and Negro spirituals as true American folk music. Of particular significance, however, was Loeb's description of Spenglerian-like stages of civilization. America, according to Loeb, was still in the youthful stage—the "formative-creative art epoch"—and it was still searching for ways to express itself culturally and artistically. This process meant that America and the mysticism of money had not yet arrived at maturity, but were still coming of age. As they came of age, moreover, one idea, according to Loeb, should remain paramount: "America must not imitate Europe" (p.115).

Thus Harold Loeb, founder and editor of *Broom*, was clearly a nationalistic explorer. He believed in his country even as he exiled himself from it, and he especially believed in America's newness, superiority and originality.

Matthew Josephson was another proponent of these same ideas. He joined *Broom*'s staff as assistant editor in 1922, and, like Loeb, his nationalistic interests motivated him as exile and as artist. Born in Brooklyn in 1899 and graduating from Columbia University's College of Liberal Arts in 1919, Josephson was an outspoken critic of the pre-War Victorian culture and an enthusiastic supporter of modernism, literary experimentation and artistic excellence. During his college years, he became acquainted with others who shared his views, "iconoclasts" like Malcolm Cowley, Kenneth Burke and William Slater Brown. Later, Josephson lived in Greenwich Village and continued to be involved in the avant-garde world of artist, newness and challenge which Loeb and Kreymborg had also enjoyed. As Josephson would later write of himself:

My curse has been extreme versatility; I began as a poet and belle-lettriste, have written one novel; numerous biographies; short stories that were precieux; essays on political questions; journalism on the same; and for some years I have been a kind of historian, according to my own unacademic ideas...[15]

After the War, Josephson joined the expatriate movement and lived in Paris, the place he called his "second country," from 1921-1923. He described this experience in his autobiography, *Life*

Among the Surrealists, published in 1962.[16] During this time, he collaborated with Gorham Munson to found and edit the little magazine *Secession.* The two men, however, had quite different views about the purpose and policy of their publication, for Munson preferred writers like Theodore Dreiser and Waldo Frank, while Josephson believed that *Secession* should be "publishing and championing the adventurous experimenters of America, translating the work of the avant-garde in France and Germany, and vigorously assailing the Mrs. Grundies of literature" (*Life,* p. 154). Unable to accomplish this in the pages of *Secession,* Josephson turned to *Broom.*

Because Josephson was, at different points, a champion of many European art movements—dadaism, surrealism, symbolism, imagism, constructivism—*Broom*'s German issues reveal the impact of these avant-garde "isms." It is important to note, however, that Josephson saw these European developments, particularly dadaism, as influenced by American materials and American popular art. In his autobiography, Josephson best formulated what he had been arguing as early as 1922 when he announced that many Continental art forms were "derived in great part from American source materials" (*Life,* p. 190). As one example of this, he commented that the American cinema greatly influenced French poetry, especially the works of Guillaume Apollinaire, Blaise Centrars, and Phillips Soupault. He quoted Soupault as one illustration of this influence:

'Those darkened halls...became the living theatre of our laughter, our anger, our pride. In those miraculous crimes and farewells our eyes read the poetry of our age. We were living with passion through a most beautiful period of which the U.S. cinema was the brightest ornament' (*Life,* pp. 123-24).

Similarly, Josephson observed how Marcel Duchamp had abandoned Cubist painting and had gone to live in America, thus ultimately affecting the direction of the European art movements.

He collected bits of rubbish, absurd machines, dummies, clothing racks, and other such disjected membra of America's 'ready-mades,' offered them as artifacts selected and signed by himself. The troubling humor with which this great mystificator attacked the art of the past—a humor inspired largely by the American environment favoring such activity— made a profound impression upon the Dada and Surealist cults in Europe (*Life*, p. 124).

Furthermore, Josephson pointed to a young France that was "passionately concerned with the civilization of the U.S.A., and stood in a fair way to being *Americanized*" (*Life,* p. 125). This realization prompted him to read Apollinaire as a visionary, a man whose ideas "were nothing if not Whitmanesque and American in tone": "Is there nothing new under the sun? For the sun perhaps so—but for man everything!. . .The poet is to stop at nothing in his quest for novelty of form and material; he is to take advantage of all the infinite new combinations afforded by the mechanism of everyday life" (*Life,* p. 125).

Because Josephson believed that European art was influenced by American art, *Broom*'s associate editor was convinced of the magazine's need to be more American in its contents, contributors, and attitudes. He felt that *Broom*'s literary tendency "was all too catholic," and he intended to "bring it [*Broom*] home to the U.S.A" (*Life*, p. 188). This, in fact, he would accomplish, for *Broom*'s German issues were succeeded by a series of American numbers published in New York City.

Josephson's contributions to *Broom* focused upon his belief in America's cultural superiority. For example, to the June, 1922 issue he contributed an article entitled "Made in America" which emphasized the technological aspects of American culture. For Josephson, the machine was "our magnificent slave, our fraternal genius, and because it was indigenous to America and reflective of the nation's emerging identity, it was worthy of both praise and celebration.[17] This technological wonder was "made in America," and therefore it was alive, it was valuable, and, most important, it was superior to any other culture's products or symbols.

Similarly, in the November, 1922 issue, he published "The Great American Billposter," an evaluation of this indigenous

American art. He suggested that the advertisements which surrounded the American people were, in fact, the "folklore" of modern times, and as such composed "a faithful record of the national tastes, the changing philosophy, the hopes and fears of a people."[18] He cited several examples to illustrate this position.

The American is emotional and generous, but at the same time he is thrifty:
USURY.
Six per cent is considered a fair rate of interest; too high a rate of interest is condemned as usury. Yet there are several thousand American homes in which an IDEAL TYPE A HEAT MACHINE is paying back 33 per cent on its cost—so great is the proportion of fuel saved and so little does it depreciate in comparison with cheaper heating plants (p. 308).

Similarly, the American is "far more amenable to suggestion, to hypnosis rather than to logic":

ASK DAD HE KNOWS
ASK THE MAN WHO OWNS ONE

or better this:

DAY BY DAY IN EVERY WAY
I AM GETTING BETTER AND BETTER (p. 308).

Furthermore, the American possesses an "uproarious self-assertion":

ZIEGFELD FOLLIES
GLORIFIES THE AMERICAN GIRL (p. 309).

This billposter phenomenon, according to Josephson, was definitely "art":

The art of people is a two-edged sword: it spring [sic] from the moods and virtues of that people. But we have learned recently to extend the meaning of 'art' inasmuch as modern man expressed himself in a far greater variety of manners than did prehistoric or classical man. An ethnological study of a group such as the Americans (of the United States of America) could no longer restrict itself to its politics, sculpture, and mythology; for, thanks to the aggressive application of the arts to new inventions, we find that the automobile is on the road to becoming a thing of beauty and that the advertisements contain the fables of this people. We would, thus, be obliged to observe the motion picture, the sports, the machinery, and many other aspects of the group's behaviour in order to really know its culture (p. 304).

This rationale provided the basis for Josephson's approach to popular culture, for his belief in what Loeb had called "the intrinsic value" and "originality" of American culture. It gave Josephson a framework in which he could evaluate the style of the popular artist and thus appraise him as a new kind of poet:

The particular restrictions of this medium [advertising] make for extraordinary ingenuity in the 'copy writer'; the call for vigor of conviction and interest, are probably more stimulating by far toward creating beautiful conceptions than an intensive course in Victorian poetry at Harvard University. The terse vivid slang of the people has been swiftly transmitted to this class of writers, along with a willingness to depart from syntax, to venture sentence forms and word constructions which are at times breathtaking, if anything, and in all cases far more arresting and provocative than 99 per cent of the stuff that passes for poetry in our specialized magazines (p. 309).

Josephson, then, like Loeb, was not an embittered exile; on the contrary, he was an American who believed in his country and who tried to identify the new symbols of a new nation. He was indeed an explorer whose nationalism provided a kind of map for his travels.

Malcolm Cowley was another nationalist who joined *Broom*'s staff at Josephson's urging. A Harvard graduate, he was part of the expatriate generation in Paris from 1921-1923, an experience he later described in his book *Exile's Return*.[19] Like the other editors of *Broom*, Cowley was interested in many current ideas and involved in numerous literary endeavors, including poetry, prose, magazine work, and editing projects. Especially important for this study, however, is Cowley's nationalism, a critical yet loyal belief in America's cultural superiority which he shared with other *Broom* editors. As he commented in a recent letter to this writer asking for his attitude toward this nationalistic posture: "In general it was that of a critical patriot— it's a hell of a country, I seemed to be saying, but it's mine."[20] Furthermore, Cowley demonstrated his nationalistic belief in a manner which was similar to Josephson's. Where Josephson pointed to America's influence upon and consequent superiority over European art, Cowley began with the opposite assertion but arrived at the same conclusion: European art influenced American art because Americans built upon Continental developments to produce their own superior cultural forms. Writing to Waldo Frank in response to Frank's article, "Seriousness and Dada," Cowley explained this building process:

You have been to Paris and have brought back the gossips of Monsieur X the poet and Monsieur Y the novelist. I have been to Paris and met Messieurs X and Y. Other American writers have been to Paris. Some of them meet Paul Fort and write polyphonic prose in his manner, some meet Paul Valery and become classicists, some meet Soupault, Aragon or Tzara and write a Yankee Dada, some meet Jules Romains and his serious little groups, study his treatises on Unanimism, adopt his more solemn thoughts and some of his virtues and are proud to be called the Unanimists of America. There are also Americans who go to Paris, meet many people of many schools, take the best of each, and retain the conviction to write about their own surroundings in their own manner....[21]

Cowley announced that he was a leader in this process of merging international and national tendencies:

In this day of advertising slogans one must have a little ticket which admits one to the Sunset Limited or the Oriental Express, blue or yellow, a slip of cardboard printed with the name....I, Mr. Frank, am...the clever but not corruscant smart or swift young man who clutters our serious magazines, the American Dada.[22]

Like Loeb and Josephson, this "American Dada" contributed articles to *Broom* which revealed his interest in post-War

American values. An interesting contribution was "Young Mr. Elkins," a satire of those people who did not appreciate the inherent values of the nation's popular culture. Appearing in the December, 1922 issue, this article presented a portrait of "an American intellectual," a man who belonged "to the professionally young," who, at sixty, would retain "the discouraged deep scepticism of adolescence."[23] Young Mr. Elkins, disturbed by what he saw emerging in post-War America, by "the new feeling" engulfing the nation, tried to quell the movement of the New American culture and to channel the American energies into creating a culture that was imitative of the Continental experience.

The new feeling that is in America...it inspired young Mr. Elkins to thunder against billboards, Billy Sunday and Methodism, proportional representation, Comstock, elevated railroads. One year with a special fulgurance he thundered against the commercial ugliness of cities. American civilization listened and moved uneasily like a sleeping volcano. Stung finally to action by his criticism it spewed forth city planning commissions, commissions specially trained at the Beaux Arts and specially delegated to make Paris, Okla. the replica of Paris, France, in miniature. (p. 54).

In his efforts to reform the new America, Mr. Elkins acted from a simple principle:

Puritanism is bad; America is puritan; therefore America is bad. (Or, to state his syllogism in its more usual form: America is bad; America is puritan, therefore puritanism is bad). (Or: badness is puritan; badness is American; America is therefore badly puritan). He has never tried to define puritanism or America (pp. 54-55).

Cowley's portrait ended with a supreme touch of irony, for young Mr. Elkins, anti-American Mr. Elkins, wrote his reactionary sentiments "on a typewriter which is the most finished product of a mechanical civilization," a civilization which "howls outside his window":

...An elevated express rumbles up Ninth Avenue and an elevated local

rumbles down Ninth Avenue. Precisely under Mr. Elkins' room four
subway trains crash past each other. One of them is bound for the 273rd
Street hugest Tabernacle, where Mr. Sunday preaches that afternoon to
an audience of over fifteen thousand....Thirty stories below an
automobile skids into a shop window, killing two and a wax
dummy....A cable snaps on Brooklyn Bridge; fire spreads to the oil
tanks; on the docks a carload of dynamite explodes....

Young Mr. Elkins, annoyed by the racket, rose nervously and closed
his window (p. 56).

The America which was despised by Mr. Elkins was praised
in another aricle by Cowley, "Pascin's America." This piece is
significant more for its comments on the new American culture
than for its description of the style of the Bulgarian artist who
became an American citizen in 1914. Pointing to Pascin's ability
to paint the American people and capture the American spirit,
Cowley expressed what he believed to be the continual newness of
the American nation:

Before Walt Whitman America hardly existed; to him we owe the
pioneers, the open spaces, in general the poetry of square miles. Bret
Harte created California and Twain the Mississippi. Woodrow Wilson,
Chaplin, the James brothers; each created a separate America, an
America which frightened pleasantly or amused us, a God-righteous
America for which we fortunately did not die. America is a conception
which must be renewed each morning with the papers. It is not one
conception but a million which change daily, which melt daily into one
another.[24]

This comment is especially applicable to *Broom's* editors, the
expatriate explorers Loeb, Josephson and Cowley. Trying to
renew America, they separated themselves from the land of their
roots and searched for new ways to see, to create, to express
themselves. Their vehicle was the little magazine; their attitude,
nationalism; their posture, loyalty. They were not like Bill
Gorton's description in *The Sun Also Rises:* "You're an
expatriate. You've lost touch with the soil. You get precious. Fake
European standards have ruined you. You drink yourself to
death. You become obsessed by sex. You spend all your time

talking, not working. You are an expatriate, see? You hang around cafes."[25] Rather, they were explorers who carried within them the country they were trying to renew.

Notes

[1]Matthew Josephson, *Infidel in the Temple* (New York: Knopf, 1967), p. 4.

[2]Warren Susman, "American Cultural Criticism," (Thesis University of Wisconsin 1950), pp. 176-79.

[3]Quoted in Hugh Ford, *The Left Bank Revisited* (University Park: Pennsylvania State University Press, 1972), p. xxi.

[4]Quoted in Ford, p. xxi.

[5]James Gilbert, *Writers and Partisans: A History of Literary Radicalism in America* (John Wiley & Sons, Inc., 1968), pp. vi-viii.

[6]Malcolm Cowley, *Exile's Return* (1934; rpt. New York: The Viking Press, 1969), p. 289.

In his discussion of the expatriates, Cowley also offers the reasons for calling this generation "lost," reasons which help to illuminate the withdrawal patterns of the exiled artists:

> It was lost, first of all, because it was uprooted, schooled away and almost wrenched away from its attachment to any region or tradition. It was lost because its training had prepared it for another world than existed after the war (and because the war prepared it only for travel and excitement). It was lost because it tried to live in exile. It was lost because it had formed a false picture of society and the writers's place in it (p. 9).

[7]T.S. Eliot, *Four Quartets* in *The Complete Poems and Plays* (New York: Harcourt, Brace and World, Inc., 1952),p. 145.

[8]*The Little Magazine: A History and Bibliography* (Frederick J. Hoffman, Charles Allen, Carolyn F. Ulrich [Princeton: Princeton University Press, 1946]) is an excellent study of *Broom* and many other little magazines.

[9]Biographical information on Harold Loeb primarily taken from *The Way It Was*, Harold Loeb (New York: Criterian Books, 1959). Specific references to this book, unless otherwise noted, will be indicated by a parenthetical insertion in the following way: (*Way*, p.   ). The reader might be interested to know that Harold Loeb was Hemingway's model for Robert Cohn in *The Sun Also Rises*.

[10]Harold Loeb, "Comment," *Broom,* I (February 1922), pp. 377-379.

[11]Gilbert Seldes, *The Seven Lively Arts* (New York: A.S. Barnes and Company, Inc., 1924), p. 3.

Although Seldes did not contribute any articles to *Broom,* he did influence the magazine's position on popular arts. In Loeb's memoirs, the Broom editor recalled a luncheon with Seldes during which Seldes discussed the importance of American popular art, reinforced Loeb's ideas on the subject, and suggested some new avenues for Loeb to pursue (*Way,* p. 109).Seldes was even more influential, however, because of the general impact of his ideas upon the cultural milieu of the twenties. His numerous magazine articles and his 1924 book proclaimed the excellence of the American popular arts—comic strips, motion pictures, musical comedy, vaudeville, radio, popular music, and the dance—and his ideas had a definite impact upon the critics and artists of the decade. e.e. cummings, for example, was probably influenced by Seldes' theories when he attempted to merge high-brow and low-brow art in his play *him,* first produced in 1927. (see author's article, " 'Damn Everything but the Circus': Popular Art in the Twenties and *him,*" *Modern Drama,* [March, 1974], pp. 43-55).

[12]Harold Loeb, "Foreign Exchange," *Broom,* 2 (May 1922), pp. 176-181.

[13]Harold Loeb to Charles Allen: August 25, 1941. Collection of American Literature, the Beinecke Rare Book and Manuscript Library, Yale University.

[14]Harold Loeb, "The Mysticism of Money," *Broom,* 2 (September 1922), p. 117.

[15]Matthew Josephson to Professor Fred Millet: April 26, 1937, Matthew Josephson Papers, Yale, quoted in Paula Fass, *Matthew Josephson—A Biography* (Collection of American Literature, The Beinecke Rare Book and Manuscript Library, Yale University, 1966), p. 1.

[16]Matthew Josephson, *Life Among the Surrealists* (New York: Holt, Rinehart and Winston, 1962), p. 79. Specific references to this book, unless otherwise noted, will be indicated by a parenthetical insertion in the following way: (*Life,* p.   ).

[17]*Broom,* 2 (June 1922), pp. 266-270.

[18]Matthew Josephson, "The Great American Billposter," *Broom,* 3 (November 1922), p. 309.

[19]This book is an extremely useful and interesting study of both expatriation and the reintegration of the expatriates; because of this two-faceted approach, Cowley's study is a particularly enlightening cultural document of the 1920s.

[20]Malcolm Cowley to author: August 21, 1974.

[21]Malcolm Cowley to Waldo Frank: November 23, 1924, Malcolm Cowley's papers, The Newberry Library.

[22]Malcolm Cowley to Waldo Frank.

[23]Malcolm Cowley, "Young Mr. Elkins,"*Broom,* 4 (December 1922), p. 53.

[24]Malcolm Cowley, "Pascin's America,"*Broom,* 4 (January 1922), pp. 136-7.

[25]Ernest Hemingway, *The Sun Also Rises* (New York: 1926; rpt. Charles Scribner's Sons, 1970), p. 115.

The Family Journey to the West

Paul T. Bryant

Traditionally, one of the more dramatic aspects of the settlement of the American West is the journey westward of the pioneer family in quest of a homestead and a new life. This westering suggests a standard picture of covered wagons drawn by oxen plodding slowly across treeless plains and over towering mountain ranges. The stalwart father walks alongside the ox team with a goad in his hand, while the courageous mother sits on the wagon box and assorted children peer anxiously from under the edges of the canvas wagon cover. Perhaps a milk cow shambles along tied to the tail gate.

At night the wagons stop in a circle for protection from marauding Indians. Meals are cooked over fires fueled, on the plains, by dried buffalo chips. The men take turns standing guard, and sometimes Indian raids actually occur. At dawn everyone turns out for another plodding day, until finally the promised land—Oregon or California or wherever—is reached. There the train disbands and each family finds its own piece of land, builds its sod hut or log cabin, tills the soil, and the story ends.

Like many cliches, this picture is essentially accurate for many pioneer families, but it has perhaps caused us to overlook other significant aspects of this basic pattern and to neglect both their cultural and literary importance in the settlement of the American frontier. Historians give us the broad historical patterns while understandably neglecting individual family experiences. Writers of fiction—one thinks, for example, of A.B. Guthrie's *The Way West*—draw upon the tradition and clothe it with dramatic reality, or some may attempt to de-romanticize it by emphasizing the ignorance, squalor, and plain wrongheadedness that were sometimes features of the western migration. Here one might cite some of the short stories and sketches of H.L. Davis, for example. Even with the negative presentation, seldom does the picture vary much from the standard pattern we have come to expect.

153

One window to a more varied and detailed view of the pioneer family in its epic journey to the West is the family history. This is a form of folk literature which has received some attention as sources for local and regional history, but no notice from literary scholars. Yet these histories form a distinctive literary genre of which there are hundreds, perhaps thousands, of examples deposited in museums, libraries and archives all across this country.

Perhaps we should begin a consideration of the pioneer family history with a general definition of the genre. Such a definition cannot be absolute in its boundaries, but it can suggest the general parameters of those features, most of which can be found in any given work designated a pioneer family history.

First, of course, it is a history through more than one generation of a family that has pioneered on the western American frontier. As such, it is more than a diary, journal, or autobiography of one individual. Although it usually focuses on the generation or generations directly involved in the move to the West and the early settlement there, the history of earlier generations will be at least summarized as a necessary background to understanding the pioneers, and the experience of later generations down at least to that of the author will be included. Although the biography of one pioneer may be central to the work, the true family history will go beyond the life of an individual to give a sense of the continuing history of the family.

It must have been prepared in written form as contrasted with taped oral histories. This means that it must have been intended as a formal written document.

Many, perhaps the majority, of these histories were written by a member of the family from a later generation using as sources memoirs, letters, journals, family traditions, and the personal reminiscences of surviving members of earlier generations. Rarely, but occasionally, they will be by members of the actual pioneering generations, and sometimes they will be by local history enthusiasts acquainted with the family. A high percentage of the authors are women, the daughters or granddaughters of the pioneers. Seldom is the author a professional writer or scholar, a characteristic that may reduce the average level of literary polish but clearly adds to the "folk" quality of such works. The language may be awkward, repetitious, even ungrammatical, but it generally represents the vision and mode of expression of its author's generation and social context in the West.

The authors' reasons for writing these histories seem most often to rise from one central impulse: to record what earlier generations endured and accomplished, so that such a record might serve as an inspiration to similar achievement.

For a very numerous and significant subdivision of this genre, the Mormon family history, these temporal reasons are supplemented by doctrinal concerns regarding the immortal souls of ancestors not already in that church, and by a desire to record the blessings of God on the church and its members, and the strength and achievement possible through faith. David King Udall, for example, when he was assisting his daughter in preparing his biography, which became a family history, wrote, "I have no ambition to tell the world of our experiences—such would be vanity indeed. But deep in my heart, I do desire to bear record to my kindred and to my posterity of the goodness of God unto us, as shown in the unfolding of our family life."[1]

Such rationales, of course, are part of a common American tradition traceable back to the earliest journals and histories of Massachusetts Bay and Plymouth. Both the democratic impulse and Protestant theology have suggested to even the earliest European settlers in America that the affairs of the common people, as well as of kings and generals, are of interest and significance to later generations. At the same time, the achievements of one's own people can serve both as a guide and as a challenge to make the present measure up to the past.

These family histories are usually privately printed in small quantities for limited distribution, mostly to members of the family. Some have been printed by local history groups for somewhat wider local circulation, and some are still only in typescript or manuscript in local history collections. The works are often of book length, but not always, sometimes appearing in local history collections of "old timers' tales" and memoirs. For the most part they are difficult to locate or even to identify by bibliographic means, and copies are rare and not easy to obtain for study.

As a group, these histories form a folk literature recording family traditions and giving an insight into the experiences and attitudes of individual pioneer settlers of the West. Many present individual adventures, and of course there is a great temptation merely to relate some of the best of these for their own sake. But as a genre these family histories fall into certain patterns that illuminate the American pioneer experience in the westward journey and at the same time help define traditional patterns in a folk literature.

Two types of patterns emerge from an examination of numbers of pioneer family histories. One type is cultural, arising from the experiences of the pioneers, and from their responses to those experiences, and coming also from the cultural perceptions and assumptions which the individual family brought to its pioneering adventures. The other type of pattern is literary, arising from the techniques of narration, description, and interpretation imposed on the material by the writer. It is not always clear when the written presentation only reflects the attitudes and understanding of the pioneers themselves, and when it is the interpretation of the writer, viewing the events from a later generation, but some few patterns emerge that suggest a developed literary tradition imposed upon the original material. Examples of these two types of patterns should serve to illustrate.

Cultural Patterns

Among the cultural patterns that emerge frequently is that of continual movement on the part of the pioneer families. Modern literary treatment of the pioneer trek westward generally presents it as a single journey accomplished in one continuous effort and aimed at a specific goal, such as the Willamette Valley. Again Guthrie's *The Way West* provides an excellent example in a contemporary novel. Certainly this was often the case, as illustrated in the Powell family history of a wagon train to Oregon.[2] The prime movers of this wagon train were Illinois farmers, apparently reasonably prosperous and settled, but:

Our people had been reading of the Oregon country for a number of years, and had also received direct information from a man who had visited the Willamette Valley. In 1850 they decided to sell their farms in Illinois and seek the advantages of a milder climate and the fertile land offered by the government. When they arrived in the valley in September, 1851, and viewed the beautiful mountain scenery, the wonderful evergreens, and the valley covered with native grass waisthigh, unfenced and largely unclaimed, they felt that they had really reached the promised land....[3]

But this somewhat static impression of settled families uprooting themselves for one grand pioneering move westward, followed by permanent settlement, is quite misleading if it is taken as a totally representative pattern. Many families made the journey across the plains as only one part of a lifetime, or even generations, of footloose wandering that did not end until the close of the frontier, if then.[4] The move westward was not a single venture, but rather a part of a lifelong search for something that many families never found. Perhaps what the families said they were seeking will shed some light on their continuous movement.

One of the most commonly expressed reasons for going West, of course, was a search for greater economic opportunity. Some hoped for land, for farms that were larger and more fertile than they could hope for back east, or for ranches that had not been overgrazed and exhausted. Some hoped for business opportunities as merchants or freighters or innkeepers. And some sought El Dorado's quick wealth in the western gold and silver mines.

Better health was another benefit sought in the West by many pioneer families. Malaria, tuberculosis, asthma and dozens of other, less clearly identified ills were to be left behind in the higher, drier, clearer air of the West. The Promised Land, after all, would surely have not only fertile soil but also health-giving air and sunshine, as escape from the fever-ridden South and Midwest.

The traditional frontier search for "more room" provided a third though less distinct motivation for continuous westering, a drive that was automatically self-defeating as more and more people followed it into the "new" country. The benefits of "more room" were never spelled out, particularly when the seekers were often moving from country that was only partially settled and certainly not crowded. Most commonly those who gave this reason for westering appear to have been strong minded, self reliant individualists who perhaps were seeking freedom from social restraint. Many of these demonstrated that they were men willing to shoot first and ask questions later.

The large number of families for whom the journey westward ended only with the closing of the frontier suggests that the western dreams of Eden, of El Dorado, the search for land and health and wealth and freedom, did not come true. Social and economic pressures, human depravity and their own mortality followed them wherever they went, but the persistence of the dream itself is demonstrated over and over by the fact that they kept on moving in search of its realization. In these terms the journey westward became for many families an unending search for something more than this world can provide. It thus became the stuff of which myths are made.

These central motives, of course, were those of the male "head" of the family. Family histories repeatedly reveal that the father of the family was the one who made the decision to move West. If the opinion of the mother of the family is mentioned at all, she is likely to have been, at the least reluctant, if not downright opposed to the move, and understandably so in most cases. At the beginning of the family's westering, the father and mother were usually young. There were usually young children and more often than not the mother was pregnant—if not when the move began, at least before it was completed. Miscarriages were not uncommon and the mortality rate among young children and their mothers was high. Yet pregnancy did not appear to be a deterrent to any move the father might decide to make. It seems to have been accepted as a standard condition of life and part of the burden women must bear as they followed their husbands' search for the Promised Land.[5]

Of course, those women who successfully resisted their husbands' urge to move west would not be likely to appear in a study of pioneer family histories, but some did manage to resist.

One case in point was the wife of John Jacob Miller (the first names of many of these women are not given in the histories). John Miller was a frontiersman and hunter and spent much of his time in the West, but his wife steadfastly refused to leave their farm in Illinois. On one of his visits home (and he must have made several—the family had nine children), John secretly made arrangements to sell the farm, presumably as a way to force his wife to go west with him. Unfortunately for his plans, she learned of his arrangements and "put a stop to them" before he could carry them through. Mrs. Miller never went west.[6]

This is not to say that all women went west unwillingly. Many were willing to face the hardships and dangers if they could gain something worth the risk and effort.

Another standard assumption about the pioneer family's journey to the West is that the entire trip was accomplished in a single season. In many cases this was true, but in a significant number of instances the journey was interrupted by extended stays along the route, and sometimes the original objective was never reached.

When the Julius Sanders family set out for California in 1861, they stopped near Denver to raise a crop of corn on Wild Plum Creek. They sold the corn for travelling expenses and continued on to California the following year. Even then they did not settle. In 1863 two of the sons went to Arizona, found gold, returned to California for the rest of the family, and arrived in Arizona in 1864.[7]

Substantial delays might be caused by anticipated Indian trouble. Military posts along the trails would sometimes stop emigrant parties until they could be better equipped, or until several smaller parties could be gathered to make up a single, stronger group. Often this might mean only a few days' delay, but on occasion it might hold up a group until the following spring.

Clearly the westward journey of the pioneer family was not purely a success or disaster, "California or Bust" type of undertaking. Most of these people were resilient and resourceful, able to adapt to changing circumstances even of the most extreme kind. If California was not possible, they would settle for Colorado or Kansas or Nebraska or Iowa. If they could not

complete the journey the same year they started, they would
winter as best they might and continue the following year. The
journey westward for these families was not an interruption in
their lives, but an integral and sometimes extended part of it.

Tradition presents the mode of travel of the pioneer family as
the covered wagon, drawn by horses, mules or oxen, and the
tradition is largely accurate.[8] However, there were significant
variations. For example, migrants westward from Texas often
had large herds of cattle, or more rarely large flocks of sheep, to
drive with them. Instead of wagon trains such as were standard
on the Oregon and California Trails, the herd would be the main
element of the group, accompanied by horsemen and a few supply
wagons, in which might be riding the women and children. As the
railroads penetrated the Southwest, a portion of the journey even
for the livestock might be made by train. To keep the herds
healthy and intact, the journey might be made through two or
more seasons with planned stops for grazing the stock for
extended periods of time.

In the years after the completion of the transcontinental
railroad, families might use it to make a major part of their
westward journey, sometimes going all the way to the West Coast
and then coming back eastward into Arizona or southern Nevada
by ship around Baja California to the mouth of the Colorado and
then up that river by steamer for as far as it was navigable, or
overland eastward across the southern deserts. By rail, of course,
travel was quicker, the hazards were fewer, and the introduction
to the West more directly concentrated in the arrival rather than
being spread through weeks or months of slow travel and nightly
camping.

The travellers' attitudes toward the Indians also varied
perhaps more than is generally supposed. They range along a
spectrum from sheer hatred and terror through suspicion and
paternalistic condescension to respect and sympathy for their
plight, although such sympathy was apparently rare, and seldom
acted on.

Families venturing into the West for the first time were
naturally fearful of Indian attacks. They had heard many stories
of Indian raids on wagon trains and isolated settlements and

ranches, and these stories coupled with the element of a danger outside their previous experience often led them to expect the worst. Settlers who had lost friends or loved ones in Indian raids might have been expected to have an implacable hatred for Indians, but even here there is often a surprising dispassion in the relation of such losses. At times in such accounts, losses to Indian hostilities seem to be accepted in much the same spirit as losses to floods or droughts or other natural disasters, as if the Indians were a natural force that unavoidably went with the western landscape.

At the same time, there were whites who believed the Indian version of such events as the Skull Valley massacre in Arizona,[9] and who saw the injustice of the Kern River massacre in California.[10] Certainly even the inexperienced travellers made distinctions among the various tribes and did not regard all Indians as the same.

In Colorado a train of 60 wagons captained by Joseph Ehle, in about 1864, met an unexpected instance of fraternal cooperation from the Indians. Ehle, a Mason, was told by an old trapper that he could get through a dangerous stretch of Indian country to the south because someone had made the chief in area a Mason. Accordingly, Ehle painted the Masonic emblem on the lead wagons of the train. True to his fraternal obligations, the chief sent a group of young warriors to escort the train through his territory safely and to hunt for them. They stayed with the train for twenty days.[11]

In short, white settlers and Indians are presented in these family histories as more often enemies than as friends, but the white attitudes toward the Indians seldom match some of the more extreme present day stereotypes of white racist attitudes in the West.

Literary Patterns

In addition to these cultural patterns common to many of the family histories' accounts of the journey westward, a few conventions emerge that might be called literary patterns common in family histories. It is these more than the cultural patterns that might justify calling pioneer family histories a genre of folk literature.

One of the most striking and common of these is the idea that the urge and the aptitude for pioneering are at least a cultural if not a biological heritage. The fact that so many family histories present a continuing movement westward through several generations makes such an interpretation understandable, but it appears in these histories so frequently and in such similar terms that it becomes conventional. Albert Banta wrote, of his family, "For generations the Bantas have been pioneers....My parents, being pioneers by heredity, migrated to the Territory of Wisconsin in 1846."[12] With more emphasis on environment than heredity, another family historian writes, "Mr. Shivers was a lifelong pioneer of the West, as even his ancestors before him were pioneers of Tennessee....Mr. Shivers was fit by precept and education for the trials and difficulties of a life such as always confronts the pioneer of a new country."[13] Again, Alfred Hight went West from Delaware because he "had pioneer blood in his veins!"[14] Thus the westering of these families came to be regarded, in retrospect at least, as something like the individual equivalent of the nation's Manifest Destiny. This helps to explain the frequent interest in genealogy, and the interest of each author in writing the family's history, particularly when the author is a member of that family. The reader may be reminded here of the intricate genealogies of heroes in the sagas of northern Europe.

As might be expected in folk histories of this type, the tone is almost uniformly laudatory. Any cruelty, meanness, or questionable practices are glossed over or justified, sometimes elaborately. John Slaughter may have had a habit of ending a trail drive through cattle country with two or three times as many cattle as he had had when he started, but that was merely a "common" practice of the time. A tendency on the part of some pioneers to shoot Indians without apparent provocation was rationalized into an "understandable precaution" in the face of the supposed perfidiousness of the red man. And of course the occupation, by force if necessary, of land already held by Indians was justified as nothing more than wresting the land from the wilderness and elevating it to a higher use. Thus these family histories can not be expected to be either objective or highly analytical, but they probably reflect the justification the pioneers would have presented for themselves. Certainly these histories were written from a distinct viewpoint that is very similar from one to the next.

Pioneer family histories often draw upon the written memoirs of the actual participants in events, and from historical documents of various types, but they also draw to a considerable extent upon an oral tradition within the family, what Mody Boatright has called the "family saga."[15] This is sometimes acknowledged directly by the family historian: "This volume is part of the living tradition of a family. My brother and I heard this story, and particularly the highlighted episodes, many times during our childhood, and our children have heard them in their turn. Expressions have flowed from these experiences into the family vocabulary and have contributed to those intimate ties by which a family group develops its own characteristic patterns."[16] This same work exhibits some characteristics one might expect from such an oral tradition, distilled from memories of actual events over the years. For example, the author reports having personally observed, as a child in a wagon train along the Platte, "a prairie dog and an owl or two sitting on the rim of a hole with a rattlesnake coiled alongside." This, the author says, was "a common sight."[17] The same author reports in impressive detail a meeting between her father and Buffalo Bill in the town of North Platte in 1873. Cody's clothing, down to the silk thread embroidery of his cowboy boots, is described. Cody introduces himself as a government scout and gives a detailed warning about a Sioux village the wagon train will soon encounter on the trail to Denver. Yet not only is a government scout unlikely to have been dressed as Cody is said to have been (except in a Wild West show), but also Cody left government service in 1872 for show business. Apparently an indistinctly recollected encounter with a government scout has become embellished in the family saga with the trappings of the later show business hero and has then been set down in the family history. Similar discrepancies in the story (the 54 mile journey from Greeley to Denver, by wagon, is telescoped into a single day with arrival in the early afternoon, for example) also suggest the tendency of the oral tradition to discard the duller aspects of the story and make it more interesting and direct, a tendency common also in folklore and the folk ballad.

Similar phrases occurring in different accounts of the same events also suggest the oral tradition that often lies behind the written family history. An example of this may be found in the Powell family history, in which the narrative of the journey to Oregon written by S. Hamilton, and that written by L. Jane Powell, conclude almost identically with the observation that they arrived at their destination September 3, "having been five months to a day from our starting point in Illinois" (Hamilton) or "five months to a day since we left Illinois" (Powell). Both of these sources seem to have heard the same narrative of the family saga of the train to Oregon enough times to have absorbed the standard phrasing.

Perhaps most significant to our present consideration of the journey westward is that in most cases the family history does not focus on the journey westward either as the climactic or the central episode of the family's story. Most often the pioneering after arrival, pioneering that frequently includes a series of further moves, forms the center of the narrative. Unlike Steinbeck's "The Leader of the People," most of the actors in these family histories seem to have found challenges at the end of the journey at least equal to the challenges of the journey itself.

NOTES

[1]David King Udall, *Arizona Pioneer Mormon, David King Udall,* written in collaboration with his daughter, Pearl Udall Nelson (Tucson: Arizona Silhouettes, 1959), p. 2.

[2]James Madison Powell, *Powell History: An Account of the Powell Ancestors of 1851—John A., Noah and Alfred—Their Ancestors, Descendants and Other Relatives* (privately printed, 1922). I am indebted to Professor Gilbert Powell Findlay for giving me access to this volume.

[3]Powell, p. 27.

[4]Examples of this continued wandering are myriad. For example: Albert F. Banta,*Albert Franklin Banta, Arizona Pioneer,* ed. Frank D. Reeves, Historical Society of New Mexico Publications in History, Vol. XIV (September, 1953), p. 4; Fannie Wingfield Stephens, "A Pioneer of the Verde Valley," *Echoes of the Past: Tales of Old Yavapai,* 3rd ed. (Prescott, Arizona: The Yavapai Cow Belles, 1972),

pp. 129-135; Allen A. Erwin, *The Southwest of John H. Slaughter, 1841-1922*, Western Frontiersmen Series X (Glendale, California: The Arthur H. Clark Company, 1945); Robert H.Forbes, *The Penningtons, Pioneers of Early Arizona* (Tucson: Arizoa Archeological and Historical Society, 1919).

⁵Three instances of death from childbirth on the trail occur in a single family history: Marcia Rittenhouse Wynn, *Pioneer Family of Whiskey Flat* (privately printed,1945), pp. 6-15, 28. A copy is deposited in the library of the Arizona Historical Society in Tucson. I am grateful to the Society for permission to consult this and other material in their collection.

⁶Rachel Redden Koontz, "The Miller Story," *Echoes of the Past,* Vol. 2, ed. Robert C. Stevens (Prescott, Arizona: The Yavaplai Cowbells, Inc., 1964), pp. 11-40.

⁷Koontz, "The Miller Story," p. 26.

⁸A classic description of a traditional wagon train, giving details of equipment, food, routines, and hazards on the trail may be found in Jennie Atcheson, Wriston, *A Pioneer's Odyssey* (privately printed, 1943), pp. 24-69. A copy is deposited in the collection of the Arizona Historical Society in Tucson.

⁹Pat Savage, *One Last Frontier* (New York: Exposition Press,1964), pp. 78-79.

¹⁰Wynn, *Whiskey Flat,* pp. 109-111.

¹¹Mrs. Charles Herbert Bowers, "Joseph Ehle and Margaret Williams Ehle and Descendants," typescript in the Sharlot Hall Museum, Prescott, Arizona. I am grateful to the Sharlot Hall Museum for permitting me to consult this and other materials in their collection.

¹²Banta, p. 4.

¹³Learah Cooper Morgan, "Casa Del Rio: The Home of Hannah Shivers Postle Rees," *Echoes of the Past,* p. 3.

¹⁴Wynn, *Whiskey Flat,* p.3.

¹⁵Mody Boatright, "The Family Saga as a Form of Folklore," *The Family Saga and Other Phases of American Folklore* (Urbana: University of Illinois Press, 195), pp. 1-19.

¹⁶Wriston, *A Pioneer's Odyssey,* p. vii.

¹⁷Wriston, p. 43.

The Incorporative Consciousness: Levertov's Journey From Discretion to Unity

Victoria Harris

A constantly self-evaluating, non-static poet, Denise Levertov has developed markedly since her first book, *The Double Image* (1946). That book, as Stephen Stepanchev notes, was influenced greatly by remembered English "metrical and stanzaic patterns and rhyme schemes."[1] Bothered by the dishonesty and irrelevance of such "importations," Levertov began a concentrated effort to wean herself from poetic models, and to achieve not merely a poetic voice of her own but a relationship to reality that is uniquely hers and that informs as it makes possible her own poetic voice. This struggle, while evident in *Here and Now* (1957) and *The Jacob's Ladder* (1961), is perhaps best represented in her fourth volume, *O Taste and See.*[2]

In this volume, Levertov approaches and at times achieves that reciprocal relationship with reality made possible by what may be called the incorporative consciousness. This type of poetic consciousness encompasses both internal and external reality, integrating self, others, and nature into an organic whole. The centripetal motion which brings in the sensory landscape, its taste and sight, is met by centrifugal forces issuing from the poet herself. Organically incorporating her world, the poet's psychic awareness expands. This growth transforms the interior landscape, expanding her creative potential. The incorporative consciousness continues to grow, like a tree organically enlarging its boundaries. Her vision increasingly expanded from bringing in the world, Levertov balances these incoming energies with centrifugal energies. From the deep—and deepening—interior landscape, Levertov reaches outward, crystallizing this reciprocal motion with the gift of her perception, the verbal equivalent to that perception: the poem itself.

The necessary first step toward balancing interior and exterior landscapes involves the discovery and total integration of one's self. Such self-actualization does not involve separation from the natural world, however. To the contrary, the self must include an organic integration of all the energies and influences centripetally brought in. The poet must somehow incorporate that influx of material from outside into her private consciousness. Part of this process involves learning to distinguish addition and reflection from incorporation and creation. One must not copy the world, but energize it with dynamic involvement and inspired creations. Profound intuition, not additive memory, becomes the mode. Levertov's astonishingly honest and painful struggle to attain the "incorporative consciousness" forms an important part of *O Taste and See,* the first lines of its title poem hinting at the necessarily intense involvement with the surrounding universe: "The world is/not with us enough/O taste and see."

The journey toward poetic self-actualization recorded in *O Taste and See* involves several "matters" or concerns, some of which become stages in the poet's growth. The first is the poet's attempt to overcome dualism. This attempt often fails, a failure underscored by Levertov's use of language. Fragments and run-on sentences are employed, as though the very vehicle of creation is inadequate to convey the creator's impulse toward harmony. Of course, once Levertov discovers a language that overcomes dualism, dualism for her will have ceased to exist. Dualism and the search for a language that overcomes it, then, are two important concerns of *O Taste and See.* A third concern is the need for that authentic perception that allows the reciprocal interchange of inner and outer energies necessary if dualism is to be transcended. But such perception becomes possible only after the poet has come to terms with her own interior spaces, a fourth major concern in this volume and one which receives its fullest treatment in "To the Muse" and "Into the Interior." The fifth and perhaps most important concern in *O Taste and See* involves the poet's emergence as the fully developed "I-as-poet," an emergence signified by Levertov's discarding of poet-personae and her consequent shift to the first-person "I."

"The Ache of Marriage," the third poem in this volume, represents a good example of the first concern mentioned above, the need—in this case a frustrated need—to overcome a world of distinctions.

The ache of marriage:

thigh and tongue, beloved,
are heavy with it,
it throbs in the teeth.

We look for communion
and are turned away, beloved,
each and each.

It is leviathan and we
in its belly
looking for joy, some joy
not to be known outside it

two by two in the ark of
the ache of it.

Rooted in a field of distinctions, the poet stands bereft of the "joy" she seeks, for her marriage is marked by division rather than unity. Senses become heavy with the ache of unfulfillment; "thigh and tongue, beloved,/are heavy with it,/it throbs in the teeth." The very fact that this house of marriage is characterized by a leviathan image housing separate entities, and that the body is characterized as holding distinct senses, seemingly separate, routinely must lead to division rather than to organic joining. Quite explicitly, Levertov admits the lack of fulfillment: "We look for communion/ and are turned away, beloved." Obviously the problem is an unfulfilled expectation of harmony. The very motion toward harmony, however, may be the cause of disharmony; the fulfillment of harmony, that is, is sought through a *decentralizing* energy. The speaker and her spouse are divided "each and each," but centrifugally seeking communion. The gesture overcomes itself: harmony can not be the culmination of otherness, attained through closures big or small, be they houses, marriages, or bodies in which quantifiable distinctions are put together. Outsideness is admittedly the wrong path to the joy of harmony: "looking for joy, some joy/not to be known outside it." The "it" seems to have a double referent: the joy will be found within the leviathan's belly, but also within itself. The direction of the search must be changed, centripetally drawing the distinctions—be they different senses, or different people—into the hub, else "two by two," a mathematical compounding of one individual plus another, will additively fill up the ark with more and more pairs of distinctions, eluding the joy, continuing "the ache of it," the notion with which Levertov is left.

"The Message" continues the additive process, leading again to a failure of expectations, whereby maps, additions, and memories cannot comprise the mode to the "great Spirit." In a dream the persona receives a letter from "cross country" in which a Bard claims "seeds of the forget-me-not." The residual notion of the past comes to the speaker from "out of the sea fog," a hazy reminder from "a Bard" of a different country, apparently Levertov's native England. The message seems to be to take the seeds from this other country and plant them here on this land where they will grow. In other words, the past is come here to haunt the speaker, making not only the seeds but the speaker herself an importation. The motive is to produce a hybrid forget-me-not, thereby making a stronger variety. Explicitly, the speaker is asked to plant the seeds on this soil, then send the new seeds back to her old land, "Not flowers but/their seeds." The Bard of the other land gives the seeds, and the "Spirit of Poetry" asks for the new seeds back. The power of the image—here the generative seeds—overcomes the flatness of the message to remember. Moreover, the message comes horizontally from across the sea. The seeds come across also, but to fulfill their potential, they also need vertical space. They must penetrate beneath surfaces to transform potential into growth.

In the next stanza, the transplanted flora are metaphorically represented as a map, "The varied blue/in small compass." In multitude the distinctions among the individual herbs become blurred from "a cloud of blue, a river/beside the brown river." But the transplantation remains one of going from one spot to another, and the hazy collection of flowers is described by "compass," or "Multitude," "Beside" the real thing to which it is compared, a field gotten by a collecting and transferring process. In metaphoric relation to the seed stands the poet who is also transplanted—a hybrid—and reminded by her ancestor soil to "Remember [her] nature." Thus, her sense of poetry, she is advised, should be gotten through memory—ignoring her landscape, perception, intuition, and imagination. Then the speaker relates that this Bard-become-Spirit from across the sea speaks of her *nature* as a power; "And he bids me/remember my nature, speaking of it/ as of a power." Thus, the advice reminds the speaker of a component of herself brought across the sea. This importation becomes an integral part of her makeup and is elevated into the eminent position of a power. A somewhat paradoxical notion resides in the advice to call the inheritance from a former home, something to be remembered, a power—the former seeming fixed, the latter generative. One seems an inert part of formation; the other seems the formulator itself. Although the advice connotes collecting, the power connotes something more essentially integrative than addition. The speaker relates the further advice which itself speaks of the additive nature of the advisor: "And gather/the flowers, and the flowers/ of 'labor.'" In other words, cultivate the seeds and pick the blossoms, those of labor, through your hybrid nature in order to gain results. The flowers of labor—the poems—become the mode of fusion: "(pink in the dream,/ a bright centaury with more petals./ Or the form changes to a seapink)." But the perception is parenthetical.

The italicized lines in the next stanza—"*Ripple of blue in which are/distinct blues. Bold/ centaur—seahorse—salt—carnation/ flower of work and transition*"—comment on the distinction of the many parts, urging this dichotomized vision on the speaker, who is but blurred when leaving the dream state: "Out of the sea fog, from a hermitage,/ at break of day./" Finally, she is left only questioning whether or not she can find the "flower of work and transition": "Shall I find them then—/here on my land, recalled/ to my nature?" Surely the question proposes, at most, lack of confidence. The pun on the word "Recall" shows the poet taking the wrong path to find her own nature on her own land. Transference goes linearly back and forth, and the resulting hybrid would be an additive of memory and parts, a wrong way to the power she seeks, a power wrongly attributed to seeds of memory from past lands. Her final search shows her looking in the wrong direction, collecting (or importing) foreign seeds and seeking outwardly for the power, "O, great spirit," as if it were something "out there" and functionally separate from the "I" and "nature" of her question.

So, importations of remembrances are not the answer, leaving a distinct problem for a hybrid such as Levertov—especially with regard to language and the problems of incorporating and expanding the past, instead of merely "recalling" it. One important aspect of this poem may be that the poet is operating intuitively. Although cognitively unaware of the force which would drive the poem, the impetus for the poem itself comes from a dream. This forms the optimism undergirding the poem. Although the speaker has not yet organically assumed the role of poet, she begins to collect herself with a drive from intuition, "out of sea fog." It will be shown that she increasingly realizes herself as poet, with concomitantly increasing involvement in her poems. Indeed, she will come to swallow that "seed." She begins the poem "The Breathing" with calm resolve. "An absolute/patience" like Eastern passivity characterizes the tree with which she is in reverie. The next sentence, "Trees stand/up to their knees in/fog," envisions this splendid tree engulfed in a creeping fog—one which moves upward, and one which blurs the base or the roots, a conventional portrayal of beginnings or past. The blurring continues as the fog proceeds uphill: "The fog/slowly flows/uphill."

Not only is the persona standing apart from the creeping fog, but she doesn't have the "absolute patience" needed to wait for the change from addition to mergence. The next stanza goes from one very distinct image to the next. Still above or outside the creeping fog, the poet details "White/cobwebs, the grass/leaning where deer/have looked for apples." The distinct images are presented in a sentence fragment, thus formally showing the tension between the holistic vision and, if not the incomplete vision, then at least the inability of language to portray the insight in any but a fragmentary way. This comprises an important failure to Levertov who does not view the poet as one who first has a vision, then tries to find the words to express it. Quoting William Wordsworth, Levertov asserts that "Language is not the dress but the incarnation of thoughts."[3] It should be emphasized, then, that to Levertov, when a gap exists between feelings and the words to express them, "that is language used as dress." Poems written in such language "are not musical, though they may sometimes be superficially so. The *music* of the poetry comes into being when thought and feeling remain unexpressed until they become Word, become Flesh (i.e., there is no prior paraphrase)."[4]

Contextually emphasizing this point, the poet shows her perception of the deer, an objective correlative of the poet, looking for apples, an objective correlative of the poem, and not finding them, thus also not fulfilling their search. The lines, "The woods/from brook to where/the top of the hill looks/over the fog, send up/not one bird," suggest that the area of foggy outlines is not the place for atomistic scrutiny of distinctive images. The narrator lessens the gap between herself and those foggy places by the end of the poem, when she approaches something beyond the senses; "a breathing/too quiet to hear" concludes the poem with the sense of life rhythms which cannot be sensorially perceived. But whatever this life force may be, it remains something *outside* the narrator's consciousness. She remains outside the space from which she derives the perception; maintaining the subject-object dichotomy, the perceiver seems somehow removed from the perception of the "so absolute, it." The scene of "happiness itself," then, is finally physically separate from the viewer describing it. Yet once again Levertov approaches her intuition, the "sea fog," thereby not yet organic with, but approaching, her existence as intuitive poet.

The paradox between happiness residing in a silence, wherein even its breathing is too quiet to hear, and the very act of writing poetry continues throughout this volume. In the very next poem, "September 1961," the poet elucidates the painful process of shedding layers of memory, be they derived from either influences or words themselves. But the poem ends with the failure to fulfill the hope, leaving memory and thought to conclude the poem, excluding the narrator from her space of perception.

The beginning of the poem shows initiation of the speaker in a new territory without her previous guides, left "alone on the road." "This is the year" signals a new way. Although more than the speaker must depart from the old direction, this departure must not be clustered into a group, for the many who leave the old way still go their own. The old school will "leave us alone," thus the several leaving are going in individual "obsecure directions." This obscurity carries a double existence for the poet. Surely, she has not yet "seen" her direction. But, more positively, she moves forward without the constricting parameters of a clearly delineated path. Obscurity, then, not only suggests hiding meanings through defective expression, but also allows freedom to move in undefined directions. The inheritance to be veered away from is not only shed because it is old, but because it is passe. This inherited thought was only previously considered "great." Consider, for example, the different connotation between "great old ones" and, as the narrator calls them, "the old great ones." Anyway, one finds increasing evidence within the poem that not only are old tutors no longer adequate, but so are all referential systems through which reality must be distilled by some external criterion, such as words. Referential systems are done with, as the initiate travels with the words in her pockets. Although seemingly tucked away, these words are brought along. Old structures no longer work; those modes "have taken away the light of their presence." Words stored in pockets become lights over a hill, seen "moving away over a hill/off to one side." The "old ones," which gather more than one metaphoric attachment within the space of the poem, "...are not dying." Finally, the pocket-storing and peripheral sighting of these old ones relocate: "They are withdrawn/into a painful privacy." The impetus changes. Although the speaker initially takes the road away from them, she finally brings the words. The insistent retention of these linguistic artifacts imbues the subject with pain. But the motion, foreshadowing organicism, bears attention. Instead of additively toting the words, the speaker begins to incorporate them; she centripetally draws them in. The digestion will allow the consciousness to expand whereas the mere carryovers would challenge only the memory.

Articulating the cause of this pain, the subject begins the next stanza with the end of the sentence, "learning to live without words." When consciousness itself may be defined as language, the repercussions of its denial are indeed traumatic. "E.P.," presumably Pound, declares that "It looks like dying." William Carlos Williams declares that he "can't/describe to you what has been/happening to me." H.D. is "unable to speak." There is a double significance to the inclusion of these poets' reactions. First, they must be included in the "us" who are leaving the old ones. Each must go alone, and though their individual reactions seem similar, the privately found answers cannot transfer. To the eye of E.P., it is death. Williams is unable to deliver the message to the listener's ear. His statement pointedly negates a linear message code between speaker and listener. H.D. is not yet capable of the utterance apart from the old ones. Though disclaiming referential articulation and passive reception, the speaker's imaginative voice and conscious ear have not as yet developed.

The second significance to the inclusion of the poets is that not only are they of "us" relevance to the poet, but they are also themselves "old ones." If any of their conclusions were adopted by the speaker, such conclusions too would be referential to reality, would come between the poet and her perception, and thereby call forth passive reception of another's views instead of active individual intuition. Retention itself is the act of memory; retention of another's solutions are to this poet lies. Cognitive transferences do not allow the poet to perceive the universe unfolding around her. This simply does not do; Levertov will not accept importations, and finds herself "alone on the road, not following the direction 'old words' can give," and not led by the "light of their presence" (old words and old tutors). She is moving, but not yet arrived, as finally the speaker seems surrounded by an energetic darkness: "The darkness/twists itself in the wind." The only light remaining is that of the stars which are far and small, and of the city which is "confused urban light-haze." The poet sheds her old guides—words and mentors—but still gropes in darkness.

On her road, although she recalls the message, she ends in silence. They have laid a map for her to follow, somehow—a method of approach objectively attainable by the subject: "They have told us/the road leads to the sea." Along with the reified experience comes the inherited gift: "and given/the language into our hands." This handing down of words for shaping makes the communication a matter of manual dexterity. This notion is anathema to Denise Levertov. The poet's task is to hold in trust the knowledge that language, as Robert Duncan has declared, is not a set of counters to be manipulated, but a Power. And only in this knowledge does he arrive at music, at that quality of song within speech which is not the result of manipulations of euphonious parts, but of an attention, at once to the organic relations of experienced phenomena and to the latent harmony and counterpart of language itself as it is identified with those phenomena.[5]

The atomistic parcelling out of space, here language, seems inadequate to the speaker. This may be related by the sensory additions in the next sentence which lead to silence. We "'hear'/our footsteps each time a truck/has dazzled past us and gone." Thus, there seems to be something in the image allowing the subject to approach a despatialized time, whereby she transforms a reified map made by her footsteps into an I-in-the-world perception. The footsteps seem to remain past the time when a passing truck has gone, thus perhaps extending the subjective moment. But, unable to cope with this intuition, the poet is left in "new silence," not yet "in touch" with the organicism. Subjective involvement is implied here by the description of the silence being new; but nonetheless muteness remains.

Levertov changes the collective "us" and "we" to the singular (although abstract) "one" when she reaches her insight of negation. This road is not the fruitful path; "one can't reach/the sea on this endless/road to the sea unless/one turns aside at the end, it seems,/follows/ the owl that silently glides above it/ aslant, back and forth." Her unidirectional path becomes an unending labyrinth, which has no end. But the image augurs the reciprocal energizing movement in the later *Footprints* (1972).

Levertov tentatively suggests that "it seems" that a person alone (one) must go off the path, one prescribed and apart from the individual. Levertov pointedly advocates departure from linear modes, of both language and inheritance, at the end of this insight. First she advises, go "aslant, back and forth," at least mixing directions, skewing the unidirectional linear mode; then the poem climaxes with the one-line stanza, "and away into deep woods." Here the reciprocal motion gathers energy to create deep landscape, as back and forth transforms to "deep wood" and "across" changes to "into." Thus, Levertov presents an image for a place both internal and external, confusing the separation and the clear delineation of the road. The woods contain a more profound depth than the flat directions strung out on a linear plane even when moving back and forth. But the functional thematic anticlimax is foreshadowed by the mention of following "the owl that silenty/glides above it." Though surely the owl is seer in the night, and copes with the new silence, following from a distance precludes intuition and forebodes a negative result. One should remember the previous intention not to follow anything apart from one's own preceptions.

Thus, although singular, "one" is abstract and other; this leads to the additive motion allowing "one" to become "us" in the concluding stanza. Levertov again portrays an atomistic composite collecting on the maplike road. Levertov reinforces this additive propensity by portraying the speaker counting the words; "But for us the road/unfurls itself, we count the/words in our pockets." Even the road seems to appear apart from the poet's interaction with or choice of it as she passively notes that the road unfurled itself. The speaker is left with a nagging intuition of something beneath logical ordering. Levertov even semantically points to its logical inadequacy by concluding in a run-on and yet unfinished thought: "we wonder/how it will be without them, we don't stop walking, we know/there is far to go, sometimes/we think the night wind carries/a smell of the sea. . . ." Thus the linear path can only lead the speaker to atomistic accumulation, utilizing already given modes (the words in the pocket); although one may add and add onto the string, it remains incomplete. And the pain inside remains "sometimes." "Sometimes" is given a tension appearing first on the line with "there is far to go, sometimes," then syntactically a part of "sometimes/we think the night wind carries/a smell of the sea..." On the horizontal road there are times when she perceives a distant place, but ends on the other times when her linguistically arranged "thinking" notes sensory impressions. The speaker never relates that there is something beyond sensory perception. Moreover, she ends twice removed from an "I-enveloped-in-the-world" perception. The potential depth of the image seems constrained by the thought. The sensory perception of the smell of the sea is not perceived by the person in the world, but conceived by the thinker—apart from it—using memory. She moves closer but still is far from the sea if she perceives its smell through thought and pursues the wrong road.

Levertov moves closer to the authentic perception hinted at in "September 1961" in "The Ripple." The poem begins with a description of a tau cross lying on a piece of white linen, that white linen retaining its traditional suggestion of purity. The tau symbol aptly applies to Levertov herself. First of all, it is the Greek symbol, and Levertov admittedly has much debt to the Greeks, claiming that she may be closer to them than to her own English ancestors. Also, the symbol is derived from the Semitic letter, the Hebrew Taw, therefore applying to the poet who herself is of Jewish descent. It becomes a single symbol representing a mergence of distinct parts, itself casting shadows on the white linen. A glass jug and tumblers rise from their own shadow. The tau cross seemingly bears witness to the image of water throwing back, not a gray shadow, but a luminous one: "and luminous/in each/overcast of/cylindrical shade." The road to the river seems not so remote when the narrator now perceives an "image/of water, a brightness." This brightness begins to seem like the kind of light only suspected in the previous poem. Here the suspicion becomes more and more a perception, the anticipation of which begins to bring with it an hysteria. The light is not the luminous familiar kind, "not gold, not silver," therefore not attributable to the shiny stuff we know. Rather, a strange luminosity appears from such an unsuspected source as a shadow. The lights can be seen playing on the moving water, which is finally perceived "rippling/as if with laughter." The energy derived from what is initially a description of a shadow, seems incredible; not only are perceiver and image involved and with motion, but the motion seems to become an effervescent spilling out and around of joy.

Here may be the beginning of a new mode of perception for Levertov, when the importations seem centripetally drawn into the single image of the tau cross. From this image, the poem opens up as the motion seems to pour outward with the "jug and tumblers' rise." Then the cylindrical shades are perceived by the luminosity shining through the overcast, or shining out. This luminosity finally breaks the bounds of its physicality—beyond the shininess of even the previous metals we know, until it, itself, seems alive when its waves are rippling outward. The motion goes inward and outward, gaining energy with each turn. Tentatively, but finally, it is seen moving "as if with laughter." Thus, the mixture, which presented transplanting problems, unites appropriately in the tau cross image; this distinct image of a shadow's becoming the source of a shimmering luminescence, rising above itself, getting power from the center out, and vibrating, shows Levertov overcoming not only the shadow of the past, but the very physical structures in the present.

The light-from-darkness imagery, along with the difference from linear, that of inheritance and transference, to deep moments, that of consuming energies from sources simultaneously outward and inward, continues in the very next poem in *O Taste and See,* in which luminous glistenings of "The Ripple" become "Sparks." The poem deals with the notion of messages and incorporation of "importations," portraying a speaker who receives a poem which incorporated a carpe diem message from Ecclesiastes. Solomon prescribes, "Whatsoever thy hand/findeth to do, do it with/thy might:/for there is no work,/nor device,/nor knowledge/nor wisdom,/in the grave, whither thou goest." A first consideration may be the linear inheritance implicit here, where part of the substance of the poem itself is derived. Though from the wise man himself, and put in a new context, the message remains one of memory, and one that, like the previously cited example of a perfectly rewritten Shakespearean sonnet, has everything but the fresh perception and new intuition; thus, this message seems quite similar to the transplanted forget-me-not seeds. The speaker's reaction to a letter enclosed with the poem reveals her feelings regarding the value of receiving and storing messages. Once again, Levertov notes the problem of language. Borrowing Solomon's words is not the answer, for horizons broaden in other ways. The lines, "A letter with it/discloses, in its words and between them," suggest that the wisdom which may possibly be incorporated does not come from replanting a message. The true worth lies in the space between the lines.

The comment upon the poet's poem is inherent in the mode of perceiving the poet's words. When entering this space between the lines, one can see the self unfolding in a reciprocal kind of self-regenerative activity that counteracts the enervating experience of memorized inheritance. Non-linear, "a life opening" becomes more than logical cause-to-effect assertions. The non-linear involvement is clarified further in the next two descriptions, "fearful, fearless," then "thousand-eyed." First, the male letter writer encompasses two emotions which would objectively cancel one another out. Second, the "thousand-eyed—image suggests an infusion-diffusion type of perception from the very pores of perception, instead of an eye-to-object, one-to-one relationship. The man seems protean, now different from the poet who passes down "old great ones" in his poetry. Levertov again describes the metamorphosis with a living luminosity emerging through darkness—here "a field/of sparks that move swiftly/in darkness." And the motion, again not a hand-me-down deliverance of used materials, consists rather of a regenerative reciprocation from outward and inward energy sources: "to and from a center." The speaker's method of receiving the message itself portrays the concept with which she is dealing. First of all, one cannot derive truths from old messages. This is seen throughout this volume of poetry; so the incorporation of Solomon's message in the man's poem cannot possibly afford the best way to form a poem. Secondly, the reader cannot proceed linearly through words already laid out for his passive reception. The more active reader—the speaker here—grasps a thought through the "words and between them." Finally, not only is the thought to be grasped someone else's thought, but the very gleaning process itself inherently includes enervation. This active reader concludes, "He is beginning/to live." Thus, something living in the space involved the reader, who actively, personally, reacts with her own energy and her own insight; this perception is not derivative, but regenerative.

Furthermore, whatever she sees between the words of the letter of her correspondent, leading him to new life, is not to be adopted by her. His message of imminent doom is explicitly disclaimed: "The threat/of the world's end is the old threat." Her message, from the "Book of Delight," seems a double one, suggesting that *now* you prepare for the future world, and day by day you prepare for this world. In other words, go through your own individuation, a process through which you encompass the here and now and the other world, and a process through which time itself is subjectified. The tension implicit here is one requiring immense energy, and the energy of "sparks" is the imperative metaphor dominating this poem. No easy "passing down of" or "putting away for" will result in these "sparks." A self-emanating and self-enclosing reciprocation is the action necessary for "beginning to live."

It may be seen, then, that Levertov senses something new beginning. What is old, characterized by message, tutors, transference, inheritance, and even language, must be overcome in a continual struggle. Many of the above-mentioned poems carry with them the residual effect of a loss of spontaneous energy and original intuition. Levertov struggles with beginnings and with the necessary energy and freshness such beginnings require. The failures are many, thus the book is embroidered with run-ons and fragment. But even when the inability to express wins, an underground movement pushes its forces upward like the fog pushing up the tree in "The Breathing."

As we have seen, Levertov works strenuously in *O Taste and See* with the problems of memory and distinction, focusing on considerations ranging from a past inheritance to a reference system such as language itself. Sometimes the eschewal of scientistic referential modes seems impossible, leaving unresolved confrontations resulting in fragment or silence. The crucial necessity seems to be the incorporation of an integrated being as poet. Levertov's strides and successes are achieved through her scrupulous honesty, impelling a growing awareness and poetic revelation of herself. Levertov's gathering up of herself involves incorporating the muse in her body-house. I suggest preparation, not completion. Only when her own harmonious energy system is achieved can it mingle with the energies in the universe. Only then can she poetically participate with and reflect the energy system that is the world.

The direction and the mode of this self-realization become apparent in Levertov's poem "Into the Interior.":

> Mountain, mountain, mountain,
> marking time. Each
> nameless, wall beyond wall, wavering
> redefinition of
> horizon.
>
> And through the months. The arrivals
> at dusk in towns one must leave at daybreak
>
> —were they
> taken to heart, to be seen
> always again,
> or let go, those faces,
>
> a door half-open, moss
> by matchlight on an inscribed stone?
>
> And by day
> through the hours that
> rustle about one dryly,
> tall grass of the savannah
>
> up to the eyes.
> No alternative to the
> one-man path.

The journey of life takes the traveler across the scene. "Mountain,

mountain, mountain" begins the poem, placing the landscape monotonously and horizontally across the line. Indeed, on the next line, time seems spatialized, showing the speaker "marking time." But Levertov relieves the apprehension of a flat map world with detemporalized space and despatialized time in her conclusion of the stanza. First of all, Levertov portrays each "wall beyond wall" as "nameless," perhaps indicating no intellectual predilection about the world, which would undercut the acquaintance with it. This stanza pointedly undermines all static notions; the least resilient notion, of "definitions," here becomes "redefinitions." And such an abstract characterization as a definition of space and time relents before contactual involvement with the unfolding universe. Levertov counteracts the static characteristic of definition itself, transforming inertia into fluctuation. Here, we not only witness definition give way to "redefinitions (which would be just one step further, exchanging one inert phase of abstraction for another), but the word "redefinition" joined to "wavering" connotes a quality of awareness, rather than capitulation. The constant quality, then, is the ongoing awareness; the changing quality is the perception. Levertov reaffirms this central notion of being involved with one's universe at the end of this stanza. The traveler's movement through space unfolds the world with each step taken. The undergirding notion dominating the participation of the subject with her world asserts that reality is process. Indeed, reality is the very awareness of one's world as she moves through it. Thus, definitions such as "mountains" re-form with each step toward and away from the peak. Levertov undercuts the predisposition of the world-as-other with her "wavering/redefinition of/horizon." The very perception of the landscape, then, forms the reality. This reality fluctuates with each movement of the world traveler.

In "Into the Interior," Levertov depicts the direction of this involvement. It is, as this first stanza portrays, the movement through the world, whereby awareness remains constant but the articulation of this reality always changes. Levertov balances the motion of looking out with the centripetal motion of drawing in. Thus the time "through the months" and the time and space— "The arrivals/at dusk in towns one must leave at daybreak"—

must be pulled into the speaker in order to reach the internal resident: the poetic muse. The poet therefore must question, "were they/taken to heart?" Only then could the interior eye relish the passing universe, allowing it "to be seen/always again." This drawing-in-process preserves that fluctuation. Here the poet foreshadows an image predominant in the later *Footprints*—she herself becomes the passageway, the very spot where the motions of incoming and outgoing meet. She is Denise, Daleth, doorway— "a door half-open." The option is to bring the fluctuating world "to heart" or to "let it go." The choice is clear, and the procedure of centrifugal awareness and centripetal incorporation adumbrates the energy condition dominating *Footprints*. The poet, then, affirms her commitment as a poet, by showing how the world becomes, and what to do with it. Indeed, she must bring it "Into the Interior," as the title suggests. This will be shown as signifying the growing assurance of herself as a poet, whose muse resides internally—indeed perhaps existing as "the heart" of the being. Moreover, the walk through life is always a singular commitment: the consciousness cannot forsake its very growth by *attaching to definitions*— poetic schools, modes of vision. The odyssey is arduous and wonderful, and singular: there are "no alternatives to the/one-man path." Thus, in "Into the Interior," Levertov depicts the world, space and time, as process; the motion as centripetal and centifugal; and the commitment as unrelenting awareness along the deep singular path. This is the starting point for the odyssey—literal, symbolic, and poetic where that "half-open door" will open onto a wonderful luminescence imbuing the literal horizon with a light from the internal, spiritual muse of poetry.

Levertov designates that inner region as the residence of the muse. In an earlier poem in this volume, "To the Muse," the speaker alerts the reader in the first stanza to her suspicion that the muse is not a transient visitor—"not one who comes and goes." Instead, Levertov portrays the muse as a permanent resident of the chosen body-house—one who travels through the "garden for air and delights/of weather and seasons." The interior landscape, then, is a changeable place too, in which the muse reacts to those changes. The body-house becomes an elaborate work which must make room for the muse. Only then can the internal landscape become this reservoir of poetic insight. So, Levertov says, "Who builds/a good fire in his hearth/shall find you at it/with shining eyes and a ready tongue." That this heart-hearth must be well-lit implies that those images taken "to heart" from "Into the Interior" must be brought to a well-cared-for place. The warmth of the hearth prepares an inviting home, an apt receiver for the muse. Levertov indicates the imperative "O taste and see" of the book by the image of muse with "shining eyes and a ready tongue." The important motion is apparently the preparing for and opening up to the guest. Even if the house may seem paltry, the effort of sharing one's humblest offerings bespeaks the dignity such as that witnessed in the humble host in *Electra*. Indeed, the sharing of the humble repast brings "joy." Levertov declares that no enclosure should exclude the guest; not even should one "lock the door of the marriage/against you." Thus, the involvement with the guest becomes total. In fact, reforming the interior landscape allows the spiritual light provided by the muse to radiate. This light is hinted at at the end of the fourth stanza with the "shining eyes" and reinforced in the seventh stanza with the description of the muse's being "as/the light of the moon on flesh and hair." Thus, the human quality will gain a radiance, but one really more organic than the simile conveys, since it is an internal irradiation.

In Levertov's delightful tour through her internal corridors, she depicts an intricate system whose hidden places at times elude the host, yet become known to the muse. So, often when the host believes the muse is gone, the muse is actually hiding in places "unknown to the host." The reason for the evasion is the erection of a barrier excluding the guest. It is always the responsibility of the poet as receiver to prepare the house for the muse as guest. It must be stressed that Levertov is getting herself together as the house of the muse. Either the hearth or the table, the heart or source of nourishment, has somehow neglected the guest. Or the doors, that now apparent motif, have not "been unlocked," thereby closing off the passageway. If Levertov is to realize herself as I-as-poet, this matter must be straightened out.[6]

Her lack of preparation for the muse, as well as the lack of appropriate position afforded her, reflect a closing motion diametrically opposed to the reciprocal energizing motion. Instead of receiving, the speaker "forgets" to do so, then frantically searches elsewhere for the muse. The false direction joins emotional falsity as the joy and light beginning the poem change to accusations of faithlessness and a tone of "demanding," and finally a situation which "is intolerable." Not only does the unfulfilled poet-house become a "great barracks," but those internal garden places of "air and delight" in the human house transform into an enclosure as stifling as Plath's "bell jar." Indeed the house becomes a prison, and its intricate corridors become meaningless in themselves when the only significant feature becomes enclosing walls. Thus, "it is too big, it is too small, the walls/menace him." At last the frantic energy of reaching elsewhere snuffs out the inviting heart-hearth fire. The blaze of light, life, and spirituality burns out in the stifling image where "the fire smokes/and gives off no heat." Here, the opposite of the spiritual image, that incandescent glow, results from the poet's not meeting her joyful and continual responsibility as host to the muse. Frantically rushing elsewhere for the answer closes off those interior spaces which must be the reservoir of inspiration.

Finally, the ridiculous question of this outward seeker, "But to what address/can he mail the letters," is answered with the calm, "And all the while/you are indwelling." The discovery of the interior reservoir opens up all the wonderful qualities that the negligent host closed. First of all, the spiritual golden illumination becomes assuredly a part of the internal landscape. Twice Levertov declares "a gold ring lost in the house"; then she affirms that the glimmer of gold is indeed the muse's presence by transforming the "gold ring," subject of the previous two sentences, to "you," subject in the next. In fact, the spiritual glow emanates from the place where the muse hides, "glowing with red, with green,/with black light." The poet approaches the muse with this very intuition of her. Levertov follows the "glowing" line, with the assertion that the "gold ring/waits" in the "crack in the floor." The stifling bell-jar type image transforms into a place where a crack can open a place for the air of intuition.

Finally, the other-directed poet completely changes in motion. She exchanges frantic seeking for calm recipience, once again revealing the dignity of the humble host. With "a calm face" the poet makes ready for the muse. Importantly, not even the wise man can relate how to prepare. This is the "one-main path" previously articulated, and the speaker moves in the correct direction—internal. Once again, the body-home becomes an inviting scene with table laid, fire trimmed, and even flowers, from those garden spaces, sought. The inward direction matches the resurrection of the dominant mode of awareness. The speaker alerts herself to "be ready with quick sight." Then the spirituality can issue; then the speaker can "catch a gleam between the floorboards/there, where he had looked/a thousand times and seen nothing." Thus, the "Light of the house" is a spiritual one, kindled by the calm receiving nature of the inner-directed poet. The spiritual light joins the symbolic door at the end of the poem, setting the scene appropriately invitational. The dutiful host now has the intuition that "someone had passed through the room a moment ago," and the poem culminates with the image of spiritual radiance in the sight of the "ring back on its finger."

The spiritual glow illuminates the internal landscape only when the poet becomes increasingly aware that the muse resides internally, indeed only after the epiphany: "You are in the house!" A preparedness of the house joins the internal direction as landscape, while calm vigilance of the host comprises the mode for finding the muse. Levertov, then, has gotten her house together. She is on her way, changing the search for the internal muse to the effects of it. This reflects the increasing dimensions of her poetic consciousness.

"In Mind," significantly written in the first-person, further reveals Levertov's identification with the internal muse, and shows that this identification is not always delightful. The poem depicts two internal beings.

> There's in my mind a woman
> of innocence, unadorned but
>
> fair-featured, and smelling of apples or grass. She wears

a utopian smock or shift, her hair
a light brown and smooth, and she

is kind and very clean without
ostentation—
             but she has
no imagination.
             And there's a
turbulent moon-ridden girl

or old woman, or both,
dressed in opals and rags, feathers

and torn taffeta
who knows strange songs—

but she is not kind.

Significantly, the first more quiescent person "in my mind" is fresh, and fair, and a woman. Though "kind and very clean," she "has no imagination." The second, darker being, though introduced as a picture in the mind, somehow has dominance over the mind. Indeed the speaker cannot even distinguish whether she is a "girl/or old woman, or both." What is clear, however, is that this being differs markedly from the easily characterized innocent fair creature. Indeed, Levertov portrays her as a "turbulent moon-ridden girl" in gypsy disarray of "opals and rags, feather/and torn taffeta," suggesting perhaps the highs and lows, wealth and poverty, endemic to the poetic consciousness. Levertov reveals the most significant feature of all, however, that she "knows strange songs" in the most casual way. In this way, the fact of being a poet is shown as well incorporated into the poet's self-awareness. The question is not whether or not she metaphorically houses the poet; this seems conclusive. Here the poem ends on the effects of this internal dark lady. Indeed, Levertov states that "she is not kind." Thus, the spiritual resident is no handpatting lady, but a resident who demands, strains, and is "not kind" to her host. The commitment, then, to be the being "who knows strange songs" must be strong; the "I" reveals the poet's mature acceptance of herself as poet—dark singer of songs.

This commitment becomes clearer in the poem "The Prayer." In this poem the speaker prays for continuation of her poetic powers. Again Levertov calls upon the image of light to indicate the spirituality igniting the poem. And again this spirituality emanates from within the first-person speaker: "I prayed...that he maintain in me/the flame of the poem."

The flame remains inside the poet: "since then, though it flickers or/shrinks to a/blue head on the wick,/there's that in me that/burns and chills." With the combination of burning and chilling, Levertov repeats the kind of image seen in "The Elves," "unless a woman has that cold fire in her/called poet." This time, however, the speaker becomes first person. Levertov assumes her position as ark of the resident muse, though often this internal resident, dark and moody, causes pain. Not only does the flame burn and chill, but the speaker finds it often "blackening my heart with soot," or "flaring into laughter," or "stinging/my feet into dance." Indeed, this blackening, flaring, and stinging suggests no quiescent guest. Yet the act of prayer bespeaks commitment. There are structural similarities here to the poem "In Mind," which almost offhandedly assumes the fact of being a poet within the poem and then ends on a different note. Almost paralleling the kind of thought concluding "In Mind," that the one "who knows strange songs" "is not kind," here Levertov also assumes that "the flame of the poem" resides internally, then ends by saying that perhaps the gift does not come from the youthful, light, healing Apollo. The admission of a dual nature seems a frank self-evaluation. It becomes increasingly evident in Levertov's poems that she does not exclude herself from her scrupulously honest evaluations. Linda Wagner asserts that "One of the most noticeable expansions has been in the poet's depiction of herself...."[7] But pride is mixed with revelation of those aspects not usually admitted. Here, Levertov passes the real test of honesty with her awareness and first-person portrayal of the darker parts of herself.

A tirade against hypocrisy, odious to the woman, dominates

her poem "Hypocrite Women." Here, Levertov rails against women who pare their dreams like toenails, "clipped...like ends of/split hair." The whole feminine zeitgeist seems overcast with whorish "psychopomp" whereby roles overcome feelings. When, for example, "a dark humming fills us, a/coldness towards life," we cannot face ourselves. "We are too much women to/own to such unwomanliness." Thus, Levertov taps those coverings of role, or predisposition, hurling womankind into honest, and painful, self-discovery. Her tirade against hypocrisy is a personal one as well. Thus, she admits that the very spirituality for which she prays "is not kind," but rather is a "blackening," "flaring," and "stinging thing."

But Levertov reveals the honest evaluation of a poet who does not go through her world with the easier shell of "psychopomp." The point is that Levertov's demands for honesty extend to herself, to the incorporative consciousness housing pleasing and not-so-pleasing aspects. Perhaps this is why in her first-person poems, the "I," which includes Levertov as *poet*, openly unfolds her darker sides. Levertov very consciously uses the "I," as she suggests in her interview with David Ossman: "I think that a poet has to be skilled and experienced before he begins using 'I.' He can come to it eventually; and I'm really beginning to let myself say 'I' because I feel that now I can do it without the kind of crudity with which some people who have just begun to write poetry write about their own feelings."[8] Here, Levertov makes the prose statement similar to the poetic statements that affirm assurance of herself as a poet. The inclusion of "I," then, is organic. This inclusion in the poem foreshadows Levertov's inclusion of herself in her poems in *Footprints*. In this next volume, Levertov sparingly, but with marked effectiveness, walks into the space of her poems. The insertion of the word "I," then, looks forward to the spatial opening whereby the poet honestly confronts her universe.

The change in technique signifies an alteration in focus. *O Taste and See* shows Levertov as poet, as woman, increasingly coming to grips with herself. The "I" becomes more and more filled up; the poet increasingly realizes her space. In *Footprints* this space becomes an energy force to interact with the energies of the world. The evolving consciousness expands into its own constellation—as indicated by the many-corridored house image. Levertov imperatively asserts that the "house is no cottage, it seems,/it has stairways, corridors, cellars,/a tower perhaps,/unknown to the host." But this unknown aspect increasingly diminishes, causing a concurrent shift in focus. Now, while the consciousness never stops expanding, at least some aspects become realized—such as the I-as-poet aspect. Once realized, the poet must yet continue her life as honest endeavor. Therefore, she uses her space as poet, to confront her perceptions as a poet. This much at least is already realized. Thus this space will enter the poetry, and the walk through *Footprints* reveals the collected impressions of *O Taste and See* consumed in the consciousness of I-as-poet. I do not speak of conclusions, then, but rather indicate starting points.

NOTES

[1]Stephen Stepanchev, *American Poetry Since 1945* (New York: Harper Colophon, 1965), p.157.

[2]Denise Levertov, *O Taste and See* (Norfolk, Conn.: New Directions, 1964). All poems will be taken from this volume.

[3]Denise Levertov, *The Poet in the World* (New York: New Directions, 1973), p.16.

[4]Levertov, *Poet in the World,* p.17.

[5]Levertov, *Poet in the World,* p.54.

[6]In my discussion here and elsewhere of house imagery, I am indebted to Gaston Bachelard, *The Poetics of Space* (Boston: Beacon, 1969).

[7]Linda Wagner, *Denise Levertov* (New York: Twayne Publishers, Inc., 1967), p.56.

[8]David Ossman, *The Sullen Art* (New York: Corinth Books, 1963), p.75.

Originally published in *Exploration,* IV:1, December 1976. Reprinted with the permission of the editor and the author.

"No Time for Fainting"
The Frontier Woman in Some Early American Novels

Edna L. Steeves

Before I had read very far in the subject of this paper, I discovered that the image of the frontier woman reflected in the works of James Fenimore Cooper, William Gilmore Simms, and Charles Seasfield was very unlike that which our history books have led us to expect. In fact, the heroines of these three novelists strike the reader at first acquaintance as even more Victorian than the typical Victorian female. Of course that feminine stereotype is, perhaps, to be expected, since all three authors lived and wrote in the mid-nineteenth century. Yet the image of the frontier woman is so firmly fixed in the mind's eye that I found myself in the position of the redoubtable Sherlock Holmes who, in one of his who-dun-its, found the clue to the crime in the dog who did *not* bark in the night. After a close look at some of these heroines, one wonders how they could have survived the hazards of the American frontier.

Lowell once complained about the insipidity of Cooper's females; and Bret Harte wrote a story about a fainting Ginevra who, attacked in the forest by five wild beasts at once, was saved in the nick of time by a shot from Natty Bumppo's rifle—one shot from Killdeer killed all five beasts, naturally. Nevertheless, the women portrayed by these early writers on frontier life do manage to survive the hardships of their rugged environment.

For the purposes of this paper I have confined myself to Cooper's Leatherstocking series; to Simms' best-known novel, *The Yemassee,* and to two of his novels in the Revolutionary War series; and to three of Sealsfield's works: *Tokeah, or the White Rose,* his first novel; *Nathan the Squatter-Regulator,* a narrative of the Southwest frontier; and *The United States of North America As They Are,* a pseudo-literary, sociological document which is in effect a travelogue.[1]

Cooper's five Leatherstocking novels appeared between 1823 and 1841. Their settings vary from Lake Otsego in upstate New York in the 1740s, when Deerslayer is a youth of twenty or thereabout, to the western prairies beyond the Mississippi at the turn of the century, when Natty is an old man of four-score. However one defines the frontier, it always meant beyond the settlements, which were, originally of course, along the Atlantic seaboard. So the frontier is always in a western direction, and the term *West* to an American has a long and respected mythology connected with it. In the early nineteenth century, the terms *frontier* and *West* are practically interchangeable. As Edwin Fussell has pointed out: "The American West is almost by definition indefinite and indefinable."[2] But about the conditions of the frontier there was no question: they were wild and woolly. And the man and woman who braved them needed the strength of ten. Resourcefulness, endurance, daring, courage, skill in marksmanship and woodcraft, adeptness in handling Indians, willingness to eat-it-up, wear-it-out, make-it-do, the sheer ability to survive—these were the traits needed for life on the frontier. Cooper's Leatherstocking has all of them: he is a kind of Davy Crockett, Dan'l Boone, Kit Carson, and Jedediah Smith rolled into one. He is an idealized frontiersman. Natty does not swear, drink, or spit tobacco juice. Considering these highly desirable qualities, we marvel that Natty manages to stay a bachelor all his life. But unmarried to the end he remains, despite the fact that at least two young ladies nearly succeed in getting him into their clutches, and despite his highly romantic view of "the gentle ones"—one of his favorite phrases for the various young women who from time to time wander in and out of his orbit.

Since these are novels wound around a dominating male character, our image of the frontier woman in Cooper's Leatherstocking novels comes through the eyes of this male hero. There is little reason to think that that image differs much from Cooper's own view of woman, for Cooper was a Victorian gentleman who himself never knew frontier life.

The general ladylikeness of Cooper's heroines has often been remarked. They faint dead away on occasions when females were supposed to faint. They are, with a few exceptions, the angel-in-the-house type, or, more precisely, the angel-in-the-log-cabin. They are the moral inspiration of their men—the figurative light in the clearing. For all their distinctively feminine attributes, they do not lack courage or resourcefulness. In *The Deerslayer* (1841) Judith Hutter is a good example of the kind of frontier woman who enters into the life of Natty Bumppo. (She is, incidentally, one of the would-be Mrs. Natty's.) Judith and her sister Hetty set off alone by canoe to reconnoiter an Indian camp in order to aid the captured Natty. Because Hetty is feeble-minded, she has nothing to fear, Indians supposedly respecting the dim-witted as wards of the Great Spirit. But Judith, fair game for any Indian, decks herself out in a really fancy ballgown and boldly enters the savage camp, posing as a queen bearing a reprieve for the prisoner. The ruse does not work. On another occasion, when Indians attack the Hutter houseboat, Judith dashes out amid flying bullets and pushes the Indian about to clamber aboard into the lake. When Judith finds her scalped and dying father, she does not faint (one might excuse a lady for fainting at sight of a scalped head), but dresses his wounds and tries to make his last hours comfortable. In the course of the narrative, Judith loses her father, sister, and home, and is rejected by the man she loves, all within a few days. Yet she does not die of a broken heart, but marches off alone through the forest following a contingent of troops to the nearest fort. Since rumor had it that Judith was once interested in these same soldiers, we might read her action as more than a little ironic. But Cooper does not mean us to do so. She is, for him, a brave and tragic heroine.

There is a fainting female in *The Last of the Mohicans* (1826). Alice Munro faints after an Indian massacre in which her friends have been scalped before her very eyes. One might say it was a cutting experience. She has been separated from her father and her lover, and, with her half-sister Cora, is being carried off by Indians. Alice and Cora, tied to trees and threatened with torments, stoutly refuse to buy their lives in exchange for becoming the house-mates (wigwam-mates) of their savage captors. It's the old spirit of "I'd rather die than say yes."

In *The Pathfinder* (1840), the heroine, Mabel Dunham, shows courage and nimble-mindedness in her defense of the blockhouse against Indian ambush. With enormous daring, she dashes out of the blockhouse to seek the wounded body of her father and bring him aid or a proper burial. Mabel is no Antigone, but she is brave and resourceful—and she captured Natty's heart. In fact, Natty has a very near miss with matrimony in the person of Mabel Dunham. Unfortunately for him Mabel loves faithfully—from first sight, of course—a bonny young sailor. Mabel has many characteristics of the typical Victorian heroine, but then so has Dorothea Brooke. It is simply that one does not expect typical Victorian heroines to stand up so well to frontier conditions.

In *The Pioneers* (1823), the heroine, Elizabeth Temple, has been, like many of Cooper's heroines, educated in a finishing school in the East. Yet frontier hardships do not finish off this young lady. When Elizabeth and her friend Louisa Grant, the minister's daughter, take a walk in the forest, Louisa is attacked by a panther, whereupon she faints, not unexpectedly. Elizabeth refuses to leave her, and manages to stave off the panther (presumably by saying "Go Away, naughty Kitty!") until Natty rescues the girls with a bull's-eye to the panther's forehead. Elizabeth also is trapped in a forest fire. Naturally she is rescued, but the reader wonders how long skirts, lacy collars and cuffs, and little straw bonnets can emerge unscorched from a raging inferno.

In *The Prairie* (1927), the heroine, Ellen Wade, is a more liberated female than the typical Victorian maiden. Ellen sneaks out of the Ishmael Bush camp at night under a prairie moon to rendezvous with her lover. Unlike the creole beauty Inez, a noblewoman and heiress who has been captured by the Bush family, Ellen Wade is a believable frontier woman—her conduct, her speech, her dress do credit to a young person in her situation. Like all of Cooper's heroines, she has courage, devotion, faith in God and in her man. Perhaps Esther Bush, the squatter's wife, is as close as Cooper ever comes to drawing the frontier woman whom the history books depict. Esther and her daughters are a bunch of Amazons, always taking the long chance. With a little education and social position, Esther might have been another Dolly Madison, who, when the White House burned, tucked up her skirts and dashed out at the last moment with the Declaration of Independence in one hand and in the other Gilbert Stuart's portrait of George Washington.

Cooper's heroines, then, always ladylike and generally

clinging vines, astonish us by managing to survive frontier conditions, where Indian attacks were a daily ritual and physical hardship a part of life. Cooper's heroines are not his major achievement. That achievement, rather, lies in the fact that he is our first major novelist to deal with the American experience. The problems he portrays are part of our national history: questions of liberty vs. law; of the role of public opinion in a democracy; and of the place in society of the extraordinary man—and the extraordinary woman who shacked up with such a man.

If Cooper obviously did not know the realities of frontier life in America in the early nineteenth century, Charles Sealsfield, the Austrian monk who fled to America to escape the Metternich repression, certainly did know at first hand the American "Wild West" of the 1820s and 1830s. As mirrors of frontier life and character, Sealsfield's works and Cooper's present interesting similarities, and even more interesting differences, in points of view at almost the same historical moment and upon the same facet of the American experience, the frontier. Simms' descriptions of the Southern frontier (the settings of his novels are the colonial and Revolutionary periods) broaden the territory, but do not materially alter the details.

As the leading literary figure of the ante-bellum South, William Gilmore Simms published more than eighty volumes, including some twenty novels. He was in his day the South's most representative man of letters. Because he wrote in the tradition of the historical romance, his characters shape themselves to that tradition—a tradition dominated by Scott and Cooper. In all three novelists the background of their stories is the conflict between two cultures, the new and the old, in the course of which the old goes to the wall. The basic conflict in *The Yemassee* (1835) is between settler and Indian played out against the backdrop of the Revolutionary War.

In his extended travels as a young man visiting his father in the Southwest (Alabama, Georgia, Mississippi, and Louisiana) Simms picked up a first-hand acquaintance with Indian character. His portrait of the Indian is a very faithful one, far more realistic than Cooper's. His knowledge of frontier life and of the Indian-white conflict enabled him to draw an uncommonly

true-to-life picture of Indian life in *The Yemassee*. In his depiction
of the Indian chief Sanutee, his wife Matiwan, and their son
Occonestoga, Simms provides an insight into Indian domestic
life not to be found in the typical American romance of the period.
The noble, courageous, and devoted Matiwan is as worthy a
heroine as the nominal romantic heroine, Bess Mathews. Bess is
a model Victorian heroine, fainting at every possible occasion.
She faints when a rattlesnake attacks her, when Indians storm
her father's house, when the pirate Chorley abducts her, when the
pirate's boat overturns, and when her lover, Gabriel Harrison,
rescues her from drowning. In fact, much of her time seems to be
spent in graceful unconsciousness in some man's arms. In
contrast to Bess's helplessness, Matiwan's definitive action in
crisis is in strong contrast. The climax of the novel occurs when
Matiwan kills her beloved son to save his honor and the honor of
the family and the tribe.

The wife of the Indian trader Granger is likewise a contrast to
Bess Mathews. Mrs. Granger, like most of the "low" characters in
Simms' romances, is scarcely marked as a heroine. Yet she
manifests grim courage and resoluteness and a capacity for self-
sacrifice. But like all women in romances, she knows her place.
When the blockhouse is in imminent danger of falling to Indian
attack, she suggests to Wat Grayson practical means of defense.
"This she did with so much unobtrusive modesty," Simms
assures the reader, "that the worthy woodsman took it for
granted, all the while, that the ideas were properly his own."[3] It is
Mrs. Granger who saves the blockhouse by fending off the Indian
gaining entry through an upper window. In almost sickeningly
realistic detail, Simms describes how Mrs. Granger breaks the
Indian's arm across the sill, how the Indian faints and falls to the
ground, and how thereupon Mrs. Granger faints as the help no
longer needed belatedly arrives. But Mrs. Granger is allowed the
escape hatch of lady-like fainting only once in the course of this
novel.

Simms' other heroines in his seven Revolutionary War
romances conform to the general pattern which the Victorians
deemed proper for a young lady hoping for a husband. Let us look
first at the heroine of one of Simms' most popular novels,

Katharine Walton (1851); and secondly at the two attractive widows over whom Captain Porgy nearly comes a cropper in *Woodcraft* (1852).

Katharine faints constantly and consistently on those occasions when custom demands that she sink into graceful unconsciousness. The villain Balfour, the British commandant in charge of the garrison city of Charleston, bargains for her hand with a promise to save her father from execution. What could the proper kind of heroine do except resist to the last moment, and then sacrifice her "all" as the noose was about to descend on Papa's neck. Of course she must not be permitted to sacrifice her virgin body to this deep-dyed villain. Obviously a *deus ex machina* is needed in a hurry, and help arrives in the form of a determined young schemer, a rival for Balfour's heart, whose interference succeeds in getting Walton hanged, thus freeing Katharine from giving her hand without her heart. Since the Walton plantation is on the outskirts of Charleston, and the amenities of one of the cultural capitals of the South are part of Katharine's life, it is not to be expected that this heroine should manifest characteristics useful to frontier life. Katharine was not bred to cope with Indians or to live in a ramshackle cabin in a lonely clearing.

In *Woodcraft* (1852), the last chronologically in the seven-volume series of the Revolutionary War romances, Simms replied to the emotional anti-slavery sentiment stirred up by Harriet Beecher Stowe's *Uncle Tom's Cabin*, published earlier in the same year. Simms handles his characters in this novel always with sympathy for the South's view of its most tragic problem, slavery. As his protagonist, Simms chooses a true son of the Old South, Captain Porgy, owner of a backlands plantation to which he is coming home after the end of the War. His homecoming presents a dismal scene of rape and devastation resulting from the warring forces of British, loyalists, and partisans.

The two ladies in the life of Captain Porgy are his near-neighbors, the Widow Eveleigh and the Widow Griffin. Both ladies are notable portraitures, and both are suitable enough objects of attention from a gentleman who is himself no longer a spring chicken, though something of a gallant.

The Widow Eveleigh is the strongest character in the book—highly intelligent, refined, product of an old established Southern family of means, liberal-handed, demanding responsibility of her slaves, yet extremely solicitous of their welfare. In this respect, she is Simms' answer to the ineffectual wives of Mrs. Stowe's plantation owners, just as Porgy's black cook Tom (Simms chose the name with Uncle Tom in mind) is limned in strong contrast to the northerner's Uncle Tom. Simms' southern readers felt that he had replied effectively to Mrs. Stowe's propaganda.

The Widow Eveleigh has all the attributes commonly dubbed masculine: she is a competent manager of her plantation, possessed of fortitude and presence of mind in crisis, active in promoting her own affairs, a leader among her neighbors. As a foil to her, the Widow Griffin is dependent upon men to manage her affairs for her. Even the physical contrast between the two women is emphasized—Mrs. Eveleigh being robust, mannish, and bold; Mrs. Griffin feminine, languishing, and modest. Porgy courts them both, but succeeds with neither. Mrs. Eveleigh rejects Porgy's offer of marriage because she recognizes it for what it is: a convenience rather than true love. And when Porgy then directs his interest to Mrs. Griffin, he discovers that she has already engaged herself to another man.

Simms' purpose in this novel—to defend the South's "peculiar institution"—forced him to treat his theme with grace and humor, and the roly-poly Captain Porgy, one of Simms' most accomplished character portrayals, cannot therefore be the kind of matinee idol who inhabits the typical American romance. The two women in his life share the same ambience of humor and irony which surrounds the Captain. A single quotation from this novel (which, interestingly enough, was originally entitled *The Sword and the Distaff)* gives the clue to Simms' characteristic distinction between male and female. Porgy's old crony, Sergeant Millhouse, is advising him how to court the Widow Eveleigh:

This courtin' of woman is just the sawt of business that calls for fast usage. . . . And a woman of ixperance [*i.e.*, a widow] likes a man the better if he gives her no time for long thinking. Courtin' is like storming an inimy's batteries. Women expects naterally to be taken by storm. They likes a good ixcuse for surrenderin'. You must go at it with a rush, sword in hand, looking mighty fierce, and ready to smite and tear everything to splinters; and jist then she drops into your arms and stops the massacree by an honest givin' in....Put on your biggest thunder, cappin, and go to the attack with a shout and a rush, and dang my peepers ef she don't surrender at the first summons.[4]

Sealsfield first arrived in America in the summer of 1823, landing in New Orleans. For close to a year he traveled around the Louisiana Territory, then spent some time in the Mexican-held Texas territory, returning to the Continent for a few months in 1826 and again in 1827 to see about the publication of the books he had been writing. For the better part of six years, 1823 to 1829, he traveled around America, up and down the Mississippi, the Missouri, and the Ohio River, residing for a long period in Kittanning, Pennsylvania, and on a plantation which he had bought on the Red River in Louisiana. His first published work, entitled *The United States of North America As They Are,* was written in 1826 and published in London in June, 1827. This book was quickly followed by *Austria As It Is,* written while Sealsfield was on the Continent between January and June, 1827, and published in December of that year after he had returned to America. A third book, entitled *The Americans As They Are,* was published in London in March, 1828. All appeared anonymously, all sold well, establishing a reputation for the "unknown author," and the first and third demonstrated that author's substantial knowledge of frontier America.

Some of Sealsfield's comments on domestic life in America throw light upon the frontier woman. "The American," he writes,

treats wife and children with the same formality as he treats his neighbor. He is reserved and unimpassioned. His fireside exhibits great decency of conduct. Due to his being much in the public eye, American life is open and everybody knows what everybody else does. The wealthier families live in style, especially in New York. The women act like British peeresses, forgetting that something more is required than a Cashmere shawl, a bonnet trimmed with Brussels lace, and a London watch with a gold chain. Their forenoon is employed in dressing, playing on the pianoforte, and other trifling occupations, with visits from female friends accompanied by a dandy. They talk much scandal. Then they make the rounds of the fashionable shops until three, when they dine. After dinner they ride. Then they attend the Italian opera or the theatre. After that, supper, and a ball in the evening. The ladies are attractive, especially when a foreigner appears sporting a diamond, which brings out the fortune-hunter in them. American ladies have a certain assurance, perhaps because there are not ranks in society; they think themselves the center of a man's attention, and will even claim it as their right.[5]

In a country where so much attention is paid to the fair sex, it is to be expected that proper attention is paid to their education. The female wholly destitute of learning is seldom to be met with in the United States. . . . The wealthy families usually send their daughters to boarding schools [in the East]. The price of the first class is from $400 to $600 a year, for board and lodging, independent of tuition, which amounts to $200 or more. The instruction comprehends writing, reading, mathematics, drawing, painting, geography, astronomy, history, French and Italian, singing, pianoforte, and harp. The prevailing custom of introducing the pupils once or twice a week into the society of good families essentially contributes to the improvement of their manners.[6]

The foregoing comments, of course, pertain to the education offered in the Eastern settlements, but the settlements were rapidly spreading westward, and many a young woman with parents of means living in Cincinnati, St. Louis, and New Orleans, towns which were in the early nineteenth century on the virtual edge of the frontier, was sent East for her schooling. Cooper's heroines Elizabeth Temple and Mabel Dunham are simply two examples among many of young women who, after completing their education in an Eastern boarding school, return to their home on the frontier and to their future there.

Sealsfield's first novel, *Tokeah, or the White Rose* (1829), is a story of Indian natives and white settlers in Louisiana just before Jackson became president. The White Rose when an infant was saved from a scalping party by the Indian chief Tokeah and raised as his daughter. Her parentage is a mystery. This forest maiden at age twenty is thus described: "Soft black eye, rolling languidly, under long silken lashes...light heaving of a delicate bosom, cheek suffused with a rosy tint, the form tender, yet elastic, seeming to breathe love, exquisitely molded forehead, ruby lips delicately formed, over all an air of mild dignity and sweetness, more the air of an ethereal than a human being. Jet black hair fell in long curls round a neck of almost transparent whiteness, a dark green silk dress, closed with a girdle, veiled her form and reached down to a pair of the smallest feet, covered with scarlet moccasins. Round her neck she wore a white silk handkerchief....In her hand she carried a straw bonnet."[7] This young lady is decidedly fruitcake.

When the young English nobleman, Arthur Graham, wounded and in need of soft feminine attention, stumbles into Tokeah's camp, she falls in love with him at first sight. Her influence upon him is described thus: "It seemed as if the delicate being looked up to him with awe, but still with a dignity, a nobleness, which inspired him with sentiment not unlike that with which a pious Catholic regards his favorite saint. It was the visible power which pure, uncontaminated innocence exercises.... 'Arthur,' repeated she, musing; it was as if his name had brought him still nearer to her heart. She drew nigher to him—her hand trembled in his; its soft palpitation thrilled like electricity through his veins. The moon shed her silvery light faintly through the window....'My sweet beautiful Rosa!' exclaimed the youth, overpowered, clasping her to his bosom. She suffered the embrace with yielding tenderness; his lips sought hers—they touched—their breath mingled—it was a delicious moment."[8]

Rather surprisingly, considering the fact that he is an aristocrat and that her parentage is unknown, he marries this flower of the wilderness, to discover, conveniently enough, that she is the long-lost daughter of a Creole nobleman, Don Juan D'Aranzo, who, nineteen years before, had lost his wife and baby in an Indian raid. So although living for the first twenty years of her life with a Creek Indian tribe, the White Rose now takes her place with complete propriety in the aristocratic society of the British West Indies, where Sir Arthur owns a plantation. By some marvelous process she has learned the use of forks and bathtubs.

With both Cooper and Sealsfield, one wonders how intimately they knew Indians—or even women. But after all, this is fiction, and life on the American frontier could be stranger than fiction.

In Sealsfield's narrative, *Nathan the Squatter-Regulator, or the First American in Texas* (1838), Nathan Strong tells the story of his squatter neighbor Asa Nollins and his wife Rachel who, with four others, withstood an attack on their blockhouse by a Spanish military unit brought in by Asa's Creole neighbors who wanted his land. The attackers numbered eighty-eight to Asa's six. In the fracas, Asa was killed, but he took thirty-one of the enemy with him. As Asa prepared for battle, his wife suggested that they take time from priming the rifles to pray. Asa replied: "Ain't no time for praying, woman! I sure like praying with you, but not now. Put down the Good Book, Rachel Nollins. It's *doing* time now."[9] It was Nathan who, with his wife, his sons, and his two daughters, had squatted on a parcel of land on the Red River in the Louisiana Territory, cleared it, built a home, and successfully managed a small plantation. When France sold the Territory to the United States, surveyors came around and told Nathan to move "one house farther along." Nathan, rugged individualist that he was, picked up bag and baggage and moved to the Mexican-owned territory of Texas. There on the wide-open frontier he staked out another homestead, secure from the invasions of the land office, the land sharks, and the sheriff. Nathan always held the notion that land should be as free as air and water. As he put it: "A good rifle and a good woman by your side, and you can tell the devil to go to hell."[10] There is much in Nathan's narrative that has the smack of the real frontier about it. And Rachel Strong is a real frontier type—no moon-June-spoon notions about her.

My last quotation, from *The United States of North America*, gives a fascinating glimpse into the life of the average American farm family on the frontier.

The whole family are in motion from morning til evening. Children from six to eight years of age have their allotted tasks. As soon as school has ended, about mid-February, the sugar-boiling engages their time... The labors of the field follow; while the lads are plowing or sowing, the daughters are breaking flax, or spinning, or weaving.... The boys until sixteen and the girls until fourteen are sent to school during the three winter months. Thereafter, the parents generally let them work and thus provide for themselves. When a lad has worked from two to four years and acquired a sum sufficient for his establishment (rarely over $100), he thinks of marriage. The object of his affections he knows from church meetings or corn huskings. He repairs to her house before supper, which being ended, he approaches his beloved with his hat on. The preliminaries are short. 'Do you like my company?' If the reply is no, the matrimonial candidate moves off with a 'very well.' If the reply be 'I don't know' or 'perhaps,' that is taken as half-consent. If 'Yes, I do,' that is decisive. In the latter case, they sit up during the night by the kitchen fire entertaining each other as best they can.... The following day the clergyman is summoned, or a justice of the peace, and the couple are joined. If the parents are wealthy, a dinner provided; if not, then whisky must suffice. The long and tedious courtships of towns and cities are here [on the frontier] unknown; if the youth be of age, and the girl likewise, they marry without asking leave of anyone, and if not, they frequently do the same.... The portion of the farmer's son is a horse, a plow, and some seeds. The girl's dowry is her bedding, a cow, a few pots and pans, and, if her parents are rich, a bureau, table, and six chairs. With these, and $60 or $70, to which the wife adds $15 to $20 from her savings, the couple begin their husbandry by purchasing 100 acres of woodland at one dollar per acre. With the help of neighbors, they build a cabin and a barn, and in the course of two years they are free from debt, as they are both accustomed to work hard and lead a plain life. Their pastimes are corn-huskings, cabin and barn-raisings, and such frolics.[11]

boys until sixteen and the girls until fourteen are sent to school during the three winter months. Thereafter, the parents generally let them work and thus provide for themselves. When a lad has worked from two to four years and acquired a sum sufficient for his establishment (rarely over $100), he thinks of marriage. The object of his affections he knows from church meetings or corn huskings. He repairs to her house before supper, which being ended, he approaches his beloved with his hat on. The preliminaries are short. 'Do you like my company?' If the reply is no, the matrimonial candidate moves off with a 'very well.' If the reply be 'I don't know' or 'perhaps,' that is taken as half-consent. If 'Yes, I do,' that is decisive. In the latter case, they sit up during the night by the kitchen fire entertaining each other as best they can....The following day the clergyman is summoned, or a justice of the peace, and the couple are joined. If the parents are wealthy, a dinner is provided; if not, then whisky must suffice. The long and tedious courtships of towns and cities are here [on the frontier] unknown; if the youth be of age, and the girl likewise, they marry without asking leave of anyone, and if not, they frequently do the same....The portion of the farmer's son is a horse, a plow, and some seeds. The girl's dowry is her bedding, a cow, a few pots and pans, and, if her parents are rich, a bureau, table, and six chairs. With these, and $60 or $70, to which the wife adds $15 to $20 from her savings, the couple begin their husbandry by purchasing 100 acres of woodland at one dollar per acre.With the help of neighbors, they build a cabin and a barn, and in the course of two years they are free from debt, as they are both accustomed to work hard and lead a plain life. Their pastimes are corn-huskings, cabin and barn-raisings, and such frolics."[11]

This could well be a representative picture of the life of a frontier woman, especially if she had married a man with an itching foot. Young or old, well-born or of lowly birth, amply dowried or poor as a church mouse, she went west beside her man when the settlements became crowded and land prices soared. At the age of eighty, you will remember, Natty Bumppo had traveled from the eastern seaboard across the Mississippi to the western prairies because he could not tolerate in his ears all day the sound of the axes in the clearings. If that seems more fiction than fact, we should call to mind that Daniel Boone at the age of ninety-two emigrated to a spot 300 miles west of the Mississippi River because he felt that his home state of Kentucky, with a population then of ten people to the square mile, had become too crowded. For the frontier woman, the hardest thing to bear must have been the solitude, the fearful loneliness. She did indeed need courage, resourcefulness, and endurance—not to mention faith, hope, and love.

NOTES

[1]Quotations from Cooper. James Fenimore Cooper, *Cooper's Novels,* 32

volumes, the Darley-Townsend edition, 1859-61. Quotations from Simms. William Gilmore Simms, *The Yemassee: A Romance of Carolina* (edited by C. Hugh Holman), Houghton Mifflin Co., 1961; *Katharine Walton* and *Woodcraft* (new and revised edition from the 1854 Redfield printing), A. C. Armstrong & Son, New York, 1882. Quotations from Sealsfield. Charles Sealsfield, *Samtliche Werke,* Hildesheim, Olms Presse, New York, 1972-74, 9 volumes, edited by Karl J. R. Arndt. Vol. II includes *The United States of North America As they Are* (ed. Arndt). Volumes IV and V include *The Indian Chief; or, Tokeah and the White Rose* (ed. John Krumpelmann). Charles Sealsfield, *Die Schonsten Abenteurer—* geschichten von Sealsfield, Ausgewahlt und eingeleitet von Walter von Molo, Munchen, 1918 (includes *Nathan der Squatter-Regulator).*

[2]Fussell, Edwin, *Frontier: American Literature and the American West,* Princeton, 1965, p.4.

[3]*The Yemassee,* p.299.

[4]*Woodcraft,* pp.298-300.

[5]*The United States of North America As They Are,* pp.118-124 *passim.*

[6]*Ibid.,* pp.109-110.

[7]*Tokeah,* Vol. I, pp.137-145 *passim.*

[9]*Nathan,* p.147.

[10]*Ibid.,* p.21.

[11]*The U.S. of North America,* pp.131-34 *passim.*

Making Something of Ourselves

Making Something of Ourselves

On Culture and Politics in the United States

RICHARD M. MERELMAN

UNIVERSITY OF CALIFORNIA PRESS
Berkeley • Los Angeles • London

University of California Press
Berkeley and Los Angeles, California

University of California Press, Ltd.
London, England

©1984 by
The Regents of the University of California

Chapter 5 first appeared in a different
form in *American Political Science Review*
74 (June 1980): 319–32, as
"Democratic Politics and the Culture of American Education."
Used with permission.

Printed in the United States of America

1   2   3   4   5   6   7   8   9

Library of Congress Cataloging in Publication Data

Merelman, Richard M., 1938–
Making something of ourselves.

Includes index.
1. Political participation—United States.
2. Political socialization—United States.   3. United
States—Civilization—1945–   .   I. Title.
JK1764.M47   1984   306'.2'0973   83-5959
ISBN 0-520-04905-5

For Stephen and Diana Merelman

Contents

Preface

I think that the central impulses which animate a piece of scholarship sometimes don't really come clear until the work is over. Certainly that has been true with this book. I now realize that the shadowy notions with which I began some seven years ago come down at the end to one major goal: to advance the study of politics and culture in industrial societies to a position of rough equality with the study of political economy. The latter enterprise has occupied center stage for some time in American political science; I wanted to redress the balance and, in so doing, to find a novel way of talking about culture and politics.

To this end I was simultaneously stimulated and frustrated by recent work on my chosen subject. I found "cultural Marxism" as pursued by Raymond Williams, Gramsci, Habermas, Lukacs, and others immensely suggestive, yet ultimately unsatisfactory. But I found the "political culture" school of political science still less palatable; indeed, political culture seems to me neither sufficiently political nor sufficiently cultural. And so I have tried to find another way, one informed by structural anthropology. Whether this direction—with its conclusion that contemporary American culture neither legitimizes the power of dominant elites nor empowers effective democratic opposition—was the best choice, only the reader can determine.

Yet having chosen this particular direction, I found myself drawn to areas of culture that political scientists rarely investigate: schools, television, architecture, language, advertising. Imagine my exhilaration upon stumbling into these new fields, where my very lack of expertise could easily become the best persuader that I had in fact seen things freshly and aright. The sheer pleasure of analyzing television commercials, for example, may have given me the undoubtedly spurious feeling that I had managed to do something quite good, namely, that I had written a "synthetic" work that made sense out of diverse areas of experience. I have tried to remain conscious of the fact that I am a novice in these fields and that I may not be representing them—nor research on them—fairly. And I hope that the patterns I claim to have discovered are not the perfervid creations of an overstimulated mind, but are instead real and consequential. But the price of trying to cover a great deal of ground, I suppose, is that what one believes he has found may be less a function of the terrain than of the traveler.

I should acknowledge that this book is highly personal; otherwise it would not have taken the form it here assumes. It is, in fact, biased, but in a way, I hope, that turns bias into useful theory and worthwhile debate, rather than into partisan name-calling. And I should also have avoided the latter by offering something for almost every view, but nothing that would fortify strongly any single one.

I am extremely grateful to the National Endowment for the Humanities, whose largesse allowed me the academic year 1977–78 to get this work under way. Additional funding was provided by the University of Wisconsin Graduate School. Given the interdisciplinary character of this book, I found myself particularly dependent on friends who read the manuscript during its several permutations. My appreciation goes to Leon Epstein, Murray Edelman, Kristin Bumiller, Susan Pharr, Francis Schrag, Herbert Kliebard, Robert Lane, and Peter Eisinger. All examined this manuscript with care, and all made insightful comments, most of which I have tried to accommodate gracefully, some of which I reluctantly conceded. I want also to thank Steve Feierman, whose references to useful work in anthropology were beautifully timed, as well as Ivan Preston, who provided me with some helpful guidelines to the literature on advertising. To the many typists who have interpreted my hieroglyphics with (mostly) good humor, I am enormously indebted: Marcia Orbison, Shari Graney, Judy Lehrdal, Renee Gibson, and Norma Lynch. I also want to thank Grant Barnes of the University of California Press, whose encouragement was especially reassuring during a long period of review. Finally, I am grateful to the many graduate students who helped me think through these ideas and whose willingness to serve as guinea pigs contributed markedly to the book's publication. And David McConnell, Steve Manning, and Gary King proved extremely useful critics.

I wanted so very much to write this book for my children, and I can barely contain my joy in being able at long last to dedicate it to them.

Madison, Wisconsin
October 1982

1

THE LIMITS OF CULTURAL VISION
IN AMERICA

THE ARGUMENT

In this book I argue that the United States has evolved a particular cultural pattern—a loosely bounded culture—which, because of its distinctive anthropological character, cannot successfully perform certain vital tasks most traditional cultures
are able to perform. As a result, the loosely bounded culture
prevents Americans from controlling their political and social
destinies, for the world which loose boundedness portrays is
not the world of political and social structures that actually exists. It is, instead, a shadowland, which gives Americans little
real purchase on the massive, hierarchical political and economic structures that dominate their lives. And, thus, the democratic promise of American politics goes unfulfilled. In the
United States structure and culture—the objective world and
the subjective world—diverge, and the political system fails to
bring the two together.

The loosely bounded culture is in part a precipitate of three
failed visions of America that once figured prominently in our
history. We will shortly examine these visions and the raw materials they supply to loose boundedness. In addition, loose
boundedness emerges from typically modern agencies of culture creation: schools, advertising, television. These agencies
refine and reproduce loose boundedness. Indeed, the elevation
of a loosely bounded culture to prominence in America bespeaks a crucial shift in power in the primary agencies of American culture formation—from older institutions of church, state,
and social class to newer institutions of education, the mass media, and advertising. The decline of church, state, and class as

centers of culture in America has created unusually extreme individualism among Americans, an individualism which cannot stand on its own, but instead provides fertile ground for the germination of a loosely bounded culture in schools, the mass media, and advertising. More precisely, the cultural weakness of church, state, and class leaves the individual alone and adrift in an often alien social and political universe. Schools, advertisers, and television networks have elaborated loose boundedness in an attempt to turn individualism into a viable cultural form; but loose boundedness fails in this task. Eventually, loose boundedness constitutes a hindrance to the realization of democratic possibilities in America.

Since this book poses an argument about culture in America, the reader has a right to expect a definition of culture.[1] I intend to provide such a definition later in this chapter, but only after considering the three visions of America whose decline helps provide both the motive for and the elements of loose boundedness. Discussion of these three visions should ultimately make the formal concept of culture more meaningful than would a purely abstract discussion undertaken at this early point. I will pursue the concept of loose boundedness itself more fully in the next chapter.

The problem of cultural disarray is by no means peculiarly American. The United States is only an extreme case of a pattern that to some degree is endemic to all industrialized societies. The most powerful discussion of the problem is in fact that of the French sociologist Emile Durkheim. According to Durkheim, the primary difficulty industrialized societies face is the decline of a *conscience collective*, that set of religiously validated norms which, if violated, called forth immediate punitive sanctions undertaken in the name of society as a whole. Durkheim reasoned that modern societies would eventually develop a substitute for the *conscience collective* in the guise of an ethic of "individualism." As an ethic, individualism would replace adherence to the group with respect for the person.[2] However, the incomplete formation of such an ethic eventually drove Durkheim to recommend artificial expedients for *manufacturing* a new culture, among which were moral education, state intervention in the conduct of industry, and the development of professional codes of conduct.[3]

The perspective on culture which Durkheim originally articulated has influenced such contemporary observers of the American scene as David Reisman,[4] Daniel Bell,[5] Jules Henry,[6] Herbert Marcuse,[7] and Christopher Lasch.[8] My effort is designed to add to this theoretical legacy, although I differ from these writers in paying special attention to the consequences of America's loosely bounded culture for the prospects of American democracy.

As I have suggested, cultural disarray in the form of loose boundedness is especially pronounced in America because of the decline of three coherent cultural visions. The decay of these visions has deposited a residue — the loosely bounded culture — which is the primary subject of this book. In fact, not only has loose boundedness left many ordinary Americans culturally at loose ends, it has also deprived social analysts of explanatory frameworks for understanding what Americans try to make of their new situations. Like their lay counterparts, social scientists have used one or another of these three visions as explanatory frameworks on which to erect their theories of American life. And like their lay counterparts, social scientists find loose boundedness an inadequate substitute for these visions. So this book has a dual purpose: to interpret culture and politics in America, and to introduce a theoretical framework which social scientists may use to fashion new theories of culture and politics in America. Let us turn now to the three visions.

THREE VISIONS OF AMERICA

The Puritan Vision

The earliest coherent vision of America as a cultural entity was that of the Puritan fathers of New England. Consider the mixture of gravity and confidence in John Winthrop's famous assertion: "For wee must Consider that wee shall be as a Citty upon a Hill, the eies of all people are upon us." The sense of mission which Winthrop enunciated descended from a vision of America as a beacon of light to the righteous of all countries. From the outset, therefore, America was a unique religious undertaking, a moral project.

As Winthrop's assertion indicates, the Puritan vision combined a sense of destiny with a sense of obligation to others. Upon what conceptual foundation could so sweeping an assertion of uniqueness be made? The Puritans believed that God had established a covenant between himself and his newly chosen people, the Puritans, who were legatees both in ancestry and in belief of the original convenanted people, the ancient Hebrews.[9] The mission of the Puritans, like that of the Hebrews, was to serve as a saving remnant of saints. The Puritan saints received God's freely given grace, and thereby carried forward his work on earth. The Puritans, therefore, saw themselves and their covenanted country as sharply distinct from other societies.

As a uniquely covenanted people, the Puritans understood that their particular religious path would be hard. God, after all, asked much of them. To make matters more difficult, God dispensed grace freely to only a few souls, and these fortunate few displayed no outward signs of salvation. True saints had to be content with inward convictions of belief and devotion, for they could never be certain of their election. Added to this gnawing insecurity were the temptations to sin presented by the barren shores of New England. The Puritans—isolated from civilized Europe—found themselves simultaneously enticed and repelled by the wilderness and ravaged by the vagaries of a hard climate. No wonder saintly behavior proved difficult to attain; no wonder Puritans found each soul a battleground between good and evil.[10]

The combination of powerful injunctions to faith and strong temptations to sin gave Puritanism a peculiar edginess, helping to account for the Puritan's belief in depravity as man's common legacy since the Fall. This tension between faith and temptation also helps explain the Puritan analogy between each individual's silent struggle with good and evil, on the one hand, and on the other hand, the struggle between God's Chosen People and the sinful majority of the world. No wonder Puritans were ambivalent even about church membership, which they both welcomed as a means of binding together the beleaguered community and rejected as a device for protecting hypocrites and enriching ministers.[11] Finally, this tension illuminates the singular importance of theological debate among the Puritans. Eventually the Puritans' theological sensitivity created vicious sectarian struggles and church fragmentation over such questions as baptism, church membership, witchcraft, and the compatibility between commercial endeavor and Puritan belief.

Yet these theological dilemmas should not obscure the unusual comprehensiveness of the Puritan vision. Puritanism was not solely a religious interpretation of America; it also managed to stimulate the development of reason and science as a means of glorifying God. And it expounded a theocratic political theory, which argued that although the Bible left some areas of life free from religious control, in all matters on which the Bible did pronounce, the state must bow to the church. In this way the Puritan vision welded state and church together as complementary regulators of secular conduct. According to Perry Miller, "The theorists of New England thought of society as a unit, bound together by unviolable ties; they thought of it not as an aggregation of individuals, but as an organism, functioning for a definite purpose, with all parts subordinate to the whole, all contributing a definite share, every person occupying a particular status."[12] True, on occasion church and state did clash, but there existed no legitimate theoretical divide between the two, no constitutional separation of church from state. The secular and the sacred were one.

So firm was the Puritan vision that it actually required the practice of intolerance. The many Puritan acts of religious persecution, most notably the Salem witch-hunts, may offend the modern mind, but as Miller observed, "To allow no dissent from the truth was exactly the reason they had come to America."[13] The Puritans implemented intolerance with "a unique impersonal certainty,"[14] remarkable even in its own time for its coldness and lack of fellow feelings. One consequence of this prac-

tice was that each believer—and nonbeliever—knew exactly
where he or she stood with regard to the dominant values of the
society. The Puritan vision was organic; it bound together individual, church, community, state, and God in a joint enterprise
to which no person could be indifferent and in which every person performed a clearly delineated, necessary function.

Yet even as a host of Puritan thinkers elaborated on their
vision of America, Puritanism had already begun its decline.
The competition of other religious traditions, the rise of commerce, and the British insistence on a policy of religious toleration all limited the scope of the Puritan vision as early as the
1680s, and by the time of the Revolution the strength of the
vision was largely spent, despite infusions of revivalism both
before the Revolution and periodically since then. But the
chief sources of decline were internal to the vision. Because Puritanism had to assure a regular supply of church members, it
had to relax its doctrine of belief as the sole sign of grace.[15]
Because Puritanism couched religious faith in voluntary consent, it laid the groundwork for both a reasoned withdrawal of
consent and the founding of consent on reason not faith. Because Puritanism eventually tried to match inward belief to
outward signs of grace, it found itself forced to try to justify
hypocrisy as serving a positive religious function. Finally, because in the absence of state support Puritanism reluctantly
had to renounce the practice of intolerance, it had to entertain
the possibility that justifications of the state might lie beyond
the Bible, in a purely secular theory. And thus were planted the
seeds that would ultimately flower into the separation of
church from state, and the decline of Puritan domination.

It would be foolish to argue that the Puritan vision ever entirely lost an important place in American life. Our periodic
upsurges of religious fundamentalism owe much to the Puritan doctrine of a direct bond of faith between God and man,
unmediated by an organized church.[16] The recent resurgence
of an evangelical Christianity in America echoes Puritan
themes of salvation, man's inherent depravity, and even theocratic domination. And mainstream Protestant churches re-

tain a large membership. Yet contemporary evidence demonstrates that such central elements of Puritan theology as belief in the divinity of Jesus, in the Second Coming, in the existence of the Devil, in salvation through Christ, and in Christians as God's Chosen People now represent minority views even among churchgoers. Nor are most churches "moral communities" of the sort Durkheim envisaged and New England Puritanism briefly attained.[17] The hold of Puritanism on the American mind has clearly weakened.[18]

But Puritanism left legacies that are important to our argument. It contributed mightily to our political development, for, as Bernard Bailyn points out, the decline of Puritanism in the eighteenth century paved the way for a vision of a revolutionary, democratic America which would carry forth in secular terms the promise of the Puritan covenant.[19] And the Puritan penchant for painting on a broad canvas fed America's conception of its struggle against England as a crisis, not just for Americans, but for progressive political forces everywhere. Just as Puritan America served as a beacon for Christianity throughout the world, so revolutionary America served as a beacon for freedom and liberty throughout the world. Ultimately, Puritanism provided impetus to the "civil religion" in America, that body of beliefs which sees the United States as uniquely embodying God's will on earth.[20] As Puritanism celebrated its heroes with fulsome biographies, so also the civil religion celebrates Washington and Lincoln as America's prophets. Just as God humiliated his chosen church with Indian uprisings, famine, and smallpox, so God scourges his chosen state with civil war, race hatred, and economic depression—all retributions for our sins. "Behind the civil religion at every point lie Biblical archetypes: Exodus, Chosen People, Promised Land, New Jerusalem, Sacrificial Death, and Rebirth."[21] Finally, the liberated, driven, reasoning, consenting self which Puritanism supplied to American politics became the foundation of the vision of democratic America. And this self also became the skeleton of that liberal individualism for which Americans are famous, an individualism which, though strong

enough to sap the strength of succeeding cultural visions, ultimately proved too weak to withstand the modern emergence
of a loosely bounded culture.

The Democratic Vision

The most influential modern cultural vision of the United
States is the democratic vision. By the early nineteenth century,
as Welter shows, the United States had already come to think of
itself as an example of democracy for the world to emulate, as
much a "city on the hill" politically as it had earlier been one
religiously.[22] It was Tocqueville in the 1830s who most vividly
portrayed the emergence of the American democratic vision
when he began *Democracy in America* by observing:

> The emigrants who colonized the shores of America in the begin-
> ning of the seventeenth century somehow separated the demo-
> cratic principle from all the principles that it had to contend with
> in the old communities of Europe and transplanted it alone to the
> New World.[23]

Despite its early nineteenth-century origins, it was the period
from the late nineteenth century to World War II during which
the democratic vision flourished, only to decline after the war, a
decline that became fully visible in the 1960s.

What precisely is this democratic cultural vision? In the case
of Puritanism we have available a self-contained theology me-
ticulously construed by theoreticians and widely diffused to a
public of believers. But in the case of the democratic vision we
must cope with a rhetorical explosion that begins with the
Founding Fathers and continues to ramify through the words
of American politicians into our own time. Inevitably, therefore, the concept of democracy in popular parlance is too complex and variegated to be usable in our discussion. Luckily,
however, we can rely on the work of social scientists who, following World War II, attempted to construct an empirical theory of American democracy. Out of this body of research a cohesive American democratic theory emerged in the 1950s and
held sway among academics throughout much of the 1960s. It

is ironic that this theory captured a period in American politics that had in fact already run its course. What was meant to be a prediction of things to come turned out to be a benediction on things that had been. To put it differently: the mass and academic versions of the democratic vision lacked synchrony, a symptom of growing weakness in the American process of generating and diffusing any coherent cultural visions at all.

A key initial element of this American democratic vision is the idea of tolerance.[24] Tolerance provides opportunities for varying groups to air their differences, and prohibits such differences from entirely disqualifying any group socially. The meaning of tolerance is not that all modes of life are necessarily of equal worth, but that all deserve an equal chance to be heard. Thus, the function of tolerance within the American democratic vision is to establish inclusive, fair political procedures within a context of substantial and substantive group diversity.

Yet tolerance is but one part of a democratic vision. After all, if groups use tolerance only to pursue their conflicts endlessly and fruitlessly, the norm of tolerance would simply promote a debilitating immobility. Tolerance cannot be an end in itself, therefore, but must rather serve to promote a substantive consensus, so that decisions can be made and policies implemented. Accordingly, American political institutions are structured so as to require the formation of a policy consensus before politicians undertake major new initiatives. Equally important, consensus extends to fundamental rules of decision-making, rules for the choice of political leaders, and rules governing the institutional structure of the regime. This consensus is *constitutive* in the original sense of that word, for it embraces the very foundations of the polity, including such values as majority rule, minority rights, popular consent, political equality, and private property.

The theme of trust also occupies an important place in the American democratic vision. The importance of trust emerges particularly clearly in the work of Talcott Parsons, who sees a diffuse social trust in people as a precursor of more specific trust in political leaders. In a sense—and this is Parsons's own analogy—trust in government is like a political bank reserve jealously hoarded by the political system and to be used only when temporary circumstances force politicians to demand much sacrifice from citizens.[25] At such times trust in government functions as a sort of reservoir of political support which sustains the operations of the political system. When decisions adversely affect particular groups—and every decision distresses *some* groups—policy makers can draw upon resources of trust in order to carry on.

While Parsons emphasizes the defensive role of trust, others use trust more assertively. William Gamson, for example, argues that "trust is the creator of collective power,"[26] by which he means that public trust in government permits leaders to extend their influence and turn government toward necessary innovations in policy. Indeed, according to Gamson, groups that trust government actually demand that government take an active role in improving society.[27] Thus, trust creates a symbiosis between public demands for governmental action and the natural disposition of policy makers to expand their range of initiative. It is worth noting how nicely the theme of trust fits the theme of inclusiveness that we earlier identified in our discussion of tolerance. Because trust permits people to join together in collective enterprises, it helps people to see their similarities rather than their differences, thus making inclusiveness an attractive social norm.

To summarize: in the American democratic vision tolerance functions as a dynamic imperative pushing toward the inclusion of diverse social groups, first under procedural guarantees (fair trial, free speech, etc.) and then under substantive policy agreements. Tolerance thus encourages the formation of a substantive political consensus. In turn, the formation of consensus disposes people to trust each other. Once people have no need to fear each other on political grounds, they find it easier to trust each other throughout the entire range of their social contacts. Eventually diffuse social trust gives policy makers a crucial margin of maneuverability in a political system which, like any political system, is inherently riven by scarcities and in which, at any moment, some groups enjoy advantages denied others. The democratic vision thus supplies a happy solution to the problem of political order.

Necessarily, however, there must be elements of competition, conflict, and confrontation in a democratic vision, for otherwise citizens can enjoy little effective choice among alternatives and little incentive to shape their own fates. Any democratic vision assumes political conflict to be normal and tries to invent methods for the peaceful resolution of conflict. The American democratic vision therefore includes elements of conflict as well as elements of consensus, trust, and tolerance.

Robert Dahl's theory of democracy effectively states the argument: within the procedural consensus formed on such rules of the democratic game as popular sovereignty and minority rights there exist divisions on policy issues and political ideology. These differences are represented in the policies that political parties offer to voters. Fortunately, the prevailing context of procedural agreement prevents such differences from "getting out of hand," that is, threatening to upset or paralyze the regime. Indeed, under these conditions policy differences actually contribute to the success of the regime, allowing political leaders to identify areas of policy weakness, adopt curative measures, and gradually build a policy consensus. Outside a context of procedural consensus policy differences could harden into debilitating cleavages, but inside such a consensus they give the polity resilience, adaptive capacity, representative qualities, and the opportunity to better the lives of its people. An additional benefit of substantive policy competition is that it prevents political elites from perpetuating themselves in office as profiteers, rather than as public servants, and thereby causing a horizontal cleavage between elites and masses as damaging as any vertical cleavage between social groups themselves.[28] We can see, I think, why conflict is so important an aspect of the democratic vision.

But just as the Puritan vision of America began to decompose almost as soon as it had been constructed, so the democratic vision of America constructed by academics in the 1950s and 1960s also quickly decomposed. In some respects this vision was simply an inaccurate conception of how American democratic politics operated at *any* time, while in other respects it captured aspects of American democratic politics that had operated from the late nineteenth century to World War II, but that had al-

ready changed by the time the academics got around to codify-
ing the vision. Thus, the vision proved conceptually untrue to
the intricacies of contemporary American politics. Most important from our perspective, like the decomposition of the Puritan
vision, so also did the decomposition of the democratic vision
contribute to a liberal individualism which has proved incapable of withstanding the loosely bounded culture.

A primary conceptual problem of the democratic vision re-
sided in the connection between democratic politics and
American social structure. Take the element of trust, for example. As Geraint Parry observes, the democratic vision assumed
that political trust reflects an enduring social trust that is
widely diffused throughout the American public. However, as
Parry points out, the reasoning linking the two realms is by no
means compelling, and, on the empirical side, the connection
between political and social trust remains obscure.[29]

Despite appearances, the problem is not merely a bit of arid
conceptual hairsplitting. A political system founded on a reservoir of social trust would perhaps possess roots deep enough to
create the kind of cultural solidarity that industrialized societies so evidently lack. But a political system that can generate
trust only from its own internal operations lacks deep cultural
roots, and may find itself easily shaken when political and economic debacles, such as the Vietnam War or persistent inflation, stem the flow of political support. It is not surprising,
therefore, to find recent evidence that the public's trust in government has sharply declined in recent years,[30] an indication of
the decline of the democratic vision.

Other major aspects of the vision proved simply to be
figments of theorists' imaginations rather than secure elements of a democratic faith deeply embedded in the public
mind. For example, as early as the 1950s Prothro and Grigg
detected a large and embarrassing gap between the public's abstract professions of tolerance and its often intolerant practices.[31] And apparent advances in tolerance through the sixties
and seventies prove illusory when allowance is made for attitudes toward the political right as opposed to the left. Indeed,
as Sullivan and his associates note, American tolerance seems

always to be low for whichever groups are currently seen as controversial.[32] Thus, the practice of tolerance does not appear strong enough either to hold a political system together or to support fruitful policy debate. Americans therefore face occasionally the unpalatable choice of either excluding controversial issues from political debate entirely (thereby limiting the choices available to the public) or risking the escalation of policy conflict into uncontrolled cleavage. In either case, stable, controlled, group-based debate on policy proves elusive, and the question of whether tolerance ever lived up to its role in the American democratic vision remains open.

Research on consensus has also proven troublesome for the democratic vision. Again the problem is partly conceptual, for "consensus" is not a unitary phenomenon.[33] Worse yet, what should we use as an acceptable index of consensus? If we could tie any single measure of public opinion to concerted political action, the problem would solve itself, but apparently no such relationship exists. Therefore, the idea of consensus often provides an unreliable guide to political action.

The consensus argument also suffers from empirical problems. Using a 75 percent level of public agreement as a reasonable measure of the concept, Devine detects a strong consensus on such elements of the American political process as the values of popular rule, elections, the "rule of law," legislative predominance in policy-making, federalism, and a decentralized party system.[34] But Michael Mann reports a widespread *dissensus* on beliefs about the American opportunity structure, the harmoniousness of society, the extent to which ordinary people can influence political decisions, and the desirability of equality.[35] Lacking a conception of how democracy without *full* consensus might function, the democratic vision is perforce limited in view of such contradictory evidence.

The stratified pattern of consensus is also disturbing. Simply put, upper-status Americans share more consensually in the democratic vision than do lower-status Americans. More upper- than lower-status Americans take part in politics, extend tolerance readily, find themselves wedded to the procedural rules of the democratic game, and feel efficacious and trust-

ing.[36] American consensus is thus class-based, a point that encourages critics to argue that the democratic vision is, in reality, nothing but an ideological facade behind which a dominant
class hides its power. Upper-status support is undoubtedly a
crucial factor in keeping the democratic vision alive, for the
well-off possess enough power at least to sustain, if not to advance, the vision. But a political vision can hardly claim to be
entirely democratic if so many of the least fortunate members
of the community reject it.

As with the concept of tolerance, so with that of consensus:
we cannot be certain of the status of consensus throughout the
period from the late nineteenth century to World War II. The
findings do suggest, however, that during that period neither
consensus nor tolerance operated in the ways later academic
codifiers of the vision imagined.

Finally, the place of policy debate in the democratic vision
also appears dubious in light of contemporary research and
current political trends. For example, the vision announces a
central role for political parties in organizing and packaging
such debate. Yet in recent years the party system has shown
signs of decay and "dealignment."[37] The lines of cleavage between Republicans and Democrats have become unclear, and
large numbers of voters have chosen to opt out of the party
system entirely, by not voting at all, by voting unstably, or by
splitting their tickets. The proportion of the public that reports
itself strongly partisan within the bounds of the democratic
vision has fallen.[38] It is possible that the disaggregation of the
party system may be a prelude to party realignment (as the
Reagan administration clearly hopes), but at the moment all we
can be sure of is that dealignment significantly inhibits the
democratic vision's aspirations toward cohesive policy alternatives for public choice.

Partisan dealignment does not necessarily indicate public
inattentiveness or disinterest in political issues, however. Indeed, "issue awareness" may well have increased in recent
years;[39] the problem for the democratic vision is that increased
awareness of issues does not attach itself stably to party programs. Instead, issue awareness—like party dealignment—

contributes to political fragmentation rather than to political coherence. A democratic vision that cannot produce methods of organizing the public effectively through issue coalitions or political parties leaves the individual citizen radically free to pursue his own ends in or out of politics. Again, therefore, just as the decline of the Puritan vision produced a dynamic but undirected American self to find its own way in religion, so the decline of the democratic vision creates a dynamic but undirected political self. Together the decay of the two visions forces the individual to try to create his *own* culture. The result of this effort is loose boundedness, which has become the characteristic American connection between politics and culture in our own time.

To summarize: during the 1950s and early 1960s American academics described an American democratic vision. This vision appears partially to have operated at the mass level from the late nineteenth to the mid twentieth century; its primary content consisted of partisan competition and trust in government. But other aspects of the vision appear from contemporary evidence to have been either weak or entirely absent from the outset; these include tolerance and consensus. Whatever the strength of the vision prior to the 1960s, we can say with some confidence that the democratic vision appears to have declined following World War II, and that it no longer seems to propel American politics. And so the individual has escaped from the vision, but only to fall prey to the loosely bounded culture.

The Class Vision

According to Arthur Marwick, "However confused the image, the unabashed resort to the language of class distinguishes American books, newspapers, and television programs in the late sixties from those of the previous decade."[40] It is not hard to understand why a modern class vision of America might emerge to take the place of the democratic and Puritan visions of America, particularly in light of the American debacle in Vietnam and domestic discord in American cities, a discord interpretable in class as well as racial terms.[41] But as it slowly emerged during the Great Depression and came to fruition in the 1970s, the class vision remained primarily an academic rather than a popular conception of American life. The class vision, even more than the democratic vision, fell prey to the ravages of loose boundedness. Indeed, the strength and richness of the academic statement of the vision varied in exactly inverse proportion to the vision's weakness among the people it purported to describe. By the late 1970s loose boundedness had fragmented *any* coherent visions of America.

Nevertheless, the class vision did represent a brave attempt to locate American life on a scale of tension somewhere between the brittle religious dogmatism of the Puritan image, on the one hand, and the relaxed consensualism of the democratic vision, on the other. The class vision was our last attempt to discover and invigorate a pattern of socially regulated group conflict endemic to American life, a pattern of conflict that would give some purpose to the American enterprise.

In its academic manifestations the modern class vision of America is a compound of orthodox Marxist ideas and neo-Marxist modifications. The orthodox Marxist element of the vision is its assertion of inherent antagonism alienating workers from capitalists, an antagonism that cannot but increase as capitalism encounters one economic crisis after another, of which the current "stagflation" and unemployment afflicting the American economy are the most notable examples. The vision then argues that opposed class interests lead to divergent class interpretations of American life—that exploitation by a dominant capitalist class eventually congeals the diffuse resentment of the working class into a coordinated ideological rejection of the American enterprise. In turn, this rejection is reproduced and reinforced by class-based socialization of children and by class-based differences in attitudes toward opportunity and well-being in America.[42]

The first question to be asked, therefore, is whether the objective inequalities that American capitalism undoubtedly generates also create class-based visions of America. Few people any longer doubt either that our economic inequalities are real and enduring or that it is possible to understand such inequalities in class terms. But do people really interpret these inequalities by constructing class visions?

It is tempting to answer this question affirmatively. Certainly class differences in key aspects of thinking are known to exist. Thus, for example, working-class children have lower educational expectations than middle-class children, develop more slowly cognitively, and have less confidence in their ability to thrive in school.[43] Indeed, class differences extend even to language patterns.[44] But these forms of class-based thinking do not seem to flower into a public vision of class per se; instead, they remain confined mainly to evaluations of personal rather than social or political life. Class differences in levels of *personal* efficacy, for example, exceed by factors of two and three times analogous class differences in *political* efficacy.[45] And awareness of class itself occupies a place of marginal importance for most people, especially when compared with race awareness.[46] Finally, just as the middle class has adopted the democratic vision more fully than working-class or poor people, so also (and paradoxically) is the middle class more likely to actually manifest class consciousness.[47] Class awareness is itself stratified, in other words.

It is difficult to sustain a thesis of class-based political visions in America when we look at key behavioral indicators. Paul Abramson shows that since the New Deal class polarization in voting has steadily declined, a decline only temporarily broken by particular elections, such as that of 1976.[48] The same thing holds true for partisan affiliation.[49]

But voting and partisanship are only sporadically of political importance, and may therefore be poor indicators of a class-based political vision. A more important test involves class-based and class-relevant political attitudes across a wide spectrum of issues. Here again the evidence does not reveal the existence of a class vision at the popular level. Richard Hamilton locates the main line of cleavage in American political attitudes between a small upper middle class and the bulk of lower-middle and working-class persons—a line of cleavage that does not fit the class vision.[50] And while class apparently does produce quite divergent views of the political system's responsiveness, people of all classes continue to share common aspirations for their children and to evaluate class position and "respectability" in similar ways.[51] Indeed, even during the Great Depression, when economic deprivation was higher than it ever has been in modern American history, the poor, the working class, and the unemployed resolutely declined to develop a distinctive political vision for themselves.[52] If anything, in fact, a growing number of Americans identify themselves as middle class, rather than as workers.[53]

Understandably, given this body of discouraging data, the academic version of the class vision has had to pursue a new course. It has found that course by modifying traditional Marxist theory in order to develop the concept of false consciousness. The theory of false consciousness proposes that classes remain as opposed objectively to each other today as they ever were; however, recent technological innovations in capitalism conceal class antagonisms. The argument asserts that the educational, commercial, and media revolutions of the twentieth century have armed capitalists with ever more effective means of influencing the consciousness of workers. The ideology of capitalism now dominates working-class life, appearing to the exploited not as a contestable rationalization of class domination, but rather as a "neutral" scientific description of reality which people of all classes must naturally accept. Workers thus internalize ideas that are opposed to their deepest interest.[54] It is false consciousness which prevents the economic antagonisms of capitalism from expressing themselves clearly in a class vision of American life.

We cannot ignore several weaknesses in this argument. Initially, of course, the theory of false consciousness is self-validating. Obviously, if sharp value differences dividing social classes should perchance emerge, the class vision appears to be vindicated, but if—as is typically the case—such differences do not emerge, their absence can be explained away as "capitalist domination." Thus, the argument has it both ways; put more negatively, in neither condition can a convincing argument for or against the class vision be adduced. The theory of false consciousness admits of no contradictory evidence.

Even if we accept the idea of false consciousness, we need not see the phenomenon as peculiar to capitalism, nor as convincing evidence of the assertions of a class vision. As John Diggins has pointed out, anthropologists have long identified processes by which those with power attempt to influence the ideas of those without power, even in traditional societies.[55] False consciousness therefore precedes capitalism, and apparently need not depend on a capitalist-class base of political power. In short, the existence of false consciousness may not be seen as evidence either for the existence of class domination or for such a class's effective suppression of class consciousness.

The class vision also exaggerates the degree of value homogeneity among capitalist agents of ideological formation. The "bad guys" are just not uniformly bad. In fact, such agents regularly disseminate ideas that are hostile to their own interests. As we will see, this is especially true of advertising and the mass media.

Moreover, even when pro-capitalist values do dominate a medium, they are not necessarily effective. Evidence suggests, for example, that many working-class children resist tenaciously the messages that schools attempt to convey,[56] and many working-class adults reject the tempting morsels of middle-class culture which the mass media dangle before them.[57] Or consider the reactions of blacks, who steadfastly opposed the mass media's interpretation of urban riots in the 1960s. Indeed, television's depictions of the riots actually seemed to stimulate or legitimize participation of blacks in riots, an odd outcome for a medium supposedly dedicated to protecting the status quo; the more time people spent viewing the riots on television the more positively disposed they themselves became to rioting.[58]

The theory of false consciousness also overlooks an incongruity between the production of ideas and the content of ideas. The theory asserts that ideas "reflect" social structure, by which it means that ideas mirror the economic realities from which they presumably spring. But this assertion is clearly dubious with respect to the educational, advertising, and mass media organizations supposedly responsible for the diffusion of capitalist ideology. Each of those institutions differs mark-

edly from the others in organizational and economic foundations. Yet each diffuses similar messages. Might this fact not
suggest that ideas are somewhat independent of the economic
bases which class theorists believe responsible for producing
them? Let me go further: I believe that the loosely bounded
culture, which is the dominant set of ideas in advertising, television entertainment, and the schools, actually subordinates the
structural and economic differences among these institutions.
In sum, ideological "superstructure" occupies a status at least
equal to that of economic "base."

Finally, the theory of false consciousness overlooks the possibility that certain older American attitudes—rather than
changed economic or political circumstances—may help explain the weakness of class consciousness in America. As Michael Lewis points out, Americans have long espoused an "individual as central" psychology, which holds the self responsible
for success or failure and which resists arguments that attempt
to subordinate the self to impersonal social forces such as class.[59]
The "individual as central" psychology is as much a legacy of
failed Puritan and democratic visions as it is of contemporary
economic forces. Unfortunately, this psychology leaves the individual without stable group attachments and identifications
other than those of his own creation. It therefore provides the
conditions for America's loosely bounded culture, a culture
which dominant contemporary agencies of culture formation—
schools, television, advertising—strongly reinforce, but cannot
by themselves be charged with having created. And it is this culture which effectively prevented the class vision from ever having proceeded very far beyond the minds of its academic codifiers between the 1930s and our own time. Thus, the class
vision represented little more than the pious hopes of intellectuals searching for a coherent culture to stem the growth of loose
boundedness. But hope is no substitute for cultural rootedness.

American Visions as Cultural Codes

The three visions of America we have discussed share certain characteristics. Each, for example, portrays the individual

as securely related to society, and each provides a clear identity for its protagonists. The Puritan believer could oppose himself sharply to nonbelievers; the Puritan knew where he stood theologically and socially. The democrat can oppose himself sharply to nondemocrats, and leftists can differentiate themselves clearly from rightists. Within the class vision the subordinate class stands clearly opposed by economic position and ideology to a dominant exploiting class. All three visions therefore define coherently the basic identities of those who embrace them, while each vision affords a broad but sensitive lens through which adherents can interpret their society.

Each vision also stimulates the actions of certain organized, overarching groups or institutions. Puritanism demands a militant church. Democracy demands that voluntary organizations such as the American Civil Liberties Union protect basic liberties, and that cohesive political parties articulate clearly the left-to-right political spectrum which energizes public choice. The class vision encourages unions, political parties, and social movements to express and promote the basic interests of each class. Thus, each vision stitches individual identity tightly together with group membership and mass action.

Finally, each vision describes mechanisms whereby groups and individuals working together can gain control over the structure of power in society. Each portrays strong groups possessed of a firm hold on their members as becoming effective levers of power which help people to realize their destinies. Each vision implicitly recognizes that the individual alone, bereft of group identifications and unsure of ideological commitment, can be no match for large bureaucracies, corporations, and governments. Therefore, each vision draws individual, group, and social structure together in an articulated ensemble capable of controlling those massive organizations which threaten to oppress the public. It follows, then, that the weakness of these visions as comprehensive guides to contemporary American life deprives the public of tools that might protect them against concentrated, organized power structures. And these abound in the corporation and the state, each massively hierarchical and each bureaucratically impersonal.

The ultimate appeal of these visions lies in the fact that each is a kind of cultural blueprint or a suggestive road map to American society. They exemplify what structural anthropologists call cultural codes, systems of meaning akin to language which schematize the main features of a given society.[60] It follows then that the fragmentation and decline of these visions deprives Americans of the cultural formulae that might allow them to exert a greater measure of control over their futures. In response, Americans have found it necessary to fall back on the loosely bounded culture. If my formulation of this argument seems a little unusual, it is because I refuse to see culture simply as a shackle that society forces on individuals. The notion of culture as solely a matter of restraint is itself a typical example of how we have come to think under the influence of loose boundedness. I prefer to see culture also as a set of ideas which may empower the individual *against* social constraints. Cultural codes are as often indispensable stimulants as they are unjust and uncomfortable constrictions.

In order to appreciate fully how these visions function as cultural codes, we must investigate briefly the theory of culture that structural anthropologists have developed. As I have suggested, this theory asserts that cultures are composed of codes of meaning analogous to those the linguist deciphers in the analysis of language. Recurrent social practices appear as the content of the code. Consider the practice of totemism, for example, which is best understood as a practice that arranges social and natural phenomena in an homologous relationship to each other. "Totemism is but one specialized variety of universal human activity, the classification of social phenomena by non-social means."[61] Totemism aligns the classification of animals with the classification of social structure and thereby joins the natural and social worlds together symmetrically. Initially, therefore, like any language, cultural codes formally distribute the content of reality into a restricted number of equivalent classifications.

How do cultural codes accomplish the formal construction of equivalent-content classes? How is one classification formally related to another? Indeed, how do we know that we "see" a class at all? At its most compact, the process of cultural classification depends on the construction of "a pattern of opposed dualities."[62] We know where things fit in any cultural code only by opposing classifications to each other—Puritans vs. nonbelievers; democrats vs. nondemocrats; Republicans vs. Democrats; liberals vs. conservatives; workers vs. capitalists. A classificatory system thus appears when we group together in one classification all those things which bear a relationship of opposition to things in a contrasting classification. Thus, the three defining characteristics of any cultural code are: (1) two or more classificatory sets, each composed of items formally identical to each other; (2) a pattern of tension, contrast, or opposition between the sets; (3) some logical, psychological, or physical boundary separating opposed sets.

The persistence of classifications in a cultural code depends almost entirely on the strength of the boundaries separating opposed sets. The strength of these boundaries may be protected in several ways. One method, common in traditional cultures, involves perceptions of danger, magic, or sacredness. Consider the subject of time, for example. According to Edmund Leach, all cultural codes divide time into periods when we occupy a *settled* status and periods when we are *unsettled* because we cross cultural boundaries into a new time zone.[63] During transitions we exist in a kind of limbo which suspends our normal sense of ourselves and therefore leaves us vulnerable to fear and anxiety. All time codes attempt to control and regularize these periods of boundary crossing, not only to reduce the individual's sense of transitional insecurity, but also to maintain the important social distinction between different time statuses. Leach describes the time codes of culture as including the following metaphorical equivalencies: normal/abnormal::time-bound/timeless::clear-cut categories/ambiguous categories::at the center/at the edge::secular/sacred. "A boundary separates two zones of social space time which are normal, time-bound, clear-cut, central, secular, but the special markers which actually serve as boundaries are themselves *abnormal, timeless, ambiguous, at the edge, sacred.*"[64] Breaching the boundaries of normal time segments therefore forces us to traverse an abnormal, sacred time zone in which anything can happen because the normal rules associated with "stable" time do not exist. It should not be surprising, then, that science fiction writers so often remove their protagonists from normal time in order to make them vulnerable to new and unexpected events "in the fourth dimension." Nor should it be surprising why dreams, which defy our waking sense of time, should have been a source of anxiety in so many societies.

Of course, only a few people at a time participate in any particular instance of passage from one status to another. Occasionally, however, boundary ambiguities force themselves on an entire community and may thus threaten the entire cultural code. Mass migrations and mass immigration are cases in point. What happens under such conditions? How does the cultural code survive? Mary Douglas argues that societies utilize beliefs about pollution and other moral strictures to help manage large-scale, unavoidable, conceptual ambiguities. Consider the concept of "dirt," for example. Douglas argues that, while "the discovery of pathenogenic organisms is recent . . . the idea of dirt antedates the idea of pathenogenicity."[65] It follows, therefore, that the concept of dirt cannot be understood solely as a matter of hygiene. Douglas explains that dirt is "matter out of place. . . . It implies two conditions: a set of ordered relations and a contravention of that order. Dirt then is never a unique, isolated event. Where there is dirt there is system."[66] And, also, where there is dirt there is moral opprobrium. The concept of dirt as a pollutant becomes meaningless outside of a system of moralized cultural order, an order protected and reinforced by our disposition to stigmatize dirty people and dirty work. Therefore, invoking pollution beliefs directly protects the boundaries of cultural classifications.

So far so good, but haven't we ignored one puzzling aspect of cultural codes? Leach writes: "Individuals do not live in society as isolated individuals with clear-cut boundaries; they exist as individuals interconnected in a network of relations of power and domination. . . . The logical paradox is that (1) I can only be completely sure of what I am if I cleanse myself of all boundary dirt, but (2) a completely clear 'I' with no boundary dirt would have no interfaced relations with the outside world or with other individuals. Such an 'I' would be free from the domination of others, but would in turn be wholly impotent."[67]

In short, we cannot live as social beings without continually torturing the logic of our cultural codes by flirting with and ultimately transgressing the boundaries that divide us from others and that give our cognitive world meaning. We thus put our codes and ourselves at risk by straying beyond culturally accepted boundaries. How do we manage this dilemma?

The solution to this problem, according to Lévi-Strauss and Victor Turner, is that reconciliation myths emerge which symbolically reduce the dichotomized tensions inherent in all cultural codes.[68] Consider the common mythological device that joins binary opposites together in the pursuit of some larger, more important cause. The nonbeliever becomes a necessary part of the Puritan code, because without him the believer could not test his saintliness. Republicans and Democrats, left and right, become necessary to teach other if people are to be allowed to search out all political paths. Even capitalists become necessary in order to produce the machinery and productivity an eventually egalitarian society will require. In the Puritan code, believer and nonbeliever are the conjoined instruments of God. In the democratic vision, partisans serve the public interest. In the class vision, conflict between dominant and subordinate classes serves the march of history toward a widening of human freedom for all. Thus, in summary, a cultural vision is a code of meaning containing a bounded system of dichotomized, opposed social classifications; a depiction of individual, group, and society united organically; mechanisms of individual influence over economic and political structures; and a mythological aim or mission to which all segments of society—even those opposed to each other—make indispensable contributions.

The contemporary weakness of Puritan, class, and democratic visions in America leaves us without a cultural code capable of empowering the individual against modern hierarchies of power. Of course, there do exist other dualisms in the United States which help us organize our ·perceptions: city life vs. country life; white Anglo-Protestants vs. Catholics; North vs. South; and, most crucially, blacks vs. whites. Historically, these classifications have embodied rich cultural connotations. Nevertheless, major tendencies in American life have increasingly delegitimized these dualisms, just as they have dismembered our three primary cultural codes. Racial desegregation delegitimizes racial classifications; suburbanization and gentrification of cities blur the city-country divide; industrialization of the South and the nationalization of Southern art forms such as country music reduce North-South tensions; intermarriage, ecumenism, and the acceptance of Catholic political leaders defuses Protestant-Catholic tensions. As with the full-blown cultural visions we have considered, so also with these more partial dualisms: the raw materials of traditional cultural codes must fight to survive in America.

Americans are now forced to make something of themselves without much help from traditional cultural codes. The product of their efforts is the loosely bounded culture, which dominates contemporary institutions of culture formation in America. Let us now turn to that subject.

2

THE LOOSELY BOUNDED FABRIC
OF AMERICAN CULTURE

The task of this chapter is to describe American culture as loosely bounded, to explore the differences between loose boundedness and the three cultural visions we have just examined, to speculate about several main contributors to American loose boundedness, and to provide an historical "periodization" of loose boundedness. I will then illustrate loose boundedness by reference to American English and American architecture, two important forms of culture creation and transmission.

To accomplish this task let us return briefly to theories of culture in anthropology, and let us begin with an early anthropological theory relevant to our purposes: that which is contained in Durkheim and Mauss's *Primitive Classification.*[1] Durkheim and Mauss argue that culture is a unified cognitive whole which represents the social structure as a basic symbolic model or ideational template. As cognitive creations, cultures display formal correspondence between objective social classifications and those same classifications as subjectively experienced. The principle of correspondence even embraces scientific categories and systems of logic, for, as Needham puts it, "The first logical categories were social categories."[2] Durkheim and Mauss use the example of totemism to illustrate how cultures formally align different social classifications cognitively. In addition, totemism bridges the gap between the individual and the group, because the totem animal represents both the group and the individual. In totemistic societies, therefore, "individualism" or "egoism" is restrained by group identity.[3]

Latter-day followers of Durkheim and Mauss have expanded their masters' homology or correspondence argument in fieldwork. A good example of such an effort is Tambiah's study of Thai village culture. Tambiah argues that Thai marriage rules, cooking prescriptions, animal classifications, and residential architecture together express a small number of common underlying cultural themes. As Tambiah puts it, "There is . . . a close correspondence between the marriage and sex rules pertaining to the human series and the house categories which say the same thing in terms of living space and spatial distance. The house and the kin categories are linked in turn to an animal series."[4] The formal correspondence of these substantively different realms assures the reproduction of culture, for no matter where a person looks, he or she gets the same formal message. Repetition assures that eventually the message will be transmitted effectively. As a result, there is little deviance, disharmony, or conflict in Thai villages. The principle of cultural correspondence or homology encourages social stability.

Lévi-Strauss's development of structural anthropology constitutes an effort to reformulate and reconsider Durkheim and Mauss's theory of culture. Lévi-Strauss too begins by studying totemism, but he claims that totemism is an expression not of the cognitive *unity* of culture, but rather of culture's *partitioning* of society into a collection of opposed social segments.[5] Totemic systems are representations of social polarities which, paradoxically enough, resemble each other formally. In a totemic system, "the natural species are classed in pairs of opposites, and this is possible only on condition that the species chosen have in common at least one characteristic which permits them to be compared."[6] Thus, to Lévi-Strauss culture accomplishes its task of uniting people, not by presenting formal identities underlying different symbolic realms, as in Durkheim and Mauss, but only by presenting complementary, opposed symbolic classifications organized into formally identical binary sets.

Lévi-Strauss's argument has influenced many recent anthropological formulations. For example, Victor Turner claims that a primary opposition which holds some cultures together is the conflict between ideas of community and ideas of hierarchy, two richly symbolic classes of meaning which Turner believes alternate in any social group.[7] Transformations of community into hierarchy, and hierarchy into community, occur in part by the interposition of liminal rituals and liminal persons between the two types of action. Liminality functions as a symbolic switch, first cuing the transition from one cognitive classification to the other and then signaling the accomplished transformation of hierarchical into communal patterns of action. Turner is bold enough to call alternation between the two modes of meaning and action "dialectical," and he argues that

> no society can function adequately without the dialectic. Exaggeration of structure may well lead to pathological manifestations of communitas, while in certain religious or political movements of the leveling type, communitas may be speedily followed by despotism, over-bureaucratization, or other modes of structural rigidification. . . . Communitas cannot stand alone if the material and organizational needs of human beings are to be adequately met.[8]

To those who espouse this "polarity" conception of culture, patterned, reproduced tension permeates all societies and all bodies of symbolism. Inevitably, the polarity takes on an evaluative quality. Robert Hertz argues, for example, that there exists constant tension between the demonic, inferior, evil qualities in society, which people often symbolize by left-handedness, and the sacred, superior, propitious qualities in society, which people commonly associate with right-handedness.[9] And Needham supplies a number of descriptive studies which seem to substantiate Hertz's insight.[10]

The cultural representation of society in terms of a small number of homologous, paired, opposing classifications can obviously develop most fruitfully when a few social groups embrace and shape the total lives of their members. Under such conditions group membership automatically erects a sharp boundary between members and nonmembers. Churches, political parties, mass movements, ethnic groups, unions, neighborhoods, and occupations can all provide the basis of firmly embedded cultural codes. To be a strong Catholic, for example, is to go to mass regularly, to live in a Catholic neighborhood, to marry a Catholic, to read Catholic literature, to have mainly Catholic friends, to enjoy Catholic art, and so on. In this case, the polarity between Catholic and non-Catholic draws allied social categories together.

The contemporary weakness of the Puritan, democratic, and class visions of America has released large numbers of Americans from comprehensive group identifications and from firm cultural moorings. The liberated individual, not the social group, must therefore become the basic cultural unit. Although many people continue to be members of and identify with groups, they believe their group identities to be matters of individual choice, which can be changed without stigma. Group membership thus becomes voluntary, contingent, and fluid, not "given," fixed, and rigid.[11]

Individuals attempting to make sense of their social worlds without the secure guidelines of comprehensive, enduring group identities and memberships are the building blocks of a loosely bounded culture. These individuals face a peculiar dilemma, for, in the absence of group cues, they cannot assume that any group-based rules of social intercourse or value preferences govern their encounters with each other. Group characteristics no longer inform people about what to expect of others, what they can legitimately require of another, what to fear about each other, how far they can advance with another, or how they can be protected from each other. Each new person is "special," and each such person must be met anew. It follows, therefore, that the weakness of group identifications forces each person to make a concerted effort to get to know others whom he encounters, and to attempt hastily to "make friends." Lacking group-based guidelines about what to expect from other people, the individual reacts by loosening the boundaries between himself and others in an attempt to establish a personal relationship that will at least neutralize danger and, if all goes well, will endure and satisfy. Thus, paradoxically enough, friendship becomes most desirable in a society when loose boundaries between individuals place so heavy a burden of insecurity on all relationships as to make real friendship most elusive. We therefore crave most what we find increasingly difficult to obtain.

People may react in two ways to the loosening of boundaries between themselves and others. I have already described the normatively approved response: for people to narrow the distance between themselves and others, and, in so doing, to believe in a world in which there exists easy, open, trusting intercourse between the most casual acquaintances, and where strong emotional bonds can be expected to emerge quickly. A darker aspect of this response is the realization that, should circumstances dictate, personal bonds can easily unravel, and new friends and partners must be sought out. Thus, though a loosely bounded culture opens persons to each other, it also makes relationships fragile as people "hedge their bets." In the United States recent emphasis on the need to "share" experience and ideas—with its many connotations of egalitarian, quickly formed, if often superficial relationships—captures well this normatively approved form of loose boundedness.

A normatively disapproved response to loose boundedness also emerges, however, because group boundaries prove too weak to protect vulnerable individuals from people they would rather avoid. To the strong of heart, to the self-confident, to the gregarious, loose boundedness provides a pleasurably diverse range of social contacts, but to the fainthearted, the shy, the introverted, loose boundedness becomes a nightmare of exploitation by heartless others. Americans capture this aspect of loose boundedness in demands for "one's own space." And thus in loosely bounded cultures, while some people crave their own "space," other people take every opportunity to "share" their experiences with sympathetic friends. Still others want both space and sharing, which become the basic classifications of a loosely bounded cultural code.

The American press toward quickly formed, superficial relationships creates an incentive among individuals to play down or obscure their distinctiveness. Both boundary ambiguity and the resulting need for individuals to protect themselves from others contribute to the blurring of intellectual and social distinctions. The absence of convergent group-based classifica-

tions also obscures distinctions among people. This is so because it becomes impossible to assume anything about what
others believe and how they will act from knowing any particular thing about them. For example, a Catholic resident of a
Protestant neighborhood may have mainly Jewish friends. Religious, friendship, and residential codes thus diverge from
each other, and this divergence forces us to assume little about
the character of the people we meet.[12] The nonconvergence of
group classifications among individuals reinforces the ambiguity of meanings and relationships and makes it doubly important for us to believe that "people are people" and then to find
out as much about the others with whom we must deal as rapidly as we possibly can. In a loosely bounded culture a little
information does not go a long way. Therefore, the dominant
personal dynamic is inevitably intrusive; it becomes foolhardy
to respect any particular boundaries at all, for all boundaries
may deceive.

Myth is a major casualty of the loosely bounded culture.
Myths flourish when groups are sharply polarized along convergent cultural axes. Under these conditions myths serve to reconcile symbolically the potentially dangerous group oppositions
which threaten to rip society apart. But mythology becomes
shallow in loosely bounded cultures, for the multitudinous anxieties attendant upon individual relationships in such cultures
can never be reduced to a few sharply defined group polarities.
Loosely bounded cultures produce, therefore, a sensibility of individual sentiment, rather than a mythology of group-based
ideological, philosophical, and religious traditions. The only really compelling myths in loosely bounded cultures picture "individual" against "society"—each equally abstract and feature-
less—rather than specific churches, classes, or parties arrayed
against each other. Personal "styles of life," as opposed to group
customs, become central elements of such a sensibility. The idea
of a "style of life" represents a loosely bounded culture's emphasis on superficial individual choices, whereas group customs and
conflicts reproduce a more tightly bounded culture's emphasis
on social control in such areas as marriage and career.

The weakness of America's three cultural visions leaves our

culture predominantly loosely bounded, with a loose bound-edness that contemporary agencies of culture production por-tray. Loose boundedness is also embedded in more durable cultural forms, such as American speech and architecture. Be-cause the cultural template of loose boundedness appears in schools, advertising, television, speech, and architecture, the full range of loose boundedness will not become clear until we have surveyed each of these spheres. Before undertaking our survey, let us briefly discuss some of the factors which have con-tributed to the contemporary dominance of loose bounded-ness in the United States.

CONTRIBUTIONS TO A LOOSELY BOUNDED CULTURE

Most of the factors that contribute to loose boundedness in America appear in the work of other writers. Rather than their being a cause for consternation, however, the very familiarity of these arguments should be seen as a positive contribution to the present undertaking, for if these disparate arguments come together without strain under the large umbrella I am constructing, the umbrella itself gains stronger support. More-over, viewing these factors as joint contributors to a loosely bounded culture gives them a parsimony that discussion of them seriatim lacks. When seen from the perspective of loose boundedness, these seemingly disjointed phenomena become a system of cultural explanation.

Like the decay of our three cultural visions, these other con-tributors to the loosely bounded culture in America are also historical. But other writers have seen these factors as contrib-utors to liberal individualism rather than to loose bounded-ness. However, liberalism is only *one* form of individualism; loose boundedness is another. Loose boundedness turns indi-vidualism into a consumption-oriented, morally flexible, un-certain cultural course, whereas liberalism makes of individual-ism a highly efficient, rigid, productive, purposeful force. Loose boundedness transmutes individualism from the realms of politics and the economy to the realms of the social and the

personal. In the former realms it works well; in the latter it
does not. If liberal individualism was the faith of our fathers,
then loose boundedness is the faith of their children. Liberal
individualism and loose boundedness are kinfolk, children of
the same parents. The same factors that encouraged liberal individualism in our early history paved the way for contemporary loose boundedness. Let us trace this development.

Consider, for example, American frontier settlement, which
contrasts so vividly with its European counterpart. In America
the frontier was constantly in motion, restricted by few national
boundaries, open to the dynamic capacities and proclivities of a
growing population. In America the concept of the frontier denoted only temporarily unsettled land. By contrast, the European frontier denoted fixed national boundaries that held people in rigid cultural compartments. In contrast to Europe, the
boundary between frontier and civilization in America was always weak, and the transition between the two zones gradual.[13]

The ambiguous distinction between civilization and frontier
in America can be illustrated in two ways. First, the pattern of
frontier settlements was spotty. Temporary settlements inter-
mingled haphazardly with wilderness, farms, and permanent
towns, thus obviating any sharp geographical demarcations.[14]
Second, on the American frontier no legal barriers, customs
officials, passport checks, or walls regulated or symbolized passage from one category of territory to another. Lines of demarcation became spatially blurred, not politically hard-edged.
The frontier began "at the edge of the forest" or at a mountain
range or at the river bank. These spatial markers constantly
changed as settlement patterns changed, and outmoded markers were soon assimilated to the growth of civilization.

This particularly American frontier experience becomes
significant in view of the distinction between the savage and
the domesticated that is central to Lévi-Strauss's theory. Lévi-
Strauss argues that important cultural symbolism depends on
this contrast. But where nature is as pliable as on the American
frontier, the dichotomy between savagery and domesticity
must inevitably appear to be comparatively weak, and a clearly
polarized set of cultural perceptions will have difficulty emerg-

ing. Therefore, the frontier experience may have accustomed Americans to think of boundaries as temporary and permeable, and to distrust any sharp distinctions that appear to hinder the march of civilization and progress. Liberalism could turn the energies thus unloosed to productive advantage in the development of a modern economy and polity. Liberalism thus harnessed the energies of the wild to domesticated reason. By contrast, loose boundedness turns matters around by subordinating reason to an unrestrained emotionalism.

A second historical factor instrumental in producing a loosely bounded American culture is our particular pattern of age grading. Although age stratification in America is quite strong, *deference* to age has always been relatively weaker than in Europe.[15] Bernard Bailyn has argued that European deference to age could not easily survive in the United States, where elders commanded few ideas useful to their children's survival in an untamed land that lacked traditions.[16] In America each new generation had to compile its own stock of wisdom, thereby relegating its predecessors to unplanned obsolescence. Bailyn also observes how attractive an option escape to the frontier became for young people who could not get along well with their parents. Unlike their European counterparts, American youngsters did not have to work out the complications of age and deference unless they chose to. For this reason American parents never enjoyed the kind of automatic acquiescence and respect from their young that their European cousins enjoyed.

An additional factor in the breakdown of age-based deference in America may have been the early emergence of a nuclear family structure in which grandparents usually did not live with their children.[17] Contemporary evidence suggests that in three-generation residential families authority respects generational lines,[18] while this is less true in two-generation families. The absence of three-generation families in the United States undoubtedly retarded the development of sharp generational boundaries. While such freedom from family constraint poured labor power efficiently into a liberal economy of growth in the nineteenth-century, it also opened the way for the twentieth-century triumph of sheer sentiment over blood ties in a loosely bounded culture of family life.

Another relevant historical factor was the American pattern of ethnic immigration. Although the United States never actually became a melting pot, the polyglot ethnic character of many urban areas forced ethnic groups to coalesce with each other for political purposes. Not only did the urban party-machine broker ethnic coalitions, it also trained ethnic politicians in the art of crossing group boundaries for political reasons.[19] Thus, the habit of ethnic subordination may have emerged in the political machine.[20] And ethnic subordination not only serves to enhance liberal individualism, it also makes of ethnicity itself the sort of voluntary identification so crucial to loose boundedness.

To these three specific historical phenomena may be added several others of primarily technological character. One is the early dominance of the automobile in American life. Automobile travel minimizes the psychological experience of spatial boundaries, for there are no demarcations between a "station" and open country as there are with the railroad or the bus. In addition, we can "house" the automobile in the family garage, not in a separate place. No fences separate cars from people, and no one takes or sells tickets as a condition of automobile travel. Automobiles are not bound to tracks, nor need they follow predetermined, invariant routes and schedules. One need not carry identifying luggage in automobile travel. Indeed, airplane transportation carries this trend toward boundary ambiguity even further, for although airplane travel does require baggage, hidden facilities within the terminal screen the baggage from sight. The average plane passenger can therefore appear indistinguishable from the average pedestrian. There is no special class of people marked by "red caps" who separate visually those who are plane or automobile travelers from those nontravelers who simply happen to be in the vicinity. In short, sharp visual distinctions occur less frequently in either plane or automobile travel than in train travel.

Other boundary cues are also absent from automobile travel. For example, automobiles do not carry food-dispensing facilities or sanitary supplies as do trains and planes. As a result, passengers must disembark along the way to eat and eliminate waste, and in so doing, they merge with their surroundings. Automobiles are thus not self-sufficient worlds sharply separated from the terrain they traverse. As if to complement this automotive theme of merger, most American cities are now surrounded by a transitional "strip"—neither urban, suburban, nor rural—containing fast-food restaurants, motels, and amusement facilities intended to serve automobile travelers. This strip softens the passage from city to countryside, cushioning the shock of transition and blurring perception of urban-rural distinctions. Moreover, because vital life functions are dispersed among a number of specialized units along the road, the car cannot become a sharply bounded, self-contained space at odds with a distinctive external world.[21] Here the relevant contrast is with the ocean liner, which of necessity contains all its own life-support systems. Even automobile design reflects this evolution toward blurred boundaries. The design of the automobile has moved from enclosed, rectangular internal spaces to fluid, flexible interiors in which passengers enjoy ample window space, and in which they ride on aerodynamic frames that adjust flexibly to the outside world. This design evolution from rectilinear boxes to curved and fluid lines accentuates the cultural merger between landscape, automobile, and passenger.

The example of the automobile demonstrates the way in which technological factors complement historical factors in the production of a society's basic cultural matrix. And surely we need do no more than note the automobile's contribution to the labor mobility necessary to an economy built on liberal principles, and also the automobile's contribution to the free flow of intimate sentiment that fuels a loosely bounded culture. Again, the identical phenomenon encourages first liberal individualism, then loose boundedness.

Another example emerges in the work of Jack Goody, who argues that the displacement of oral by written forms of communication contributed to the creation of sharply demarcated cultures containing polarized opposites. As Goody puts it, "Writing, and more especially alphabetic literacy, made it possible to scrutinize discourse in a different kind of way by giving oral communication a semi-permanent form; this scrutiny favored the increase in scope of critical activity, and hence of rationality, skepticism, and logic to resurrect memories of those questionable dichotomies."[22] Goody then asserts that such graphic devices as lists, tables, recipes, and formulae encourage the presentation of ideas in hierarchical or linear order, with each item standing in fixed, permanent, formal, opposed relationship to every other item. The list, for example, "has a clearcut beginning and a precise end, that is, a boundary, an edge, like a piece of cloth. Most importantly, it encourages the ordering of the items, by number, by initial sound, by category, etc. And the existence of boundaries, external and internal, brings greater visibility to categories, at the same time as making them more abstract."[23] Who can doubt that such developments aid in the production of the competitive entrepreneur and the rational citizen so central to a nineteenth-century liberal individualism?

But when we turn to communication today we are struck by the growing role of visual, not print media;[24] and visual media clearly undercut many of the boundary-creation qualities which Goody attributes to print media. Therefore, if Goody is correct about the cultural contributions of communication technology, it must be that visual domination of communication in America supports a loosely bounded culture. Consider the following factors: First, people forget visual media more easily than they do print media, because the former disappear as soon as they are seen, and are therefore hard to reference.[25] Second, while readers can control the rate of information flow, and can therefore meet the written word on equal terms, the uncontrollable stream of visual communication often floods the viewer, overwhelming his or her capacity to use information rationally. Finally, visual media usually communicate by encouraging viewers to identify themselves sympathetically and intuitively with the images they see, rather than by encouraging them to stand back critically and evaluate information according to a set of durable intellectual standards. Advertisers on television sell their products by breaking down the boundary between viewer and commercial, not by respecting this boundary. They attempt to make the advertisement as "entertaining" as possible in order to elicit good feelings about the product; not surprisingly, therefore, they make advertisements that closely resemble entertainment programs. They thus create a tendency toward the homogenization of media form. The American practice of inserting advertisements in entertainment programs reinforces this tendency toward fuzzy visual boundaries. Thus, the visual communication experience becomes a continuous flow of more or less unbounded images, resembling in form our impression of the terrain as we drive through loosely bounded suburbs.[26]

Goody also points out that some written forms, such as lists, accustom us to think in quantitative, relative terms, rather than in qualitative terms.[27] Lists group items together under single qualitative rubrics and then force us to focus on the marginal differences between listed items. Rarely do we consider carefully the larger qualitative differences between the categories that undergird lists. An accumulation of such graphic devices as lists thus distracts us from thinking in terms of sharply bounded, opposed categories of incompatible meanings. And just as lists become indispensable to the rational management of any business enterprise, so also does the relativistic mentality they encourage pave the way for a loosening of cultural boundaries.

A similar refusal to accept qualitatively opposed dichotomies emerges from the dominance of science over religion in the contemporary United States. Science proceeds by reducing qualitatively absolute differences to quantitatively manageable "variables," and then by inventing appropriate formulae to transform these variables into each other. Science searches for common denominators, not for qualitative differences. Scientists also use analytic tools which array objects in like or equivalent measurement units along a continuum, instead of being content with tools that group objects in sharply bounded dichotomies. An example cited by Goody is the mathematical formula, which converts terms into equivalent—indeed, identical—expressions.[28] Another more specialized example is the indifference curve in economics, which transforms formerly unrelated "tastes" into equivalent values, thereby reducing preferences and desires to a common quantitative denominator. Such tools are indispensable for rational management of the polity and the economy, but they are also stimulants to the relativistic impulse on which loose boundedness thrives.

Thus, in ways both subtle and obvious, technological development contributes to the breakdown of binary oppositions. Even arcane developments in linguistic philosophy contribute to the same process. Consider, for example, Saussure's early theory, which, according to Petit, assumes that "language is . . . a set of words which are systematically differentiated from one another, in sound and conceptually."[29] This description of language, useful in the development of linguistics, ran into difficulty early in this century, and was superceded by Wittgenstein's analysis, which argues that apparent commonalities among words in the same categories turn out to be illusory when examined. At best, words bear family relationships to each other, relationships of overlapping likenesses in which no single specific property characterizes any element of one word class, nor is any word wholly segregated from the words of allied classes. Language sprawls; it does not group itself neatly into tightly bounded, opposed compartments of meaning.[30]

The etymology of particular words and word classes reveals precisely this property of boundary violation. For example, Raymond Williams documents the elasticity of sociological language, its refusal to be circumscribed, and its defiance of clear oppositions. This is particularly true of the concept of social classes. Indeed, Williams shows that the same word may actually include opposed and contradictory meanings. An example is the concept of power, which means both an expansive personal quality and a restriction on individual development.[31]

To the extent that the Wittgensteinian approach has altered our traditional conceptions of language it has also weakened our tendency to see culture in terms of sharply opposed ideas and meaning systems. For example, it is Wittgenstein's linguistic insight that advertisers intuit in their own use of language. Advertisements succeed, in part, by expanding and obfuscating the meaning of words. The advertiser uses language as a source of profitable play, not as a means of rational, bounded discourse. And the same practice which sells goods in the name of entrepreneurship in a competitive economy undercuts the linguistic stability that would anchor a culture and prevent its drifting into loose boundedness.

The American tendency toward loose boundedness has also been encouraged by shifts in the very markers we use to demarcate our social worlds. In former times and in America through the nineteenth and early twentieth centuries, people relied primarily on concrete spatial, temporal, or kin signs to classify each other. We "understood" people by their regions of origin or residence, their language, their church affiliation, or their skin color. Although these markers continue to be important, we must now increasingly rely on abstract differentiations—such as the sorts of jobs people have or the beliefs they hold. These newer forms of differentiation present problems of boundary definition which the older devices avoided. The place where one has one's home, the color of one's skin, the sound of one's language, the look of one's clothes—these are unambiguous signs around which a consensus on identity can easily form. But job designations and personal beliefs are more difficult to conceptualize and explain, because they provide few agreed-upon and widely understood indicators. They therefore create the sort of ambiguity on which loose boundedness feeds.

The social centrality of the scientist in America also promotes the weakness of American cultural boundaries. In societies where a traditional clergy defines truth, priests are typically set apart from the rest of society, creating a sharp cultural divide between the laity and the clergy. Priests usually live in visibly marked, consecrated places, wear easily identifiable uniforms, perform special rituals, and forego certain common activities, such as marriage. Despite their special status, some clergy may become deeply involved politically, but at least when they do so they become most conspicuous. The social distinctiveness of the clergy symbolizes the distinctive ideas which the clergy propounds. And this separation of clergy from laity symbolizes the larger polarity between the sacred and the secular worlds.

By contrast, in American society—as in most industrialized societies—it is the scientist, not the priest, who defines the truth. But scientific knowledge must be open to public scrutiny, empirical test, and disconfirmation; it is therefore too tentative to support a sharply differentiated social status for the scientist. Scientific knowledge thus creates communities of citizen-scientists, not monasteries filled with initiates or illuminati. Scientists are free to live among us in unmarked houses, to wear the same sorts of clothes we all wear, and to choose for themselves whether to marry or not. Most important, the scientist transmits and receives his ideas publicly; unlike the priest, his knowledge is protected by no exceptions based on his guardianship of a miscreant's guilty secret. Scientific knowledge is fluid, changing, and above all public; religious dogma changes but slowly, and then behind closed doors. Should we be surprised that American cultural codes—which absorb advances in scientific knowledge—become fluid and flexible? And the very scientific knowledge that fueled the engines of a flourishing nineteenth-century liberal individualism has moved today from politics and the economy into the realms of the social, the cultural, and the personal, and there undercuts those certainties that keep a culture tightly rather than loosely bounded.

A quick review of the factors we have discussed—the frontier, truncated age-grading, immigration, the triumph of the automobile, the growth of visual media, the ascendance of science, the emergence of abstract classification, and the growth of a flexible theory of language—demonstrates the arbitrariness of trying to pinpoint a single moment when loose boundedness came into its own in America. After all, the leveling of age grading was a precolonial phenomenon, whereas the automobile is a twentieth-century phenomenon. It is therefore best to see loose boundedness as slowly forming under the accumulating weight of all these factors, along with the decay of Puritanism, democratic pluralism, and the class vision. Loose boundedness came into its own when the principles of liberal individualism—which these same factors stimulated in the nineteenth-century—attempted to penetrate the culture of the twentieth-century. This penetration failed, for the identical factors that encouraged liberal individualism in politics and the economy encouraged loose boundedness in culture. And so the polity and the economy continue to be influenced mainly by liberal individualism, while culture has succumbed to loose boundedness. At least since the 1950s, ours has been a divided social world, with liberal individualism's reason, prudence, calculation, inequality, and unending competition ruling our public world, while loose boundedness's sentiment, rashness, spontaneity, equality, and transient cooperation rule our private world.

ARCHITECTURAL EXAMPLES OF LOOSELY BOUNDED CULTURE

Architecture is the deliberate design of living and working spaces. Architecture therefore crystallizes deep cultural tendencies, for as people divide, order, and reorder residential and occupational space they cannot refrain from projecting their image of themselves and their society onto the natural world.[32] Let us examine American architecture to see if it supports our conception of the United States as slowly creating a loosely bounded culture, which is now in full view. It should be understood that many of the architectural tendencies I identify can be found in other cultures as well. My argument, however, is cumulative; the loosely bounded pattern I describe emerges as a unique combination of elements in architecture, in language, in advertising, in television, and in schools.[33] Each of these domains supplies a piece of the puzzle we are attempting to assemble. As for architecture, we may describe salient features under three rubrics: styles, forms, and innovations.

Styles

One feature of loosely bounded cultures is their penetrability. American architecture provides an excellent example of this feature in the style called Eclecticism, which dominated American architecture from the 1870s to the 1930s. As Walter Kidney describes it, Eclecticism represented an attempt to import into American architecture specific elements from many countries and periods, and thereby to construct through the medium of other building cultures an artificial historical "tradition" of American architecture.[34] Thus, in a single home subject to the influence of Eclecticism one might encounter a pastiche of pieces from various architectural styles and periods all cheerfully jumbled together. The late-Victorian American mind threw different styles and periods together in the conviction that doing so would do no real violence to the integrity of individual styles. Such a practice could only continue because of the belief that the borders between styles—indeed, architectural integrity itself—need not be respected. Perhaps the best example of the Eclectic impulse at work is Armsmear, a house built near Hartford, Connecticut, between 1855 and 1862. Armsmear combined the dimensions and "presence" of an Italian villa with the domes, pinnacles, and extravagant ornamentation of a grand Turkish residence, all in an English-park setting.[35]

As this description may suggest, Eclecticism aptly expressed in architectural terms the rise of American business power during the late nineteenth century. Many newly rich businessmen turned to Eclecticism—and thus to Europe and to the past—in an effort to purchase cultural respectability for themselves. The architectural demands of this new class not only supported Eclecticism, but also helped create the school of Beaux Arts architects, Americans trained in France to adapt classical, massive designs to modern conditions.[36] It was the Beaux Arts architects who designed the grand but derivative homes of New York's newly rich on Fifth Avenue during the 1890s. However, Eclecticism and the Beaux Arts were not simply artificial attempts to magically create historical continuity from the jumbling together of historical styles. Instead, these two styles represented an effort to create an American public order in which the newly created strength of American commerce would express itself in appropriate architectural shape. It was not surprising that the Beaux Arts architects turned to imperial Rome for their inspiration, and fittingly, given the economic base of American wealth, the Beaux Arts style as a public form expressed itself most purely in two railroad stations—the Pennsylvania in New York and Union Station in Washington.[37] Train travel symbolized not only the economic foundations of American wealth, but also the fluidity of American cultural boundaries and the openness of American culture to penetration and novel connections. Above all, the massive Roman arch—which symbolized fluid continuity as opposed to sharp angles and divisions—formed the centerpiece of these structures. The arch perfectly articulates the dynamic, expansionist, confident public order of late-Victorian America.

The spirit of Eclecticism also dominated city planning and city redevelopment during this period. Leading the way was the Columbian Exposition of 1893, where imperial facades and wide boulevards evoked the Roman pattern of open town planning as a way of dazzling and engulfing the citizen. Shortly thereafter, model turned to reality in the massive boulevards and monumental prospects Burnham and Root incorporated into their turn-of-the-century reconstruction of Chicago, the city which, as a railroad and industrial center, perhaps symbolized more than any other America's ascendance in the world.

Two aspects of Eclecticism bear particular attention from a cultural standpoint. First, the incorporation of traditional styles in new combinations usually produced an efflorescence of nonfunctional ornamentation, giving spaces an unusually cluttered effect.[38] In turn, excessive ornamentation disturbed visual bounding and sharp spatial delineation. Such an architectural strategy can be explained only on the dubious assumption that sheer quantitative display will eventually produce a qualitatively distinct architectural style. The architectural reduction of qualitatively bounded separateness to quantitative agglomeration is therefore consistent with a deep impulse in a loosely bounded culture to obliterate traditional aesthetic distinctions.

A second important feature of Eclecticism is captured by Carl Condit, who observes, "What distinguishes this work is a carefully controlled ornamental extravagance and a generosity of space and detail that were skillfully calculated to explore every possible means of visual excitement."[39] The Eclectic movement and the Beaux Arts aimed to entertain and to daz-

zle people by their Roman scale and their deliberately excessive detail. But display had a larger purpose; the visual excitement of the work demanded that people be drawn into the
architecture, enlivened by it, and most of all, engulfed by it so
as to create of building and person together an ensemble of
emotional expression and sympathetic identification. Display
for the sheer sake of display thus signified both an unwillingness to be constrained by functional limitations in architecture, and a desire to overcome functional limitations of *life*,
such as the limitations of inequality, class division, religion, and
ideological conflict. In an ornamental culture all can share the
same exciting visual experience. Thus, Eclecticism and the
Beaux Arts expressed the modern American desire to transcend sharply defined occupational, class, and racial divisions.

In our own time the growth of loose boundaries in American architecture has been stimulated and reinforced by the decline of Eclecticism and the ascent of Modernism, as seen most
vividly in the work of Le Corbusier and Wright during the
1920s. According to Condit, this transition produced a new
concept of architectural space: "Space is defined by an asym-
metrical association of volumes or weightless screens freely
disposed in a pattern meant to suggest movement and continuity, as opposed to the traditional static symmetry and gradation
that symbolized an older, more stable, and more simply ordered cosmos."[40] Where Eclecticism continued to celebrate history and tradition, albeit in a somewhat bowdlerized fashion,
Modernism moves rapidly toward loose boundedness by eliminating history, tradition, and architectural references to the
past. The Modernist movement clears out the architectural
space in favor of open, uncluttered vistas, which lack fixed spatial markers to bound the visual world. The result is a loosely
bounded prospect in constant motion.

Of course, the Modernist movement is not confined to
America. Indeed, the major impetus toward Modernism appeared first in the work of Europeans, such as the Bauhaus
architects and Corbusier. But it is in America that Modernism's
architectural mobility has proven most appealing and has been
generalized most widely. Consider, for example, the effort that

Americans have devoted to the design of our time's primary image of motion and dynamics: the automobile. We crave automobile designs that are sleek, low to the ground, uncluttered, aerodynamic—and which thereby express in form the psychological freedom and escape from boundaries that we wish automobiles to secure for us. Americans have always lavished attention on the design of movement. As one astute observer commented in the late nineteenth century, "The American . . . has unwittingly, in some objects to which his heart equally with his head has been devoted, developed a degree of beauty in them *(sic)* that no other nation equals. His clipper-ships, fire-engines, locomotives, and some of his machinery and tools combine that equilibrium of lines, proportions, and masses, which are among the fundamental causes of abstract beauty."[41] Modernism has helped Americans to make the designation of motion ever more appealing, thereby confirming our deep cultural disposition toward the extension, blurring, and breaking of inhibiting social boundaries.

It is not surprising, perhaps, that our impatience with boundaries impels us to join the automobile—with its promise of freedom and independence—to the home, with its promise of comfort and security. Again Modernism helps us. Consider, for example, the large part of many Modernist-influenced homes which is given over to the attached garage. The cultural importance of the American residential garage stems from the fact that it links the principle of movement (the automobile) to the principle of stability and order (the home). The garage allows us to absorb the automobile into the home physically, thereby obliterating the boundary between the outside world and the inside world, between movement and stasis, between the dead machine and the living family. The garage makes a place for our most valued artifact of freedom—the car—within the space we reserve for our most intimate natural impulses—the home. Small wonder, then, that Mumford should characterize the garage as a modern temple.[42] And small wonder that the sleek designs of Modernism should have recommended themselves so thoroughly to designers of motion.

These same tendencies toward exalting motion while blending it with security can be found in other vehicle-related developments. We try to design automobiles that can fulfil as many home functions as possible while in operation, thereby allowing us to move without restraint in an atmosphere of security. Automobiles which contain stereo sets, telephone, and reclining chairs that convert into beds express this impulse. The apotheosis of the tendency is found in the modern camper or mobile home, where almost all the comforts of the hearth are in constant, if screened, motion. Paradoxically, some large mobile homes remain tethered and never move at all; still, because we know these homes can *become* mobile, they retain the promise and allure of movement. It is difficult to understand why so many Americans prefer anchored mobile homes over conventional residences until we reflect that living "permanently" in a stationary mobile home perfectly reconciles our love for movement with our need for security. Small wonder that Scully describes the mobile home as "everything we most believe in and can handle well: mass production, mobility, the automobile,"[43] and, we might add, our nostalgia for roots in a rootless land.

Thus, the movement from Eclecticism to Modernism is a movement from an incoherently organized architectural world in which history and tradition continue to play a binding role to a coherently organized but unbounded architectural vacuum from which history and tradition have been expelled. In the Modernist world the individual stands alone, uninhibited by the past, yet paradoxically unsure of where to go and what lies ahead in the open space that, for the first time, he can fully spy.

Much American architecture now opens us up to the scrutiny of others in preparation for the rapid formation of new social connections. To this end the loosely bounded architecture of Modernism blends cultural opposites, reduces distinctiveness, and elevates observation of others to the level of a social norm. A brief historical reconstruction of American domestic architecture reveals these tendencies clearly.

Inside, colonial American homes contained sharp interior divisions between rooms; outside, acute angles separated the home clearly from its landscape setting. The prototypical house was the New England saltbox, in which kitchen, bedroom, and living functions were rigidly separated from each other. Quite early, however, there arose a tendency toward horizontal extension and merger of the house with its lot at the expense of rigid distinctions between interior and exterior. Simultaneously, though more slowly, the interior boundaries of the characteristic New England home began to give way. And today house design places emphasis on the continuous interplay of domestic functions within the same space, to facilitate the sense of "flow" that pervades loose boundedness.

A primary early example of the American fascination with extension and multifunctionality may be found in Jefferson's masterpiece, Monticello, in which, as Scully puts it, one finds a "struggle between the fixed European past and the mobile American future, between Palladio and Frank Lloyd Wright, between a desire for contained, classical geometry and an instinct to spread out horizontally along the surface of the land."[44] It is, of course, a long way from Jefferson to Wright, whose Modernist emphasis on the harmonious blending of indoors and outdoors is certainly more marked than Jefferson's. Nevertheless, the tendency toward loosely bounded openness, extension, and multifunctionality is already present in Jefferson. Similarly, it is a long way from the Puritan's saltbox, his Congregationalist orthodoxy, and his rigid division of the world into saints and damned sinners, to the contemporary suburbanite's ranch house, his picture window (which opens occupant and passerby to mutual scrutiny), and his "laid back" family members who "share their feelings" with each other and let it all "hang out" so as not to be "uptight." The openness of contemporary American architecture complements the loosening of cultural, familial, and religious boundaries in the United States. And Modernism completed the process.

Forms

The Eclectic and Modernist impulses have also shaped alterations in the forms of American architecture, thereby extending the architectural template of loose boundedness. By "forms," I refer to the invention of new types of structures that express loose boundedness especially well. For example, the Eclectic spirit continues to display itself in automobile-related forms. Consider the typical drive-in restaurant, such as Howard Johnson's. Howard Johnson's architecture combines a New England style of church spire, an English style of sign, interior design features reminiscent of the English country house, and a facade drawn from an American town hall.[45] As a final touch, the formal landscaping that fronts the restaurant imitates the American suburban home. Meanwhile, inside Howard Johnson's, "the dominant impression is one of smoothness. The laminated menus, the plastic woodgrain surfaces of walls and tables, the marbled formica counters, vinyl booths, and smooth ice cream are combined with the languid Muzak of Mantovani and the unruffled service of tranquil waitresses who smile continuously.... There is the sense that nothing disturbing has ever happened here or ever will happen."[46] Here we see the openness that so characterizes Modernism. In Howard Johnson's—as in the loosely bounded culture generally—openness is meant to create a smooth, continuous flow of expression, with no threatening discontinuities of experience.

We have also designed our urban landscape to accommodate the mobility the automobile brings. Such new forms as the drive-in restaurant and the motel provide life support systems for automobile passengers, and thereby make it possible for people to move continuously over long distances. These ancillary structures thus blur the boundary between home and the external world. The drive-in restaurant's "take-out" food turns the automobile into a family dining room; the motel room transforms the automobile into a chamber of seduction. Whereas seduction and dining were once confined to homes or other stable spaces, now, as if to express the instability of even our most vital functions, they merge with the automobile and thus with loose boundedness.

Other formal developments also express the openness of a loosely bounded culture. Indeed, in their most distinctive and unique forms, American buildings sprawl across vast spaces, sometimes accommodating themselves snugly to the terrain—as in Frank Lloyd Wright's buildings—sometimes deliberately violating the organic integrity of the terrain through which they extend. The "ranch house," which has become the prototype for so much suburban development, is the formal example which typifies this tendency toward extension. The ranch house represents a permanent architectural crystallization of a loosely bounded culture's tendency toward dynamic expansion.

As both Mumford and Scully point out, the formal extension of American architecture complements our frontier experience spatially.[47] On the frontier the ready availability of cheap land created what Mumford calls a kind of permanent "land-hunger," which stimulated Americans to build transient structures without regard for the organic integrity of the landscape.[48] Movement was the rule of life on the frontier. Why then trouble oneself about deficiencies in structures one was soon to abandon anyway? Why not instead use the abundant land to build new structures or to add to and thus "perfect" existing structures? The result of these tendencies is a preference for long, low residential structures of seemingly unbounded extent, in which quantity of space replaces quality of design.

Our preference for extension has also shaped our attitudes toward the form of cities. Although Americans adopted a bounded, urban grid system early in our history, we have been unable to withstand the pressure loose boundedness exerts toward the indefinite extension of urban form. Typically, therefore, we have dispersed vital functions and selected populations to unbounded suburbs, and we have refused to fortify a vital, attractive downtown core. The tendency toward unbounded extension also reproduces itself within the pattern of suburbanization itself. Most suburbs lack stable commercial centers to complement their residential areas. Hence they lack the capacity to function as "defended communities." So we pile residential area on residential area, one after another, and thus create an architecturally continuous, but organically insecure, residential ring. We abandon the city and its sharply defined neighborhoods, shopping areas, and grid plan in favor of unbounded extensions of comparatively homogeneous suburban development.[49]

Yet another formal innovation which illustrates the American tendency toward extension can be found in the use of commercial signs as highway markers. The commercial strips which surround most American cities are essentially unbounded spatially. Strip architecture depends for demarcation purposes only on the altitude of commercial signs that announce the functions of buildings,[50] but the buildings themselves provide few clues to their function. Most strip buildings are interchangeable. There is an economic aspect to this formal development, for signs are cheap to erect, and so permit commercial strips to extend indefinitely outward without sacrificing the identity of particular buildings and firms. Nevertheless, the situation contrasts markedly with the enforced compactness of an urban commercial core, where the shapes of buildings signal uses by distinctive architectural markers (the church spire, the stock exchange facade, the department store window), rather than by signs alone. In strip architecture the sameness of buildings and the cheapness of signs facilitate indefinite extension and loose boundedness, while in the urban core expensive architectural markers restrict extension and facilitate tight boundedness.

Innovations

As we have seen, Eclecticism borrowed extensively from the architectural styles of other societies in an attempt to create a uniquely American architecture. This tendency toward absorption, distortion, and engulfment of cultural styles is a typical feature of loosely bounded cultures. The tendency expresses itself strongly in architectural innovations within traditional forms, as well as in the creation of entirely new forms. Consider, for example, the modern American museum. Museums have existed for a very long time, but as Mumford puts it, "In contrast to the local museums one still finds occasionally in Europe, which are little more than extensions of the local curio cabinet, the imperial museum is essentially a loot-heap, a comprehensive repository for plunder."[51] The museum in America throws together under one enormous roof the cultures of many formerly distinct societies. In doing so, the

American museum creates its own type of synthetic culture, one composed of artifacts torn from their original cultural moorings. This tendency toward mixture, absorption, and artificial grouping is an example of how fully the Eclectic impulse toward loose boundaries has influenced architectural innovation in America.

The visitor to a museum—like the visitor to the Columbian Exposition of 1893—feels overwhelmed by the visual riches on display. The variety of stimuli proves bewildering, and the viewer reacts with awe and giddiness. This reaction testifies to museum architecture's invasion of personal space, and to the annihilation of distance between viewer and object. The feeling of personal "flooding" is yet another symptom of loose cultural boundaries.

The architect who best expressed American tendencies toward architectural engulfment was Henry Hobson Richardson. Richardson's unique blend of eclectic and native themes in the late nineteenth century permanently altered American architecture.[52] His use of large arches and horizontally continuous rows of windows creates a feeling of constant movement and magnetic appeal. Even Richardson's smallest buildings tend to engulf the observer, as evidenced particularly by his train stations, which combine themes of speed, fluidity, and functionality with a sense of inner security and womblike serenity. As Scully puts it, "Richardson's work summed up the main conflicting aspects of modern and peculiarly American, middle-class aspirations: to be free and protected all at once."[53]

The American desire to create a total unbounded environment both within buildings and between buildings and their surroundings is a logical outcome of a loosely bounded culture which distrusts inside-outside distinctions. Of course, technological innovation must also cooperate. Advances in the technology of heating, lighting, and ventilation now permit us to create buildings which, by simulating the outside world within a single building, totally seal off the individual from the outside world. Modern designers have also replaced older, sharp-edged, hard, angular office furniture with furniture that is rounded, soft, flexible, and comfortable. These innovations in interior design treat offices as homes away from home, not as functionally specific spaces. The cultural significance of the new office designs is not that they create a more comfortable environment for the worker, but rather that they break down the traditional distinctions between office and home, work and play, effort and leisure, and that they thereby embody architecturally the sense of flow and continuity that is characteristic of a loosely bounded culture.

A virtual revolution in interior decoration has stimulated this tendency toward creating engulfing, multifunctional interior spaces. Interior decorators of schools and offices now employ lightweight materials, movable partitions, and a bare minimum of fixtures. These features enable educators, for example, to rearrange furniture and accessories easily to suit new teaching needs and tastes. Consider, for example, "team teaching" classrooms in American schools, where lightweight partitions permit quick rearrangement to facilitate changing pedagogical demands. The result of these innovations is an absence of sharp, permanent demarcations between students or between classes. Architectural innovation thus complements alterations in our view of the permanency of social arrangements.

Another architectural innovation which expresses the American tendency toward loose boundaries is the "family room" in the contemporary suburban home. The family room combines children's playthings, father and mother's library, a television set, various "family games," perhaps musical equipment (record player, instruments), and even spare beds. By making it possible for the family to spend its leisure time together in a single space, the family room encourages a pleasurable atmosphere of informality. The family room thus works best when it frees the inhibitions of family members in their relations with each other, thereby creating family unity by breaking down older, architecturally symbolized barriers of age and authority.[54]

These innovations, of course, require highly mobile, multifunctional architectural and interior materials. In these respects, modern architecture resembles theatrical scenery. Mumford comments on the resemblance between the modern office or home and the stage set when he writes, "What is the bare interior of a modern office or apartment house but a stage, waiting for the scenery to be shifted, and a new play to be put on. It is due to this similarity . . . that modern interior decoration has so boldly accepted the standards and effects of stage-design."[55] But if modern architecture borrows so heavily from the stage, with the latter's temporary, playful settings, may not the human relationships within these settings also take on the evanescent character of the stage? Might a fluid architectural setting reinforce tendencies toward fluid, unstable, shallow, personal relationships?

Or compare the Las Vegas gambling casino with its more traditional predecessors. Venturi describes the effect:

> The gambling room is always very dark; the patio, always very bright. But both are enclosed: the former has no window, and the latter is open only to the sky. The combination of darkness and enclosure of the gambling room and its subspaces makes for privacy, protection, concentration and control. The intricate maze under the low ceiling never connects with outside light or outside space. This disorients the occupant in space and time. He loses track of where he is and when it is. Time is limitless, because the light of noon and midnight are exactly the same. Space is limitless, because the artificial light obscures rather than defines space. . . . Space is enclosed but limitless, because its edges are dark.[56]

The gambling environment ministers to a financial purpose, of course. The disorientation that Venturi describes encourages the gambler to part happily with his money and to take risks that the "bright light of day" will reveal to have been foolhardy. The constant half-light and soft music is relaxing and uninhibiting, resembling very much in effect the contemporary dentist's office, so beautifully designed to reduce the discomfort of tooth repair. More important, however, the Las Vegas gambling room exists within a larger hotel environment that is itself overwhelming. Within the confines of the aptly named, magical Aladdin Hotel the patron can satisfy all his urbane needs. And where Aladdin exists *anything* might happen. So an economic motive extends a cultural impulse beyond its original confines.

Yet another example of our tendency toward the indefinite extension of space and self may be found in the modern American living room. As Kurtz puts it, most living rooms group together functions that could easily be partitioned off into separate, specialized spaces. But the living room becomes instead a reluctant depository of casual, misplaced functions, and must be "tidied up" (i.e., provided with strong boundaries) before company arrives.[57] Here again the convergence of architecture and culture becomes obvious. The design of the living room does not encourage "company" or formality, because we associate formality with rigid boundaries, and to provide such boundaries in the American home is an unwelcome and onerous task.

No structural innovations better reflect the American anxiety to obliterate sharp cultural distinctions and to forge new social connections than those associated with the ancient art of bridge building. Bridges symbolize the impulse to find harmony between opposites and to bring people from different backgrounds together in a common cause. Americans have lavished attention on bridge construction and engineering. And we have led the world in this endeavor. The major breakthrough was the Brooklyn Bridge, which remains even today the finest American example of the suspension bridge. Mumford refers to the Brooklyn Bridge as "not the first work of engineering to be a work of art; but . . . the first product of the age of coal and iron to achieve this completeness of expression."[58] Other American bridges—the Golden Gate, the George Washington, and the Mackinac Straits—now stand with the Brooklyn Bridge among the finest bridges in the world. Or consider the Gateway Arch of St. Louis, which, though not a bridge, still ties together east and west for purely symbolic purposes.[59] The Gateway Arch is especially significant, for its obvious *lack* of function reveals more clearly our willingness to embody loose boundedness architecturally.

The American desire for connection and continuity between potentially conflictual cultural elements has spread even into institutional settings, which would appear to make openness a liability. Thus, for example, the culture of education is in many respects inevitably hierarchical and sharply bounded. Some ideas are judged qualitatively "better than others," more sophisticated, more demanding, cleverer. Knowledge is a basis for social stratification in most societies, and it is theoretically the sole basis on which the stratification of pupils in school depends. Yet our educational system aims to be democratic. Lay persons serve on school boards, voters approve (or reject) school bonds, and parents regularly confer with teachers. In many ways we try to impose the world of the lay person—which is the world of democratic politics—on the professionalized, hierarchical order of the school. And we advocate measures to open up the school to the community, as symbolized by the attempt of the parent-teacher associations to "build bridges" between home and school.

We also express these democratic impulses through the design of schools. Adaptations of Modernism to school design express our egalitarian impulse toward extension and openness. Open architecture in schools grew as educational Progressivism, with its emphasis on intraschool democracy, became the dominant pedagogical creed in America. The key year was 1940, when Eero Saarinen's Crow Island Elementary School in Winnetka, Illinois, opened. Crow Island became the style-setter for new patterns of American educational architecture. The building featured low-slung, heavily windowed units, with rooms divided into flexible modules, open to the world. Today's school is deliberately designed to be multifunctional, and thus shrinks the distance between home and school, between knowledge and "the people." As Mumford puts it, "The new school houses are neighborhood centers as well as educational buildings."[60] Potential tensions between the school and the community—between knowledge and the citizen—thus become subordinated architecturally in the hope that they will disappear culturally. If such tensions continue to exist, it is certainly not for lack of architectural effort.

LANGUAGE AS AN EXAMPLE
OF A LOOSELY BOUNDED CULTURE

If culture is similar to language, then language itself should be expected to reveal some of the more salient qualities of the cultural code. Although the Sapir-Whorf theory of linguistic determinism is overstated, no one denies that language is an important method for transmitting culture, nor that language condenses many salient characteristics of the larger culture.[61] Therefore, it is not surprising to find in American English many features we have already identified in American architecture. In its own way American English recapitulates aspects of the American language of space. Particularly noteworthy is its strong emphasis on connectives, its intolerance for sharp linguistic distinctions, its comparative uniformity, its unusual absorptiveness, its emphasis on euphemism and inflation, and its sheer inventiveness. Together these qualities make American English a virtual model of a loosely bounded culture.

Connectiveness

In the course of a recent polemic against the deterioration of English usage among Americans, Richard Lanham pays special attention to the word "contact," which, he claims, has become an object of particular abuse.[62] "Contact," he argues, covers a wide variety of vague meanings to which it need not and ought not refer at all. How has this situation come about? Why is the word "contact" such a good candidate for deterioration? One possibility is that "contact" directly taps the ubiquitous impulse in a loosely bounded culture for people to stay in close touch with each other: in business ("making contacts"), in social intercourse ("having contacts in the community"), or in intimate affairs ("we don't have much contact anymore"). In a society where boundaries are insecure and always open to renegotiation, the persistence of social bonds cannot be taken for granted. Naturally enough, the idea of contact becomes a kind of cultural pressure point, gathering to it many of the culture's deepest structures of meaning.

A word with an even greater vogue in recent years is "share." Contemporary American English uses "share" to refer to everything from a quality of intimate relationships to its traditional meaning: the distribution of wealth. "Sharing" of one's feelings is a sure sign of "caring" about people, of being "related," and of staying "in touch" with others rather than being isolated. Typically, therefore, in institutions that specialize in culture transmission, "sharing" appears as a central theme. Elementary school teachers in American schools are eager to "share ideas" with parents and to have their students share their feelings with the class. Advertisers and pastors "share" ideas with their audiences in an often clumsy attempt at influence. The language of sharing and contact is particularly appealing because it conforms to our conception of ourselves as equals. "Sharing" is a relationship between peers, and the term thus legitimates linguistically the efforts of schools, the mass media, and advertisers to transmit a democratic culture. Our language thus describes the culture as loosely bounded, although the actual structure of schools, advertising, and the mass media is hierarchical rather than egalitarian.

These examples give us some sense of the emphasis on connectedness in American English. A more formal example appears in the characteristically American disposition to tie separate words together into compound expressions. David Gold offers the example of "frypan," a compound of frying pan.[63] Mencken argues that the tendency toward compounds in American English originated in political speech, beginning with the nationalization of American politics during the early 1800s. A good example of the political compound is "gerrymander," though other political compounds might also be noted.[64] Related to the tendency toward compounds is the practice of creating entirely new verbs by adding suffixes to nouns or other parts of speech, thus demonstrating the capacity of a loosely bounded culture to extract dynamism from formerly static categories. Recent political examples include "prioritize," "finalize," and "demilitarize."

Whence arises this American style? In an economically dynamic society the division of labor consistently outdistances moral integration. Language struggles to keep pace with the process of change. In particular, economic change transforms stable relationships into newly minted systems of action. Put differently, in a dynamic society static relationships and traditional social classes (in a linguistic sense, nouns) suddenly find themselves undercut and forced to change (turned into verbs, in a sense). New and unexpected connections join novel occupations together with formerly unrelated groups. The invention of compounds gives this quality of change a special linguistic form.

The American tendency to produce compounds—and thus to violate the traditional boundaries of words—takes a particularly brutal form when we simply dismember two older words and join together their stumps. The resulting term contrasts strongly with a true compound, which brings intact words together. Perhaps we should not be surprised that these hybrid words describe especially fluid, unstable processes. Appropriately enough, Marckwardt finds many examples in the aerospace [*sic*] and communications fields: "cablegram," "travelogue," "newscast," "hydramatic," "paratrooper," "motel," "minicam," and "Amtrak."[65] These hybrids signify an extreme violation of linguistic boundaries, for they destroy the integrity of their original words.

The Intolerance of Sharp Distinctions

A loosely bounded culture distrusts sharp distinctions. The language of such a culture should reflect this tendency, and so it does in the American case.

Characteristic grammatical aspects of the process appear in the way American English describes time. The English of two or three hundred years ago contained a plethora of "perfect" forms which distinguished clearly between periods of time past. But in our society, where change is so ubiquitous that things become "old-fashioned" before they are actually old at all, the past can easily become a blur. Our language reflects this tendency. As early as the 1920s Mencken detected a peculiarly American proclivity to eliminate perfect tenses, a tendency which sets the past "close" in time to the present linguistically. Mencken provides an example of the verb "I have eaten," which has given way to the apparently contemporaneous expression "I'm through eating."[66] The American tendency to eliminate past time distinctions has proceeded apace since Mencken's time. An extreme example of this tendency may be found among midwestern teenagers, a group whose tender age disposes them to find the past unpleasantly constraining. The practice consists of employing the simple present tense to describe events which took place in the recent past. For example, a fourteen-year-old speaking to a teenage friend will say: "I say to Mom, let me have the car." "She goes, 'You can't.'" "I go, 'Why not,'" and so forth. The practice aims to make past events dramatic by portraying them as if they were happening at the very moment of speech. This portrayal of the past as if it were still in "play" is an extreme version of boundary violation through language. A related example transmutes the older term "teenager" (a remnant of the 1950s) into the more contemporary "young adult," a term which conveys prestige to the young at the cost of precise age distinctions.

The American distrust of sharp linguistic distinctions extends also to parts of speech. As Mencken noted, Americans tend to disregard the distinction between adjectives and adverbs.[67] We often use adjectives as if they were adverbs, thereby relegating the adverbial form to archaic, esoteric, or vestigial uses, which may actually stigmatize the user. A good example is the common use of the word "real" as if it were an adverb. To do something "real well" is now widely accepted usage, and if one insists that something must be done "really well," one cannot help appearing somewhat priggish, as if linguistic precision were being employed to make a negative comment about those who speak "real well." Linguistic precision should never be allowed to serve as a surrogate for high status in a loosely bounded culture. The balance of movement across the adverb-adjective divide increasingly tilts from the adjectival to the adverbial form. The resulting imbalance reflects our proclivity to see things as fluid rather than static, and thus illustrates linguistically the deeper cultural theme of instability which infuses all aspects of a loosely bounded culture.

The conversion of adjectives into reluctant, awkward adverbs is but one part of a general movement toward American English's breakdown of syntactical distinctions. As Marckwardt has written, "English . . . has lost its inflections to such a degree that transitions from noun to adjective, from verb to noun, from adjective to verb, and in fact, in almost all conceivable directions, are made constantly. They are so thoroughly an ingrained part of the language that a word such as 'down' may actually perform five different part-of-speech functions, preposition, adverb, adjective, noun, and verb."[68] Under these conditions it is not surprising that American English lacks the tonal variation and subtlety one finds in British English. Once parts of speech lose their distinctiveness and time tenses blur, the spoken language must also become monotonous. The "flatness" of American speech to foreign ears—its lack of sharp articulation, pitch variation, clipped vowels, or sound variations among words ("wanna" for "want to")—is no illusion; it is instead a reflection of the linguistic melding that so characterizes American English. As one might expect, in more traditional regions—the South or New England, particularly—these tendencies are somewhat mitigated, for in such places the linguistic variety of traditional English symbolizes a still-surviving, if residual, system of social ranks.

A final example of linguistic blurring is the common absence of number agreement in American English.[69] Expressions like "How is they?" and "He ain't here" have always driven American English teachers to distraction. But it is important to consider the cultural function this recurrent "mistake" performs. One possible interpretation is that the mistake reflects the rapidity of change in a loosely bounded culture. Where the division of labor moves so rapidly that it escapes normative rules and cultural visions, unexpected conjunctions of unpredictable numbers of persons regularly occur. The number-agreement mistake perhaps expresses this fluidity. Consider the change in the status of marriage, which has now become a process of serial monogamy for many people. Small wonder that confusions between number and verb emerge in the attempt to catch up with and capture such a process linguistically.

Uniformity

Regional distinctions in American English continue to exist, but the tendencies I have described reduce regional linguistic distinctiveness over time. In part, of course, our perceptions of this issue depend on our point of departure. Thus, as Marckwardt points out, the majority of American colonists in the seventeenth century had been highly regionalized in England, and it was natural that as they came into contact with each other in America their distinctive English dialects should have begun to erode.[70] Today, according to Mencken, despite the streams of varied immigration to America and despite the great physical expanse of the country itself, there are fewer regional dialects in America than in most small, more homogeneous countries.[71]

In recent years the movement from local print media to national visual media has hastened this process. National visual media must use a language that people in all regions can understand. Print media, such as the local newspaper, need to be understood by fewer people, most of whom reside within the same locale. Therefore, print media often reinforce rather than subvert local usage. Word-of-mouth communication, of course, most faithfully reproduces regional usage. Thus, the initial substitution of print media for oral media, and then the subsequent substitution of visual media for print media, reduces regional variation in language. Perhaps it is not surprising, then, that the visual media hire speakers who are regionally unidentifiable in their speech patterns. The media prefer midwesterners, whose flat direct speech complements the flatness and spatially unmarked character of the Midwest itself.

Other factors have also contributed to a uniform American English. Language education in American schools has always presented a "standard brand" of American English intended to reach anyone, regardless of social origins. The command of standard American English became an invaluable resource for ambitious, immigrant children who wished to make their way in the American world. Equally important is the comparative absence in America of a distinctive linguistic pattern organized by social class positions. One explanation of this class homogeneity in American English is the predominantly commercial origins of the American upper classes. No matter how wealthy the businessman, he still must sell products on a mass market to anonymous potential buyers. He has no choice but to speak in terms that are readily understood by all. Therefore, the American upper class may never have been able to isolate itself from the general public long enough to develop a truly distinctive linguistic style.

Absorptive Qualities

American English is uncommonly receptive to novel expressions. Ethnic minorities have found it comparatively easy to get their words absorbed into standard American English, as words like "pizza," "schlep," "macho," and "delicatessen" indicate. Mencken claims in his usual vigorous style that Americans are considerably more willing to accept new words into the lexicon than are the British.[72] The ready absorption of new words reflects and reinforces the flexibility of American group boundaries. Words flowing from minority to majority help pay the price of admission to the larger American cultural show. Among the several functions the ready acceptance of foreign words serves in America, two stand out. First, as Dillar points out, in America the adoption of the language of despised minorities is a form of symbolic naturalization.[73] From this perspective, the recent popularity of "Black English" among white Americans takes on special interest. Many Black English words have found their way into standard American usage, mainly through the entertainment media and through black entertainers, such as jazz musicians, who often find themselves near the bottom of the American heap. Acceptance of Black English signifies not only that blacks are now able to "speak" to the white majority, but also that blacks possess some concepts and modes of behavior that should be appealing to whites. Blacks, for example, have "soul." Whites lack soul, but they can partly make up for their deficiency by eating "soul food" (or by talking as if they have), by listening to "soul music," and by having "soul brothers." Language can thus transform the special sensitivity ("soul") that comes with being downtrodden into a source of symbolic prestige for blacks.

Additionally, a dominant group that adopts the language of minorities is portraying itself as democratic and tolerant. Usage of Black English allows whites to reject symbolically the conventions of white civilization and to elevate linguistically a subordinate culture. Linguistic absorption may thus pave the way for social change, particularly if the children of the dominant group adopt the language of the despised minority in order to frighten or to liberate themselves from their parents. The younger generation's costless linguistic rebellion may thus become costly indeed for their elders.

Functions, however, do not explain origins. Where does the absorptiveness of American English originate? From a host of contributing factors, three in particular stand out. The first involves the pattern of settlement in America. As the line of settlement expanded westward, settlers encountered new flora, fauna, and peoples. Each new situation presented a novel mix of climate, topography, and people. Hosts of new words made their way into the American vocabulary so as to make life on the frontier viable. The settlers naturally tended to adopt the words of the region into which they moved — usually words of Indian or Spanish origin — to describe the new things they encountered in those regions. Thus, linguistic absorption became a concomitant and a facilitator of frontier expansion.[74]

A second contributing factor was the intermixture of settlers themselves. The frontier brought together diverse ethnic groups from many different lands or even from different regions within the same land. These people suddenly found themselves dependent on each other as they tried to survive on the frontier. Linguistic differences had to be subordinated to the goal of survival; thus, linguistic accommodation became the rule. Linguistic absorption did not obviate strong group hostilities, of course, but it did make possible mutual aid for minimal purposes of protection.[75]

Finally, in modern times the mass media have become major agents of linguistic absorption. The mass media are insatiable users of "material" as they try to entice a large audience of viewers, readers, and listeners. The sheer number of scripts that make up a year's worth of broadcasting on even one of the major television networks staggers the imagination. As a result, all sorts of language becomes grist for the media mill; new or "catchy language" is especially prized as a way of attracting and holding an audience. Thus, entertainers who popularize linguistic formulae may not only succeed themselves, they may also diffuse new experiences to the audience. And, given the prominence of many minority entertainers in the mass media, it is not too farfetched to see the media performing today a linguistic function similar to that which the frontier performed in the nineteenth century.

Word Inflation

Another American linguistic characteristic that illustrates our distrust of fixed boundaries is our use of honorific or exaggerated language. American English expands meanings far beyond the terrain specifically denoted by the words themselves. For example, Americans regularly bestow honorific terms on people who do not possess the legal credentials to sustain such honorifics.[76] We use such terms as "the Honorable" very loosely, following it with the person's given name rather than, as in England, with the name of the position rather than the person. In this way our language makes individual persons rather than the position the person holds the object of respect, thus humanizing and personalizing honor by removing it from designated, fixed statuses. The same practice applies to some military titles, such as Colonel, which we award to many people who have either military experience at some lesser rank or no military experience at all. The ready use of honorifics symbolically inflates the social position of the individual, thus creating the artificial mobility of persons across barriers of status.

The ready availability of honorific titles not only expresses a democratic impulse, but also represents the uniqueness of occupational evolution in America. In many parts of the country there were for a long time no professional schools or occupational certification procedures. Honorifics thus became a kind of linguistic certification device for persons who, while able to practice a skill competently, could produce no legal or educational credentials to sustain their claim. Honorific titles came to signify the *bona fides* of such practitioners.[77] The use of the honorific helped diversify the occupational structure before more modern devices could come into play.

Our tendency toward glorification also extends to folklore. Unlike other peoples, who offer the "little people" to childish imaginations, Americans gravitate to the mythological giant (Paul Bunyan, for example). As Marckwardt explains it, a big country requires big myths, for it takes large projects to domesticate a frontier.[78] And it is worth observing how our mythology still venerates those who "expand the frontiers" of knowledge or sport. We always look for "new frontiers," as John Kennedy perceived. Thus, the Daniel Boones are the forerunners of the Jonas Salks, each of whom pushed back his own particular frontier a little way.

Word inflation is most revealing when it extends beyond the genuinely grand achievement in order to laud the commonplace. It is in this latter respect that Americans excel. Ordinary apartment houses, through the magic of hyphenation, become chateaux. A crossroads village becomes a "thriving metropolis"; the championship game in professional football becomes a "Super Bowl." The glorification of the mundane has many roots. Marckwardt comments, for example, that in pioneer communities "life . . . was both hard and dull. . . . Small wonder, then, that the settlers permitted their imaginations to clothe their drab and commonplace surroundings with the salient features of the life they had known before."[79] The observation is poignant, for many of our early settlers could no doubt see sharp distinctions between the European capitals and cathedrals they had known and the raw American towns and prairies to which they came. Perhaps linguistic glorification represented for them both a remembrance of the past and a hope for the future.

Innovation in Language: Savor or Banality?

As should be evident from this account, American English is highly innovative. But innovation can take several different directions. For example, we can invent new names for the novel occurrences thrown up by social change, or we can stretch the boundaries of old words to cover these occurrences. The latter strategy is likely to lead to banality and confusion, while the former holds the promise of freshness and creativity.

Our capacity to invent appealing new words has a long history, taking us back to the very origins of American settlement. Many varieties of pidgin English developed through the maritime contact of diverse peoples early in American history,[80] especially in the slave trade, where West African dialects encountered English, Spanish, and French. The result of this encounter was a multitude of pidgin dialects functioning alongside or perhaps underneath standard American English. And the pidgin tradition still lives.

The pidgin tradition is an example of pungent, savory innovation in language. At the same time, as Mencken pointed out, Americans show a strong preference for extending words mechanically and tediously to cover new meanings.[81] An example is the word "laundry," which originally denoted only the place where dirty clothes were cleaned, but now denotes in addition the soiled garments themselves. The alteration no doubt reflects the fact that commercial laundries have recently been superceded by home washing machines and clothes dryers. This kind of mechanical extension of language adds little of interest to our speech, and sometimes actually creates confusion.

Or consider the increase in our use of euphemisms, those words which deliberately obfuscate and sanitize reality. "Termination" rather than "death," "letting go" rather than "firing," "deprived child" rather than "poor kid," "media coordinator" rather than "public relations man"—these are but a few examples of obfuscating euphemism. Every reader can supply dozens more. Euphemisms take the sting out of what they name by providing even the most noxious phenomena with acceptable, nonthreatening phraseology. Euphemisms express in extreme form both the flexibility of American English and the tendency of American English to absorb meanings at the cost of clarity. Tocqueville, who first noted this characteristic of American English, explained both tendencies by reference to democratic pressures toward equality and conformity.[82]

Euphemisms conceal unpleasant structural realities and inequalities in American life. After all, the division of labor continues apace, as does the concentration of social and economic power in large organizations. Income and educational inequalities remain a stubborn fact in American society, as do racial and ethnic tensions. Yet a legitimate language to describe these unpleasant structural realities eludes us. And thus we encounter a basic problem which will increasingly concern us as we turn to the analysis of television, advertising, and schools, namely, how can an egalitarian, flexible, loosely bounded culture cope with highly stratified, comparatively rigid, sharply bounded institutions? Does this uneasy conjunction of inegalitarian structure and egalitarian culture create tensions that Americans do not have the words to express?

3

TELEVISION: STRUCTURE VERSUS CULTURE

Architecture and language are durable sources of culture. Loose boundedness appears more obviously and dramatically, however, in distinctively modern creators of culture. Of these, television has been most noteworthy. Television has been the subject of thousands upon thousands of commentaries. No other segment of the creation of contemporary American culture has been the subject of so many words, from testimonials to celebrations to jeremiads. Therefore, any consideration of politics and culture in America can hardly ignore television.

This outpouring of critical attention springs from many sources, some convergent, others conflicting. Among these the most important, I suspect, have to do with the rapidity of television's growth, the size of its audience, and its relationship to other media. But most important is television's sheer intrusiveness. Television penetrates deeply into American life, into the home, into the family. Therefore, television represents the extreme lengths to which a loosely bounded culture permits culture creation to go. Not surprisingly, therefore, the study of television raises questions about loose boundedness.

The celerity of its development accounts for much of the fascination television holds for academics and lay persons alike. Although the technological facilities for television dissemination had been put firmly in place prior to World War II, the expansion of television did not really begin until the 1950s.[1] But the growth thereafter was phenomenal. In the space of a generation television receivers went from a position of novelty to near ubiquity. Many homes have multiple receivers. Nor do television sets sit idly serving as coffee tables; they are switched on and are watched, more or less, approximately six hours a day on the average.[2]

The magnitude of television's ascendancy can be most easily grasped by a comparison with the arrival of print media in the Western world. The diffusion of print was constrained by the painfully slow growth of literacy in the West; it was over three hundred years after Gutenberg before a genuine "mass" audience for popular writing and newspapers developed. The novel could not develop as a form until the nineteenth century, for it was not until then that a large middle-class readership finally came into existence.[3] In fact, print coverage has never been total; many people are simply not full partners in a culture of print. The same cannot be said of television, for television watching makes fewer demands than do print media.

Of equal interest to observers is television's impact on other media, particularly on media treasured by intellectuals. As early as 1956 Dwight MacDonald argued that television produced and abetted "mid-cult," which bowdlerized "high culture" (Shakespeare, the classics) in order to feed a mass audience.[4] And there is also much research into the effects of television on other *mass* media. Frank Mankiewicz and Joel Swerdlow, for example, claim that newspaper reading has dropped to an average of half an hour a day among those who still read newspapers at all; they blame television.[5] Television undeniably undercut popular-magazine reading; indeed, the mass-magazine market collapsed primarily because of television.

But the most fascinating and disturbing aspect of television is the ease with which it penetrates family and home. Unlike the performing arts, which usually require family members to step out, television makes entertainment immediately available within the home. As Jerry Mander has put it, television moves formerly outdoor functions indoors.[6] One need only flick a switch to have the world (or its simulacrum) enter one's own living room. Television has "access," which is why Robert Lewis Shayon, in his evocative phrase, characterizes television as a "crowd-catcher."[7] Television gains entrée with ease—more ease in fact than the next-door neighbor, who must knock before entering. Yet, paradoxically, television comes from hundreds or thousands of miles away, while the neighbor merely walks across the yard.

Television's capacity to penetrate through familial boundaries disconcerts as many people as it comforts. Even a loosely bounded culture needs *some* barriers, although such barriers lack full legitimacy. The discomfort elicited by television centers particularly on the young, who are thought susceptible to television's depiction of violence. Violence on television creates unease because it violates two especially intimate boundaries— first, the boundary between the person inflicting violence and the person suffering violence, and second, the boundary between the peaceful child and the violent outside world. Small wonder, therefore, that the "effects" of television violence so trouble us, for televised violence represents the subtle dangers to which a loosely bounded culture is prone.[8]

Especially intriguing in the debate over the effects of television violence on children are the terms of the argument itself. The structure of the argument typifies what we would expect of a loosely bounded culture where, increasingly, culture is treated as a commodity which large organizations produce for "consumers." It is natural to think in terms of effects and vulnerability only if one assumes that television is uniquely efficient and powerful. But why should we automatically make such an assumption? The assumption seems natural because we think of television as being more on the order of a business corporation than on the order of, say, an individual craft. The business model leads us to think in terms of effects, for we know that business has major effects on comparatively unprotected customers. But why are people unprotected? Because, as we have seen, people exist in loosely bounded cultural contexts that provide them with little legitimate cultural opposition to the penetration of either commerce or television entertainment. Thus, our expectation of loose boundedness sets the terms of our debate about television.

Defenders and critics of television share this culture, and therefore they share the approach to television's effects which I have described. They differ, of course, in the effects they single out. Marxist critics, for example, are interested in the "effects of television" on class perceptions and on class solidarity.[9] Some argue that working-class persons are unusually vulnerable to the effects of the media. By contrast, non-Marxist critics are concerned about the effects of television on individual rationality—whether in the marketplace or in the voting booth. But the question whether television violence makes youngsters irrational or deprives them of class consciousness becomes sensible only if we treat television according to an industrial-business model of efficiency and if we believe children to be Rousseau-like natural creatures easily spoiled. The former conception assumes great cultural penetrability on the part of television; the latter assumes individual openness to communication. Both assume a loosely bounded culture.

In order to place television in the theoretical framework that we have adopted we must move beyond the debate about effects. One way to do this is to think of culture-manufacturing agencies, such as television, advertising, and schools, as vehicles both for *expressing* embedded cultural themes and for *embellishing* and *shaping* those themes. Obviously, these agencies modify the themes they express, but they operate within a preexisting cultural matrix. And, as we shall see, television expresses very well the conflict between stratified organization and loosely bounded culture in America, a conflict which renders our culture a poor means of controlling structures, organizations, and institutions.

CRITICISM AND DEFENSE OF TELEVISION

Some of the most pungent critics of television are Marxist writers. While non-Marxists have their own criticisms of television, they also defend the medium, at least in part because many gravitate toward pluralism—a political theory which appeals to those with power in America, including those who control and profit by television. Marxism, on the other hand, defends the interests of those who are comparatively powerless vis à vis television. Thus, Marxism and pluralism function as ideologies—the former to those who lack power in and over television, the latter to those who control the medium.

A Marxist critique of television appears succinctly in Gaye

Tuchman's formulation: "American television perpetuates hegemony; it adumbrates political and intellectual discourse. It not only buries dissent; it buries the possibility that new ideas may emerge."[10] To Tuchman, television diffuses the ideas of a ruling economic class that controls television production and program dissemination. In an attempt to support their arguments, Marxists analyze both the ownership structure and the program content of television.

On the ownership issue, Erik Barnouw, the foremost historian of television, describes the evolution of American television as a growing convergence of the economic interests of the owners of local television stations, the television networks, and the large corporations that rely on television to advertise their products and, in so doing, purvey their own version of American life.[11] The process of convergence has been marked by a growing centralization of network power over programming. In the early days of television, individual programs were owned and shaped by their sponsors who, though themselves large capitalist enterprises, were at least numerous, occasionally diverse in interest, and sometimes even interested in "quality programming." By the early 1960s, however, television programming had come almost exclusively under the control of networks rather than of advertisers, much less of "sponsors." The networks standardized television production, played down program diversity, and ultimately reduced the quality of programs.[12]

The Marxist critique stresses the extraordinary profits of television networks. The networks are at the very top among corporations in profits even while the rest of the economy goes downhill. And, according to Richard Bunce, the networks and their local affiliates are increasingly owned by large conglomerate organizations, which use television to market the goods produced by other corporations in the conglomerate. For example, the conglomerate of which the Columbia Broadcasting System is a part also develops instructional material for schools. CBS stations help sell this material indirectly by showing programs about the "crisis" in American schooling. Meanwhile, Westinghouse-owned stations show programs about deteriorating urban transportation in order to help Westinghouse sell its mass transit inventions.[13]

The networks owe their great power largely to their ability to neutralize federal government regulation. The Federal Communications Commission has regularly favored the networks and station owners against consumers, public interest lobbies, and even television artists. The networks, their affiliates, and their sponsors have even made use of American foreign policy to gain lucrative foreign markets for American television programs and receivers. Barnouw charges that the networks and their advertisers used blocked Marshall Plan funds in the 1950s to supply programs to foreign television markets. They could do this because they knew that American cold war policy would protect their foreign investments. Foreign marketing of American television receivers, transmitters, production facilities, and programs have linked the networks to such firms as the International Telephone and Telegraph Corporation and the American Telephone & Telegraph Company, so as to make American television an important force for American cultural domination abroad.[14]

If, according to its critics, television ownership is best understood as a species of monopoly capitalism, program content is best understood as also favoring the interests of capitalists. The best-known Marxist cultural critiques of television emerge from the neo-Marxist Frankfurt school. According to Oskar Negt, members of the Frankfurt school believed that mass media produce a mechanical culture which both destroys the romantic, liberating force of art and politicizes aesthetics itself. The Frankfurt school saw the commercial element of the mass media as a series of "secondary rituals," which "were all the more suitable for the effective deception of the masses."[15] The main economic function of the media was to "pursue the business of universalizing commodity production. In this process the entire cultural heritage is drawn into the capitalist nexus of utilization and domination."[16] In short, by harnessing art to the selling of goods, the mass media obscured all liberating or revolutionary components in traditional high culture.

Because television and the mass media in general degrade possibilities for political change, they also delegitimize tension and conflict. In terms both of production and of content, according to its Marxist critics, the conception of tension and conflict decays. On the production side, what pretends to be free enterprise and lively competition is in fact a very restricted oligopolistic process indeed, since the three networks "snap and bite at each other while fighting for an identical, virtually agreed-upon audience."[17] Network oligopoly and the standardization of the audience eliminate vital competition among television producers, who therefore turn out a narrow range of programs which, in turn, reduces the awareness of conflict and choice in the audience. A complementary process of tension reduction may be found in the content of single programs. Thus, according to Adorno, television dramas lack tension because the audience knows beforehand who must win and who must lose.[18] This knowledge reflects a society in which life is predestined. Meanwhile, to Adorno's influential colleague Marcuse, television contributes mightily to the closed circle of discussion that produces "one-dimensional man."[19] The formulae of the situation comedy and the melodrama simply do not permit genuine tension and unexpected resolutions to emerge, so real conflict and genuine change is foreclosed from the outset.

Critics also charge that recent innovations in television serve to consolidate the power position of the networks and the advertisers they serve. Both Barnouw and Rose Goldsen argue that advances in survey methodology by the Nielsen company now give networks and advertisers a clearer picture of their audiences than they ever possessed before.[20] As a result, the "demographic composition" of the audience now dominates programming decisions, and programs that reach only poor or elderly audiences become undesirable, for such audiences lack purchasing power. Therefore, the new availability of the "demographics" gives program ratings greater power than ever before over television decisions. Low-rated "quality" programs cannot survive under these conditions.

Defenders of television often cite responsiveness to the ratings as proof that television is sensitive to public tastes, but Goldsen argues that the "democracy" of the ratings is deceptive, for in television some viewers are more equal than others. The rich in the audience call the tune. The ratings determine program decisions because mass audiences "must be broken up into negotiable economic units" for delivery to advertisers, who pay the networks according to a sliding scale of prices depending on the size and composition of the audience. The bigger and wealthier the audience the more the network can charge for commercial time.[21] The inevitable result of this system, according to Goldsen, is a devaluation of programs for minority audiences and minority tastes.

According to television's Marxist critics, the working class is the main loser in the centralization of network control over the media. Some critics argue that the absence of working-class consciousness and of opposition to capitalism can be traced to unfavorable television portrayals of the working class, portrayals which the working class itself all too readily accepts. Piepe, Emerson, and Lannon provide evidence that working-class Englishmen watch more television in a haphazard fashion than do middle-class people.[22] This pattern of viewing leaves the working class particularly vulnerable to media effects. In addition, working-class people use television less for information-seeking than for sheer escape, a form of viewing almost certain to turn them away from productive political involvement. In sum, television stimulates ideological fragmentation among working-class people and adulterates class cultures. In David Sallach's summation, television perpetuates the ideological hegemony of a dominant capitalist class by preventing the working class from translating its experiences of exploitation and deprivation into politically usable form.[23]

As might be expected, defenders of television dispute most of these arguments. Defenders do find some faults in television, but prefer to focus on different aspects of the medium from those discussed by Marxists. Moreover, defenders of television interpret the medium's internal operations, ownership structure, and program content quite differently from Marxist critics.

Defenders of television usually begin with the observation that all the media in America are sequestered from governmental ownership or control. Television's dependence on commercial sponsorship of programs, though a hindrance to full television freedom, nevertheless protects the medium from a worse fate:

use by government for propaganda purposes. They then conclude that what is lost from commercial sponsorship is less than what is gained from the absence of government interference.

Defenders also make three other points about the organizational structure of television. Some argue that the ratings, though not freeing television from capitalist control, nevertheless introduce an element of "consumer sovereignty" over the medium's presentations. Television must respond to the feedback the ratings provide, for otherwise the networks and their local affiliates will be unable to sell their commercial time at a profit. Therefore, sensitivity to the ratings insures that programs satisfy some genuine public desire.

Defenders also argue that the Marxist critique misrepresents the operating structure of television. Although television ownership does conform closely to a picture of monopoly capitalism, and although the medium may serve the plurality of financial interests of advertisers, actual programming decisions and policies are set by many groups, not all of whom share capitalist perspectives. Even Tuchman admits that "decisions about content are made on every organizational level," and include professional television staffers, writers, directors, and, in some cases, interest groups representing the "grass roots."[24]

Particularly relevant to the question of control is the confusion within television itself over its self-definition. To some in the medium, television is an "industry," and should be understood as simply a very effective device for selling products. To others—including many network executives—television is a form of "entertainment," a particularly appealing compound of salesmanship, escape, and craftsmanship. Still others believe that television already is, or at least has the potential to become, a real art form; supporters of this view find the Marxist critique least appealing. In any case, as these divergent views suggest, the Marxist critique can be accused of ignoring the tensions within television between those who create and develop programs and those who choose programs for viewing and then market them.

Evidence of this tension emerges from the observations of Ben Stein, whose extensive interviews with Hollywood television writers and producers revealed a deep sense of hostility, isolation, and estrangement from the financial centers of the medium. Most television writers despise the corporate structure of television; some even espouse a conspiracy theory of history, in which Nazis, businessmen, and politicians are all united against them and against the American public. If Stein is correct, those who actually create television programs are seriously at odds with those who run the networks. Moreover, some of these hostile views succeed in making their way into programming. Thus, the values actually displayed in television programs do not uniformly support a capitalist structure. In sum, as Stein puts it, "The people who are in a position of creative authority in television feel very much at war with the power centers of American life."[25]

Stein's analysis of division within the medium is supported by the work of Cantor and Ravage. Cantor reports that television producers, who are primarily responsible for the development and selection of programs, have little real conception of the audience that their shows reach. Instead of feeling constrained by the "demographics," most employ their own taste in an attempt to reach a quite undifferentiated, poorly conceptualized public.[26] And in his study of television directors, Ravage reports a widespread view that television contains no ideological bias whatever, other than the desire to gain a large audience. Those responsible for programming will air anything that promises popularity, regardless of political or social message.[27] If Ravage is correct, television's willingness to devote so much attention to apparently counter-system messages, such as protests and demonstrations, becomes clearer.

Finally, its defenders argue that television content is far more diverse than Marxists admit. Recent years have seen the regular treatment of subjects touching formerly forbidden areas—sexual relations, delicate family problems, racial, ethnic, and sexual stereotypes—all of which convey messages that certainly disdain tradition, if not dispute capitalist hegemony itself.

These debates about television have so far been inconclusive. Inconclusiveness is in part a function of disparate and unsatisfactory research findings, but the problem runs deeper.

The two versions of television are offshoots of the quite different visions of culture in industrial societies that Marxists and pluralists propound. The two versions of television therefore manifest all the problems of the larger theories from which they depart. The argument I intend to pursue attempts to synthesize the two within the framework of the theory I have laid out. I believe that Marxist criticism is a useful tool for understanding the organizational structure and some of the program content of television, but that it fails to account for all the messages television portrays. The pluralist defense is helpful in the latter respect. But the real message of television is the inconsistency between its structure and its culture, an inconsistency which, by reproducing loose boundedness, helps keep Americans from appreciating the organizational constraints on their own lives. In order to sustain this argument we must first analyze the structure of television, and then turn to matters of form, content, and culture.

THE STRUCTURE OF AMERICAN TELEVISION

The major organizational components of American television are local stations, most of which are affiliated with one of the three commercial networks, the networks themselves, advertisers who attempt to sell goods over the airwaves, writers, directors, actors, producers of television programs, and public regulators, of whom the most salient is the Federal Communications Commission. The principal actor among these groups is the network, whose control over time and access comes very close to that described in the Marxist critique.[28] In brief, television is a centralized, hierarchical, oligopolistic, but internally competitive program-distribution agency whose primary concern is the making of profits from commercial advertising. The role of the network is central in this process, even though the networks themselves create few of the programs and commercials they transmit. But although networks are mainly conduits for the efforts of others, they nevertheless enjoy control over these others. For this reason, television perhaps comes closer to fitting an orthodox Marxist model of exploitation than do either of the other two culture-creation structures we will consider.

From the outset of their development in America the electronic media have depended for their main financial support on the sale of air time to advertisers. This operation poses problems, given that the *public* owns the channels through which radio and television transmissions move. The anomaly is that, while the public may own the air, private interests—local stations and the networks themselves—own the facilities necessary for transmission. Other than its facilities, the station owner owns nothing but an operating license, renewable by the Federal Communications Commission every three years, which makes legal transmission to the general public.

In actuality, however, despite the legal rule of public control and the regulatory function of the FCC, the core of television lies in the private relationship between the local station, the network, and the commercial advertiser. Although stations are usually owned by local groups, most are "affiliates" of one of the three national commercial networks. The profitability of the affiliate depends on its capacity to transmit commercial messages which reach a large local viewing audience. The station's venture becomes profitable because of the twin properties of simultaneity and anonymity "that constitute the very heart of advertiser-supported . . . television."[29] "A message that advertises a product—no matter how expensive that message is to produce or buy time for—can more than pay for its cost by being transmitted simultaneously to anonymous multitudes via a television screen that has the extraordinary power to keep [people] hypnotically entranced."[30] In short, local stations are simply the means by which advertisers attempt to reach a large market efficiently.

If stations are to operate profitably, they must attract an audience. Otherwise, advertisers will put their money elsewhere. Television programs, therefore, are the indispensable means of attracting the necessary audience. Thus, from the perspective of station owners and network executives, programs are best understood simply as unavoidable and irksome means to corral an audience willing to watch commercials. Programs are themselves economically valueless; indeed, they constitute the main operating costs of television. The perspective of the average television station owner is almost completely the reverse of

the average viewer's. To the viewer, no matter how artfully constructed, a commercial is a necessary evil; viewers see commercials primarily as tiresome means to the desirable end of program viewing. To the owners, programs are the necessary evils
that serve the larger good of the commercial. Thus, there is a
basic conflict of interest between television's owners and network executives, on the one hand, and the public, on the other.
The television executive would like to reduce the amount of
money spent on programs and raise the amount spent on commercials; the public would like them to spend more money on
programs and less on commercials. The balance of power in
this conflict favors the executive: per minute of air time, far
more money is spent on commercials than on programs.

The network functions primarily as a middleman in the organizational structure of television. The network coordinates
the production and distribution of programs and advertisements for its local affiliates. In part, the power of the network
stems from economies of scale. The network is a centralized
booking agency with whom advertisers deal in the placement
and distribution of commercials. Were it not for the network,
advertisers would have to make literally hundreds of separate
contacts and contracts with local stations. Similarly, networks
provide most of the programs that local affiliates show, because
the cost of creating enough television programs to fill the number of program hours each day is prohibitively expensive for
the local affiliate. Affiliates have some choice in whether to run
programs supplied them by the network; in the case of some
locally "controversial" programs they have exercised their option to refuse network programming. But as a practical matter,
most affiliates lack the financial resources and production facilities to provide much alternative programming for themselves. Therefore, they remain dependent on the networks.

Another basis of network power is technological: the networks exercise control over the transmission lines through
which television pictures travel. The National Broadcasting
Company is a part of the Radio Corporation of America,
which, along with the American Telephone & Telegraph Company, owns the transmission lines through which programs go.

Because local affiliates require access to these lines in order to transmit programs, they must depend on the networks.

Meanwhile, advertisers contract for showing commercials with both the network and, in local markets, affiliates or independent stations. Advertisers pay for the use of air time according to a sliding scale of costs per minute based on the size and composition of the audience for programs in which the commercial appears. Although advertisers make use of advertising agencies to help in the development and placement of their commercials on television, they themselves retain legal title to the commercials. In a sense, therefore, advertisers "sponsor," not programs, but commercials. Advertisers pay the entire cost of commercials, usually to independent producers of commercials, although a few large companies contain in-house production facilities to develop commercials.[31]

Given the huge cost of producing television commercials, one would naturally expect commercials to be a substantial financial burden to advertisers. But this is not necessarily the case, for, as Barnouw points out, "For tax purposes the cost of making and showing commercials is generally deducted as a business cost—which means that the citizen is in effect subsidizing much of the barrage of argumentation aimed at him."[32] Thus, while the public has little direct control over the program decisions of networks, stations, and advertisers, it still must pay much of the costs that the three production units generate. And, as if to compound the double jeopardy, the public is then asked to buy the products it has helped advertise.

The complex interplay between local station, advertiser, and network has a profound influence on the character of television programming. For example, as Shayon points out, "It is highly desirable that . . . audiences be delivered by the crowd-catcher [television] to the sponsors in a mode that is receptive to the latter's commercial messages. This means essentially a relaxed, comfortable, happy state of mind."[33] Commercial considerations thus limit the amount of tension, of unresolved conflicts, and of depressing endings the audience can expect to see on television. Creative personnel pay a large price in this process. Television's inhibitions on tension and conflict give writers and directors little room for maneuver. The role of the television director shrinks to that of a transient inheritor of ongoing programs or scripts over which he or she exerts little artistic control. Indeed, the lack of artistic demands or opportunities helps to explain why television series are able to rotate directors freely, and why directors rove from show to show on a free-lance basis. Directors are usually hired for established programs that contain fixed, well-defined characters. Additionally, the director of a single episode works under tight constraints of time. Preexisting budget arrangements place a rigid ceiling on costs and thus reduce script maneuverability. The director simply moves the bodies around. The result is a certain "standardized," somewhat repetitive directorial product in television.[34]

Network power of the magnitude I have described is a recent phenomenon. In its early years television program ownership and development followed the pattern that had evolved in radio. Sponsors developed and owned most programs, and sponsors also put up the money for program creation. These advertisers typically contracted to make their programs available, with commercials included, as single units to networks. The process gave the advertiser or the sponsor considerable power over programming. Networks negotiated with advertising agencies and sponsors from a position of weakness; their schedules were at the mercy of the unpredictable programming tastes that sponsors sometimes displayed. Some programs, such as "The Bell Telephone Hour," survived despite their catering to minority tastes, because they became popularly identified with the sponsoring company and with quality presentations. These programs enjoyed a special power to defy network alterations in format and distribution. Most sponsored programs occupied regular time and day slots, further limiting the network's maneuverability.

It was this situation that encouraged the legend of sponsor censorship of television programs. The legend is partly true. Sponsors were the moving force behind television blacklisting in the early 1950s, a period in which many suspected former Communists disappeared from television view and in which program themes were carefully scrutinized. Some organiza-

tions, such as the anti-Communist group headed by supermar-
ket magnate Lawrence Johnson, threatened to boycott the
products of sponsors who continued to employ "unreliable"
people in their programs. Given the crucial role of supermar-
kets in product distribution, Johnson's was no idle threat. Even
today, according to Cantor, producers of television shows occasionally fight sponsor censorship and intrusion.[35]

But in recent years the power of the network has grown at
the expense of advertisers. The changes are many. No longer
do advertisers sponsor whole programs, and it is the network,
not the advertiser, which decides where to place advertising.
Sponsors of whole programs exist now in only special cases. Advertisers no longer control particular time slots. Fewer advertisers produce programs themselves. Few have much control
over program content. Networks now finance most program
creation, and it is the network's standards—not the advertiser's—that must be met before programs appear on the air.

The ascent of the network and the decline of the sponsor
may be explained by a number of different factors. The details
go far beyond what can be discussed here, and the legal and
financial technicalities are tedious. But several points deserve
mention by way of example in order to indicate the process of
network ascension. The key period in the process was the mid-
to late 1950s when, through adroit use of fortuitous opportunities, network executives succeeded in making networks the
power centers of television.

An initial factor of importance was that during the mid-
1950s television and the movies finally agreed that it was better
to work together than to fight each other. As part of the ensu-
ing arrangement the studios made available to the networks—
at huge profits to themselves—hundreds of movies for television showing. Two important results of this policy emerged.
First, television and movies became partners rather than an-
tagonists, and made-for-television movies constitute a large
part of every film studio's output today. Second, and more important from the network's standpoint, the new-found availability of movies relieved network dependence on programs
developed by sponsors. Not only could the networks decide for

themselves when they wished to show particular movies, they could also control advertising time during the movies. Naturally, the power of the network vis à vis the advertiser increased.

Of greater importance, however, were the quiz show scandals of the late 1950s. The quiz shows were the most popular programs of their era. All were owned by commercial advertisers who had developed them under contractual arrangements with independent producers. Most important, all were identified in the public mind with particular sponsors. The networks themselves claimed to have had little control over the programs, and in fact to have entertained some misgivings about their quality. When it turned out that the quiz shows were rigged and that contestants had been given answers, the networks felt that their own credibility, as well as that of the sponsors, had been seriously damaged. Astutely, they used this debacle to argue that they would no longer take responsibility for programs over which they exercised no control. So, in Barnouw's words, the networks "would no longer permit sponsors to own or control shows, and they squelched any further notion that an advertiser had about his 'franchise' or his right to any time period; the networks produced or bought the programs."[36] Since the late 1950s a variety of policy changes have permitted the networks to consolidate their control. For example, networks now determine their own advertising fees and remunerate their affiliates at a flat rate for carrying commercials. The networks pocket as profit the difference between the costs they charge advertisers and the flat rate they pay affiliates. None of these enormous profits would have been possible without program control.

The rise of the network and the centralization of network control over programming predispose us to agree with Tuchman's assessment that television "reflects a corporate economy" in its organization.[37] At the same time, however, the Marxist critique underemphasizes aspects of this process which reduce the network's apparently monolithic control. Marxists overlook the fact that television is a highly unstable structure internally. Program executives, writers, directors, actors, and network management feel themselves under overwhelming and constant pressure to produce highly rated programs. But the sad fact is that most programs fail in this respect. It is not surprising, therefore, that the rate of personnel turnover within the television industry is perhaps as high as turnover in any capitalist structure. Turnover is particularly high among the creative personnel. This instability has created an individualistic, entrepreneurial, self-help ideology in television despite the centralization and bureaucratization of network structure. As Stein notes, television producers are still largely on their own in developing and selling programs; their insecurity causes them to project great plans to make money quickly, to become lucky or ambitious, to strike it rich with a successful program.[38] Their mentality resembles far more that of the primitive capitalist adventurer or the frontiersman or even the prospector for gold than it does that of the careful bureaucrat in a centralized communication system. Within television, insecurity reigns as an entrenched, centralized bureaucratic structure competes with venture capitalism and aesthetic values. The Marxist critique misses this struggle.

A number of factors have created the insecurity and boom-and-bust psychology of television. The most important single factor is the high rate at which programs fail. In this respect television's "products" are far inferior to the products of other corporations. Each year the networks and independent producers spend millions of dollars on new programs, most of which never even get to the "pilot" stage, much less into full production. The few programs that do appear as series may pay off eventually for their creators, but the money spent on unproduced pilots is simply wasted. Moreover, despite much advance testing to gauge likely audience reaction, the majority of new series also fail to make money for their producers and creators. This sorry record of product inefficiency hardly bespeaks real "hegemony" or wholly effective, frictionless class domination of the sort a Marxist critique envisages.

The same sorry record applies to the financial lifeblood of the entire enterprise—the commercial. Only one-eighth of the potential viewing audience actually sees the typical television program. Of these viewers only one-fourth recall the commercials on the program.[39] Whether, and how, these commercials influence buying habits remains unclear. This low level of audience appeal coupled with the great cost of producing commercials does not signify great success. Instead, most studies of effects and awareness strongly dispute any simple argument that television is a highly efficient process of communication. Quite the opposite is nearer the truth.

Explaining this discrepancy between centralized, rationalized organizational form and limited communication success is a question that reaches to the heart of our inquiry. Part of the "effects gap" undoubtedly stems from a breakdown between communicators and the public.[40] Despite the "demographics" and the massive audience research available to them, television producers and network executives really have very little idea of the tastes of the audience for which they are programming. They still rely heavily on rules of thumb internal to television itself or on their own professionally tutored intuitions. This is as true on the news side of television as on the entertainment side, according to Gans and Schlesinger.[41] Small wonder, therefore, that programming efforts should often misfire.

For the political scientist interested in culture and politics, television news is of special importance. The presentation of news brings cultural predispositions directly to bear on political perception. I propose no detailed account of television news organization in this study. As might be expected, however, economic considerations determine important characteristics of television news.

Until recently, the conventional television wisdom considered news and public affairs broadcasting an economic loss. Therefore, broadcasters reduced such programming to the lowest level compatible with FCC regulations. Thus, for example, between 1966 and 1971 very few local stations devoted more than 20 percent of their air time to news and public affairs; most devoted far less. The operating dictum carried with it a set of self-fulfilling prophecies. For example, because advertisers assumed that news audiences are sophisticated and therefore resistant to sales messages, they were naturally unwilling to place their advertisements on news programs. As a result the news programs were underfinanced and operated at a loss, a fact which, in turn, discouraged producers from sinking money into such programs, thereby dooming them to continue doing what they had been doing: reaching a small, commercial-resistant audience.[42]

This formulation might lead us to expect that financially successful stations will be willing to put more money into public-interest and news programming. The evidence, however, does not substantiate the claim. Thus, after looking at the fifty largest television markets, Robert Prisuta concludes, "The data indicate that markets which feature a relative surplus of advertising revenue will stimulate stations to utilize that surplus in increased commercial time, as opposed to increased public interest programming."[43] Nor does the concentration of station ownership or so-called cross-ownership (where stations are owned by other media outlets, such as newspapers) alter this pattern.[44]

In recent years, however, things have changed somewhat. A few news programs and some regular news "magazines," such as "60 Minutes," have unexpectedly become money-makers. Although there is considerable speculation about this alteration in viewing habits, some critics argue that news producers have purchased these larger audiences at the cost of factual value and reportorial accuracy. News magazines seem increasingly to adopt program techniques developed for the entertainment side of the medium, thereby reinforcing the formulaic logic of television, a logic that is antipathetic to "hard news."

TELEVISION: FORM AND CONTENT

There is a conflict between the concentrated organizational power of television and the fluid cultural form and content that television programs evince. Organizationally and economically, as we have seen, television is a centralized, hierarchical, internally competitive structure in which profit is the major goal, and in which program failure is common. Culturally, however, both television form and television content depict a decentralized, egalitarian, democratic society in which individual success is common. Thus, the culture of television is at odds with television's organizational structure.

Most analysts of television agree upon certain of its formal characteristics. They agree that television conveys comparatively little real information, primarily for technical reasons. Television also places great emphasis on speedy transmission in terms of message rate, viewer attention, and technological gadgetry. Although television expands the public's awareness of distant places and events, it mediates such awareness in artificial ways. Television personalizes experiences, emphasizes action over explanation or evaluation, and elevates the ephemeral at the expense of the durable. Finally, despite its fascination with "personality," television portrays the growth of personality poorly. It therefore displays a conception of personality continuity in the midst of constant environmental flux. [45]

We begin this analysis of program form by focusing on the simplest factor: information. Consider television news, in which the transmission of information is central. According to Diamond, "A newscaster speaking at a normal broadcast quality pace can deliver no more than 120 words a minute; the average high school educated person can read about 250 words a minute." [46] The same general ratio of information transmission holds true throughout television. Simply put, whatever the content, print media transmit information in less time than does television.

Given these severe constraints on television's dissemination of information, among those who put programs together there is a natural emphasis on not wasting precious program time. Schlesinger, for example, shows how preoccupation with making optimum use of time becomes an obsession among British Broadcasting Corporation newscasters, who depend on elaborate formulae to translate broadcast time segments into sentence patterns. [47] There is no margin for temporal error in television; given the medium's slow rate of transmission of information, economy of words, simplicity, and directness are vital. And "dead time," when no one speaks, is the greatest curse of all.

The problem of a constrained flow of information is particularly significant given the other major temporal property of television: its pacing through the control of the transmitter rather than the viewer. As Diamond puts it, "Television is a very demanding mode of communication. . . . There is no way for the viewer to go back over material, in the way a newspaper reader or book reader can glance back over the page."[48] Given this property, it is not surprising that television producers should be preoccupied with making their every word and image count. In practice, the resulting technical requirements eliminate subtlety and inflection from the medium, for subtlety might miss (and thus lose) viewers, who would require explanation or repetition in order to get the message. And, economically, television simply cannot afford to lose viewers.[49]

An additional consequence of time limitations in television is a great reliance on visual information. Because the eye can process visual images more rapidly than the ear and the brain can process speech, programmers naturally speed up the rate at which they convey visual images. Time limitations are particularly significant in commercials, which must tell a complete story in as little as thirty seconds. It is not surprising, therefore, that commercials have pioneered new techniques for quickly conveying visual information. As Price puts it, "Culturally, commercials have trained our eye to accept fast cuts, dense and highly paced imagery, very brief scenes, connections that are implied but not spelled out—in brief, a new style of visual entertainment."[50] Television has also speeded up our perception of the visual world by developing innovations that make possible such "technical events" as animation and superimposed images. According to Mander, there is a generally accepted rule that in a commercial a "technical event" should occur every six seconds in order to stimulate viewer interest.[51] The result of these efforts is an impression of speed, movement, and "import," despite the absence of much real information. Many of these techniques have spread to successful entertainment programs, such as "Laugh-In," to "learning programs," such as "Sesame Street," and even to television politics, which makes use of many techniques developed in spot commercials.

The manipulation of time is equally significant to the construction of entire programs. The standard story line must develop from premise to resolution within a half hour or an hour—hardly time to convey much serious information. All program episodes and segments must fit the demands not only of the time slot as a whole but also of the commercial breaks within each program. As a result, situations that in real life develop naturally over varying periods receive a standard, short, artificial treatment in television. Television regularizes our experience, encouraging us to think of the serious and the trivial as equally important in terms of time, if not in the mind's eye.

Not only does television fail to differentiate well between the serious and the trivial, it also trivializes complicated problems. This too it owes to time constraints. As Newcomb puts it, television "creates the illusion that our lives can be made whole within a sixty-minute time slot—interrupted only by eight minutes of commercial message."[52] This tendency to pose easy, unrealistic resolutions to serious problems confronts television with a dilemma. Either television attempts to treat serious problems for what they are—serious—and therefore broaches solutions which the audience on reflection must recognize to be impossible and unworthy of the problem (as if, for example, Macbeth could wash the blood off his hands with Irish Spring Soap), or else television must portray such problems as less serious than they actually are in order to make program resolutions believable. In practice, television adopts the latter option. The primary formula of the situation comedy involves making what in the real world are anguishing problems of family life and social relations appear comedic and, because they are reduced to comedy, soluble. Laughter is television's best medical prescription.

Another way in which television attempts to solve this dilemma is by portraying the most ordinary means for meeting problems as if they possessed almost magical powers. Thus, simple decency and politeness suddenly become powerful devices for problem solving, rather than the straightforward social facilitators they actually are. Television magnifies the ordinary into the extraordinary in order to mask the discrepancy between problem and resolution that is inherent in its format.

Goldsen has summarized the problem well:

Television programs face a continuing dilemma. To hold an audience, they must evoke human feelings, stir human emotions, engage human passions. Yet as soon as viewers find their intellectual curiosity awakened, as soon as they allow themselves to be gripped by fear or anxiety, love or hate, terror or revulsion or rage, as soon as they are on the way to being overcome by laughter or engulfed by tears, the program delivers them to commercials.[53]

The difficulty is that people emotionally stirred by real problems could hardly be expected to welcome commercials; they could be expected, instead, to resent commercial intrusions into the action. Paradoxically, television has an inherent interest in dampening the emotional engagement of the audience. As Mander puts it, "The ideal relationship between program and commercial is that the program should be just interesting enough to keep you interested, but not so interesting as to actually dominate the ads."[54]

There is one emotional response, however, which television most desires to unleash: viewer demand for a product. The financial health of television depends on viewers who believe that advertised products are worth having. In order to convey this message, television constantly praises people who give in to impulses of all sorts, especially to acquisitive impulses or impulses to consume. The message is that people who give in to emotions eventually gain, even though in the short run they may suffer.

How can impulsiveness be made compatible with emotional restraint? Shouldn't people who are always being encouraged to "give in" and "take it all off" expect and desire real emotional gratification from programs? Not necessarily. Indeed, the question itself represents a good example of how a loosely bounded culture shapes perceptions, for the question assumes that the restraint of emotion is equivalent to the absence of emotion. The question ignores the fact that in *tightly* bounded cultures restraint and ritual coexist with and in fact stimulate great depths of individual emotion and sentiment. But the culture of television, with its encouragement of uncontrolled behavior and shallow emotions, typifies a loosely bounded culture. By contrast, tightly bounded cultures encourage controlled behaviors and deeply rooted emotions.

To get across its message of uncontrolled demand, television derogates the idea of order, even of natural order. As Mander points out, the television commercial proceeds on the assumption that the natural endowments of individuals are always deficient.[55] Nature unnecessarily limits human perfectibility and happiness. Nature makes people perspire, get dirty, move awkwardly, age unattractively. Television sells products that promise to correct nature's faults and, in so doing, to push aside natural limits and barriers. Television thus spreads the gospel of human perfectibility, with nature just one more moving frontier to be driven back by pioneering characters using innovative products.

These observations bring us to the argument that television "personalizes" events. Observers usually have in mind several different meanings of personalization, some that focus on how the right combination of "personality" traits can solve social problems, some that focus on television's fascination with "celebrities," and some that focus on television's promise that advertised products will "improve" character. This complexity about the meaning of personalization is symptomatic of the ambiguous position personality itself assumes in television.

Consider the question of personality stability, for example. In one sense, the personality of the television character is unusually stable. Indeed, it is this very character stability, with its resistance to fundamental development, which some writers believe to be the cause of shallowness in television. Newcomb argues this position most persuasively. Newcomb also believes that character stability is one of the primary ways television falsifies real life.[56] Although real people do change, television pays no heed. Season after season major television characters remain rooted in time—ageless and changeless—while the technological qualities of television itself constantly stimulate our sense of change.

How can character stability in television be explained? One explanation is that the static quality of television characters caters to the medium's norms of economic logic, which states that the way to make a television series popular is to establish audience identification with a character at the very outset of a series and then to crystallize the character indefinitely. The conventional wisdom in television claims that audiences dislike changes in character, although the same wisdom claims that audiences crave changes in the social situations in which characters find themselves.

The problem with this argument is that it ignores a type of character change which *is* common on television. Consider the following example. In a recent episode of "One Day at a Time," the heroine—a divorced mother of two teenage girls—experiences the following events in the space of a scant half hour: (1) her older daughter announces that she is shortly to be married to a man whom the mother has never heard of; (2) the mother argues vehemently with her daughter about the wisdom of the impending union; (3) the daughter decides at the last moment not to marry; (4) it is revealed that a friend of the daughter's former fiancé loves the daughter, and that the daughter reciprocates. Action, energy, and change abound in this episode; the events pile one on top of another as the mother in "One Day at a Time" struggles to cope. Understandably, the mother's moods change rapidly as she tries to keep up with this flood of unsettling events. And yet, once calm has returned at the end of the episode, the mother is not really altered at all. Despite the apparent trauma of these events, she seems fundamentally no different at the end of the program than at the beginning. Situational challenge and emotional response are ubiquitous; character development is totally absent.

This example serves to refine our conception of character on television. The ideal television character is able to absorb rapidly changing, unpredictable events without losing emotional balance. True, events occur unpredictably and rapidly; there is never a dull moment. But characters almost always cope. The larger question, of course, is what sort of character can operate in this way, and the answer appears to be the kind of distinctly modern, flexible, open character described by Robert Jay Lifton.[57] Yet the price paid for personality flexibility is a certain shallowness. It is hard to believe that characters with truly deep attachments, ideals, and commitments could respond so rapidly and unflappably to severe challenges to their beliefs. Instead, there is a convergence of character "development" on television and the broadcaster's ideal of a wholly responsive audience. Both character and audience should be open enough to try and perhaps be converted to new products or new situations, yet not so deeply involved as to become fundamentally wedded to their shallow conversions.

The pattern of shallow, flexible characters adjusting to rapidly changing, potentially traumatizing situations can better be understood by placing it within the single most important and distinctive formal quality of television. Raymond Williams puts his finger on this quality when he writes:

> In all developed broadcasting systems the characteristic organization, and therefore the characteristic experience, is one of sequence or flow. This phenomenon, of planned flow, is then perhaps the defining characteristic of broadcasting, simultaneously as a technology and as a cultural form.[58]

In other communication modes, such as books, newspapers, plays, or painting, the audience cognizes separate, discrete, detailed items. On television, however, one program succeeds another with no break in time and usually with little continuity in content or theme. From the perspective of the viewer this miscellany of images is comparatively undifferentiated. In fact, television broadcasters work on the assumption that people watch "television," not a particular program. This sort of assumption differs markedly from that entertained in other media.

Williams's description sketches a communication experience where primary emphasis falls on a whole *process* of communication—the television experience itself—rather than on the *substance* of any particular program or set of programs. As a result, argues Williams, television conveys diffuse moods or messages, rather than sharply differentiated meanings. Over the course of an evening's viewing a set of loosely linked themes may emerge, but the relevant viewing unit is "television this night," not a particular program or a sharply defined idea. What is central to this process is a feeling of continuous flow from program to program, like an onrushing river. Television is a stream of entertainment sweeping an audience along, rather than a set of discrete programs, each with a different, perhaps even conflictual message. As a cultural form, therefore, television elevates process above substance, mood above message, flow and movement above locus or stasis.

Often, vague themes that emerge from an evening's programming are meant to reproduce the sense of continuous flow. Consider, for example, programs like "The Dating Game," which deliberately stylize ordinary social pastimes in order that they may be absorbed readily into the flow and thus metamorphosed into objects of entertainment. In "The Dating Game" the everyday facts of romance—meeting, dating, marriage, and children—assume entertainment value. The events themselves may be common and mundane, but they are made to appear uniquely valuable because they can entertain others. In television, the intrinsic quality of an event or a personality has no value. Intrinsic values give way to the extrinsic evaluations audiences place on the facts. The moral of the story of continuous flow is that, if something is fun, it must be good, and that if what is good is not fun it simply is not good enough.

Television's format of continuous flow reflects characteristic American assumptions about knowledge and about audiences. As to knowledge, consider recent alterations in television news. In many places "show doctors" have invented a news format that emphasizes friendly interactions among the members of a "news-team," at the expense of "hard" news.[59] The news-team makes use of rapidly panning cameras, informal conversation, and short, rapidly shifting stories which often distract attention from the news items themselves. Within this format, "the anchorman is someone who is asking the audience to invite him into their homes."[60] The news-team plays down the intrinsic importance of particular stories, as well as the expertise of individual news-team members. In place of expert specialization we encounter an atmosphere of informal conversation about an apparently undifferentiated stream of news into which all team members dip as equals. Indeed, we can easily envisage news-team members exchanging roles when the situation requires it. Thus, the format removes from "news," sports, and weather their specialized character and turns them into objects of equal general interest and consumption. The format implies that knowledge is not a matter of disciplined investigation in which some are experts and others are not, but is, instead, a pool of easily accessible, superficial knowledge which all can assimilate equally. The process of continuous flow blends bodies of knowledge together, breaking down institutionalized competencies and status barriers.

Similar assumptions guide television's expectations about the audience. Mankiewicz and Swerdlow argue that broadcasters accept the theory of the "least objectionable program."[61] Adhering to Herbert Krugman's argument that television encourages "learning without involvement,"[62] theorists of the "least objectionable program" claim that audiences apply only relative standards of quality to television. People do not judge programs against a fixed scale of quality, but settle instead for the least objectionable program available at the moment. To be successful a television program need not be "good" in any absolute sense so long as it is less objectionable than its competitors. The assumption is that, once ensconced in the continuous stream of television watching, viewers will find it easier to stay than to leave. At root, the argument claims that the audience wants to be a playing part of a moving process, rather than an isolated referee applying fixed standards of quality. Ultimately, interchangeability among bodies of knowledge and among "experts" relativizes audience perception, with the result that the *process* of television rather than its substance becomes uniquely and exclusively valuable.

TELEVISION AND THE LOOSELY BOUNDED CULTURE

Our discussion of television's form should have suggested affinities between television and a loosely bounded culture. The paradox is that in both form and content television is predominantly loosely bounded, but its corporate setting is entirely at odds with such a loosely bounded culture. As we have seen, structurally, television is tightly demarcated, inegalitarian, competitive, and centralized. Yet this tightly bounded corporate world portrays a social vision which in both form and content is comparatively undifferentiated, markedly egalitarian, decentralized, hostile to authority, personalized, and open. In this sense, therefore, television's structure and culture are at odds with each other.

A convenient place to begin this analysis of loose boundedness in television culture is to look at status boundaries as they appear in television programs. Consider, for example, portrayals of the family, certainly the most ascriptive and traditionally bounded of social institutions. But as it is portrayed on television, family life is striking for its voluntary, unrelated quality, not for its traditional, regulated quality. Television families are often transient institutions composed of voluntary participants who are unrelated legally or by blood. Typical family members share a unique structure of feeling rather than a formally binding relationship. Consider, for example, series such as "Three's Company," "Mannix," "Ironside," and—perhaps the foremost example of the genre—"The Mary Tyler Moore Show." In all these cases television's preference is "for showing the country people who are co-workers on the job but who relate to each other as if they were a family."[63] In fact, this observation does not go far enough, for in each of these programs co-workers become the family of choice and the workplace becomes a home, while blood relations and residence are made to appear dull, impoverished, or conflictual. Television's preference for a flexible family of choice above a static family of blood relationships stands out vividly in the revealing history of Rhoda Morgenstern, "Mary Richards's" friend. It is Mary who is Rhoda's family of choice, as Rhoda herself admits when contrasting Mary's friendship with her own mother's unwelcome meddling. And when Rhoda finally does acquire a legal family for herself in the person of a husband, the marriage fails, and Rhoda must construct a new makeshift family for herself.

This view of family as a shifting unit of voluntary participants who share a structure of feeling, rather than an involuntary, status-ascribed, hierarchical unit of age-graded blood relatives, manifests itself in two other prominent characteristics of television portrayals. First, intact families and marriages have increasingly become the exception rather than the rule. Today's "One Day at a Time" takes the place of yesterday's "Father Knows Best," reflecting an alteration in television expectations about the durability of American family life. The point here is not that American families are or are not actually unstable, but rather that the portrayal of family structure on television legitimizes a concept of the "normal" family as a loosely bounded structure of individual choices.

An allied factor has to do with the authority relationship between parents and children on television. American mass culture has long idealized children, often by portraying adults as incompetent bumblers whom only the child's natural wisdom can rescue. As long ago as 1950 Wolfenstein and Leites detected a pattern in American movies whereby children appeared to be as uniquely innocent as they were instinctually wise—uncorrupted by self-defeating neuroses, unbought by vicious corporations, and thus able to overcome their compromised parents.[64] The same pattern of expectations persists in television, even in such programs as "The Waltons" and "Family." More often than not, children lead their parents out of error, rather than the other way around. This inverted structure of authority emerges most vividly in the situation comedies of Norman Lear, especially in "All in The Family" and "Maude," where sensible children patiently and kindly lead their less-educated, foolish, bigoted, or silly parents toward a new, sounder view of life. In such presentations the relationship between parents and children has become as unsettled and negotiable as relationships among adult family members. The fundamental dilemma of families in these portrayals is their inability to reconcile two conflicting axes of solidarity: one of which favors children's power (an expectation that children know what is best for them, are fundamentally good, and therefore need not be controlled—a loosely bounded conception), and one of which favors parents (an expectation that age and blood relationship automatically conveys legitimate authority and higher status—a tightly bounded conception).

A similar denigration of status boundaries emerges in countless other ways. Indeed, even egalitarian status distinctions are illegitimate. Almost never do we hear "Mister" or "Miss" or "Missus" or "Miz" used on television, for such formal modes of address only impede such access. Similarly, as Goldsen points out, television violates boundaries of linguistic sub-cultures by quickly disseminating subcultural terms to a general audience, thus using language to bring different groups together.[65]

In such a loosely bounded setting—where intimate markers of family, language, and address cannot operate effectively—television concentrates on what Kisova calls the mobilization of the individual personality. Television supplies multiple values for the liberated person to choose from.[66] The individual character's freedom of choice is the sine qua non of television, for no longer is identity supplied legitimately by previously ascribed status or by vital subcultures. Thus, television attempts to be as variegated and miscellaneous as possible, for the premise of free choice requires it to make available a broad and diverse menu of values.

Television's dissolution of status constraints occurs within a context of action that also dissolves history. Such program types as situation comedies and police dramas draw on no historical context which could move them beyond an essentially intimate, personal contest of wills or conjunction of accidents. Even television's dramatizations of *real* historical events, such as the Jonestown mass suicide or the march on Selma, Alabama, in 1963, usually concern themselves primarily with the motivations of leading participants and ignores historical or sociological factors. This pattern of programming is inevitable, since the slow development of major historical forces is impossible to portray effectively on television.[67] Instead, television simply extracts representative historical vignettes from their chronological or social settings, reproduces them, and embeds them in the flow of programs. Television thus creates a new, artificially assembled context of events which competes with the old, historical context. Thus, for example, instead of the march on Selma following logically from the long line of civil rights protests that began with the Birmingham bus boycott, television audiences see the march as following from "Three's Company." The two settings convey very different meanings.

Replacing status, history, linguistic distinction, and traditional roles on television is, above all, the free play of individual personality. Indeed, idiosyncrasy, uniqueness, or "personality" take the place of traditional rules in bonding people together. Arthur Berger noted an extreme example of personality assertion in his discussion of Frank Sinatra. As Berger puts it, Sinatra is willing "to strip away the veneer of gentility and geniality that pervades our society and daringly expose himself."[68] The ideas of "stardom" and of the "special" television program put great pressure on performers such as Sinatra to carry a program by the sheer power of their extreme, revealing behavior. A Sinatra who dramatically unbuttons his shirt collar or tosses away his formal jacket symbolically reveals self and soul, thus loosening the boundaries between audience and performer. The behavior complements his songs, which are also highly personal expressions of "feeling." The singer's emotional surrender to the music—vividly signified by various gyrations or by mugging—is the cultural equivalent of his or her informal attire and willingness to speak confidentially with the audience about "personal" things.[69] Thus, demeanor, song, dress, and speech are interrelated parts of a single cultural ensemble. And the presentation extends even farther when performers mix with members of the audience. As the star mingles with the audience, or as members of the audience reach out to touch the star, or as the television camera pans the audience and juxtaposes audience responses to star performance, the identical message is conveyed: the barrier between real life and performance, audience and star, needs to be pierced in the interest of emotional expression. This form of personalistic assertion may be contrasted with the behavior of dance band singers of the 1930s and 1940s, who dressed soberly, deferred to the band's performance, and minimized revelations about their personal lives or feelings at the moment.

Television's emphasis on the exaggeration of personality and the revelation of spontaneous feeling reflects clearly the perspectives of those who write and produce television programs. As Stein points out, television writers and producers believe themselves to be in a dog-eat-dog competitive world in which they must advertise themselves if they are to survive. They argue that humility, modesty, and the acceptance of limitations are hopelessly old-fashioned qualities. Those with talent must flaunt their skills, for otherwise they will be overlooked.[70] The emphasis on personality in television programs is therefore a projection of the larger dilemma of creativity in the medium.

Why are television writers so sure that talent unadvertised and unflaunted will go unrecognized? The answer lies in their belief that most people—even television professionals—possess no intrinsic standards of quality with which to identify real talent. It is noteworthy how this assumption implicitly recognizes the ubiquity of loose boundedness in America, for standards of quality depend on powers of discrimination encouraged by, if not actually embodied in, *tightly* bounded cultures. When a cultural code works against refined discrimination and the perception of distinctions, it becomes natural for performers to resort to extreme demonstrations of their selves. Performers must connect with audiences quickly, and in the absence of audience standards all becomes a scramble of display.

The importance of vividly demonstrating feeling in television programs should now be clearer. The acting out of feelings signifies to the audience that performers are not just actors doing a job, but are themselves—like their audiences—involved as whole people. The result is a closer connection between audience and performer. The practice even extends to the handling of news. For example, Michael Arlen finds it puzzling that purportedly objective television reporters should find it necessary to ask the people they are interviewing how they feel about the often tragic events which have happened to them. This intimate inquiry appears wholly unwarranted, says Arlen, because the reporter and the unfortunate interviewee usually have never met before and will never meet again.[71] The assumed intimacy becomes intelligible within the loosely bounded culture, however, for how else can the interviewer prove to his audience that he is not just a status-ridden reporter but is also a "genuine" human being "sympathetic" to the unfortunate person he is interviewing? And, for that matter, how else can the person being interviewed make contact with the millions of anonymous viewers at home? This display of feelings resembles the exchange of tokens in a primitive society.

In sum, in a loosely bounded culture the demonstration of feelings—indeed, even the simulation of feelings—symbolizes emergent social relationships, good will, and "authenticity and sincerity." The person who holds nothing back becomes trustworthy, for he or she no longer has anything to hide. This motif of loose boundedness appears particularly vividly in the behavior of television stars who contrive to lose control, but it is also a general program motif consisting of ill-assorted characters who are held together by emotional bonds rather than by intellectual understandings, shared values, or traditional status relations. An example of this type of relatedness, as Arlen points out, may be found in "All in the Family" as well as in other Norman Lear programs. It is true that many Lear programs capitalize on traditional formulae, such as the device of mistaken identity and other misunderstandings to which the audience is privy, but the characters are not. These devices do not break with tradition, nor with the fiction of a culture in which an audience can be omniscient, objective, separate, and impartial. But traditional formulae of this kind are ultimately incongruent with the fragmentation of a loosely bounded culture, and thus new formulae enter the scene.

In the traditional situation comedy, for example, humor and drama both arise from the omniscient observer's possession of knowledge which the characters themselves lack. By contrast, in Lear's situation comedies the audience often lacks such knowledge, but instead takes part in a particular mood or feeling. For example, as Arlen points out, a primary characteristic of Lear's comedies is anger, "but it is a curious, modern, undifferentiated anger, which serves to provide the little dramas with a kind of energizing dynamic—sometimes the only dynamic."[72] In Lear's work, as in much other such programming, strong emotions—anger, fear, love, sympathy—engulf all the characters and bring them together, even when they have little else in common. It is almost as if Lear is contending that, in the absence of a culture held together by traditional status obligations or value agreements, people must share emotional states, even if those states are embarrassingly revealing.

Anger is a perfect emotional expression of loose bounded-ness, for people who are angry at each other, though divided along lines of values or logic, at least share the same emotion. Thus, mutual anger, like mutual love, expresses the dominant theme of the culture: not to let intellectual differences or status divisions separate people who are willing to give of them-selves—even if all they have to give is hostility.

It is not surprising, therefore, that television programs should pay so little attention to ideas. Indeed, Stein is correct in his assertion that television portrays education as useless and deep thought as a waste of time.[73] After all, the intellectual or contemplative life is, by its very nature, somewhat isolating, and therefore alien to loose boundedness. Moreover, contempla-tion often encourages the sober examination of values which in a loosely bounded culture are almost always poorly defined and shallowly rooted. Values of this sort stand up poorly to ex-amination. Therefore, education, reason, and intellect contra-vene the main dynamic of loose boundedness, a dynamic that involves a display of emotion aimed at transcending diversity in order to forge new social relationships.

A primary characteristic of the loosely bounded culture is absorptiveness, a quality we have already examined in the con-texts of language and architecture. Absorptiveness also ap-pears on television in a number of ways. So far as commercials are concerned, the prominence of food and drink symbolizes the metaphor of absorption, encouraging us to associate inges-tion with good character. The commercial urges us to "get the gusto out of life," an injunction which in practice parallels the absorption of exciting new experiences with the enjoyment of gustatory pleasures. The metaphor of absorption also appears in program content. As Arlen points out, in recent years televi-sion programs have begun to examine formerly tabooed sub-jects, such as infidelity, drug addiction, and illegitimacy.[74] Why should such topics have become appealing, particularly given their problematic role in the real world? The answer lies in part in the curiosity the audience may well feel about the bi-zarre and the exotic. In this sense, by treating yesterday's taboos as today's normal viewing, television serves to domesticate and regularize the culture. Equally important, however, is the fact that such controversial subjects provide innumerable chances for characters to emote and, thus, to let down their guards. Television here exploits the fact that people on the fringes of society have suffered emotionally devastating experiences; therefore, to suddenly treat the dispossessed "honestly" insures the expression of extreme emotions. And, as we have seen, emotions are the lingua franca of a loosely bounded culture. Therefore, the portrayal of formerly tabooed subjects insures the representation of social relations along lines of "shared" feeling. It is particularly comforting to a "straight" audience to know that the "deviant" has the "same" (perhaps even stronger) emotions that they themselves have, for emotional displays become a means of meeting new people on common grounds. The deviant's breakthrough of emotion thus becomes a rite of passage from social isolation to social integration, much as, in the psychiatric interview, the doctor interprets the patient's tears as a sign of progress.

It is, of course, impossible for a society to expand its periphery without bending its cultural boundaries. It is not surprising, therefore, to find television preoccupied with cultural expansion and flexibility. Three examples serve to illustrate the expansiveness motif in action. The first example is technological. As Price notes, commercials increasingly employ animation to alter the shape of products and persons. Thus, to depict an upset stomach in need of treatment by Pepto-Bismol, animation distorts the sufferer by blowing up his stomach to grotesque proportions.[75] Technology thereby accustoms the viewer to the sudden expansion of boundaries and experiences.

Paralleling this technological innovation is a corresponding set of motivational innovations. As Barnouw has pointed out, commercials are unnecessary to sell goods that people genuinely need; such goods generate their own demand.[76] Therefore, the logic of the commercial becomes a logic of expansion. The commercial attempts to imbue the trivial with the same qualities as the necessary. Thus, it portrays comparatively unimportant goods as if they possessed great power to alter the lives of those who use them. We can see, therefore, that the animated alteration of media images is but a technological expression of a larger cultural dynamic: the expansion of audience appetite and the distortion of audience perspective.

The technological and commercial levels of meaning, in turn, represent a still deeper symbolic stratum: an all-embracing metaphor of openness and diffuseness that is television's primary theme. For Arthur Berger this peculiarly American television theme comes through clearest when contrasted with English television. Berger writes that in English programs such as "Upstairs/Downstairs" (a sharp binary distinction is already explicit in the title), "the relations between the masters and servants are dignified and proper on all sides. There is respect all around and the servants all have an essential dignity that is admirable. That is the irony of it all, as far as Americans are concerned. We are all masterless men who serve no one, but we feel a strong sense of alienation and de-individuation. Because we respect nobody, nobody respects us, and our supposed freedom seems to offer little except isolation."[77] In our theoretical terms, Berger argues that in a loosely bounded culture the basic social unit is the free individual constantly faced with a choice between unbearable isolation and emotional bonding through the exaggerated and often contrived display of self. Neither of these alternatives carries with it stable rules or understood roles. Nevertheless, the culture decrees that we must expand ourselves, whether through "self-actualization" or through "media hype" (a medical metaphor brilliantly expressive of television's attempt to exaggerate the mundane). Thus, under the mask of freedom, loose boundedness places severe stress on individuals.

Television thus presents several levels on which the patterns of a loosely bounded culture emerge. But loose boundedness is not television's dominant characteristic, for in fact television also reproduces mythic elements of a traditional binary cultural code. And to some observers of television, these mythic binary oppositions—not loose boundedness—are television's dominant depiction. For example, some observers note the stubborn survival of primitive good-guy/bad-guy depictions in television western dramas, while Horace Newcomb argues that television portrays a pristine world where pollution and innocence are rigidly separated.[78]

Arthur Berger goes further. He sees the spaceship *Enterprise* in "Star Trek," for example, as a "smoothly functioning society ... penetrated by some force, evil or good, and some kind of solution is found in which the foreign elements are controlled, one way or another. The *Enterprise*, as a system, resists contamination and flies on to new adventures."[79] The *Enterprise*, Berger claims, serves as a metaphor for the United States. Berger also claims that the program "Kung Fu" embodies a classically dialectical cultural conflict between oriental and American conceptions of life. In "Kung Fu" a contemplative, spiritualized, historically entrenched, civilized East confronts a savage, pragmatic, individualistic, dynamic West. The synthesis of this polarity is Kung Fu himself, a hybrid, half savage and half sage, who utilizes the wisdom of the East to domesticate an anarchic West.[80] Berger is undoubtedly correct in his contention that domesticating violence, chaining unbridled power, and controlling a frontier mentality is a central motif in American television westerns. Nevertheless, television's proffered reconciliation of opposites still remains the reconciliation of individuals within a loosely bounded culture. The traditional mythic elements which Berger and Newcomb identify find themselves embedded within an alien tradition: that of the loosely bounded culture. Television's American mythology is but a pale replica of the mythic meaning systems we find in traditional societies. Berger states the problem well:

> The classical American problem is that of creating a natural community ..., and the way we have done this is by defining society as an abstraction, which stands for a multitude of individuals each pursuing his private destiny. The links between people are tenuous: they live in the same territory and have certain rights to be protected, but few have any sense of solidarity with their neighbors and there is little in the way of social consciousness.[81]

This "natural community of abstract individuals" is exactly the modal pattern Varenne discovered in his anthropological investigation of a midwestern town.[82] It seems clear that the mythic resolutions which structuralists claim hold cultures together are not entirely absent from television. Nevertheless, they must contend against our loosely bounded culture. Eventually, loose boundedness softens their dialectical oppositions, reduces the rigidity of their boundaries, diffuses their meanings, and personalizes their status classifications. Tradition on television cannot do its job, and myth becomes only a muted theme within the loosely bounded culture of television.

THE THEMATIC STRUCTURE OF TELEVISION'S LOOSELY BOUNDED CULTURE

A loosely bounded culture does not favor enduring group conflicts mediated by myth systems. Instead, a loosely bounded culture prefers to construe its conflicts as soluble, temporary differences of opinion between essentially like-minded individuals. From a theatrical standpoint, therefore, melodrama replaces drama and situation comedy supplants farce. An examination of television's news programs, situation comedies, crime programs, and children's shows illustrates the ubiquity of these cultural messages.

In a loosely bounded culture, television news and documentaries are especially important because such a culture cannot draw on legitimate group differences to set the terms of political conflict. Group conflicts do exist in such a culture, of course, but their foundation in stable material interests and primordial characteristics must stand unacknowledged. As a result, groups become less vital in setting political agendas. Group tensions may generate the real political conflicts of our time, but groups rarely define the framework by which such conflicts will be interpreted or understood. Instead, it is the mass media which perform this function. The media take what may originate as essentially parochial issues and place them in a context suitable to a loosely bounded culture.

Recent research clearly reveals the effectiveness of the mass media in performing this function. Frustrated in their fruitless search for specific effects of television news on opinions, attitudes, and voting preferences, media researchers in recent years have hit upon a more general "effect" of the media. Observers now contend that television news and public affairs programs help define the political universe of Americans by shaping the relative salience of political issues. McCombs and Shaw, for example, discovered a strong correlation between issue emphases in the mass media and voters' ranking of major campaign issues.[83] Voters did not selectively perceive the news in order to protect positions important to themselves or their groups, but instead depended on the media to define the political world for them. Agenda-setting is particularly important from our perspective, for it shows how group ties erode under the influence of television in a loosely bounded culture.

It should not be concluded that agenda-setting turns television into an effective educational device. There are few enough such devices in loosely bounded cultures. Television creates little besides an *impression* of importance. As Diamond observes, people recall far less from watching television news than from reading comparable newspaper stories. Indeed, most people recall only a single story from television news programs. They thus carry away from their viewing less a full *agenda* than a vague impression of "how things are going." Nor does television news help people develop sophisticated conceptions of the issues. Margaret Conway finds that among adolescents high exposure to television news increases sensitivity to personalities in politics, but has no effect on a person's abstract understanding of political issues.[84] This finding too makes sense, given a loosely bounded culture's primary emphasis on personality as opposed to sharply bounded and perhaps static group and issue conflicts.

That television news should dominate the political communication process thus symptomizes the domination of a loosely bounded culture. The next question to probe is how television depicts politics. Since politics involves conflict, three questions emerge: how political conflict is presented; what viewpoint television takes toward conflict; and how conflict is resolved. In each of these instances we see the domination of a loosely bounded culture.

Television's version of political conflict pits individual politicians against each other in confrontations of character. Television searches desperately for vivid personalities who can illustrate political conflicts effectively for a viewing audience. Indeed, political campaigns, which ostensibly debate issue differences embedded in contrasting party platforms, actually appear on television to be gladiatorial contests between candidates who are lovable or hateful by turns, but whose connections to groups, coalitions, or issues come through poorly.

Some have argued that television's political personalism erodes authority by making those in authority appear undignified.[85] It has been alleged that this kind of reporting characterized the Watergate affair, in which television's portrait of Nixon the President denigrated the office of the presidency. But there is little evidence to support this charge. In fact, Pride and Richards demonstrate that, so far as pollution policy is concerned, television news has treated governmental authority more favorably than it has business leadership.[86] However, the argument itself misses a particularly important point: the personalization of political issues serves to humanize the process of leadership. By portraying complicated issues as somehow under the control of flesh-and-blood leaders, television moves leadership close to the public and makes our response — whether love or hate — intensely emotional. A loosely bounded culture does not encourage people to *judge* their leaders according to a set of settled standards; it encourages them to react spontaneously to events in an open fashion. Television's personalization of authority thus transforms the perception of political conflict.

What viewpoint does television news adopt toward the conflicts it portrays? In America — as in Britain — television news strives to present itself as truly neutral in reporting the conflicts it detects. Both Gans in his study of American television news and Schlesinger in his study of the BBC document the extreme sensitivity of broadcasters to any charge of bias.[87] Indeed, only in recent years has local television news felt safe enough to take editorial stands.[88] Some observers find television's stance of neutrality convincing and laudable. Others, such as Michael Arlen, only find it irritating. Arlen writes, "The trouble with network

news isn't mainly its politics, or its slant, or its show-business
quality. The trouble is that it has become a bureaucracy news; an
impersonal high-level news; an establishment news."[89] Still others charge that the stance of neutrality is deceptive and illusory;
in practice neutrality represents covert adherence to an ideology that shunts dissenting minorities and deep conflicts out of
camera range. Schlesinger argues, for example, that the BBC
uses its doctrine of neutrality to play down the bitter sectarian
conflict in Northern Ireland.[90] And Tuchman complains that
"balance" in television news "means in practice that Republicans
may rebut Democrats and vice-versa,"[91] but that only unrepre-
sentative and easily dismissed spokespeople, such as the feminist
Kate Millet, are permitted to speak for dissenters from the liberal consensus.

Empirical evidence supports the view that television in
America lives up to its protestations of neutrality within the
range of two-party politics. Studies of the 1972 presidential
campaign, for example, provide good evidence of balanced,
fair coverage. On the whole, the networks appear to live up to
their own standards of neutrality.[92] The larger question, however, is the role that television's neutrality plays within a loosely
bounded culture. From Arlen's perspective, television's stance
of neutrality appears to create a strong barrier between the
medium and the political world. Certainly this is the impression television itself desires to convey. Television sits proudly
outside the fight, jealously guarding its opportunity to report
the facts fairly. From a different perspective, however, the
stance of neutrality subtly reinforces the loosely bounded culture. The studied calm of neutrality conveys to the audience
the impression that political conflict is neither so intense nor so
divisive as to force fair-minded people into sharply bounded,
opposing camps. By claiming always to be "above the battle,"
newsmen perhaps suggest that the conflict itself is not very
deep or important. The stance of neutrality thus reinforces the
loosely bounded culture's personalistic portrayal of conflict,
for if persons and not principles are the sources of conflict, it
becomes easier for observers to report on the conflict without
having to choose sides. Neutrality thus encourages us to see our

culture as a process of open negotiation, ongoing accommodation, and exchanges between persons free to choose their roles in pursuing solutions to "problems," rather than confined to fighting enduring, destructive political wars.

The final aspect of this formula is the nature of "problem" resolution, which also conforms to the emphasis of loose boundedness on personal involvement in superficial issues. What television construes as a personal disagreement can always be settled by the right combination of persons harboring goodwill. Television news coverage thus places primary emphasis on a focal problem-solver rather than on organizations and groups. As Frank points out, television news favors persons rather than institutions, executives rather than legislatures or courts, voluntary organizations rather than bureaucracies.[93] More often than not, television singles out the large group or agency, the fixed status or role, as the enemy of the individual. It is "bureaucracy," "big business," "inflation," "unemployment," which create our problems. The impersonal abstraction becomes the bête noire of American politics. Meanwhile, it is the courageous individual—the all too rare bureaucrat who blows the whistle on her boss, or the compassionate welfare worker who stands up for his clients—whom television most admires. Through television news—as indeed, in the loosely bounded culture as a whole—Americans attempt, like Lévi-Strauss's *bricoleur*, to *construct* a culture out of the idiosyncrasies of individuals.

This effort at culture construction is not peculiar to television news. Adult and children's entertainment programs contain these same messages in different forms. As Newcomb points out, most situation comedies treat conflict as the result of confusion through mistaken identity, or of disrupted communication, or of flawed personality.[94] The cure for conflict therefore becomes easier, for what at first appears to be a deeply rooted conflict is in fact not serious at all. The characters have no enduring antagonism to each other. Indeed, the contrary is true: people are always potentially in harmony. It is circumstance—particularly the system of communication—which is actually at fault. If only communication can be fostered and boundaries between people broken down, then what appears to be serious problems will turn out to be illusory. Story plots based on confusion or misidentification thus become subtle commercials in favor of communications media like television itself, which can serve as mediators in a loosely bounded culture.

Programs animated by the personality deficiencies of protagonists also convey the messages of a loosely bounded culture. In such programs lacerating conflict disappears with a "change of heart" among the protagonists. This alteration usually occurs because a new bit of information convinces one protagonist that he or she has misjudged another or that another protagonist is a good person after all or that the original protagonist actually is a better person than he or she thought. The message here is complex, but reinforcing to loose boundedness; it tells us that we ought not to judge quickly or harshly, for appearances may deceive; that we must be flexible; that people can change for the better; and, finally, that if change is genuine, others will accept it. These messages question all deep-seated differences and all enduring moral commitments. In television, personality change becomes its own morality.

By contrast, crime programs appear to resolve conflict in a very different manner, namely, as Barnouw points out, through the villain's attempted escape followed by capture or death.[95] The theme of attempted escape conveys subtle messages within a loosely bounded culture. For one thing, loose boundedness creates many zones of neutrality and islands of isolation where a wrong-doer can hide. Escape therefore becomes feasible. In addition, the motif of escape suggests that conflicts can be avoided and need not necessarily be accepted. Unlike classical mythology, which attains tragedy because of the hero's inability to overcome an inescapable conflict, a loosely bounded culture makes escape a real possibility and thus defeats tragedy. Finally, the capture or death of the escapee reflects the dynamic absorptiveness of the loosely bounded culture. Real escape would also supply a rigid boundary which the fugitive could cross once and for all. But these qualities clash with those of a loosely bounded culture. Ultimately, the death of the fugitive symbolizes the illegitimacy of genuine opposition to loose boundedness and also reflects widespread uncertainty about the real worth of the culture. Murder will out because neither reasoned adherence nor principled opposition has a place in the culture, and therefore emotion rules.

Evidence suggests that this television scenario, which legitimizes aggression against cultural opponents, has a gradual but important influence on children. Research by Drabman and Thomas and by Snow, among others, shows that children who watch much television aggression become more likely to tolerate aggression in real life than do nonwatchers.[96] Thus, television does convey the message that a loosely organized culture cannot tolerate real dissent for long. The cultural sanctioning of aggression against deviants hardly appears to square with the easy tolerance that we described earlier as part of loose boundedness. Nevertheless, the two reactions are but different sides of the same coin. Both are ways of destroying genuine, deeply rooted cultural politics. Both are therefore examples of how subtly but importantly television contributes to the dissemination and reproduction of the loosely bounded culture.

4

ADVERTISING AS A CULTURAL CODE

The millions of Americans who watch television regularly and imbibe its cultural system unavoidably encounter advertising in the form of commercials. Like television programs, commercials are deliberately manufactured images designed to appeal to a mass public. As such, they play an important role in the manufacture of American culture, and they help fill the gap between the exaggerated individualism produced by the imperfections of American cultural visions and the need for political and social consensus in American life. In short, commercials provide their own version of the loosely bounded culture.

Of course, mass advertising long preceded television. Advertising has played an integral part in American business since the late nineteenth century, in such forms as magazine appeals, billboards, newspaper copy, movie trailers, window displays, and circulars.[1] The character and volume of advertising fluctuates over time as a function of many different economic and noneconomic factors; it is these fluctuations in volume and character, rather than the cultural significance of advertising, that have occupied most writers on the subject. The dominant approach to advertising has thus been an economic not a sociological approach.

It is natural that the economic approach should have become dominant; after all, reliable information about advertising expenditures, alteration of forms, and costs in relation to sales receipts is easily obtainable. The availability of such statistical information encourages the economic mode of analysis. Moreover, the economic approach makes sense when viewed from the central purpose of advertising: the sale of goods at definite prices in a market. Advertising, even more than television entertainment, has a close connection with economic variables of product demand and supply. Again, advertising lends itself readily to an economic mode of analysis.

My analysis is primarily cultural. I believe that, whatever its economic functions or effects, advertising cannot be understood solely as an economic force. More specifically, although advertising may perform economic functions, it can do so only through the prism of culture, that is, through portraying products in culturally shaped and distorted ways. Mary Douglas makes the same point when she observes that in modern societies economic goods serve as vital cultural markers of status and respectability.[2] For this reason, many economic "rules" that apply effectively to the production of goods are not equally effective in explaining the consumption of goods, for consumption is as much a cultural expression as it is an economic fact of life.

Of course, writers on advertising have not *entirely* ignored its cultural role. Both its critics and its defenders have something to say about the cultural role of advertising. Its critics generally pursue a three-phase argument. First, they claim that advertising plays a crucial role by allowing producers to sell their products by reaching a mass market through impersonal means.[3] Once capitalism has reached a high level of mass production, producers must not only create large markets but sustain them over time. The old-fashioned personal contact between a corner-store salesman and a neighborhood clientele can no longer do the job. Advertising thus plays a crucial intermediary role in mass marketing.

Second, critics claim that advertising sells products, not by altering the buying habits of the public, but rather by shaping crucial parts of public "consciousness." For example, Connell argues that advertising sells "feminine" products only by reinforcing traditional stereotypes of femininity; advertising both capitalizes on preexistent sex-role stereotypes and reproduces such stereotypes by embedding them in product consumption.[4] And Goffman, in his insightful study of advertising's sex-role stereotypes, provides empirical support for such a view.[5]

Indeed, advertising exploits even the most intimate aspects of life—including sexuality itself—to sell goods. Advertising thereby alters our entire concept of sexuality. Connell concludes—following Marcuse—that advertising has "turned teenage sexuality into a highly profitable business."[6]

Finally, its critics charge that advertising not only shapes values toward specific institutions—such as sex roles or family life—but also influences the most fundamental values people develop: concepts of self and concepts of the social order of which the self is part. Through advertising, Ralph Miliband argues, "business is able freely to propagate an ethos in which private acquisitiveness is made to appear as the main if not the only avenue to fulfillment, in which 'happiness' or 'success' are therefore defined in terms of private acquisition, in which competition for acquisition, and therefore for 'happiness' and 'success' is treated as, or assumed to be, a primary law of life."[7] Advertising, of course, portrays the acquisition of specific goods by private consumers. But the larger message of advertising is not the selling of any particular mix of goods currently available on the market, but rather the selling of acquisition itself as a mode of life.

Complementing its image of the consumer is advertising's portrait of the producer: the corporation, the businessman, and the salesman. This portrait, critics charge, is unrelentingly benevolent. The rise of institutional advertising has made the selling of the corporation as an entity in itself a primary element of advertising. For example, Robert Freedman claims to have detected close collaboration between the United States government, large corporations, and the Advertising Council in developing a massive advertising campaign intended to sell American capitalism during the late 1970s.[8] And Miliband argues that advertising's twin visions of the happy private consumer and of the responsible, benevolent producer are symbiotic parts of a single cultural message:

> The *firm* is soulful, benevolent, public-spirited and socially responsible. This being so, the *individual* may, therefore, safely remain private-oriented, acquisitive, predatory, and be content to enjoy the blessings which are showered upon him.[9]

Stuart Ewen's *Captains of Consciousness* offers us the most penetrating contemporary attack on advertising. Ewen attempts to understand advertising both economically and politically. Although, economically, advertising began solely as a means by which mass producers could reach a newly formed mass market, it was advertising's political role that was most important. Advertising, according to Ewen, took an initially recalcitrant working class, which was resistant to the extension of capitalism, and helped transform that class into docile consumers, willingly acquiescing to capitalist hegemony. What capitalism could not create solely through expanded productivity, through full employment for workers, or through the suppression of worker resistance, it brought about through advertising, which appealed to the emotions of the worker and falsified his real economic interest. Basing his argument on a careful historical analysis, Ewen states:

> The factory had not been an effective arena for forging a predictable and reliable work force. More and more it appeared that proletarian integration might be effected within the realm opened up by increased productivity and the need for broader markets. As a result, the business community now attempted to present an affirmative vision—a new mechanism—of social order in the realm of daily life to confront the resistance of people whose work lives were increasingly defined by the rigid parameters of industrial production and their corporate bureaucracies.[10]

Thus, advertising attempted to persuade workers that consumption—the positive side of capitalism—compensates for the alienated labor that capitalist production requires workers to perform. Ultimately, advertising inhibits the emergence of revolutionary tendencies among workers.

Critics have also discussed the psychology of advertising. They argue that advertising works through *persuasion* and the exploitation of irrationality. If advertising is to sell a product, or a conception of human nature, an entire economic system or a sex or class stereotype, it must be highly emotive.[11] Advertising is both persuasive and manipulative, appealing to the heart not the head. Critics argue, for example, that the large portion of every commercial which is purely dramatic or aesthetic rather than informative is actually the very heart of the message, for this is the part that persuades. And aesthetics has nothing to do with such rational questions as the real value of a product. Therefore, the persistence of advertising must be explained by its powerful appeal to the irrational.[12]

Defenders of advertising deny the charge of irrational persuasion. They admit that advertising has cultural significance, but they claim that the culture of advertising serves to further the vision of a liberal polity. Advertising, they argue, is an indispensable system for providing consumers with information necessary to a rational choice among products. Product advertising plays the same role in the pluralist defense of the market that political campaigns play in the pluralist defense of American electoral politics. Both processes are alleged to promote consumer sovereignty, as signified by the word "campaign," which denotes both the run for office and the employment of advertisements to sell a product. To its defenders, the cultural significance of advertising is its contribution to public knowledge, clearly a good to those believers in the democratic vision. From this perspective, information not persuasion becomes the best way to approach advertising.[13]

Neither these criticisms nor these defenses of advertising stand up to scrutiny. Advertising cannot be understood solely as a form of manipulation or as a form of information dissemination. Advertising is not simply corporate "brainwashing" of isolated individuals for private profit and potential hegemony, nor is it the "neutral" provision of information useful to consumers. Most of all, advertising is not confined to its manifest subject—products for sale—but also extends to a latent subject: the social context in which products are embedded. The "message" of an advertisement embraces far more than the information the advertisement conveys about a product. Advertisements are symbolic models through which, in a loosely bounded culture, people attempt to overcome their isolation and make common cause with each other, at least in fantasy. Advertisements both model a loosely bounded culture and also propose solutions to some of its more vexing problems. Advertising thus resembles television entertainment and public schooling as a cultural device. Before elaborating this argument, however, we must discuss both criticisms and defense of advertising in greater detail.

A CRITIQUE OF CRITIQUES

If the criticisms of advertising we have reviewed were correct, we should expect some or most of the following things to be true: (1) advertising penetrates deeply into the working class; (2) advertising works smoothly with business corporations; (3) advertising is well organized and internally cohesive; (4) advertising is effective in selling products; and (5) advertising is effective in gaining public acceptance not only for the products it sells but also for the process of selling. To a greater or lesser degree, however, these propositions do not hold up. Advertising's place in capitalist hegemony, therefore, remains debatable.

As we have seen, Ewen argues forcefully that advertising has as its primary mission the socializing of the working class to accept capitalism, an economic system which, on objective grounds, workers should reject. There is little evidence, however, that low-income populations are uniquely susceptible to advertising. Workers do *see* more advertising than do upper-income populations, but this is primarily because workers spend more time with television. However, a careful analysis of evaluations of advertising among middle- and low-income populations revealed no significant income-related differences.[14] Indeed, if anything, low-income groups were slightly more likely than middle-income populations to reject advertising. Ewen and other critics forget that advertising may be double-edged. Product advertisements must be directed mainly to those with the money to buy; in the process, they may sour those without money. In any case, the evidence does not support this first proposition of the argument against advertising.

Do advertisers work harmoniously with corporations and industry? The answer is uncertain. Most advertising in America is developed by specialized agencies which handle dozens of corporate accounts. Few businesses create their own advertising, although all large corporations monitor closely the ad agencies that handle the corporation's account.[15] Corporations always retain control over the choice of an agency and over the use of any particular advertisement. However, most agencies go to great lengths to exercise full creative control over their accounts, arguing, reasonably enough, that as experts in advertising and as experienced salesmen themselves, they alone should judge the worth of any particular advertisement. If an agency is to be held responsible for results, it naturally feels that it should have full freedom to carry out an advertising campaign according to its own professional judgment.

What little is known about the relationship between corporate clients and advertising agencies disputes the position of those who believe in a ready convergence of interest between the two. Bensman, for example, writes of the frustrations advertising executives continually feel because of client interference, which often destroys the sales potential of an advertisement.[16] The agency must accommodate the client's whims if it is to retain the account; yet accommodation often produces an advertisement that is less successful than the client expected. Tunstall, in his study of English advertising, also expands upon the poisoned atmosphere between corporate clients and ad agencies.[17] One reason for the prevalent disharmony is the internal structure of the advertising business. Unlike television, where three large corporations dominate programming, advertising is a high-risk field in which many small agencies compete viciously against each other. Naturally, therefore, each agency fears that other agencies will snatch away its clients if it does not do a good job. As a result, "account executives in conversation frequently complain about the ignorance or lack of ability of their client opposite numbers [but] . . . they have to be very careful to hide these opinions from the man concerned."[18]

On first reading, this description supports the view that monolithic corporations are able to force their messages upon weak and disorganized advertising agencies. This conclusion is premature, for in fact recurrent conflicts between advertisers and clients disrupt the effective transmission of messages that corporations particularly desire to convey. Clients continue to depend on advertisers even as they place pressure on them, and these contradictory forces make for neither an easy relationship nor the ready transmission of capitalism's message.

A brief survey of the internal structure of the advertising profession deals the image of a monolithic corporation-advertising complex a serious blow. What is most striking about advertising as a profession is its extreme instability.[19] New agencies are able to emerge with considerable ease, and every agency suffers from much turnover as executives switch to competing firms. One reason for the high turnover and fragmentation of the profession is the multiple pressures to which personnel must respond. Advertising work is divided into specialties, such as layout, art, captioning—and specialty groups feel a great loyalty to their specialty. This loyalty often proceeds from a youthful identification with art and a continued sensitivity to artistic standards. Thus, when faced with unpalatable client demands, "the individual specialist is . . . almost always placed in a cross-pressure between specialty and account."[20] Loyalty to one's team or to one's skill collides with obligation to the account, thus making dissatisfaction and turnover a chronic problem.

Other aspects of the relationship between advertising executive and client also cause friction. In Bensman's description the relationship is one of patron and courtier. "Being in a business where one's very existence depends upon the 'favors' bestowed on one by the client gives advertising a court-like atmosphere."[21] Competition for the favors of clients creates guilt and disgust, powerful stimulants to job instability.

Another source of instability and turnover within advertising lies in the structure of specialty teams themselves. Relationships within teams are intensely personal; however, because it is difficult to trace the contributions of individual members to the team's success, continued jockeying for position within teams is practically foreordained. In particular, the theft of ideas becomes a way of life. It is not surprising, therefore, that festering jealousies and misunderstandings should regularly erupt, causing the destruction of teams.

An additional organizational source of insecurity and turnover in advertising is the political structure of the advertising agency. Advertising is one of the least bureaucratized of professions. Instead, advertising agencies are unusually democratic structures, where one encounters great flexibility in lines of organization and responsibility.[22] Although this structure greatly improves innovation and adaptation to changes in client demands, it also complicates the assignment and monitoring of tasks. The fluidity of the environment encourages private arrangements, cabals, and cliques, with the result that individuals can rise or fall quickly within the agency. Bureaucratic regularity and rule-making does not stabilize the advertising career.

One final element contributing to the instability of advertising is the division between talents useful for the creation of advertising (chiefly artistic ability) and talents useful for the placement of advertising (salesmanship). Rarely is the same person equally talented in both endeavors.[23] As a result, complicated negotiations must take place between the business and artistic segments of each agency, and many opportunities arise for the development and perpetuation of hostilities, with creative personnel accusing the sales side of undervaluing the artistic components of a commercial, and sales personnel accusing the creative side of artistic "self-indulgence."

To summarize: Because of the extremely competitive nature of the endeavor, turnover and job insecurity are frequent in advertising. The advertising profession is composed of many small firms which compete with each other in a classical free market. Advertising agencies resemble corner grocery stores in a medium-sized city more than they resemble either the three commercial television networks for whom they design commercials or the corporations for whom they labor. Ad executives dissatisfied with their current positions can easily sign on with competitors if they choose to pull up stakes. The internal dynamics of the advertising agency further encourage the tendency toward fragmentation. Finally, since advertising is labor intensive rather than machine intensive, fragmentation usually increases the number of new firms. A new firm needs only a few talented people and a few contracts to get started.

It could be argued that this highly competitive, unstable structure should increase the efficiency of advertising in transmitting pro-business messages. Isn't competition always a source of efficiency in a market economy? Not so in the case of advertising, however. The problem is that in advertising, instability and competition cannot be connected closely to efficient operation, primarily because there exists no reliable information about how individual workers are doing. As Mayer points out, there is a long, complex, problematic connection between any particular ad executive and any particular set of sales receipts for advertised products.[24] The relationship between an advertisement and its audience is impersonal, compared, say, with the relationship between an individual salesperson in a store and his or her customers. In the latter case, the effects of personal salesmanship can be accurately indexed by commissions, sales, and customer reactions; but there exists no such information to link advertiser and consumer.[25]

The anonymity of the advertiser's relationship with the public encourages a highly irrational structure of expectations in advertising. Given the imperfect nature of their information, ad people understandably consider the marketplace and the individual consumer to be mysterious and unpredictable. Not surprisingly, therefore, an atmosphere of gambling eventually permeates each ad agency. The inability to cite specific instances of success, failure, or unusual individual contribution creates a gold-rush, boom-and-bust psychology where hunch and fear turn handsprings. In such an atmosphere there is plenty of room for false starts, mistakes, errors, and failures.[26] Such a picture hardly resembles the fully rationalized system of capitalism painted by advertising's critics.

According to Price, the characteristic attitude of the advertising executive toward the consumer is warlike.[27] The ad executive feels engaged in a never-ending struggle to gain the attention of an audience. Worse yet, this is a war fought largely in the dark, for no one in advertising feels confident about what makes a commercial or an advertisement "work" nor even about what "work" actually means in advertising. Still, the war must be fought, and so myths grow up: "An idea works like a grenade: a flash, a loud noise, and then the shrapnel slices deep into our brain."[28] The frustrations of advertisers are understandable, for the figures on audience attention to advertisements are not at all reassuring. Price cites a study which shows that only one-fourth of those who see a commercial recall anything whatever about it, and of this one-fourth only a small proportion actually rely on the commercial in making buying decisions.[29]

Thus, the structure of advertising both internally and externally disputes the proposition that advertisers and corporations work together harmoniously. Moreover, aspects of advertising as a profession render it internally divided, unstable, and highly inefficient. Its contribution to capitalist hegemony therefore seems problematic.

THE EFFECTS OF ADVERTISING

Its critics argue that advertising demonstrably increases sales, helps maintain corporate power in the economy, and sells capitalist values effectively to audiences. In fact, however, these arguments remain undemonstrated. Evidence does not support the proposition that advertising is a very effective pro-capitalist force in any of the aforementioned respects. It follows, therefore, that any analysis of advertising must search out other viewpoints.

To begin with, does advertising, as some of its critics contend, increase the concentration of firms in an industry, thereby limiting competition and increasing the power of a few large corporations? The answer is uncertain. Lambin, for example, argues that advertising does not reduce competition over price and quality. Advertising, he claims, is far less a determinant of market performances than are the price and quality of goods; the market situation of large corporations improves because those corporations can keep prices low (if they so choose) and innovate to produce items of higher quality, not because they spend large amounts of money on advertising. As Lambin puts it, "Artificial product differentiation based solely on advertising appears to be fruitless."[30] The most knowledgeable student of advertising economics, Julian Simon, argues that the close connection between advertising expenditures and market concentration is explainable simply by the fact that large companies can afford to advertise more than can small companies, because of economies of scale in advertising expenditures.[31] Thus, advertising expenditures do not cause greater market concentration; the causal chain actually runs in the opposite direction.

If advertising has not been shown to increase market concentration, surely advertising must stimulate sales by making products appear attractive to consumers. Here again, however, the evidence is ambiguous. Lambin, for example, concludes that a 1 percent increase in advertising expenditures increases sales only .1 percent in the short run and .025 percent in the long run, a finding which he interprets as an indication of advertising's "limited power."[32] By contrast, Harry Block reports that "there is a strong positive relationship between profit rates and advertising intensity."[33] However, he qualifies this argument to apply only to current expenses of advertising; as a long-term investment, advertising does not appear to be very profitable. Certainly, evidence does not support the view that advertising increases overall spending in the economy (the aggregate consumption process), although advertising for particular goods may have some effect on sales of the goods in question.[34] Still, as Demsetz puts it, "The statistical relationship between advertising and profit rates remains a puzzle."[35]

The problematic effects of advertising on product purchases may surprise advertising's critics, but it comes as no surprise to ad executives. After all, uncertainty is the operating code of the advertiser. Even Price admits that although advertisements sell products "often enough so business can time the upsurge of sales from the minute their spot is aired," it is still only the rare commercial that seems to cause a dramatic upsurge in sales; most advertising effects are small, short-lived, and inexplicable.[36]

Finally, has advertising established itself as a legitimate component of a capitalist structure? Only in part. In a cross-national study Thorelli and his associates found that Americans accept advertising only as a necessary evil in a competitive economy. Americans decry the persuasive power of commercials with the same avidity as do people in any other country.

Most people in all countries feel that advertising is often untruthful, that it persuades people to buy unnecessarily, and that it insults the intelligence. Yet the same people believe that advertising is a necessary means of learning about the existence of new, desirable products.[37] Thus, Americans do believe that advertising performs a useful function, but they reject major elements of the advertiser's message, and they distrust advertisers themselves.

How should we summarize this body of research? On balance, it is hard to disagree with Arndt's assessment that "findings relating to advertising effects have been shown to depend heavily on the research design. Contrary to the general belief, almost nothing scientifically valid is known about the effects of advertising."[38] Arndt's conclusion is certainly more judicious than Simon's, who argues that the economic effects of advertising have been considerably overrated. It is true, however, that the critic's image of advertising as a smoothly functioning, efficient, and successful component of a monolithic capitalist structure does not stand up under scrutiny. Instead, what becomes particularly striking is the diversity of culture-producing institutions in the United States. Thus, from a structural standpoint, advertising agencies and commercial television networks differ considerably; therefore, if we discovered that they transmitted similar cultural messages we would be warranted in concluding that, contrary to an orthodox Marxist position, culture imposes itself uniformly, no matter what the structure or economic function of the institution in question. In Marxist terminology, "super-structure" molds "base," rather than the other way round.[39] The suspicion emerges that perhaps all institutional roads lead to the loosely bounded culture.

A CRITIQUE OF ADVERTISING DEFENSES

James Cary lucidly sums up the position of those who defend advertising. He writes that advertising "is an institution designed primarily to provide information on economic goods and services."[40] Its defenders claim that because advertising gives consumers information they need if they are to make rational choices among products, it presents no ethical or moral questions.

It is far easier to attack the "information" defense of advertising than the persuasion or manipulation criticism we have just examined. Four lines of argument suffice to discredit the information argument. These four involve the actual informational content of advertising, the way consumers interpret advertising content, the particular conception of rationality that advertising reflects, and the role the brand name plays in advertising.

If in fact advertisers are anxious to convey useful information about their products to consumers, it is only reasonable to expect advertisements to contain much useful information. But advertisements do not actually contain much useful information, at least so far as consumers themselves are concerned. According to Marquez, consumers "rate less than half of all advertising as informative."[41] In short, consumers believe that advertisements are primarily persuasive rather than informative.

Even if advertising were mainly informative, consumers would hardly be able to use the information they provide to make rational buying decisions. Raymond Bauer and Stephen Greyser argue that "modern products are sufficiently complex that the individual consumer is in a rather poor position to judge their merits quickly and easily."[42] And, as if to support this view, Marquez cites studies which indicate that consumers rarely search for pertinent information about the products they intend to buy. Even those who are anxious to locate useful information are uncertain about the kind of information that would be useful to them. Most consumers "neither know how to process or use" what little factual information advertisements provide.[43] Indeed, even the briefest consideration will suggest the weakness of the "information" defense; products as complicated as automobiles, say, surely require more than the thirty seconds or a minute most advertisers allocate them if such messages are to be useful to consumers. Thus, even if advertisers had the best will in the world, advertising could not function effectively as an informative device.

And what of the argument that advertising increases "rational" choices among consumers? The concept of rationality is fraught with ambiguities, but it still remains possible to show how poorly advertising measures up to even the most generous definition of rationality. The critical point is that advertising never simply *describes* a product, it actually adds to it a spurious, wholly artificial value. Advertisements function by associating products with salient cultural symbols, often in a thoroughly illogical way. For example, Ivan Preston notes that most automobile advertisements attempt to link the product to high status. Yet, "we can examine an auto all day without finding intrinsic evidence that it can provide status."[44] The trick of association permits the advertiser to argue, illogically, that the status value inheres in the automobile itself, rather than in the product's symbolic role in the culture. The effect of the appeal is thus to increase *irrationality*, rather than to enhance informed, rational choice. It is this dynamic which underlies and motivates the multiple confusions Jules Henry captures in his fertile phrase: the "pecuniary philosophy" of advertising.[45]

Finally, the "information" argument ignores what is, in fact, the advertiser's major goal, that is, selling a brand name rather than a product. As Preston puts it, "In the twentieth century mass markets have changed . . . from selling products to selling brands. The marketer's goal is to make the brand appear to the customer as though it *is* the product."[46] Do advertisers invite us to crave "soft drinks?" Of course not. They call us to thirst after Cokes, Pepsis, or Dr. Peppers. We are enticed by Fords, Buicks, and Chryslers, not "cars." The primary concern of the advertiser, therefore, is to establish product *differentiation* through packaging and brand names, rather than through product type or quality. Preston thus explains the growth of advertising very differently from Ewen: "Manufacturing increased to the point where supply overtook demand and passed it. The individual producer became threatened with an absence of markets, and began seriously to compete for those which remained available. As this competition heightened in the late nineteenth century, producers became painfully aware that the non-distinctiveness of their product was a liability."[47]

Advertising aims to inflate minor brand distinctions into

apparently vital matters on which sales should turn. To do so, they emphasize things other than factual product information, for they know that factual differences are rarely sufficient to create brand name identification. It follows that the thrust of advertising directly contradicts the arguments of advertising's defenders.

THE CULTURAL ROLE OF ADVERTISING

Attempts to interpret advertising in terms of its informational or persuasive effects on an audience provide an incomplete view of the subject. Let us investigate another line of analysis, one which sees advertising as an expression of meanings deeply embedded in American culture. From this perspective advertising crystallizes certain conflicts we have already encountered in our analysis of the loosely bounded culture. To repeat, the basic problem of a loosely bounded culture is how to surmount diversity and extreme individualism and construct a system of cultural order without the aid of such traditional bonding mechanisms as ethnic homogeneity, religious convergence, racial purity, political ideology, class endogamy. Advertising depicts in highly symbolic terms two phases of this process: the first is a portrait of diversity necessary for the marking off of goods for sale, and the second is a transcendence of diversity through the medium of these same goods. The ultimate result of the process is a defense of the loosely bounded culture.

Many writers have commented on myth-like representations of diversity in advertising symbolism,[48] but few have observed the way in which advertising overcomes diversity symbolically. Only in its initial phase—its economic phase—does advertising play a traditional mythic role. Here, as we shall see, it depicts a status-ridden society.[49] But in its second phase it constructs a loosely bounded culture out of the diversity it depicts. We will examine both aspects. True, from a strictly structuralist perspective in anthropology, advertising does at first appear to be a set of structured oppositions in which a coherent, static, cultural order emerges out of materials similar to the myths and folktales that structuralists are fond of analyzing. But, as we shall see, this kind of analysis leaves the most critical aspects of advertising untouched and ignores the loose boundedness of advertisements.

That advertising appears at first to create tight boundaries and sharp distinctions between social groups may be explained by four basic factors. First, advertising differentiates brands; the advertiser thus emphasizes structured comparisons and polarities. At first viewing, advertisements appear to sharpen distinctions rather than to surmount them. This is a particularly appealing interpretation because goods serve as status markers in all consumer societies.[50] The unequal costs of different products help create and symbolize social hierarchies. Thus, by differentiating brands, advertising stratifies consumers. Advertising helps arrange people in status hierarchies according to who owns what advertised brand of what valued good. Without advertising, status allocation in any modern society would become somewhat more difficult.

Second, advertising appeals to deeply rooted psychological tendencies toward differentiation, competition, greed, and envy. Many ads cater to our acquisitive instincts; others play upon our desire to humiliate our fellow humans in order to buttress our own fragile self-esteem. A particularly good example is the television commercial in which one man condescendingly chides another for the latter's insistence on keeping his money in a bank that pays comparatively little interest. The viewer is left with no doubt about who is smart and who is dull in this advertisement, as well as in the countless others that resemble it in plot line.

Third, all advertisements picture the product as a sort of fulcrum around which action revolves. The goal of selling the product directs the advertisement toward predictable ends and thus imposes on advertisements a coherent formal structure easily analyzable within the framework of structural anthropology. Indeed, commercials are usually easier to analyze for their cultural content than are entertainment programs on television.

Finally, advertisements include many elements that anthropologists have identified in the myths of traditional societies.[51] For this reason it is tempting to view advertisements as "no

more than" the symbolic crystallization of static cultural oppositions. In this view, the advertisement sells either because it
represents and reinforces traditional distinctions or because it
mediates such distinctions through appeals identical to those
that myths employ in traditional societies.

Let us illustrate this latter argument. Consider, for example,
the traditional theme of pollution, with its emphasis on eliminating dirt, cleansing boundaries, and purifying souls. Douglas
has shown that this is a primary theme uniting the myths of
many traditional societies; further, the pollution theme not
only underlies symbolism but also serves as a social control.[52]
The pollution theme reappears in the cultural system of modern advertising. How else to explain our preoccupation with
detergents and soaps, and, more important, advertising's loving depiction of these cleansing products. Soap advertisements
depict in graphic form a few simple mechanisms for cleansing
the self of pollution and marking oneself off from those who
are dirty and polluted. It could be argued, therefore, that our
society's preoccupation with detergents, soaps, and bodily
cleanliness symbolizes the survival of a *tightly* bounded culture's
concern with status demarcations. Perhaps there is less loose
boundedness in American culture than I have suggested.

Or consider the many commercials that capitalize on our
fear of bodily excretions. Sanitary pads absorb menstrual
fluids; razors, shaving creams, shampoos and hair treatments
eliminate "unsightly hair and dandruff"; "Pampers" mop up
baby's feces and urine; manicure sets trim up finger and toe
nails; deodorants kill germs which could defile the body;
mouth "fresheners" sweeten the breath; and air deodorizers
eliminate cooking odors from the dining room. Like traditional myths, advertisements warn us to respect the boundary
between dirt and cleanliness, waste and worthiness. And it is
the advertised product itself that shores up this vital boundary.

Notice, however, the difference between the way advertisements depict pollution and the way traditional myths depict
pollution. The advertisement argues that an inanimate, dispos-
able product is enough to transport us from defilement to purity. By contrast, traditional myths tell us that purification de-

mands a complicated, drawn-out, occasionally risky series of rituals, which make use of multiple incantations and perhaps even spells and witchcraft. The contrast is glaring. The advertisement fiercely condenses the mythic message in time and space. Thus, though the advertisement and the myth deal with the same cultural theme, they are quite different formally. As we shall see, their differences are just as important as their similarities.

Another traditional mythic theme that appears in advertisements is that of the fate of the stranger or the foreigner. Many myths center on the sojourning of heroes in foreign lands— their travails, their danger, their survivals, or their deaths. Examples include the myth of Israel in Egypt, of Jason and the Argonauts, and of Dorothy in the Land of Oz. The same theme appears in many of the advertisements for travelers checks and credit cards on American television. In one such advertisement, for example, a disconcerted and disheveled American couple find themselves mired in a decrepit, dirty hotel room in the Arab quarter of some ancient city. They have just come from an Arab meal that is not sitting well. They do not like their room. In fact, they are frightened to death. The wife timorously expresses her discomfort to her husband, who reassures her by pointing to the Citibank office just across the street. They are not really alone and vulnerable. Here the product—the credit card—becomes the passport from danger to safety.

Or consider yet another traditional mythic element in advertising: the theme of ritualized eating. Meals promote the selling of foodstuffs, of course, but they also connote far more than simple ingestion. The meal is a central metaphor for the quality of social relations in any society, and the frequent televised coupling of meals with products—even products which are not themselves foodstuffs—cannot be accidental.[53] Frequently, meals in American commercials reunite long-dispersed families, thus reinstating tradition and selling products at the same time. An example is the Coca-Cola commercial in which a family reunion includes a picnic featuring Coke. Another example is the Inglenook wine commercial in which an important ritual—marriage or college graduation—is celebrated with a family meal, which Inglenook helps transform from an ordinary repast into a festive ceremony replete with toasts. The centrality of the meal shows that many advertisements continue to employ traditional mythic material in a distinctively modern cultural setting.

We can thus agree that traditional cultural themes—pollution and purity, foreignness and security, eating and kinship—infuse contemporary advertisements, indicating that advertisements may in fact depict a cultural system that is old and unchanging. But we can go even further along this line. A central function of myth and ritual in all societies is the imposition of order on a confusing cultural scene. Thus, for example, purification separates dirt from cleanliness so as to stabilize social arrangements and status categories. This same scenario—the extraction of order out of apparent disarray—is the basic plot of many advertisements. Several examples will illustrate the point. A territorial version of order is the central thematic thread of most lawn-mower advertisements. These advertisements typically begin by displaying an unkempt lawn, and then proceed, with the assistance of the lawn mower, to transform the lawn into a manicured, carefully bounded, and eminently respectable territory. Such commercials equate unkemptness not only with disorder but also with ugliness. It is noteworthy also that the owner of the advertised lawn mower is as neat and clean as his or her newly mowed lawn. Not a hair of the owner is out of place, and not a blade of grass is out of place on the lawn. Thus, the commercial constructs a homology between human beings and territory, a homology mediated by the mower.[54]

Another advertisement that provides a similar vision of differentiated, tightly bounded order is that for the American Express Card. The plot of the American Express commercial is the card's capacity to provide instant identification to otherwise identity-less persons traveling abroad. The commercial appeals to our fear of losing our identity (and ourselves) when we travel. The card prevents the potential diffusion of identity and reinstates personal boundaries.

A tightly bounded commercial with special social relevance

is that for a national real estate service. Because personal property is, virtually by definition, an intimate, charged form of territoriality, we should not be surprised to discover that real estate advertisements take us from territorial disorder to territorial order. This particular commercial is especially subtle, however, for it equates territorial order with social order, so as to advantage not only the financial well-being of the advertised firm, but also that of the entire real estate industry. The commercial begins by showing the audience one black and one white family, each searching for a home. Both families are perplexed, disorganized, uncertain, and harried. However, thanks to the intervention of the real estate salesman, each family finds its "dream house," which, in a particularly significant twist, turns out to adjoin the other in a well-kept, integrated, middle-class neighborhood. In the final frame the audience sees the two families strolling happily down their respective entrance-ways, smiling gaily at each other from the safe distance their adjoining territories provide. Thus, they are connected territorially, but safely apart as persons.

This commercial skillfully unites traditional themes of social and territorial dislocation. Being "homeless" (the process of house hunting) is equivalent to being in a dangerous liminal state of the sort Victor Turner describes.[55] Thus, although the house hunters in the commercial are separated by race, they are actually united in discomfort and vulnerability. Their mutual vulnerability shows us that "people are people" no matter what their skin color. The commercial depends on the fact that blacks and whites are from different, mutually hostile cultures, which have been in stark conflict for the past generation. Therefore, finding adjoining homes for the two couples not only resolves their own individual problems of liminality but also epitomizes a vision of a harmonious racial order founded on Robert Frost's observation that "good fences make good neighbors." The real estate man sells each couple not only a home but also a sense of security; he manages to keep them far enough apart across the lawns to protect them from each other, yet assures them through his salesmanship that they are social equals. The salesman demonstrates in practice what the Supreme Court could not in theory: that "separate, but equal" actually works, and that the races can be peacefully combined in an integrated territory. Small wonder that the commercial concludes with both couples gratefully saluting the real estate man, who has accomplished in one brief transaction what the American political system has been unable to accomplish for 120 years.[56]

The traditional function of myth in rescuing a social order from disorder and confusion often involves religious symbolism. The same thing is true in advertisements. Advertisements treat brand names as religious ikons whose adoption will reinstate traditional moral values. The religious character of the product becomes the mechanism whereby order emerges out of disorder. Advertisements make the following intertwined religious appeals: they apply religious symbols to products; they attribute religious powers to products; they portray product use as a religious rite; and they claim that product use has "uplifting" religious effects. Let us examine each of these appeals.

Hallowed symbols of both secular and religious origin permeate advertisements. An example is Prudential's Rock of Gibralter, which symbolizes family stability by invoking the biblical association between rocks and steadfastness, courage, and safety. What could be more trustworthy than a company that insures against death by emphasizing the rock of enduring life?[57] Henry observes that even our most sacred patriotic figures, Washington and Lincoln, have been mobilized in the fight to sell goods. "An important social function of the Franklin, Lincoln, and Washington sagas is to make Americans ready to patronize any institution or buy any product bearing their names."[58] Henry dubs this practice the "monetization of values,"[59] a phrase which denotes a process whereby religious values have their sacred quality compromised by being reduced to monetary equivalents in the form of products for sale. But might not Henry have it backwards? Perhaps the products gain value by being associated with sacred symbols; and in this way the realm of the sacred expands rather than contracts. Finally, Tankard argues that "the exploitation of sacred words and symbols" has extended even to the appropriation of themes sacred

to the counter-culture, such as "love" and "peace."[60] In a society
that creates new traditions as promiscuously as it borrows from
old, advertisers will stop at no sacred tradition. In this way advertising domesticates the periphery of society.

But religions—whether traditional or counter-cultural—are
not the only source of sacred symbolism in advertising. Advertisers reach back to the "natural symbols" characteristic of
primitive societies in an attempt to imbue their products with
sacred qualities.[61] Martyn, for example, comments on the widespread use of animal symbols in advertisements. Consider the
Esso tiger, or the practice of naming automobiles after animals,
or the use of "unpolluted" country appeals to sell cigarettes.[62]
Elsewhere Sullenberger investigates the use of folklore in
American advertising. "'The Jolly Green Giant' who helps sell
vegetables is . . . a throwback to the numerous European fertility symbols or spirits of vegetation."[63] The Keebler cookie company invents elves to sell its products, and in an invocation of
mythical associations between sexuality and knighthood, the
Ajax White Knight magically "explodes" dirt with his lance.[64]
Finally, in some advertisements natural symbols appear very
explicitly, as with the Firebird of Russian mythology, a name
that now graces an automobile which resembles the mythic
firebird only in the most heated imaginings of the ad's creator.

Another natural symbol in advertisements is communion as
a source of personal power or grace. Not surprisingly, communion appeals abound in ads for drinks. Like the wafer and wine
of the Catholic mass, so also Coke "adds life" by infusing those
who drink it with new energy. Dr. Pepper drinkers become so
energized by their communion with the product that they
break into song and dance, and thus turn a quiet citizenry into
a bunch of whirling dervishes on the first leg of a contemporary
children's crusade in pursuit of pleasure. Communion does not
necessarily require drink, however. The lovely woman who
wakes after a blissful night's sleep on her Sealy Posturepedic
mattress feels so good that she literally bounds from her bed
and skips through the neighborhood, enchanting children as
she goes. In these advertisements traditional promises of salvation and freedom through communion become attached to the

product. The product "carries a punch" because it possesses a power far beyond its physical qualities. It infuses life because Life infuses it.

Skolimowski and Leavis and Thompson argue that the ritualistic aspects of advertising transcend even the simulation of communion.[65] They claim that advertisements portray consumption as a state of grace. As consumers, we "become worshippers of objects,"[66] but these objects are not to be adored, contemplated, or avoided—as in traditional religions—they are to be grasped, used, and finally used up. Leavis and Thompson argue that because material acquisition is the religion of modernity, advertising in fact offers the sacraments to people by transforming mundane acts of buying and selling into religious rituals.[67] Perhaps this is why so many ads linger so lovingly over the acquisition of the product, instead of simply describing the virtues of the product itself. In any essentially religious endeavor there are a definite succession of steps leading to a spiritual climax. Thus, one can't just purchase a good; one must first make oneself worthy through purification, sanctification, and ritual.

Finally, advertising promises that the product will not only create a power for the buyer, but will also deliver a spiritual experience akin to enlightenment or insight. In Leavis and Thompson's words, advertising offers the buyer "vague uplift," and an infusion of warm sentiments that "spill over" into enhanced fellow feeling.[68] Communion with the product thus produces power, and power in turn creates exemplary behavior toward others. The lovely woman just arisen from her Sealy Posturepedic is not suddenly just a "fun person," but is in fact a model adult for children to follow. Children don't just play with her—they learn from her. And the father who successfully sells insurance in the insurance advertisement becomes a "better father" for it. In a sense, therefore, advertisements promise us that products will effect a moral reform of society which will permit us all to live up to our ideals. The Coke drinker not only has more fun at the picnic, but on the job he also becomes a more efficient worker. Thus, advertising vivifies traditional statuses in a tightly bounded cultural code where "old-fashioned virtues" still abound.

The most complete theory of advertising as a traditionally structured, tightly bounded mythic expression appears in the work of Varda Leymore. Leymore sums up her argument in the following way:

> Advertising is a multi-layered construct, each of which may have its own level of meaning. While the surface level is devoted to product characterization and consumer benefits, and the intermediary level to semiconscious messages, the underlying dimensions of an advertising system are exhaustive statements, which reduce all the diverse appearances into simultaneously abstract and simple binary relations.[69]

Leymore's method, as one might expect, lies well within the tradition of structural anthropology. She identifies a number of specific structuralist devices in commercials: the existence of a "deep structure" lying underneath the surface content of the advertising message; the existence of homologous messages organized into binary sets; and the existence of mythic resolutions of these binary tensions. Leymore contends that "advertising is a degenerated form of myth,"[70] which helps integrate a society cognitively along the lines of tightly bounded cultural codes.

In pursuit of her thesis Leymore analyzes several types of advertisements in detail. She argues, for example, that advertisements for baby foods pose the polarity of life against death, where the food stands for life, and the absence of food for death. Advertisements for English cheese associate the product with stable order, and portray non-English cheeses as deceptive interlopers. The cheese advertisements thus play upon the inside/outside tension so vital to traditional cultural systems. Leymore claims that these binary sets constitute "Exhaustive Common Denominators," which underlie all commercials for a product. Leymore thus argues that to analyze any set of commercials requires the researcher to identify the Exhaustive Common Denominator.[71]

Advertisers are *not* mainly concerned, Leymore argues, with selling a particular brand name. Rather, advertisers concentrate on a type of product. The product forges the mythic resolution of any message's polarities. Without product identification, no brand will sell. Thus, for example, cheese as a product becomes appealing when advertisements show it mediating between animal and man. Although cheese comes originally from an animal in the form of milk, it becomes separate from the animal. Thus, by consuming cheese humans come into indirect touch with animals, but not in a directly threatening way. Similarly, perfumes mediate the tension between civilized and primitive women, and between nature and sophistication — polarized categories necessary to each other, yet irreconcilable without the product's intervention. Perfumes promise to bring the best aspects of the natural together with the sophisticated, thereby reconciling the conflictual elements of the nature/civilization dichotomy. The woman who uses the perfume is naturally sensuous, yet almost preternaturally civilized.[72]

Leymore claims that the Exhaustive Common Denominator in a commercial determines the advertisement's selling power. She presents data which show a significant statistical correlation between the frequency of Exhaustive Common Denominators and fluctuations in sales volumes for selected products. Leymore claims that although the audience may not perceive the underlying binary structure and closed-meaning system of single commercials, the cumulative effect of a set of commercials is not explicable without a structuralist interpretation of the sort she provides.[73]

Leymore's structuralist interpretation clearly suits the tenor of our present discussion of advertising as a traditional, tightly bounded cultural form. To it we could add supportive material, such as the persistence of racial stereotypes in television commercials. Racial boundaries obviously fit neatly within a tightly bounded cultural code. We could also cite evidence that advertisements encourage children to purchase the particular brands advertised as well as to overlook deficiencies in the product they buy.[74] These effects suggest a socialization function for advertising akin to the socialization function anthropologists identify for cultural codes generally. Thus, advertisements do in many ways resemble a traditional cultural code.

ADVERTISING AND THE LOOSELY BOUNDED CULTURE

To discuss only those aspects of commercials concerned with
product differentiation, sharply bounded oppositions, and traditional cultural themes would be to distort the cultural role of
advertising. We would be equally misguided to interpret advertisements solely in terms of status differentiation along
Veblenesque lines. Even Mary Douglas, who is otherwise drawn
to Veblen's analysis, cautions that, while goods serve to differentiate people from each other, they also serve as common media
of communication—a kind of lingua franca in industrialized
societies.[75]

Our earlier discussion of the loosely bounded culture should
also have suggested the inadequacy of this traditionalistic interpretation. A major problem of all industrialized societies,
especially in the United States, is the construction of social integration despite the ravages of a refined division of labor and of
extreme individualism, both of which undercut those complementary binary oppositions and synthesizing myths which
hold traditional societies together. Although traditional phenomena persist in attenuated forms, an ethic of impersonal,
meritocratic egalitarianism dominates American life. People
are encouraged to compete individually for jobs as equals, undifferentiated by group attachments of blood, race, religion,
and class. The function of modern artificial culture—the media, advertising, schools—is to provide models of cultural integration in the face of these developments. Advertising thus
seeks to bring Americans together and connect them with each
other, rather than simply to differentiate them from each
other. Put dialectically, an advertisement's first "moment" separates people from each other through product usage; however,
this differentiation creates tensions that the advertisement's
second "moment" resolves as the product ultimately reunites
people with each other.

A primary function of products in advertisements is the creation of new, unforeseen relationships out of differentiated
and unpromising circumstances. The product becomes the
magnet that draws people together. The operative rule is that

the advertisement should never leave people separated and alienated from each other. An example should help to clarify the argument. In one AMF sports equipment commercial we are introduced to an obviously bored, silent, overweight couple staring vacantly at a television set. Each partner is preoccupied with his or her own thoughts. The two clearly have nothing to say to each other. The portrayal obviously expresses symbolically the social malaise a refined division of labor and extreme individualism create in even the most intimate relationship.

Suddenly, however, the AMF logo appears on the couple's television screen followed by AMF's line of recreational products—bicycles, boats, and so on—and immediately a rainbow dawns outside the couple's window. Color floods the formerly drab living room. Husband and wife visibly brighten as they ride off on bicycles along the rainbow that AMF products have created. Their new recreational equipment has reunited them; no longer are they separated and alienated from each other. In countless commercials this same theme appears.

Of course, a married couple is not much of a challenge for an advertisement. Husbands and wives may be bored and temporarily out of touch with each other, but the married state supplies fertile ground on which the commercial can erect a more vital relationship. AMF has an easy task. But forging relationships on less-fertile ground is no more daunting to ingenious advertisers.

Even the touchiest personal problems eventually yield to the appropriate product. Consider the life insurance commercial in which the insurance salesman's attendance at a wedding smooths over differences between a new father-in-law and his son-in-law. All that is required is for the salesman to sell the groom insurance, just as years before he had sold the father-in-law insurance. The insurance forges a bond of trust between father-in-law and son-in-law during a time of tense transition. In-law relationships, as we all know, are often touchy at their outset. The function of life insurance in the commercial is not only to provide financial support for the newlyweds, but also to reassure the father-in-law that his new son-in-law is responsible, shares his values, and deserves respect. The salesman therefore insures more than the life of the groom. He insures the life of the family itself.

Advertising's contribution to the construction of satisfying relationships appears in two other components of the message. As a number of writers have observed, advertising's portrayals almost always separate goods from the process of production. Rarely does an advertisement actually show us products being made, except for an occasional glance at an oil rig or an assembly line.[76] More often the product stands entirely apart from any productive context. Products serve as ikons for contemplation, or more often as objects for use or consumption. Advertisements thus associate products with consumption, not with production.

The usual explanation for this kind of representation is economic. After all, ads sell products to consumers, so advertisements must feature the process of consumption. Equally important, if less obvious, however, is a culturally relevant difference between the structure of social relations in production and consumption. Production is a differentiated, highly organized, tightly bounded, hierarchical process, in which people relate to each other, not as unique persons, but as often interchangeable workers possessing greater or lesser amounts of power. To place a product in a productive context, therefore, is to imbue it with a differentiated, separate, inviolate meaning, as symbolized by the final divorce between the product and the process of production. Ultimately, the finished car rolls off the assembly line and out of the lives of its builders forever. Separation is the primary cultural motif of such a commercial.

By contrast, consumption is an absorptive, incorporative process which brings the product into touch with its users in an undifferentiated diffuse fashion. Consumers are essentially equals, at least as their use of the advertised product brings them into connection with one another. And, because they are equals, consumers can potentially come into touch with each other as easily as they come into touch with the product. The product aids in this endeavor, for it draws people together freely and pleasurably. Thus, by picturing the product in its consummatory mode, advertising creates illusions of intimacy, freedom, and pleasure, which are the very emotions appropriate to a loosely bounded society.[77]

To this representation advertising appends an appropriate conception of human nature. The ideal personality type for a society that values meritocratic structural differentiation is one of rational individuals who assess facts for themselves, including those facts relevant to the buying of goods. Merle Curti discerns this conception of an independent, rational buyer dominating the first period of American advertising from 1889 to 1905. However, in the period 1910–1930, Curti's analysis of advertising content reveals a growing tendency to see human nature as malleable and fearful of nonconformity. During this period advertisers conceptualized human nature as irrational and dependent, vulnerable to fears of ostracism. Most recently, Curti sees a partial return to the older, rationalistic conception, but still most advertising conceives of human beings as subject to dependent impulses that not only are uncontrollable, but actually should not be controlled if pleasure is the aim. Thus, the independent customer has given way to the dependent consumer in advertising's portrait of human nature.[78]

Hence it is no surprise that contemporary advertising plays upon the liberation of impulse and the breakdown of inhibitions. In commercials "hang-ups" create barriers between people (indeed, the hang-up is usually a spatial barrier between persons); "letting it all hang out," on the other hand, is the royal road to workable human relationships. The function of many advertised products is to remove hang-ups so that communion between equals can take place.

Although there are few legitimate status barriers between persons in a loosely bounded culture, the problem of constructing satisfying relationships is more complex than we might think. Indeed, the very absence of status barriers causes some people to become fiercely protective of their "selves," for they lack legitimate status defenses against the intrusions of others. Their "hang-ups" thus become interior, consisting of phobias against intimacy or preternatural sensitivity to "offensive" personal habits. These pathologies of loose boundedness are deeply embedded, primarily because they constitute a last thin line of defense for the self.[79] As a result, many commercials and products strive to alter the individual's state of consciousness in order to surmount these last stubborn barriers to intimacy. Consider the many glossily produced ads for such mind-altering products as sleeping aids, liquor, "intoxicating" perfumes, and tobacco. Many other goods may not actually alter consciousness physically, but promise to do so symbolically. These include, for example, Noxema shaving soap, which gives its user a "clean shave" so he can "take it all off" with lovely young women. Here again we see the advertising dialectic at work: from initial differentiation (shaving and cleanliness) to the implicit formation of an egalitarian sexual bond.

The many barriers which advertisers try to sweep away in our loosely bounded culture are tributes to people's residual fear of becoming vulnerable to each other in such a culture. Such vulnerability often elevates trivial relational factors to matters of great significance. This too the advertiser detects and attempts to correct. Thus, it is "bad breath" (not bad faith) that drives lovers apart; "wrinkles" (not death) that cause depression; dandruff (not worry) that causes sleeplessness. In a loosely bounded culture the minutiae of appearance take on the sort of critical importance that more tightly bounded cultures ascribe to traditional barriers of race, education, class, language, and ethnicity. At the same time, however, the commercial promises to overcome these disorienting personal characteristics if people will just use the product. Once the product does its job, the ideal of instant and all-encompassing "togetherness" can be realized. The problem for the advertiser, therefore, is not whether the product "works," but, rather, getting the reluctant and timid consumer to "try it, you'll like it." And so the advertiser becomes physician to the uneasy American soul.

Advertising's emphasis on consumption employs a number of interconnected psychological and structural appeals. In fact, advertisements depict a kind of consumption cycle. As we have seen, advertisements promise relatedness among formerly differentiated and separated individuals. However, this appeal is perforce restricted because, once consumption has taken place, the relationship so recently stitched together may easily unravel. Therefore, just as relationships develop quickly with the appearance and use of the product, so also they collapse quickly when the act of consumption has ended. This is the problem the consumption cycle attempts to solve.

Advertising's solution to the problem is to argue that personal relationships must continually be renewed by recurrent acts of consumption. Characters in advertisements always start at ground zero with each other; no matter how hard they may have worked to forge a relationship, they must work again. With each viewing of a commercial we see the same relationship develop again and again. The need to cement relationships thus becomes the motivational dynamic that creates new products and sustains old. The evanescence of personal relationships in advertisements thus mirrors the economic function of advertising (to create consumption), a function which can only be satisfied by making sure the product serves the loosely bounded culture's need for satisfactory, if transient, relationships. The economic and cultural meanings of the commercial thus fuse, and symbolic consumption begets real consumption.

The products that advertisements picture help create satisfying relationships in many different ways. For example, the many cameras advertised on television create relationships because they make it possible for some people to observe others closely. In Polaroid commercials, for example, the camera's operation is a metaphor for the widespread openness to scrutiny that is common in a loosely bounded culture. And photographer and subject's joint admiration of the just-taken photograph provides them with the basis for a new relationship. The camera thus becomes a way of associating visual scrutiny with personal intimacy.[80]

Openness to scrutiny in a loosely bounded culture plays an important role in many commercials. Openness, after all, places a priority on appearance, and appearance is served by such products as cosmetics and shampoos. The purpose of these products is to help people package their exteriors so as to attract others and gain their friendship. The packaging of the self parallels product diversification and brand differentiation, neither of which alters the effectiveness or quality of the product, but both of which increase visual appeal. The message of commercials for products that improve self-packaging is that superficial cosmetic alterations of the self can create new relationships. Distinctiveness of scent or look is but the prelude to new solidarities.

Another method by which advertising promises new relationships is by altering not the appearance of the product's user, but his behavior. The product must stimulate movement, for the explosion from stasis into action symbolizes the destruction of differentiation, isolation, and alienation, and installs intimacy in their place. Commercials for the drink Dr. Pepper begin, for example, with a group of self-absorbed, isolated people confined within the conventional roles of civil society. But the appearance of Dr. Pepper creates an explosion of activity—a dance, in fact—which becomes a kind of communal recreation, breaking down isolation. There is much complementarity between movement in this commercial and other aspects of a loosely bounded culture. In such a culture relationships need not be long-lasting or confining. Therefore, the forging of relationships in the midst of movement—though difficult from a logical standpoint, since deep relationships take time and space to develop—is entirely consistent with a loosely bounded culture. Movement expresses both the development of a relationship and the dynamic, ever-changing quality of that relationship in a loosely bounded culture. Additionally, movement precludes much serious discourse; the new relationship is thus founded upon shared *activity* and emotional expression, not upon the measured exchange of ideas or values. In a loosely bounded culture where ambiguity in relationships is a constant danger, common understandings cannot be constructed by probing possible sources of discord and diversity. It is far safer to play together than to talk together. Better share a framework of action rather than a framework of meaning. In a sense, therefore, the very inarticulateness and childishness of advertisements is the most important message they have to give. The commercial's mindlessness is its most important idea.

A final appeal that advertisements make to the consumer is the metaphoric equation of satisfying personal relationships with the expression of impulses, usually represented by visual images of softness and sensuousness. Commercials associate hardness with severely differentiated, isolated, unhappy persons who must yield to impulse and breach their boundaries if they are to forge satisfying personal relationships. The superiority of softness to hardness appears in countless commercials.[81] For example, a bathroom tissue, we are told repeatedly, is "cottony soft" and therefore desirable. The best tobacco is "mild," not harsh; mild-smelling tobacco appeals to others, while harsh tobacco makes us expectorate, and thus repels and expels in the same act. Light, smooth beer is better than heavy, strong, harsh beer. Indeed, today "light" beer is low in calories as well as light in flavor, thus slimming us down so we can become attractive. Automobiles give "smooth" rides, which allow passengers to snuggle softly and comfortably into their seats. "Hard" rides, on the other hand, bounce us around uncomfortably and thus separate us from each other.

Advertisements also picture human relationships evolving from hardness to softness, from restriction to unbounded action across newly permeable boundaries. An example is the television commercial that begins by presenting us with a prototypically "hard" situation: a runner sweatily finishing a highly competitive marathon, isolated from other runners and also from the opposite sex. Here task, perspiration, dirt, and odor combine to create "overdetermined" separation from others. But this isolation soon dissolves with the help of a soft product, a smooth beer, which the newly cleansed and sweet-smelling athlete drinks convivially with former competitors and present women friends in the equally convivial atmosphere of the bar room. No longer offensively odoriferous, our hero merges into the bar-room crowd, hugged by his woman friend and grabbed at by his friends. Or consider the shaving cream ad where we are first presented with a man's hard, unyielding, stubby, unattractive whiskers, which alienate him from women and co-workers. This time a hard implement intervenes (a razor), but it is actually a soft product—a shaving cream—which transforms the hard whiskers into an easily shaveable condition. The result: a clean, soft, attractive visage suitable for nuzzling.

This particular commercial—like others we could analyze—interestingly joins a traditional culture's purification theme with the modern qualities of a loosely bounded culture. The purification theme involves cleaning up dirt in the form of whiskers, thereby differentiating sharply between man and nature. But the real lure of shaving in the commercial is the hoped-for connection between man and woman. Thus, purification serves the ends of a loosely bounded culture. Cleanliness is simply preparatory to connection.

EXAMPLES OF THE CYCLE OF ENGAGEMENT

Two television commercials are especially notable for the clarity with which they depict a behavioral cycle from purification and cleanliness (a sharply bounded theme), to sexual engagement across barriers (a loosely bounded theme), to pollution through the sexual connection, and finally back to purification. The entire cycle becomes an occasion for product consumption. Consider first an ad for Foamy Shave Cream. The ad begins with a bewhiskered man shaving with Foamy while a lovely lady implores him to "take it off, take it all off." All double entendres in this commercial are fully intended, but what is the real message of the commercial?

The act of shaving with a white, foamy soap is, on one level, an act of ritual purification. Whiskers are errant hair, and therefore constitute, in Douglas's terms, "matter out of place." Therefore, to shave is to make oneself clean and pure. In the first instance, therefore, the act of shaving separates the shaver from nature and draws him away from threatening boundaries. But the ad also recalls distantly the Sampson legend, where hair stands for virility, and the absence of hair, for weakness. Thus, shaving, while a necessary ritual purification, is also a risky act, for it plays dangerously with virility, thus courting separation from and humiliation by others.

This is only the first phase of the commercial, however, for in fact shaving is only a preparation, not a consummation. "Foamy" lather prepares the way for sexual conquest and the permeation of the delicate boundaries between men and women. A young woman nuzzles the man as he shaves, as if to assure him that what happened to Sampson cannot happen to him. Indeed, shaving promises to produce more rather than less sexual gratification. The mechanism through which the transformation from isolating differentiation to pleasurable connection takes place is the medium of softness. The woman yields to the man because the man's beard yields to the soft soap, which in turn makes the man's face soft and lovable. Hardness becomes softness; bristles make way for smoothness; and isolation prepares the path for sexual yielding. At all times the product, Foamy, mediates the relationship.

The sexual act itself (which we obviously do not see) transgresses personal boundaries. Time passes, and soon a new set of whiskers appears. The result is that the soft, yielding quality so necessary to the sexual relationship vanishes; in its stead appears a renewed need for Foamy to clean one in preparation for yet another satisfying engagement. And so the cycle continues.

Similar messages appear in advertisements for English Leather, a cologne for men. In one such commercial a deliberately provocative and apparently liberated young woman remarks that women no longer need to accept a passive status vis à vis men. Instead, they can now take the initiative in making fulfilling connections. She then associates this new freedom for women with English Leather. She tells us that "men who can cope" with women's new freedom are self-confident and wear English Leather. These are, she tells us the men she likes; indeed, she assures us that "all my men wear English Leather—or they wear nothing at all."

This commercial contains multiple interlocking messages. At one level, the advertisement attempts to convince men that the practice of using a cologne—a practice traditionally associated with women—is not emasculating or effeminate, but has instead become the essence of masculine success with women. The interesting thing is that the commercial makes this point by paralleling the transition of perfume from female to male status with the transition of women themselves from passive to active roles. Thus, both the product itself and the theme of role reversal place boundary alteration and permeability at the center of the commercial.

At another level the commercial portrays openness by coupling cologne with nudity and the "baring" of self. To use the product is to gain access to the woman, as she makes clear by joining the product to the theme of nudity. We thus receive three parallel messages about permeable boundaries: (1) a message about a product's movement from female to male status; (2) a message about changes in sex-role behaviors; and (3) a message about the removability of clothes as a metaphor for openness both sexually and socially.

One advertisement that succeeds particularly well in associating the theme of speed with the formation and sustenance of relationships is that for Pepsi-Cola. The commercial begins with a baseball player crossing home plate to the wild cheers of a crowd and the ecstatic greetings of his teammates. The action of rounding the bases climaxes in a scene of reconciliation with teammates. The symbolic association between movement and relationship is thus firmly established from the outset. Next we see the young man traveling home on a train, and the entire town turns out to greet him. His family, all his friends, and his woman friend wait silently, motionless at the station. Here, as in the first sequence, movement takes the young man home again, just as it did when he hit the home run. But now he's returning to his real home. The hero finally arrives, and the crowd explodes into action; the man hugs his mother and father, who shed tears of happiness, and the entire company toasts his homecoming with Pepsi-Cola. The Pepsi vanishes quickly, just as the train moves fast, and just as the young man hurries around the bases to his waiting teammates. Of course, the faster the Pepsi disappears, the more quickly the relationships it symbolizes may crumble. The young man had better hit another home run soon in order to reinstate the pleasure of friendship.

Yet another depiction of a product taking people from a tightly bounded, constraining, isolating set of relationships to a loosely bounded, active, free, voluntary, and pleasurable set of relationships is one for Miller Light Beer. Especially interesting is the way this ad associates "natural" beer—with its connotation of nature generally—and domesticated conviviality; the beer is the medium through which we make the transition from nature to society, but to a society of shared pleasures rather than divided statuses. The ad also cleverly associates order, organization, and sequencing with a tightly bounded culture that must be surmounted. Indeed, the ad—and the product—actually satirize order. The ad begins with the comedian Rodney Dangerfield attempting to pose Miller Light Beer "alumni" (celebrities of various sorts who have appeared in previous Miller commercials) in preparation for a formal group picture. Just as the celebrities finally settle down into static poses, Dangerfield tells them to act "natural" for the photographer. The predictable result is explosive action and noise, which destroy the order that Dangerfield had so laboriously constructed. The picture, needless to say, is never taken.

In this commercial the projected picture is a satire on the Victorian family photos of the nineteenth century, which depicted a static family order of uncomfortable people confined as tightly within their roles as they were within the tight corsets and high collars that the portraits display. It is this traditional order which Dangerfield strives so unsuccessfully to construct. But a traditional status order is clearly inappropriate in a loosely bounded culture. When Dangerfield tells his charges to act "natural," he lets free the natural conviviality and informality embodied in the "natural" taste of Miller Light. The beer thus becomes the medium which destroys the old, tightly bounded order and creates a new vision of loosely bounded connections. It is hardly surprising that the picture is never actually taken, for a still photograph cannot capture the fluid relationships of a loosely bounded culture. Only the television camera can do the job properly.

The commercial which most successfully combines all the themes we have been discussing is one for Bell Telephone long distance.[82] In this commercial—perhaps as successful as any in recent times—we first see a mother talking long distance with one of her children. The conversation begins, and behind it we hear a song telling us to "reach out, reach out and touch someone." As the conversation continues the mother becomes more and more animated and lively, whereas her husband, buried behind his newspaper, sinks slowly into torpor. By the end of the commercial the husband has fallen asleep with the paper draped over his face like a funeral shroud.

The theme of crossing boundaries between separated individuals is the centerpiece of this commercial. The telephone, of course, is the indispensable medium through which communication and the renewal of relationships occurs. And, since all relationships are a source of life-giving energy in loosely bounded cultures, it is not surprising that the elderly woman should look younger and healthier the longer she talks. The telephone is a kind of Fountain of Youth. Nor is it surprising that we never see her husband's face; an isolating, lonely medium—the newspaper—literally walls him off from us, just as it separates him from his wife and even his child on the line, a thousand miles away. The father as a newspaper reader is a remnant of an old, tightly bounded culture, sulkily out of phase with loose boundedness. So naturally enough, as his wife becomes animated—for the phone enlivens her—he falls ever more out of contact. His sleep is the death of a culture. Indeed, his wife is in closer contact with her child a thousand miles away than she is with her husband, only three feet from her. After all, you cannot create a new culture without altering the family structure, even if this means symbolically killing some of its members. In America, you can't make a cultural omelet without breaking dads.

5

THE STRUGGLE FOR A POLITICAL EDUCATION

A school is a place where culture in the form of normatively regulated ideas, beliefs, and behaviors emerges from the organized and coordinated actions of teachers and students. In some respects, American schools resemble the mass media and advertising, each of which is a particularly modern means of contriving, packaging, and transmitting ideas to mass audiences. All three create expectations about the world and the self. Most important, all three reinforce the basic pattern of a loosely bounded culture.

Yet schools differ in important ways from the two other culture-creation institutions we have examined. These differences cause the loosely bounded messages embedded in American schools to take quite subtle forms. Schools are unique in three respects: in what they transmit, in their internal organization, and in their relationships with their audiences. Because of these differences the study of American schools confronts us more directly from the outset with politics than does the study of either American advertising or television entertainment.

Although these three factors are fairly obvious, they must nevertheless be discussed, for they constitute the foundation on which the cultural character of American schools depends. I will try to be brief and not too tedious.

First, schools attempt to transmit useful knowledge, or at least knowledge that educators believe to be useful for students. For this reason the "learning without involvement" which Herbert Krugman identifies as a primary aspect of the mass media is culturally proscribed in schools.[1] Unlike the mass media or advertising, schools cannot present learning as a by-product. Involved, intentional learning is the essence of schooling. The range and variety of knowledge which educators construe as potentially useful in all industrial societies is almost boundless because new disciplines, technologies, and languages constantly appear and find a place within society's operations.[2] Therefore, internalizing useful knowledge becomes doubly effortful, for such knowledge is constantly shifting its character. Schooling can therefore not be a halfhearted, casual, or entirely pleasurable enterprise of the sort we associate with mass media entertainment or even with advertising. To put it differently, the advertiser or the television producer must justify any serious intellectual demand he or she makes of the audience, for sustained concentration may well be seen as incompatible with "entertainment." By contrast, the teacher must justify *entertainment* in schooling, for entertainment may well be seen as incompatible with the mastery of demanding material. Perhaps this is why intrinsic enjoyment, which Jencks claims to be the only real justification for contemporary American schooling,[3] never actually appears as an educational rationale, for such a rationale, if admitted, would undercut the entire educational enterprise.

Schools then aim to convey truth(s), not titillation or pleasure.[4] By contrast, television and advertising aim to entertain and to satisfy consumer preferences. Of course, in the process of doing so, television and advertising may enhance people's understanding of the world, but this is not their primary goal. They become serious only to deceive people into buying what they might not otherwise buy or, in the case of television entertainment, into accepting entertainment. But these primary functions place distinct limits on their capacity to teach.

Second, unlike television or advertising, schooling is not a matter of choice. We are compelled by force of law both to go to school ourselves and to send our children to school.[5] By contrast, we are free to leave the television set at rest in our living rooms if we so choose. No truant officer drags us in front of a television receiver if we do not reach a certain quota of television hours. And, although advertising is ubiquitous in America, we need not remember what we see. No one tests our memory of advertising. True, our purchasing decisions are analogous in some ways to examinations of classroom learning, but the analogy is strained, for we are under no compulsion to take such tests, nor do we suffer if we choose not to.

The compulsory character of schools insures that many students will be unhappy in the classroom. Schools are not subject to competitive pressures as product advertising and mass media entertainment are. Few self-respecting schools permit the preferences of students to control the behavior of teachers. By contrast, the voluntary character of exposure to any television program or advertisement gives audiences some limited check on what they see. Thus, some alienation from schooling must be counted as normal, for teachers need not take student desires into account in planning coursework. As Morgan puts it, "The learning process fails in any systematic manner to emanate from the needs or interests of the young, and the institutional functions of schooling are not primarily concerned with meeting student needs and developing student interests, despite rhetoric to the contrary."[6]

The involuntary character of schooling proceeds from the third factor that distinguishes schools from advertising and mass media entertainment: schooling's special politico-legal status. School attendance is a legal prescription, backed, as all effective legal prescriptions must be, by the power of the state. The state refrains from direct control over or ownership of commercials or television programs. These are private not state enterprises. Thus, if schools do help create and reinforce loosely bounded culture in America, it is because the state — directly or indirectly — permits the schools to do so.

Undoubtedly, it is because the state takes a hand directly in the area of education that schools must deal with "knowledge" rather than "entertainment" or "consumer demands and preferences." The state is too important to allow schools to be frivolous. But more than this is at stake, for given the state's interest in encouraging the development of a loyal citizenry, it naturally wishes to control what is defined as truth. Let other agencies play around with opinion, provide entertainment, produce discretionary goods, or show people how to recreate. But let none but the state purvey secular knowledge.

The development of compulsory public schooling in America is a topic much researched and far too extensive for us to review here. Bereday's summary of the European case also applies to the United States: "In Europe the bourgeoisie created and controlled the modern system of education."[7] But this summary conceals the fact that important changes in American public schooling have broadened schooling to cover material only tangentially connected with "knowledge" in its traditional forms. At the same time, a conflicting emphasis on the issuance of credentials and the upgrading of competence grows apace. Paradoxically, as Tapper notes, "Schools now perform some of the functions previously undertaken by the family, *and* academic qualifications are increasingly important in determining entry into prestige occupations" (italics mine).[8] Schools thus nurture their students, à la the family, and certify graduates preparatory to employment. Neither of these functions, strictly speaking, is logically derived from the traditional function of knowledge dissemination which legitimizes schooling.

How are we to understand this process of educational development? Does it fit the thesis of a loosely bounded culture in America? Of relevant theory and research we have almost more than we can handle. But of conclusions we have few.

SCHOOLS AS TIGHTLY BOUNDED CULTURES

Three arguments have convinced many writers that American schools reflect and transmit a tightly bounded culture replete with invidious status distinctions, rigid boundaries, and inegalitarian consequences for social stratification. If schools are tightly bounded, my thesis obviously suffers. Therefore, I must necessarily address these arguments before providing an alternative. The three arguments are economic, intellectual, and organizational.

An Economic Argument for Tight Boundedness

Writers who embrace the economic argument claim that the primary influence on public education in America is the economy's demand for skilled labor. Writers such as Martin Carnoy, Samuel Bowles, and Herbert Gintis argue that schools attempt mainly to provide a compliant, trained labor force for employers.[9] The history of expanded public schooling in America, they claim, was governed by labor market demands which grew beyond the capacities of private schools, apprenticeships, and primary education. How else can one explain the simultaneous growth of public schooling and capitalist enterprise? Moreover, economic demands have also governed the state's educational role. For example, the Progressives rationalized school organization, "depoliticized" school governance, and began tracking and testing children during the late nineteenth century, all because a newly mature capitalist economy could no longer afford a recalcitrant, inefficient school system. And today's growing credentialism in schools can be explained by similar economic pressures. Today the primary need is to fill highly skilled and demanding jobs with competent, certified people, and the schools play a major role in this endeavor. Thus, in Carnoy's summary, "Schools functioned to control social change (maintain order), to produce better labor inputs for more material output, and to transform individuals into competitive men and women who functioned well and believed in the capitalist system."[10]

In this economic argument schools create two important effects: upgraded technical skills in the population and low levels of opposition to a capitalist system. The economic argument assumes that advanced technical skills are quite consistent with political apathy, ideological confusion, and "false consciousness." After all, high technical skill and low ideological awareness combine effectively in the corporate workplace, and the workplace, critics claim, is the organizational model for much education. Thus, Callahan argues that the Progressives borrowed principles of "scientific management" and "efficient organization" in the development of modern schools. Schools thus became effective transmitters of technical skills and ineffective transmitters of critical-thinking skills that might question the economic logic of capitalism.[11] In short, education and corporate life increasingly converged; an efficient, individually competitive education became an education only in efficiency and individual competition.

The economic argument is highly flexible and occasionally provides ingenious explanations of educational developments that appear at first glance to conflict with the "economic needs of capitalism." For example, Maurice Levitas dismisses recent comprehensive education reforms in the following way:

> What is a matter of necessity to capitalist firms in the shifting ratio of "staff" to "hands" and a matter of unavoidable policy for the capitalist class as a whole—expansion of secondary and higher education, besides, more recently, expansion of pre-school education—can be presented as the work of a beneficent state apparatus meeting consensus opinion.[12]

It follows from this view that reforms in education which appear to respond to the expressed desires of mass publics are in reality policy changes responsive to the economic needs of industry. And thus an older function of education—producing a skilled, compliant work force—becomes allied to a new political demand: persuading people to have faith in the political systems of industrialized democracies.

The economic argument appears to be comparatively straightforward. Yet, disturbingly often, we encounter ambiguities. One important ambiguity proceeds from uncertainties on the part of the writers about whether to emphasize the economic backgrounds of students or the economic and class consequences of education. These aspects of the economic argument may in fact produce contradicting ideas about the economic "needs" of capitalism. Consider, for example, Cohen and Lazerson's version of the economic argument. Schooling, they claim, has attempted "to socialize economically desirable values and behavior, teach vocational skills, and provide education consistent with student social class position."[13] This seems an innocuous enough statement at first glance, but it becomes incoherent when closely examined. After all, in a dynamic capitalist system where the demand for novel skills and competence is ever increasing, it is literally impossible to "provide education consistent with student social class positions," since the demands of the labor market will propel many students into *new* class positions. Does the school therefore confirm existing class positions? Or does it educate people for what the capitalist economy will desire in the *future*? And aren't these two economic "needs" of capitalism in conflict? Cohen and Lazerson are unclear.

Those sympathetic to the economic argument often cite evidence suggesting that not only do capitalist enterprises profit from the skilled labor outputs of schools, but that they also call the political shots in education. Wirt and Kirst, for example, report that in the late 1950s roughly three-fifths of all school board members were "either business owners, officials, and managers or they rendered professional technical services."[14] In short, the majority of the personnel charged with making school policy were either capitalists themselves or servants of capitalists. More important is Wirt and Kirst's conclusion that this proportion had not changed fundamentally since the 1920s, despite political intrusions into a "free economy," intrusions which might have been expected eventually to alter the power balance between capitalists and workers in school politics.[15]

In sum, the economic argument views the school as reproducing the economic and class inequalities inherent in capitalist economies. Since social classes are sharply divided by interest and power into conflicting status groups, the school helps produce a tightly bounded culture, not a loosely bounded culture.[16]

An Intellectual Argument for Tight Boundedness

If the economic argument lays primary emphasis on the school's contribution to class stratification, the intellectual argument lays primary emphasis on the way schools distribute knowledge. In this argument the distribution of knowledge becomes the medium through which the economic functions of schools are performed. More succinctly, the function of schools in economic stratification parallels the internal stratification of educational knowledge. This is because schools can stratify students occupationally only by allocating different kinds of knowledge to different student clienteles. Thus, in Bourdieu's formulation, ideas are the intellectual "capital" of schools, and like economic capital, they provide the school with power: specifically, power over student futures. It follows that the internal structure of educational knowledge reproduces the class structure of occupations.[17]

The stratification of educational knowledge—and thus of the students who possess different types of knowledge—proceeds in several ways. Bourdieu argues, for example, that above all, schools teach taste, that is, standards that distinguish between the worthwhile and the trivial, the ennobling and the meretricious, the valid and the vulgar. By exposing the dominant classes of capitalism to worthwhile knowledge, the school produces taste classes as well as economic classes. The chief line of division separates the ennobling liberal arts from the stigmatizing vocational and mechanical fields. Thus, according to Bourdieu, we have a "duality of culture" because education divides rather than unifies.[18]

But taste and its cultivation are not the only stimulants to knowledge stratification. There is also the comparative complexity of different kinds of knowledge. Certain skills—the mastery of advanced mathematical or artistic ideas, for example—are simply not made available to all students, because they are believed to require unique abilities and a long, demanding sequence of education. Therefore, the stratification of educational knowledge may proceed as much from the differential demands placed on learners as from standards of good taste. Stratification of this kind is twofold: first, stratification within a field of specialization (for example, ranking a student of general mathematics lower than a student of calculus); and stratification among disciplines themselves. The more rarified and prestigious the field the more it must be taught as a self-contained specialty set apart from other fields of knowledge. The result is horizontal differentiation in the curriculum and a tightly bounded educational code which isolates different disciplines and specialists from each other. Bernstein has termed this a "collection" curriculum, and he describes carefully how such a curriculum generates the stratification of knowledge.[19]

A final stimulant of intellectual stratification is the self-interest of educators. Schoolteachers depend for their power on the public's belief that they are authoritative, dispassionate arbiters of specialized truth. If the teacher is to enjoy legitimate power, he or she must command an expertise which others (especially students) do not command. In the process of demonstrating and sustaining this claim to power, the teacher becomes a primary force in the stratification of knowledge.

At the very least, teachers must argue that they are in a privileged position to know the difference between truth and error in the field of their professional training, experience, and expertise. Teachers signal their special competence by claiming the right to organize curricular knowledge into learnable sequences, to examine students, and to evaluate test results fairly. To buttress their claims to authority, teachers argue that knowledge is inherently complex, sequential, and cumulative and, therefore, that it imposes an inevitable hierarchy upon students who stand at different levels in the sequence. Teachers may even argue that grouping students according to demonstrated competence is in the student's interest, for grouping facilitates learning. Most important to the teacher's case, however, is the argument that the teacher has already accomplished what the student is only now undertaking and, therefore, that the teacher deserves legitimate power over students.

Elements of a tightly bounded school culture fairly leap out of these rationales. Self-contained tracks of students; distinctions between types of curricula; specialized disciplines; and distinctions between those students willing to "try" to absorb demanding material and those not willing to try—these all are examples of tight boundedness. Thus, to the extent that the school is a tightly bounded culture, as keepers of the intellectual flame teachers may make it and keep it so. And the motives of successful students who have mastered the curriculum reinforce the teacher's power, for good students will want to protect the cultural capital that gives them a head start in the race for status. To protect their capital is to defend their teachers.

Just as those who advance the economic argument for tight boundedness cite supportive evidence, so also do those who embrace the intellectual stratification position. For example, teachers are quite resistant to reform proposals that threaten the distinctions between specialized fields or stratified tracks of students. In addition, despite the overwhelming evidence that grouping of students by ability retards learning, few teachers have altered their tracking practices. In fact, grouping of students is as common now as it was fifty years ago.[20] Similarly, McAulay reports that the "new social studies," which emphasize interdisciplinary thinking and encourage the student's active participation in the classroom, have received a cool reception in most places. Of 120 social studies programs he scored on the basis of five "new social studies" criteria, the average score was between one and two. McAulay concludes simply that "local schools refuse to implement such programs."[21]

An Organizational Argument for Tight Boundedness

The intellectual argument, as we can see, places primary emphasis on the demands certain types of knowledge make, and more directly on the ways teachers use their power over knowledge to sustain a tightly bounded school culture. However, this argument must cope with the fact that many teachers and curricula simply do not fit the pattern. For example, Morgan describes several "active open" social studies teachers who do not rank their students invidiously and who actively embrace interdisciplinary ideas.[22] Other studies identify similar groups of maverick teachers; indeed, in Metz's sensitive study, the mavericks outnumber all other teachers.[23] In fact, some subjects, such as painting and music, can perhaps be best taught without imposing on them a sequential, graded format.[24] Significantly, these subjects encourage comparatively egalitarian teacher-student relationships. Therefore, if a tightly bounded school culture is the norm, aspects of school-ing in addition to those inherent in structures of knowledge or teacher self-interest must be identified.

It is necessary to distinguish in particular between *teacher* de-mands based on educational arguments and *school* demands based on the imperatives of a formal organization. Mary Metz makes this point best when she writes, "Public schools have a paradox at their very heart. They exist to educate children, but they must keep order. Unless the children themselves are inde-pendently dedicated to both these goals, the school will find that arrangements helpful for one may subvert the other. Yet to sa-crifice either for the other is to default upon a school's most fun-damental responsibilities."[25] In short, like any formal organiza-tion concerned with stability and predictability, schools contain purely organizational stimulants to tight boundedness.

The school's problem of order is, after all, acute. Schools bring together a large, heterogeneous mass of cognitively and emotionally volatile, physically active young people, none of whom have freely chosen to be in school, most of whom barely know each other, and all of whom are encouraged to compete against each other for grades when, outside of school, they would as likely cooperate in the pursuit of pleasure as struggle for status. Keeping order under these conditions is difficult, and it is therefore not surprising that order should be upper-most in the minds of school administrators.

From these organizational imperatives springs the theory of the "hidden curriculum," which attempts to uncover the true source of tight boundedness in schools. The hidden curricu-lum encompasses the many practices of schools which allegedly teach respect for order and authority. Such practices include ability grouping,[26] surveillance of students by teachers and ad-ministrators,[27] competition and conflict,[28] delay and queuing,[29] the division of class periods into standard units, the age-grad-ing of students, standardized testing, control over student movement in classrooms and corridors, and finally, control over noise. The practices which constitute the hidden curricu-lum differ from writer to writer, but all have in common that they are not educational subject matter, that they are practiced implicitly, and that they teach hierarchy and submission to authority. The hidden curriculum allegedly stratifies and differentiates the student body, creates tight boundaries between different groups of students, isolates teachers and students from each other, and carefully labels different groups of students according to differential moral evaluations.[30]

The organizational argument asserts that the personal interests of teachers and the organizational interests of schools reinforce each other. Teachers argue that unless students obey the school's demands for order, teaching will be ineffective. Meanwhile, administrators argue that unless the power of the classroom teacher over students is preserved, school order generally will be placed in jeopardy. Thus, the intellectual argument and the hidden-curriculum argument support each other; ultimately, the argument claims, knowledge will appear genuine only if it conforms to the demands of a hidden curriculum and is so presented to students. Eventually students come to associate "true" knowledge and successful school performance with an ordered setting in which the hidden curriculum holds sway.[31] Under such conditions, even should teachers wish occasionally to relax the hidden curriculum, they will find it difficult to do so, for their students will interpret any such action as a signal that what is being taught is frivolous or a matter of opinion, and therefore provides an opportunity to "shoot the bull" rather than to learn.

THE BASIC SHAPE OF SCHOOLING

Our considerations thus far allow us to identify a basic shape of schooling which emerges from the intersection of the hidden-curriculum argument and the organizational argument. The basic shape of schooling consists of the hidden curriculum's hierarchical practices as legitimized by arguments about the indispensability of hierarchy to the acquisition of useful knowledge. The basic shape of schooling therefore becomes a legitimate hidden curriculum which administrators and teachers strive to imbue in students. To the extent that teachers and administrators succeed, schools will in fact embody tightly bounded cultural codes with the basic shape of schooling at their heart.

Hidden-curriculum theorists cite many practices by which teachers attempt to incorporate the basic shape of schooling into their everyday classroom activities. Thus, for example, Nell Keddie argues that teachers profess to reward intelligence, not social background, in their contacts with students; to avoid ability grouping; to eschew IQ tests as unreliable; and to prefer integrated to specialized curricula in their mode of teaching. In reality, however, teachers expect their weaker groups to continue to be deficient, and they regularly and illogically rely on the moral qualities of their students (particularly their attitudes toward authority) to judge their cognitive skills. Teachers thus incorporate the school's demand for order in their evaluation of student educational performance.[32]

Similarly, Estelle Fuchs argues that in the course of their first year of teaching, novice teachers gradually adopt the view that students from different backgrounds will have different reading aptitudes. Such a view not only creates a self-fulfilling prophecy that reinforces the child's stratification position, but also allows teachers to rationalize their failures in teaching reading to the "hard cases" they themselves have already unconsciously written off.[33]

Finally, Cicourel and his associates argue that teachers "typify" or classify students by employing terms such as "immature," "bright," "behavior problem," and "independent." Teachers then depend on these typifications as bases for tracking decisions. Cicourel claims that these typifications function primarily to protect the power of teachers themselves and do not reflect accurate *global* evaluations of students outside the teaching context.[34] Ultimately, these typifications grossly stereotype and distort student behavior.

We can summarize the economic, intellectual, and organizational arguments in support of the school as a tightly bounded culture containing a "basic shape" by imagining these arguments as homologous expressions of a single binary, tightly bounded cultural code. Each argument poses a binary logic in which the boundary mechanism is sharp, boundary transgression difficult, group control over the individual tenacious, and tension the rule between classifications. The appropriate depiction appears below:

The Tightly Bounded Cultural Code of Schools
The Basic Shape of Schooling

	Intellectual Argument	Organizational Argument	Economic Argument	Political Argument
Homology:	Teacher/ Student	= Administrator/ Student	= Employer/ Worker	= State/ Citizen
Mechanism:	(the structure of knowledge)	(the hidden curriculum)	(credentialing)	(hegemonic domination of knowledge)

In this view the structure of knowledge, the hidden curriculum, the process of credentialing, and the state's use of schools to dominate the transmission of knowledge all become mechanisms that produce a tightly bounded culture. These four mechanisms parallel each other, and each contributes its share to the basic shape of schooling, which is the primary mechanism by which schools create a tightly bounded cultural code.

ARE SCHOOLS TIGHTLY BOUNDED?

Together these three arguments for schools as tightly bounded institutions are formidable. Yet they tell only part of the story. To put it differently, American schools may strive to sustain their basic shape, but they do not succeed. In order to understand why schools do not succeed, we must first examine carefully the argument for tight boundedness. Its flaws will point us toward our own reconceptualization.

Consider the economic argument for tight boundedness. If in fact schools served the economic interests of a dominant capitalist class, we should expect at least some of the following things to be true. First, schools should be effective in selecting students for future occupational positions. Second, schools should persuade students to accept the capitalist order and to value the diligence and self-discipline necessary to success. Third, school performance as certified by schools should predict occupational futures effectively. Fourth, those who have succeeded in school should be zealous in their support of schools, for they will naturally wish to reciprocate the school for the benefits it has gained them. Fifth, capitalist "interests" should control schooling. Certainly not all of these arguments need be true, but, as it happens, on all five of these points the evidence is either inconclusive or downright inconsistent with the argument for tight boundedness. Something therefore appears to disrupt the basic shape of schooling.

For example, the evidence does not strongly support a belief that schools effectively select students for different occupational futures. Although there is a sizeable correlation between educational attainment (years in school) and occupational placement, the correlation is far from perfect. Jencks shows in both his earlier work (1972) and his more recent work (1978) that correlations between educational attainment and occupational success fall between .50 and .70. Thus, there is considerable slippage in the connection between schooling and the occupational world.[35] The result of this imperfect match is that employers—supposedly those with power under capitalism—must provide costly on-the-job training for their workers, during which times "the cream" presumably rises to the top and the dross slides to the bottom.

It is also doubtful whether schools are becoming more efficient in their selections of students than they used to be. Indeed, the opposite is nearer the truth, for as schools strive to keep a more heterogeneous student body in school longer, their capacity to select for effective future occupational allocation falls. Many years ago, when few students attended college, these lucky few came from select secondary-school backgrounds, where teachers could perform a more effective process of selection than they now can. By contrast, teachers today must sort people out from a more diverse population in more diverse schools. Inevitably, there will be more errors.

Do students learn to embrace capitalism and its supposedly

supporting attitudes (diligence, competitiveness, obedience to authority)? Again the evidence gives us pause. Surveys do show that students believe strongly in our economic system, but whether they know exactly how that system works is not clear. And there is also evidence that "big business" commands relatively *little* respect among students.[36] Occupational ideals among young people have moved considerably away from the capitalist entrepreneurial model of the late nineteenth century. Schools may have once succeeded in transmitting capitalist ideology, but they do not seem especially effective in that regard today.

As for attitudes like diligence and competitiveness, the evidence is again ambiguous. The productivity of American labor has declined in the last several years, a result hardly to be expected if diligence were widespread. And, while competitiveness does contribute strongly to success in school and on the job, in both arenas many people reject the race entirely. As early as 1961 James Coleman detected a strong predisposition among American high school students to de-emphasize academic competition in favor of cooperative peer group relations, a cast of mind which perhaps paves the way for informal peer group restraints on productivity at the workplace.[37]

It should also be pointed out that competitiveness fits a loosely bounded conception of culture as well as it fits a tightly bounded conception. People of the same status who compete with each other weaken class solidarity in the interest of individual mobility. The result is a loosely bounded stratification system. Thus, an economic argument which views competition as compatible only with a tightly circumscribed class culture is sadly deficient, as Runciman pointed out some years ago.[38]

Do credentials (diplomas chiefly) accurately predict occupational futures? Again, the evidence is ambiguous. Many employers complain that they can tell less now about the real skills of prospective workers from their educational credentials than they once could. Not only is it hard to understand how a purportedly powerful capitalist class could permit such a situation to emerge, but it also becomes necessary for businesses to provide remedial education for their workers, thus making themselves rather than the schools primary agents of stratification. Finally, occupational status, including first-job placement, depends on more than just educational credentials. Appearance and conduct count for much, and these are inevitably subjective phenomena. The effects of subjective impressions are generally unrelated to the paper credentials that prospective employees bring with them. Therefore, an economic argument that focuses solely on credentials is deficient.

Educational credentials are important in the allocation of first jobs, but become progressively less important thereafter.[39] Job allocation and mobility within and between occupations is a continuous, fluid process in the United States, and schools do not really crystallize this process as completely as the tightly-bounded argument suggests.[40]

Moreover, academically successful students are no more wedded to the capitalist system than are their unsuccessful classmates, despite the fact that the former can reasonably expect to occupy positions of great power within that system. During the 1960s the primary challenges to American capitalism came, in the words of Richard Flacks, from the "revolt of the advantaged."[41] Nor was this revolt unrelated to schooling, for, as Edward Morgan points out, "honors track students have the most *democratic* [my emphasis] learning experiences and general track students the most profoundly undemocratic experience."[42] Why schooling that is purportedly intended to prepare the best students for positions of authority in hierarchical capitalist institutions should present a democratic face to those same future leaders can only be considered a mystery. True, these fortunate few will supposedly be controlling such institutions, and can thus enjoy relative freedom for themselves. But from a sociological point of view, habitual respect for and acceptance of authority is as important a quality for the leaders of institutions as for ordinary members. Any lapse in respect for authority among leaders may reverberate downward, emboldening subordinates to question their subordination. Disrespect for authority among leaders may become a powerful and dangerous lesson for those below. If anything, schools of the 1950s and 1960s trained future leaders to *question* and *reject* capitalism, not to embrace it.

Equally suspicious is the fact that workers often seem to espouse "capitalist" attitudes more fervently than do leaders and employers. Here too the role of the school is unclear. Paul Willis demonstrates, for example, that many working-class English school-leavers can barely wait to begin a factory job. They need the money, of course, but they also believe that the job is the "real world." They intend to work hard although they know that they probably will not "rise."[43] Where do they get such pro-capitalist attitudes? Not from the school, for they ridicule what they believe to be childishness in schools. Ironically, it is in part because they *reject* school that they embrace work in a capitalist system. And to believe that schools deliberately turn such students off in order to force them out into the world of work is to ignore the havoc these disaffected students wreak on the schools. Why would teachers deliberately perpetuate the conditions that make their work lives so unpleasant?

One reason for these deficiencies in the economic argument is its tendency to oversimplify the relationship of objective to subjective "interests." Despite the objective structuring of class in capitalist systems, subjectively classes are composed of quite heterogeneous points of view. The economic argument overlooks the diversity of perspectives within any social class and within the academic groups supposedly based on class.[44] As a result of this oversimplification, the economic argument often encounters anomalies.

Lastly, do we discern the controlling hand of capitalists in school politics? The disproportionate representation of business people on school boards is at best suggestive, for we need to know whether school boards actually wield much power. And this is itself a problematic question. In fact, many studies in the politics of American education turn up little convincing evidence that capitalists generally get what they want in school politics.[45] For example, Peterson argues that in Chicago, control over schools is shared among machine politicians, administrative staff, teacher unions, and reformers dedicated to widening opportunities for minorities. If "the people" have little direct control over this process, the same is true of businessmen. Indeed, in Chicago, business interests were either entirely uninvolved in school policies or were actually losers when they chose to participate.[46]

The strongest single group in school politics appears to be the superintendent and the administrative staff.[47] The school board rarely challenges this professional establishment. It is tempting to dismiss superintendents as mere surrogates for business interests, but this too would be incorrect. Recently, professional educators have introduced many programs over the vociferously expressed unhappiness of the business community. These include some curricula that question the legitimacy of business power in American politics, and other curricula which seem to businessmen "frills." In short, the observable power of business in school politics is not strong enough to rescue the economic argument.

Many problems also afflict the intellectual argument for tight boundedness. Often the argument is simply not conceptually clear. Some authors, for example, run economic and intellectual considerations together in confusing ways. Thus, Bourdieu never makes clear whether its monopoly of privileged knowledge (refined taste, for example) legitimizes the dominant class or whether the dominant class *defines* privileged knowledge by choosing to pursue certain ideas. My guess is that Bourdieu has the latter view primarily in mind, since the most he will claim for the *independent* power of knowledge is that it creates a code by which the dominant class communicates. But he never claims that these codes themselves create class divisions. Therefore, what appears at first to be an argument based on the inherent qualities of knowledge becomes only a gloss on the economic arguments we have already analyzed.

Any argument for knowledge as a basis of educational stratification must place teachers as custodians of knowledge at the center of the process. Such an argument should meet some, if not all, of the following predictions: First, teachers should be of high intellectual quality, for otherwise they can hardly serve as effective models of the intellectual stratification order. Second, mastery of subject matter and sheer brilliance should be primary determinants of student evaluation and placement. Students should also respect knowledge for its own sake and, thus, esteem their teachers whose superior competence they acknowledge. Third, teachers should generally agree among themselves on their profession's need to reward intellectual competence. They should also agree on standards of student evaluation. Otherwise, they will hardly be in a position to enforce the stratification criteria they are alleged to create. Fourth, teachers should believe that knowledge is stratified, sequential, and hierarchically complex, for such a belief legitimizes the status they confer on their more successful and disciplined students. Finally, the teaching profession should be a powerful socializing organization; experienced teachers should inculcate new teachers with the norms and beliefs stated in the previous four conditions.[48] Only in this way will teachers retain a dominant stratification position.

Of these five predictions not one has been confirmed within the American context. To begin with, most teachers are not of high enough quality even in their fields of specialty to serve as intellectual role models for their students. The evidence suggests that American public school teachers constitute a distinctly mediocre intellectual reservoir.[49] Studies show that the grade point averages of future teachers fall below the averages of their college peers.[50] Significantly, mediocrity is most common among teachers of social studies, the field of instruction uniquely germane to the concept of stratification itself. Mediocre teachers of social studies will hardly teach the concept of stratification well nor legitimize intellectual stratification through their own efforts. Thus, teachers are not capable of making knowledge the basis of social stratification either in school or in the occupational world, although it is true that their intellectual lassitude may prevent their becoming critical of capitalism itself.

Second, although sheer brilliance and comprehension of subject matter contribute heavily to the placement of students in school, other factors also play an important role. Anticipation of how students will likely perform, given test scores, racial background, or economic status, is an important influence on teachers' decisions, as the provocative research of Jacobson and Rosenthal has demonstrated.[51] Such personal qualities as docility, obedience, pleasantness, and a willingness to defend the teacher's prerogatives also play a role in student placement. Thus, the intelligent student with a touch of unruliness may not accomplish as much as his or her "potential" might predict, while the able, uncreative, but cooperative student might gain the rewards that the intellectual stratification model would hypothesize. Factors other than intellectual ability or achievement thus impinge heavily on the process of academic stratification. Nor do knowledge and intellect rank especially high among students as a basis for their own internal prestige order. Instead, other qualities—athleticism, friendliness, beauty, humor, even "wildness"—become desirable characteristics. Thus, students have not internalized the intellectual stratification model as a basis for their own status rankings.

And there is no consensus among teachers on how to evaluate students. Sheer intellectual competence must compete with other criteria, such as hard work, effort, dependability, and helpfulness. Metz argues that teachers fall into either "incorporative" or "developmental" types, the former who believe they should teach subject matter, the latter who teach children. The two types differ in the standards they apply to students.[52] Lortie documents similar differences among teachers over goals and even methods of evaluation.[53] It is the rare student who does not have to endure several different and often conflicting forms of evaluation during his or her scholastic career. Such evaluational inconsistency cannot fail to alienate some students from the schooling process entirely, or at the very least to create doubt about what "real" competence is and about the way teachers define competence.

The problem is that teachers do not share a pedagogical theory which they uniformly enforce. Because teachers disagree about how to teach, they also disagree about what to reward among students. As Gage pointed out many years ago, studies in the psychology of education and in developmental psychology rarely yield reliable guidelines to classroom teaching techniques.[54] Indeed, most fledgling teachers simply discard the pedagogical theories and findings they worked so hard to master in their training.[55] Most complain that their methods courses are of limited help on the job. In addition, some recent theories of education, particularly those drawn from the work of Jerome Bruner, specifically dispute the idea of a fixed, sequentially patterned program of learning. Brunerian theories support an open, "individualized" pattern of education, a conception which commands assent among a significant number of teachers who reject the idea of hierarchical, uniform, lockstep classroom teaching.[56]

Lastly, teachers appear not to be powerful controllers of their peers so far as evaluation of students and conceptions of curricula are concerned. Jaros discovered, for example, that teachers in a number of Kentucky high schools were very weak influences on each other in the teaching of democracy.[57] Most teachers avoid confrontations with each other, either by retreating to the isolation of the individual classroom or by observing an informal norm not to evaluate or pressure each other. And when coalitions of teachers do form around different conceptions of effective teaching, conflict, not reasoned debate, ensues. Teachers guard themselves against these dangers by avoiding discussion of teaching with each other. When teachers congregate they prefer small talk, gossip, banter, and the pleasurable denunciation of unruly students. They actively avoid enforcing teaching norms.

Let us now briefly examine the organizational argument for tight boundedness, which, it will be recalled, attributes to American schools an imperative—embodied in the hidden curriculum—to control a mass of volatile, resistant students in risky settings. The result of the school's efforts to protect itself is alleged to be respect for authority among students. This conception of American schools is, I believe, descriptively and conceptually inaccurate.

To begin with, American students do not evidence widespread respect for authority. Although administrators and teachers attempt to create an ambiance of respect, they fail as often as they succeed. The reason for their failure is the existence of norms which legitimize student resistance in most American schools. The evidence of resistance is ubiquitous.

First, there is the abundance of noise in American schools: in the halls as students move from class to class, in class itself, and on the playgrounds. Noise not only retards learning, it also works against organizational efficiency, consuming the time and effort of teachers and administrators. Yet the inability to reduce noise gives it a quasi-legitimate status in most schools.

Second, contrary to hidden-curriculum theory, students do not spend most of their time working diligently at classroom lessons. Any reader of Philip Cusick's *Inside High School,* an ethnographic account of a middle-class American high school, cannot help but be impressed by the amount of freedom students carve out for themselves in school. As Cusick puts it, "The school . . . provides an enormous amount of time when students are actually required to do little other than be in attendance and minimally compliant. It is this that provides them [the students] with the time to carry on their group activity, and their group activity seems to consume over half the school day."[58] Indeed, it is no misstatement to observe that informal and unsanctioned student activity appears to be as much a "hidden curriculum" in schools as is the authoritarian hidden curriculum that school critics usually describe. This is not to suggest that resistance creates a parity of power between students and teachers, for we find forms of resistance even in slave-master relationships.[59] Still, tenacious resistance does dispute the accuracy of the hidden curriculum's characterization of American schools.

A third form of student resistance takes the form of an effective, antischolastic peer culture. Consider, for example, Willis's working-class English students whose "matiness" mixes a fondness for racism, sexism, and violence into a potent brew of rebellion against school regulations and classroom activities.[60] In comparison with these students' atavistic values, the awkward autocracy of the school's hidden curriculum becomes, if anything, a blow for democracy rather than a blow against "democratic" students.

Peer-coordinated opposition to the hidden curriculum is by

no means confined to the academic cast-offs Willis describes. In his path-breaking *The Adolescent Society*, James Coleman described the "dating and rating" game, the stress on appearance and, for boys, athletics, the sacrifice of scholastic performance for social popularity, and the appeal of fraternities and sororities—all middle-class American counterparts to the violence, racism, sexism, and pseudo-masculinity of Willis's English students.[61] Both patterns of student life depart radically from the submissive surrender to authority that the hidden curriculum of the school supposedly engenders.

A final and dramatic form of resistance to the hidden curriculum, of course, is overt student violence against fellow students, teachers, and administrators. Evidence suggests that violence is on the rise in American schools, and that teachers in greater numbers than ever before worry about their safety.[62] No clearer evidence against the hidden-curriculum argument can be imagined.

It is important to note in passing a further descriptive inaccuracy in the theory of the hidden curriculum. From the student's viewpoint, there is nothing at all "hidden" about the hidden curriculum. The attempted imposition of classroom order fools no one. In fact, as Apple and King point out, American public schools have gone to great lengths to *emphasize* their intention to teach discipline, obedience, and conformity.[63] Teachers continue to explain at length and with heat the benefits supposedly to be derived from student acceptance of the "hidden" curriculum, such as the virtues of promptness, neatness, and submission to authority. If such exhortations fall on deaf ears, it is not for lack of effort. Such clumsy exhortations almost always backfire anyway, for they unintentionally suggest to students that sloth, laziness, and defiance are excellent ways of challenging the hidden curriculum. The marvel is that a hidden curriculum so unsubtle should ever actually be expected to succeed.

Students have also observed recent adult intrusions into school operations and policy. Students now have available to them the history of agitation for new treatments of minorities and women in their courses, for new offerings in bilingual education, and for new approaches to American history. They know it is possible to change things on a more prosaic level, for they continually hear their parents criticizing schools and teachers. Many know from their own experience that their parents will intercede for them, and that they need not be cowed by teachers. In short, as often as not, students are warranted in believing their teachers to be weak rather than strong.[64]

More significant, perhaps, is the fact that cues signaling the legitimacy of opposition to the hidden curriculum originate within the school itself. Dreeben points out, for example, that many teachers aim primarily to develop students who will be active, purposeful, forceful, and assertive in their pursuit of academic goals.[65] Students with these attributes can hardly be expected to accept authority unquestioningly. Instead, they will demand that their teachers provide a logical grounding for the ideas they purvey. Thus, salient teaching goals interfere with the hidden curriculum's supposed encouragement of submissiveness and passivity. Paradoxically, teachers themselves manufacture some of the ammunition that students use against them.

Lastly, the hidden-curriculum argument is damaged by the fact that the brightest and most academically promising students resist authority most successfully. Metz points out, for example, that students in the top academic tracks regularly challenge both the teacher's expertise and the school's control over behavior.[66] And we should not forget that in the wake of the Vietnam War it was the most successful students who led rebellions against the school. Surely a hidden curriculum which cannot control the recipients of its abundant bounties is hardly in a position to create a tightly bounded culture.

BENDING SCHOOLS OUT OF SHAPE THROUGH LOOSE BOUNDEDNESS

Although schools appear at first to provide fertile ground for the creation of a highly stratified, tightly bounded culture, most American schools are not tightly bounded. Something disturbs their basic shape. Our task now is to investigate this puzzle.

It is tempting to explain why American schools are bent out

of shape by reference to apparently unrelated impediments, deviations, or accidents that detract from an "ideal type." But this would be a misreading of the real situation. Schools, like other cultural agents in America, manifest strong tendencies toward loose boundedness. The collision between the basic shape of schooling and these tendencies creates much confusion and indecision in American schools. True, schools manifest tight boundedness more explicitly than do advertising or television entertainment, but even so, schools cannot overcome the patterned attacks of a loosely bounded culture. Instead, we find that schools are the setting for a virulent struggle between tight and loose bounded conceptions of culture.

An important source of loose boundedness in American schools is the American political system. Paradoxically enough, the state—the very institution radical critics identify as one source of tight boundedness and educational stratification—acts simultaneously to stimulate loose boundedness in American schools. But we should not find this paradox surprising, for by now we must surely realize that any institution contains several elements of a larger cultural code. Occasionally, these elements may in fact oppose each other. Thus, while with one hand the state legitimizes hierarchy and authority in American schools, with the other it promotes educational democracy and decentralized power. Democracy in its many and subtle forms serves as a primary vehicle by which loose boundedness disrupts the basic shape of schooling.

The state introduces democracy into American schools in three ways, each of which bends schools slightly out of shape. First, the state mandates a democratic form of political control over American public schools. Second, the state requires schools to teach democratic values as subject matter. Third, the state promotes democratic practices and customs in schools. This three-pronged attack on the tightly bounded culture of schools is neither well coordinated nor fully successful. It does not necessarily promote good schooling. In fact, the loosely bounded culture is hostile not only to authority but also to intellectual excellence in education. It follows that poor schools—which first appear to be unfortunate by-products of the state's efforts to "teach democracy"—actually should be understood as the heart of the educational process in America. That which educators and political scientists constantly lament—the comparative weakness of American schools as agents for education and value socialization—is in fact a predictable adjustment to the cultural imperative of loose boundedness. "Failure" in educational terms is a cultural adaptation to loose boundedness, and because it *is* an adaptation, it naturally reproduces itself from generation to generation.

Of these three elements of democracy in schools, democratic political control is the least contributory to loose boundedness. Despite a pattern of decentralized school districts in which boards of locally elected citizens nominally make school policy, public control over schools is almost everywhere weak.[67] This weakness does not mean that American public school politics resembles a tightly bounded, two-class system of partisan conflict where business and the working class fight it out over such issues as curricula, expenditures, or tracking. A tightly bounded class pattern characterizes English schools, according to Peterson, but it hardly describes the American system.[68]

Instead, Americans have insulated schools from the English style of partisan, class politics. We have used the electoral mechanism in decentralized school districts to diffuse such conflicts. But if we have avoided class politics in education, we have not attained real popular control over schools. Writers as diverse as Michael Smith, Zeigler and Jennings, and Norman Kerr argue that popularly elected school boards mainly legitimize the power of school professionals, and especially the power of the superintendent.[69] Professional control over schools frustrates popular sovereignty and reflects aspects of tight boundedness.

Still, Wirt and Kirst are able to cite a number of studies in which school politics become pluralistic and open.[70] Recent public protests about such diverse issues as busing, sex education, school prayers, ethnic studies, and bilingual education demonstrate that public pressures can occasionally be effective. Public resistance has also been effective in reducing expenditures on schooling. And, as a declining school population

forces the closing of some neighborhood schools, with attendant threats to neighborhood integrity, the public has another
issue to energize it. In sum, therefore, American public schools
oscillate between democratic, decentralized, fragmented, and
spasmodic reflections of loose boundedness and "neutral" bureaucratic or professional controls that reflect tight boundedness. At the very least, the ideal of democracy legitimizes the
public's occasional transgression of educational boundaries.
Even superintendents cannot deny the legitimacy of the public's forays, for they realize that they too must operate within a
predominantly loosely bounded culture.

But it is the federal government that imposes the most demanding democratic pressures and pluralistic incentives on local schools. Contrary to an analysis which sees school politics as
tightly hierarchical at its national apex, we find federal author-
ities joining some teacher groups and minority organizations
to sponsor programs such as Operation Head Start, ethnic
studies, the mainstreaming of handicapped students, and bilingual education. These federal initiatives respond to demands for better protection of the excluded and deprived in
the schools. Thus, the federal government has forced schools
to respond to pressures from below, and in the process, to become more pluralistic and loosely bounded. The most critical
effort in this direction, of course, was the abolition of school
segregation, a system of education structurally and ideologi-
cally wholly at odds with a loosely bounded culture. School desegregation represents an attempt to break down boundaries,
not only between divided school systems, but also between divided racial groups whose continued conflict has become incompatible with loose boundedness.

The other two aspects of educational democracy—the mandate that the schools teach democratic values, and the mandate
that schools practice democracy—have a somewhat greater influence on the basic shape of schooling. The influence is the
greater for so often being overlooked in comparison with the
more conspicuous policy initiatives of the federal government.
These two mandates—the former the legacy of our history of
diverse ethnicity, the latter a remnant of Progressive educational
theory[71]—take seven forms in schools. Each of these forms de-

rives directly from loose boundedness. Loose boundedness in these seven forms does not entirely obviate tight boundedness in schools. Instead, loose boundedness and tight boundedness are so evenly matched that they neutralize each other and thus disrupt any clear educational messages schools might send. The primary losers in this conflict are tight-bounded messages of intellectual discipline and excellence, and loose-bounded messages about democratic values. We produce neither distinguished minds nor democratic activists among our students. What we *do* produce awaits later discussion.

Loose boundedness in American schools takes these seven forms: First, loose boundedness attempts to treat dissimilar or opposed groups and ideas as similar and compatible. The result is forced homogeneity in American schools. Second, because it assumes that authority separates people from each other, loose boundedness undercuts authority. In a loosely bounded culture people often equate authority with authoritarianism, a patterned mistake of logic that Metz accurately describes in her study of teachers.[72] Third, because loose boundedness is hostile to enduring differentiation, it is suspicious of the sharp logical distinctions, classifications, and organizations of experience that make for intellectual excellence. Fourth, loosely bounded cultures support high levels of individual contact, access, and sociability, manifold examples of which we find in American schools. Fifth, loosely bounded cultures contain an absorptive dynamic which attempts to engulf potential critics or dissidents. American schools contain many examples of such absorptiveness. Sixth, loose boundedness is expansive even when there exists no potential opposition to be co-opted. Again, American schools provide many examples. Finally, group and individual barriers are weak in loosely bounded cultures, and can therefore be breached without polluting or defiling consequences. The penetrability of such boundaries also characterizes American schools.

Homogeneity and Standardization

Americans value political equality, a concept generally congenial to loose boundedness. After all, political equality is de-

signed to place all Americans on an identical, standard footing
with regard to collective decisions. Of course, no political system—not even one supported by a loosely bounded culture—
can attain full political equality, but the concept remains a basic
guideline by which Americans judge their system's political
performance. Not surprisingly, therefore, we attempt to teach
political equality in schools.

Yet we do not seem to be as successful as might be expected.
Political equality—along with many other democratic values—
does not seem to take firm hold through the school's efforts.[73]
It would be tempting to assume that concepts like political
equality are not taught at all. But this would be a mistake. We
do teach such concepts, but primarily as practices and habits
rather than as intellectual constructs. Indeed, we are forced to
teach democratic values in this way, for to teach them as the
deeply reasoned and demanding ideas they actually are would
pose a threat to the organizational order of schools. To give
students a precise understanding of political equality would allow them to challenge the legitimacy both of their teachers and
of the school as a whole. Therefore, we prefer to teach democratic ideas tacitly, indirectly, nonverbally, and practically. How
does such teaching occur in the case of political equality?

The danger in the idea of political equality lies in its conflict
with the imperative that teachers feel to protect the sanctity of
knowledge through their grading of students. Most teachers
believe that imparting as much knowledge as they know as well
as they can to as many students as they can reach will sooner or
later require them to make potentially invidious distinctions
among students. That they feel such distinctions to be necessary is manifest in their reluctance to abandon the tracking of
students.[74] Yet these invidious distinctions impede the norm of
equality, for they spill over onto the child's general sense of confidence. At the same time, however, to teach "less well" than one
can is not only to violate one's conscience but also to compromise the knowledge base of teaching itself and, therefore, to
threaten the base of the teacher's authority. What is to be done?

A dilemma of this magnitude defies straightforward solution, but schools have developed a pattern of coping. In brief,

most teachers attempt to convey roughly the identical form and quantity of knowledge to a majority of students in any classroom. They thus standardize and homogenize curricula so as not to reflect invidiously on slow students, and they calibrate their grading practices by what they take the competence of the majority of students to be. This practice solves several problems. It assures that only the bare minimum in any class actually fail and thus become subordinated to their fellows on grounds of insufficient knowledge. It also assures that only a bare minimum will actually proceed rapidly toward difficult material, thus making certain that real intellectual success crowned by public recognition is so uncommon as not to dishearten the majority of students. Most students in each classroom thus remain equals.[75]

To aid in their endeavor, educators employ standard curriculum packages that carefully abstain from discriminating between students in terms of abilities or interests. Educators rationalize this practice by arguing that the standard package contains knowledge "appropriate" for students of a particular age. Educators also rely on IQ scores, innumerable studies of "reading readiness," and a panoply of supportive theory to make the same argument. A curriculum thus becomes that body of knowledge which a majority of age-graded students can learn equally well, and which this majority can share as a community of equals in a loosely bounded culture. After all, in a loosely bounded culture that favors political equality, knowledge must unite not divide people. These observations should make more comprehensible the oft criticized uniformity of mass public schooling in America, and also help us understand why public schools so adamantly resist the steps toward "individualized education" which reformers have advocated for so long.[76] Educators may profess their devotion to such lofty educational goals, but when all is said and done they know that the uniform curriculum they have contructed is too valuable a network of cultural compromises to be abandoned in the interest of "better education." Better education alone is not what American schools are about.[77]

An interesting illustration of my argument is the dreary fate suffered by recent laws requiring students to prove their academic competence before moving to higher grade levels. Many of these laws originally defined competence so restrictively that the majority of students in a class might well have failed, an outcome perhaps justifiable on purely educational grounds, but hardly consistent with the need the school feels to demonstrate equality in practice. "Too much competence" among students is as unfeasible as "too much incompetence." Predictably, therefore, initially stiff standards of competence have slackened in order to encompass the modest abilities and potentialities of most students. Slowly, like a phoenix from the ashes, the standard grading practices have resurfaced, thus permitting us to practice equality, even if to do so requires us not to talk about the concept of equality in an intellectually respectable fashion.[78]

Demeaning Authority

We have seen that teachers and administrators have vested interests in getting students to respect their authority. Therefore, we can hardly expect them to be happy in teaching values that threaten to undercut their authority. At the same time, however, American loose boundedness in its democratic manifestation demands that the school teach popular sovereignty, the value which expresses perhaps more directly than any other the historic American antagonism to centralized power. The school's adaptation to this dilemma resembles the adaptation we have just discussed. We demonstrate popular sovereignty implicitly in practice rather than confront it in theory, thereby effecting an uneasy compromise between the imperative of tight-bounded authority and the pressures of a loosely bounded culture.

Consider, for example, the recruitment of social studies teachers in American schools. Our low intellectual standards, our lax training procedures, and our generous retention policies provide a lesson in popular sovereignty as powerful as any that teachers provide in their classrooms. We do not teach popular sovereignty as a complex value requiring explicit, disciplined classroom reasoning, for a loosely bounded culture is hostile to the intellectual demands and inevitable distinctions inherent in such reasoning. Besides, teachers themselves have reason to fear those of their students who actually *understand* that they might legitimately resist authority. Instead, we teach popular sovereignty indirectly by tolerating low standards of instruction. We limit the teacher's intellectual competence, and thus promote a sense of political and social efficacy in the young, for the mediocrity of instruction reduces the gap between teacher and student, and thus serves as a practical demonstration of citizen competence to judge leaders.

I therefore propose the following perverse little hypothesis: the greater an American school system's commitment to transmitting the value of popular sovereignty, the greater will be its tendency to employ teachers competent enough to protect the profession's claim to autonomy but not so bright as to command unquestioned deference from the student. Mediocre teachers demonstrate to students that they need not fear authority. The derision the barely competent teacher creates is counterbalanced by the growing confidence in themselves that the students of such a teacher develop, sufficient to augment the practice—but not the understanding—of popular sovereignty as a mode of functioning in a loosely bounded culture. Thus, paradoxical as it may seem, every American school needs its poor teachers as much as it needs its good teachers.

I know that what I have said must seem almost coyly heretical; yet I am in earnest. Surely the evidence does suggest that American public school teachers constitute a distinctly mediocre intellectual reservoir.[79] For example, study after study shows that the grade point averages of future teachers fall below the averages of their peers.[80] Significantly, mediocrity abounds among teachers of social studies, the subject area in which, if my argument is correct, mediocrity is particularly in demand. And the measly salaries we pay teachers assure that mediocre teachers will continue to be recruited in suitable numbers. Indeed, again paradoxically, the fact that we pay so little for teachers suggests that a purely economic explanation of educational mediocrity is not sufficient, for we are willing to put out the money for excellence in many other occupations. The economics of teaching only provides the means through which the loosely bounded culture works its will.

Intellectual Differentiation

If the heart of any culture is the cognitive construction of social relations, then the capacity to make intellectual distinctions is of central importance. Such distinctions are the foundation of social classifications. Of course, there are many different ways by which such distinctions might be learned; in America, we rely heavily on the school for this purpose.

At the same time, however, the democratic values of our loosely bounded culture continually impose themselves on American schools. Despite the best efforts of the schools, these values cannot be restricted entirely to the implicit practices we have already described. They must appear somewhere as subject matter, but when they do they threaten the teacher's authority. After all, from the standpoint of epistemology such ideas as popular sovereignty and political equality are not neutral truths consistent with the teacher's claim to objective knowledge and legitimate expert authority. They are instead values that legitimize popular controls. Indeed, the better and more effectively such ideas are taught, the greater the danger that they might create controversy and tension within the school. Therefore, the greater is the risk they pose to school order and teacher power, for students who truly understand democratic values may venture to apply them to the school itself. Therefore, to teach such values complete with appropriate intellectual distinctions is to court organizational disruption.

The adaptation the school makes to this problem is to distort and simplify democratic values so as to force them into the corpus of accepted knowledge. Teachers accomplish this metamorphosis by obfuscating the logical hiatus between factual statements and normative propositions.[81] Their ignorance is fortuitously self-serving, for it permits them to treat such potentially dangerous values as political equality and popular sovereignty as if they were facts already embodied in practice by the school and the political order, rather than values which might shake up those two spheres. In short, they turn dynamic, vital ideas into torpid truisms. Their effort in this regard is aided by the fact that they read so little beyond the most pragmatic aspects of their craft that they can be assumed to confront the fact-value distinction but rarely.[82] In any case, many have had only minimal college work in the fields where they end up teaching.[83] Obviously, more work in the social sciences would help teachers distinguish between facts and values. As it now stands, however, the teacher becomes a smuggler of values, producing students who react with surprise and bewilderment when, in college, their instructors ask them for the first time to make the fact-value distinction.[84]

There is an alternative explanation of this phenomenon. Teachers may be reluctant to discuss values seriously because they make a mistake typical in a loosely bounded culture: they may equate values with superficial matters of taste to which all people can lay equal claim. In a loosely bounded culture it is easy to reduce values to the status of momentary fancies or situation-bound responses, rather than seeing them as all-embracing intellectual constructions. And since all people are in theory politically equal in a democracy, how can one person's sense of taste — even as expressed in values — be chosen over another's, particularly when both are tender children in a classroom, not hardened adults able to fend for themselves in the wide world?

Obfuscating the distinction between facts and values makes an important contribution to a loosely bounded culture. The intrusion of deeply felt normative distinctions may well create tense social divisions, which are the hallmarks of a tightly bounded culture. By contrast, a people disposed to look for factual "solutions" to what are actually normative problems naturally places a priority on "reasoning together," even though such reasoning can at best forge temporary alliances which mask the real depth of differences. Substituting an illusory language of facts for a sharply bounded language of values stretches science into scientism and dissolves genuine debate into psychiatric homilies.

Absorptiveness

A loosely bounded culture absorbs diverse ideas and forges them into a superficial consensus. American schools manifest the imperative of absorptiveness in a variety of ways. In their experiments with absorptiveness it is not content that matters (such experiments, indeed, often turn out to be failures), but rather it is the legitimacy of absorptiveness itself as a model for social life that becomes the primary aim of instruction.

Consider, for example, the periodic spasms of reform in American educational history. The most recent period of reform—from the 1950s to the 1970s—was a lesson in absorptiveness. During this period educators introduced such curricula as the New Math, innovative natural science programs, a challenging anthropology curriculum ("Man: A Course of Study"), and the Piagetian open classroom. Predictably enough, the American open classroom de-emphasized teacher control in favor of student-initiated, group projects in which teachers played an unobtrusive, guiding role. Not surprisingly, the American open classroom approach differs considerably from its British or Israeli counterparts, which place greater emphasis on subject matter and less emphasis on social interaction.[85] And the physical rearrangement of rooms—the incorporation of "wide open spaces" into the classroom—itself became a visual metaphor of the loosely bounded culture.

The school system's effort to absorb diverse groups into its culture has been equally striking. Formerly stigmatized children, such as the physically and mentally handicapped, have now been "mainstreamed," a term that vividly expresses the metaphor of a loosely bounded culture. Handicapped children used to be excluded from the "flow" of life—out of the mainstream, as it were—isolated in tightly compartmentalized, bounded institutions, such as hospitals, psychiatric wards, physical therapy centers, or "sheltered workshops." Now, however, they participate in the constant movement that is part of the loosely bounded culture, and overcome their handicaps by doing what the loosely bounded culture requires—being "themselves" like everyone else.

The school has attempted to find a home for previously stigmatized groups by broadening and revising its curricula. Thus, for example, Fitzgerald has described the almost frenetic revisions of history textbooks during the 1960s, a decade in which formerly ignored groups—blacks, Chicanos, Indians, Puerto

Ricans, women—suddenly saw themselves portrayed as major contributors to American history.[86] The attempt to absorb these groups into the life of the school reflects the political pressures of the 1960s as well as the belated recognition by textbook publishers that a market existed for new approaches. Still, despite these political and commercial factors, the trick could not have been managed so rapidly outside of a loosely bounded culture. The periodic rewriting of history can be expected in a culture that lacks deep roots and is unsure of the direction in which it is heading.

Accessibility and Contact

As we have seen, a loosely bounded culture encourages people to make contact with one another by surmounting barriers of class, race, sex, and income. The schools in such a culture reflect this tendency by widening channels of communication between teachers and students, administrators and parents, and school and community.

American schools are characterized by especially egalitarian relations between teachers and students, particularly in the early grades when teachers aim to reduce the age gap between themselves and their students. Much of this effort is rationalized by an educational doctrine that stresses the need of the child to feel emotionally secure and confident before attempting to learn truly demanding subject matter. This American pattern of quasi-familial nurturance contrasts strongly with early education in more tightly bounded cultures. For example, in France, students learn early that teachers are most assuredly not their equals, and that their emotional well-being is not the teacher's primary concern.[87] In France, the task of the school is sharply demarcated from that of the family. The school deals in cognitive and intellectual development; the family specializes in affectual well-being. By contrast, in the American school, nurture and cognitive learning overlap.

In American schools a plethora of support personnel, such as school psychologists and guidance counselors, promote the merger of nurturance and learning. Although the counseling staff also plays a role in the tightly bounded process of academic selection, it is equally important as a means of linking the student to the school affectively by circumventing academic routine. In this sense, school psychologists and guidance counselors, like other school personnel, serve both tightly and loosely bounded cultural codes. Their interaction with students reproduces the mix of equality and hierarchy inherent in the school's ambiguous operation.

American schools also provide open channels between administrators, teachers, and parents. The tradition of the neighborhood school legitimizes parental access to the school, and teachers are expected to solicit requests from parents for consultation. Of course, many teachers do not really welcome parental involvement, but unlike teachers in more tightly bounded cultures, they can not legitimately avoid consultations. One aspect of this process, not surprisingly, is reinforcement of the cultural tendency toward obfuscation. Teachers forced by cultural convention to be open to parents find ingenious ways of defusing parental concerns. For example, they often resort to educational jargon, which makes them appear to be noncensorious and nonjudgmental of their students. At some point accessibility may become counterproductive if it leads, not to the clarification, but to the obscuring of relationships. To put it differently, accessibility and imprecision are related methods by which the loosely bounded culture expresses itself in schools.

Accessibility takes an architectural as well as an organizational form. French schools are locked and barred from the beginning of every school day to the end. Parents would not think of transgressing school boundaries during the school day. In England, mothers indulgently shepherd their young as far as the school-yard fence, and at day's end they gather expectantly, waiting to enfold their young back into the bosom of the family. The fence is the boundary between two worlds, and the English child moves quickly from one group setting into another—from a tightly bounded school to a nurturant but quite separate and enfolding family. By contrast, American parents send their young children off each day as independent little individuals; most parents would feel slightly embarrassed to be seen walking their child to school. But should the parent wish to see the teacher, no barred iron gates intervene. The parent marches confidently through an open playground into an unbarred school. And why not? After all, the school belongs to the community; the parents picnic on school grounds, play softball on school diamonds, and basketball on school-yard courts. Moreover, parents support the school with their tax monies. Why should they not have the right of easy entrance and exit?

The pattern of access which most Americans take for granted is particularly prevalent among upper-middle-class persons. Many studies indicate that parental interaction with the school in America is class biased, with upper-middle-class people especially likely to demand and enjoy access.[88] Indeed, progressive private schools catering to the upper middle class provide even closer interaction between parent and teacher than do public schools. This pattern of upper-middle-class access contrasts strikingly with that of English upper-middle-class parents. According to George Male, in England, "It turns out that the better the school is, the higher its prestige, the less control parents have over the school."[89] The English pattern of separation originated in the boarding school tradition of intellectually demanding education. The point is, however, that in loosely bounded America, money buys access and mediocrity; in more tightly bounded England, by contrast, it buys competence and separation.

Expansion

A loosely bounded culture is characterized by a dynamic of expansion. This dynamic is particularly visible in a number of American school patterns, embracing teaching, course curricula, and even conceptions of education as part of the life cycle.

A primary pedagogical example of the school's expansiveness was the 1960s movement for schools "without walls."[90] Following Dewey, this conception of schooling—in which an entire community becomes the setting for education—deliberately blurred the boundary between school and community. In this conception the community becomes a kind of giant learning laboratory, extending the school's boundaries.

The movement for schools without walls was short-lived and never especially popular. Perhaps a more significant pattern of expansion in American schools involves paraprofessional "teacher's aides," noncredentialed parents who perform volunteer work under the supervision of teachers. The use of the paraprofessional suggests that teaching itself may to some degree be dispensed by noncredentialed volunteers. In other words, paraprofessionalism demonstrates that the teacher's knowledge is not sacrosanct. Weakening knowledge's privileged position is, of course, a paramount aspect of democratic loose boundedness. The possibility of delegitimation is enhanced by the paraprofessional's opportunity to actually observe and evaluate the teacher's classroom performance and to judge both its strengths and its weaknesses. The mystery that helps legitimize the power of any professional group disappears rapidly when outsiders are in a position to scrutinize professional practice with care. Thus, in an odd sense, the paraprofessional serves almost as a spy for the loosely bounded culture.

The school's dynamic of expansion also takes it into new subject areas. In recent years American schools have tackled sex education, moral education, new forms of vocational education, and emotional and psychological education in courses like "Health and Wellness." Meyer has analyzed this dynamic of expansion with exceptional insight. He argues that any specialized group that succeeds in having its specialty incorporated into a school curriculum thereby gains legitimacy.[91] Consequently, groups trying to gain a social foothold place the school under constant pressure to expand the range of its offerings. Meyer overlooks the fact, however, that expansion is already most congenial to American schools because the loosely bounded culture regularly stimulates teachers and administrators to take on novel roles and teach innovative or "relevant" courses. Many teachers complain that the schools have already been asked to do "too much," but they can discover no legitimate grounds for resisting expansion. The loosely bounded culture of which they are themselves such typical products arms them with no ideologies of refusal.

A final example of the school's dynamic of expansiveness involves the place of education in the life cycle. Rhoda Metraux observes that the United States has deliberately blurred the line between upbringing in the family and education in school. This effort is epitomized, she argues, by the school's development of "adult education," which assumes that in America education need never end. The life cycle's usual demarcation between "school days" and adulthood becomes yet another casualty of the loosely bounded culture. Metraux believes that in America education and upbringing have become interchangeable parts of a larger notion: individual development. What is striking about the concept of development, of course, is its open-endedness. In a loosely bounded culture we are all perpetual learners, and so we can always start over or find young techniques to mask our old age. As Metraux puts it, "We do not expect children to learn as their elders did, or even young siblings as did their elder ones." Therefore, "our present has very shallow roots in the past."[92]

Pollution and Participation

Political participation is widely valued in America. Participation is, of course, a necessity if people are to transcend the barriers that confine them politically. Thus, the value we place on political participation becomes another political form that loose boundedness assumes. We require schools to teach the value of participation more as implicit practice than as explicitly justified ideal. If people come from sharply divergent statuses, as do teachers and students, participation between the two groups can have a contaminating effect. Therefore, participation presents yet another danger to the basic shape of schooling. For this reason, the teaching of participation—like the teaching of popular sovereignty and political equality—takes an implicit form that compromises between hierarchy and democracy.

Teachers begin the process by making student participation

the norm in the classroom. The child who is "too quiet" becomes a particular source of concern to the teacher, as does the child who isolates himself from others, who avoids group activities, or who prefers to listen or to dream rather than to speak out. Children of this kind are deemed "shy," and teachers, parents, and counselors converge to "get the child over his shyness." As the example indicates, in a loosely bounded culture, classroom participation possesses a quasi-religious aura, perhaps to overcompensate for the fact that participation risks pollution. Participation thus becomes the reflexive obverse of pollution, just as loose boundedness is the obverse of tight boundedness.

Given its religious penumbra, participation easily becomes a ritualized end in itself. The rationale for participation—even the quality of participation—is less important than the act itself. Better the child should at least say something, no matter what, than that he or she should sit diffidently or sullenly silent and apart. Thus, as usually happens in a loosely bounded culture, movement and action displace contemplation and stasis. We teach process not purpose.

Similar pressures toward participation emerge in extracurricular activities, such as sports. American schools are notable for the range and variety of their extracurricular activities, which are designed to invite as many students as possible to participate. Sports events are particularly potent in this regard, for they bring the athletes and the spectators together into a unified participatory ritual. Indeed, the sports event is a series of expanding circles of participation: team member with team member; the team and the crowd together; and, finally, the team and the crowd as joint representatives of the community. Thus, the basic theme of participation appears in multilayered form, as is the case with all major cultural messages.

To summarize: American schools adapt to demands that they transmit the democratic values of a loosely bounded culture by de-emphasizing the academic competence of their teaching staffs; by setting their grading standards at levels low enough to insure that a majority of students perform acceptably, if perhaps poorly; by glossing over the difference between facts and values in politics; by engaging in various strategies of absorption, contact, and expansion; and by turning participation into a prescribed ritual. In short, American schools adapt by reducing the quality of education as intellectual training. Yet this adaption has its ironies. Poor teachers who apply mediocre standards to distorted social studies ideas are hardly capable of legitimizing the school's demand for order. Therefore, the practices I have described actually impede school order. Even the average student soon realizes, for example, that the little that is demanded in social studies classes can be accomplished without a hidden curriculum of order. As a result, students resist order, especially in the social studies, and when they are successful in their resistance (as Metz shows they often are),[93] they take their success as confirming their initial insight that school—particularly the social studies—is not really "serious" after all. If the social studies *were* serious, wouldn't they require order for effective teaching? Thus a vicious circle is drawn, a circle in which the school's attempt to accommodate itself to democratic values curls back destructively on the school itself.

If this argument is correct, it should follow that in a political system where democratic political socialization does not seriously threaten the hidden curriculum or the teacher's power, teachers should be able to maintain the distinction between political facts and values, and critical debate about democratic values should find an accepted place in the schooling process. An example of such a system is that of France, a society tightly enough bounded that teachers feel a level of security and competence uncommon in the United States. It is significant, therefore, that in France

> there is very little attempted control over the ideas which pupils should express. In fact, an integral part of the system is an overt attempt not to restrict or influence the ideological options open to the individual. Thus teachers in the humanities and social sciences present their subject matter in as objective a manner as possible. ... In addition, teachers try to inculcate within their students a critical bent of mind. These are clearly illustrated in the French school exercise called *explication de texte*, in which the pupils must analyze and then criticize a given passage in work selected by the

teachers—what to do and how to do it are precisely defined, but the student is given total freedom of expression. The attempt not to restrict the philosophical options open to the child is apparently successful, since the belief systems of the pupils gradually become dispersed all along the ideological spectrum.[94]

Of course, the school itself may not be solely responsible for the ideological dispersion Schonfeld describes. Schonfeld also ignores the highly restricted modes of expression that French students evince. But note that in the French case the school's demand for order and the teacher's claim to knowledge may be overtly asserted as not just compatible with but actually necessary to the process of teaching democratic values. The result is an educational pattern precisely the reverse of that which American schools adopt. The French teach democratic theory; we teach democratic practice.[95]

The confabulation of facts and values in the American social studies curriculum creates two specific limitations on political education. First, teachers who pretend that values are matters of settled fact rarely imbue such values with passion or conviction. To argue the proposition that democracy is a good thing as if it were equivalent to the proof that $2 + 2 = 4$ is to remove from the concept of democracy its singular emotional force. Much damage is thereby done to the value transmission process, for the people who internalize their political values most deeply and cleave to them most intensely are those who have felt a necessity to confront others who espouse opposed values, to argue for their own, to think through their beliefs, and through these exchanges, to explore the many applications, implications, and ambiguities of their political lives.[96] The American social studies curriculum provides few opportunities of this kind. As a result, democratic values rarely become deeply rooted in the American student's mind. Perhaps this tepid education helps to account for the well-known American reluctance to apply abstract democratic values to concrete situations of choice.[97] In this case, practice makes imperfect.

At first, all students face this problem together. But bright students soon begin to see through the ruse, eventually concluding that what the school has pretended to be fact is in reality a complex and confusing matter of debate and personal commitment. Therefore, it is bright students who find the loosely bounded school most disillusioning. And so, in every American school system, we turn many of our best students— indeed, many of our future intellectuals—against the educational enterprise.[98] These students thus come to *oppose* intellectualism to the current structure of schools. Perhaps this is the most damaging critique of all: that the American school's adaptation to the teaching of democratic values in a loosely bounded culture causes it to alienate many of its most promising students. The school thus forfeits the respect of many future citizens who should be its natural allies.

THE MYTH OF EQUAL EDUCATIONAL OPPORTUNITY

The strength of tightly bounded structures within the school setting derives, as we have seen, from organizational, professional, and economic pressures. But democratic values pursued by the school at the behest of the polity eat away at these boundaries. The tension between loosely bounded and tightly bounded interpretations of the school's role is strong—certainly stronger than any such confrontations in the mass media or advertising where, doctrinally at least, loose boundedness easily prevails. One precipitate of the comparatively equal confrontation between loose and tight boundedness in education has been the generation of a compelling myth comparable in structure and function to the myths described by structural anthropologists. This is the myth of equal educational opportunity.

That the idea of equal educational opportunity possesses mythic qualities is demonstrable in four respects, each of which relates easily to anthropological theory. First, from a logical standpoint equal educational opportunity is incoherent. Within the American context real equality is at odds with opportunity for advancement, since equality levels the incentive distinctions that lie at the heart of opportunity in America.[99] To the structuralist, the sustained appeal of a logically incoherent and contradictory doctrine is a sure sign of myth, and therefore demands close analysis.

Second, multiple attempts to clarify the concept of equal educational opportunity have succeeded in doing little more than saddling the concept with an ever-growing penumbra of meanings. Today, the concept may refer, *inter alia*, to identical starting points in the educational process, to equal access to education, to equality of educational treatment, to equal life chances in the Weberian sense, and, finally, to equal outcomes of education.[100] Confusions among these meanings have rendered the concept of equal educational opportunity intractable from a discursive standpoint, although all the more attractive as a myth. The very opaqueness of the concept increases its mythic appeal, since, as Edelman points out, ambiguity permits people to project diverse meanings onto any social object.[101] Multiple meanings and logical incomprehensibility combine to generate and sustain the myth of equal educational opportunity.

Third, like other myths, the concept of equal educational opportunity motivates actions which can succeed only in a psychological sense, not in an instrumental sense. Policies designed to secure equal educational opportunity are doomed to instrumental failure; the opaqueness of the concept decrees that those who pursue these policies will not even agree about what they are looking for. Therefore, to understand the continuing efforts to secure equal educational opportunity requires us to view such efforts as either ill-formed or symbolic, that is, serving mythic functions that never become explicit. In practice, I believe, both explanations are correct.

A last aspect of the equal opportunity concept which gives it a mythical function is its capacity to remain appealing despite its demonstrated "failures." To understand this unusual property of survival we must visualize the concept as a mediator functioning to reconcile the tensions between democracy and hierarchy, tight and loose boundedness, that appear regularly in American schools.

In order to understand how the concept of equal educational opportunity can perform these mythic roles, we will employ ideas from structural analysis. However, it is worth emphasizing again that the mythic quality of the concept depends on its logical incomprehensibility, its penumbra of ambiguous meanings, its psychological appeal to disparate groups of Americans, and its certain failure as a goal of public policy. These qualities, far from being aberrant—as they would surely appear in a straightforward political economy analysis—in fact constitute the very center of a structural analysis. Paradoxically, its many failures of logic and execution permit the concept of equal educational opportunity to perform successfully its functions of mythic mediation.

The idea of equal opportunity is composed of a binary logic linking effort to success. One-half of this logic moves from a loosely bounded culture to a more tightly bounded culture, proceeding from equality of opportunity to differential accomplishment. This is the more familiar part of the myth, as illustrated in the well-known Horatio Alger stories. In this form, the myth begins with a poor but honest and hardworking youth living in a disorganized setting, preferably a "broken" (i.e., loosely bounded) home. The youth then enters school, which is tightly bounded, and through hard work surmounts difficulties, eventually becoming rich and secure, reproducing in the security of family life the theme of economic success. Thus, the myth includes the following binary code: poverty/disorder = success/order. The result of this mythic scenario is the production of individuals who are able to surmount their social backgrounds and move successfully through social space to a safe harbor.

Less obvious, but equally necessary to the equal educational opportunity myth, is the binary opposite of the Horatio Alger scenario: the "poor little rich boy" scenario. In this case, a child born to a successful, secure, well-structured family is sent to the "best" schools—which are also tightly bounded and well structured—but the child "fails," usually because of some uncontrollable weakness, such as sloth, vice, or excessive use of alcohol. The youth thus slips across the boundary from tightly bounded success to loosely bounded, disorganized failure, with the school again serving as intermediary. In contrast with the Horatio Alger story, the poor-little-rich-boy story begins with a tightly bounded, well-organized starting point, a worthless person who does not "live up" to his status, little effort on the part of the protagonist, poor performance, and a fall into the loosely bounded, disorganized culture of poverty. The school mediates between both rise and fall; the two types of movement complement each other and thus serve to "complete" each other mythically.

We can see that the equal educational opportunity concept contains many elements that Turner and others have identified as peculiar to mythic structures. For example, in both versions of the myth the protagonists undertake long trips, both psychologically and geographically, in order to find themselves and establish their place in society. Their journeys force them to prove themselves, and thus serve to emphasize the individualism and self-reliance that is the essence of loose boundedness in America. The journeys force each protagonist to undertake a series of graded tasks supplied by the school. For the Horatio Alger figure the tasks become increasingly demanding, much like those undertaken by Greek mythic figures. For the poor little rich boy, however, the tasks become increasingly less demanding, although they are still beyond the protagonist's capacity. Finally, both stories begin with a figure in the home, move into the outside world, and then return to a very different home. The ensemble illustrates the A-B-A form so common in musical composition and apparently so psychologically satisfying to audiences.

Although the myth of equal opportunity involves movement in two directions, it retains the essential distinction between the binary classifications of the cultural code. The myth carefully separates the person, who is the center of loose boundedness, from the opportunity structure, which is the center of tight boundedness. For example, the myth is careful to argue that mobility does not *alter* but only reveals character. Mobility displays but does not distort the person. Movement thus gives the Horatio Alger figure the opportunity to reveal his real worth and to show us, for example, that he is not the sort of person who will "forget his old friends." Indeed, he would be more likely to "go bad" if he had been forced to remain in a status that did not measure up to his qualities. Similarly, the poor little rich boy does not go bad because he falls in status; rather, he falls in status because of his defective character. Character is thus kept independent of status. The myth separates personality from structure—loose boundedness from tight boundedness—while suggesting that successful transactions between the two realms are nevertheless possible.

As both midwife and judge of these transactions, the school occupies a unique position. The school functions solely as instrument; it supplies neither goal nor purpose itself. The meaning of the myth of equal educational opportunity does not derive from accepted knowledge in the school's keeping; it derives rather from the messages of success emanating from the tightly bounded structure of opportunity and from the messages of individualism, character, and mobility embedded in democratic loose boundedness. The school itself creates none of these messages. The school simply engineers mobility; the ideas it transmits are mere badges of self-display or mediums of exchange useful in the pursuit of status. The school functions solely as a mediator. Its own mythic power is derivative and artificial, like the loosely bounded culture it reflects.

In American culture the school almost always points beyond itself. It rarely justifies its efforts by appealing to the intrinsic worth of ideas or by maintaining the standard of an "intellectual life." Therefore, the myth of equal educational opportunity consigns the school to the same inglorious fate we have already observed in the collision between loose boundedness and tight boundedness in curricula, teacher recruitment, and the domain of knowledge itself. The school's weakness in pursuing the goal of equal educational opportunity therefore symbolically reproduces its weakness in day-to-day educational practice. The result of the school's efforts is a culture in which ideas per se command little value and where, therefore, people lack intellectual tools helpful to an understanding of their own actions. Americans thus live in a kind of culturally patterned political innocence that reproduces itself from generation to generation.

6

THE AMERICAN POLITY AS A CULTURAL CENTER

I have argued that in America loose boundedness has become our primary cultural pattern. Unfortunately, however, loose boundedness makes it difficult for us to comprehend and control the economic and political structures that shape our lives. Most of these structures are characterized by a refined division of labor, highly stratified, functionally specific hierarchies, and impersonal, meritocratic norms. But construed culturally, these structures appear instead to be egalitarian, fluid, highly personal—even sentimental—and, above all, open. We are therefore deceived, or, more precisely, we deceive ourselves. From the objective standpoint of efficient functioning in these structures the ideal American should be a well-trained specialist with a healthy respect for science, reason, and the limitations imposed by imperfect knowledge, restrained—though legitimate—authority, and restricted power. By contrast, from the subjective standpoint of cultural ideals the exemplary American should resemble Lévi-Strauss's "bricoleur"—a cultural jack-of-all-trades, who possesses extensive though tacit and unsystematized knowledge; who heeds instinct and impulse rather than reason; and who condemns all restraints as unjust and unnecessary fetters on freedom, opportunity, self-betterment, and the satisfactions of emotional bonding.[1]

Is this gap between American social structure and American culture irreparable? Must we end this inquiry with a whimper rather than a bang? Not necessarily, for we have yet to consider whether the state itself might gradually move to provide a coherent connection between culture and structure in America, even if television, schools, and advertising can not. Would the state make such an effort? Might the American polity construct a moral heart for American culture and, in so doing, bridge the gap between American social structure and American culture?

Durkheim, following a venerable tradition of political theory, envisaged the modern state as playing precisely this cultural role. He put it this way:

> The role of the state . . . is not to sum up the unreflective thought of the mass of the people, but to superimpose on this unreflective thought a more considered thought, which therefore cannot be other than different. It is and must be a centre of new and original representations which ought to put the society in a position to conduct itself with greater intelligence than when it is swayed by vague sentiments working on it.[2]

The question we must consider in conclusion, therefore, is whether American political institutions are in fact able to "superimpose . . . considered thought" on our loosely bounded culture, and thereby to compel society "to conduct itself with greater intelligence." I will address this question by examining two recent efforts by the federal government to perform this culture-shaping function: one involving proposed alterations in the content of television entertainment, the other involving a major social studies curriculum reform. Perhaps it is not surprising that both efforts fell far short of Durkheim's dictum and, in so doing, displayed the American polity's cultural weakness rather than its strength.

Of course, Durkheim's vision of the state's cultural role presupposed that the state possesses real incentives to actually shape culture. There are three reasons why we can justifiably infer such incentives in the American case, despite the fact that ours is a political system most thoroughly in tune with loose boundedness and, therefore, most cautious in pursuing an active cultural role. Despite the many hindrances to such a task, the American polity is motivated to produce a culture that has more coherence than loose boundedness provides.

For one thing, American political elites adhere to comparatively cohesive political ideologies. Most studies agree that the policy views of political leaders are more consistent, more comprehensive, and better grounded philosophically than are those of their followers. Indeed, some of these ideologies approach the visions of America which we considered in chapter one. Leaders often think in terms of tightly bounded, culturally coherent conceptions of America—even if they do not always allow their words to echo their thoughts. But surely they are favorably disposed toward urging their conceptions on their fellow countrymen.

Second, as we have seen, tightly bounded cultural codes—such as the visions we examined in chapter one—are formidable political mobilization devices. The group identities, myths, and values such visions contain constitute potential rallying points for an otherwise listless population. All political systems need to mobilize their publics occasionally; all must therefore call upon their people to sacrifice sometimes. But people demand a reason to sacrifice, and sacrificing solely to advance the *self* provides only a minimal level of mobilization for the *polity*. Cultural visions take people beyond self-interest into a realm of commitment where sacrifice becomes transformed into duty. And so, as political systems attempt to manage recurrent scarcities, they naturally attempt to appeal beyond loose boundedness. A coherent, tightly bounded political culture facilitates successful political mobilization; a loosely bounded culture backs the individual away from politics and directs him toward a private vision of the self in the world.

Finally, political systems always face the problem of legitimation. They must somehow make their power seem natural and even desirable to the people they rule. They must transform the unpleasantness of domination into the joy of submission. In this respect the American political system resembles other Western political systems, whose rapid growth in the twentieth century has created formidable problems of legitimation. But the American case is extreme, because loose boundedness places the burden of proof against any effort by the state to expand its cultural role. Thus, the power of the American polity lacks full cultural justification. It is only reasonable for politicians to attempt to close this gap by shaping American culture in ways more congenial to state power.

There are, however, two factors that seem likely to limit government's influence on culture in America. One is our tradition of political liberalism; the other is the haunting sense of personal vulnerability that pervades loosely bounded cultures.

The power of the liberal tradition in American politics has been well documented elsewhere,[3] and we have already discussed it in our account. The liberal tradition protects free speech, free assembly, and a free press, all in an effort to retain the private citizen, not the state, as the primary unit of our culture. Liberalism thereby sets up conditions that facilitate loose boundedness. Thanks to the liberal tradition, American political institutions undertake any new culture-shaping roles at a great disadvantage, fearing at every step to hear charges of "censorship" or "violation of the First Amendment."[4] The widespread American suspicion of any cultural role for government is a predictable outcome when loose boundedness and liberalism work together. Although this hostile environment does not prevent government from attempting to shape culture, it does alter tactics in ways Durkheim could never have imagined. Indeed, in the two cases we will examine shortly, the government moved indirectly, hesitantly, and—to its critics—surreptitiously, in contrast to Durkheim's prediction that in matters of culture the state will act directly and purposefully. In turn, the very uncertainty of its action prepared the way for government to fail in both cases.

As to the second limiting factor, let us remember our discussion of television and advertising, which alluded to feelings of vulnerability and anxiety which pervade loosely bounded cultures. Communicators in both media succeed in part because they teach people how to reach out to others, and thus how to avoid loneliness by forging new relationships. The unprotectedness forced on each person by loose boundaries requires people to choose between the Scylla of possible exploitation by others and the Charybdis of loneliness. The price of having many people potentially available to the self is one's own complementary accessibility to these others, and who can be sure that others are as well intentioned as the self? Trust and suspicion are the Abel and the Cain of loosely bounded cultures.

The latent theme of suspicion and fear occasionally leads to unexpected outcomes. In loosely bounded cultures there are many people who yearn for tighter boundaries around themselves—borders they can defend without being considered "standoffish," "snobbish," or "paranoid." The young, the infirm, the mentally retarded, the aged, the poor—these are the groups most open to victimization in loosely bounded cultures; therefore, it is often these groups which crystallize the latent misgivings about loose boundedness that all share to some degree in loosely bounded cultures. We should not be surprised to discover especially vulnerable persons or groups in loosely bounded cultures occasionally demanding that boundaries be drawn to protect them.

Often these groups call on government, first to define defensible boundaries and then to police the newly defined zones. However, the difficulty (as we shall soon see) is that these demands appear to invite an even greater evil, namely, that government—whose coercive force is unmatched—may use the call for help as a pretext to "invade" the rights of *all*. The state cannot easily answer the call of vulnerable persons in loosely bounded cultures, because, as an institution to which people are attached involuntarily, the state appears more likely to harm the vulnerable individual than to help him. In short, a political cure for the ills of loose boundedness often appears more deadly than the ills themselves. Small wonder that the state as a putative cultural center encountered rough sledding in the two cases we now examine.

THE MACOS FRACAS

An educational curriculum is a vehicle for the propagation of culture.[5] Therefore, a useful way of investigating the cultural power of the American polity is to analyze a curriculum reform effort which the federal government recently sponsored. MACOS ("Man: A Course of Study"), a social studies curriculum the National Science Foundation funded in the late 1960s and early 1970s, is therefore a worthy object of our attention.

It should be recognized at the outset that people in loosely bounded cultures possess at least two grounds on which they can legitimately resist a new curriculum. They can, of course, object to a curriculum if they believe that its content is inconsistent with those expectations and norms that are part of loose boundedness. But they can also question the procedures by which the curriculum is developed and disseminated, if they suspect that these procedures do not conform to loosely bounded expectations. And, finally, inconsistency between procedures and content may also disqualify the curriculum from ready adoption. We begin our investigation of MACOS by considering the procedures Americans normally follow in the adoption of new curricula.

In the United States the typical mode of curriculum adoption conforms to loose boundedness in at least three senses. First there is the tradition of local control. "From the beginning in colonial days, the 'local control' approach was intended to maximize the control of the local citizenry over the sensitive matter of determining the kind of instruction to be offered, and values to be fostered in the local schools."[6] Local and regional diversity in curricula, rather than state-mandated curricular uniformity, fits the loosely bounded culture's emphasis on voluntarism and citizen choice. Of course, in practice curriculum decisions today are not purely local,[7] but the cultural recipe for curriculum decision-making obscures this fact; indeed, any curriculum which does not at least pay lip service to the local control norm may be in for a difficult time. MACOS was one such curriculum.

A related procedural norm is embodied in what Weick calls the "loosely coupled system" of intraschool governance. As Weick notes, public schools in America have never fully epitomized the ideal type of ordered, rational bureaucracies. Instead, schools are "loosely coupled structures," characterized internally primarily by "impermanence, dissolvability, and tacitness,"[8] rather than by hierarchical controls, centralized decision-making, and a single line of legitimate authority. Although participants in loosely coupled systems enjoy high and legitimate access to each other, they also jealously retain flexibility and autonomy as they work out their interrelations. In loosely coupled systems organizational units are not hamstrung by clear lines of authority or inflexible specifications for tasks. It should be clear that the loosely coupled internal structure of schools expresses vividly at the level of organization the loose boundedness of the larger culture on which the school is parasitic. Within the school's loosely coupled structure students, teachers, principals, parents, and school board members mix together easily, but exert little control over each other, thereby exemplifying the cultural pattern of loose boundedness.

Loose coupling assures that curricular reform in American schools will inevitably be a time-consuming, imperfect process. Loose coupling protects the plethora of interest and occupational groups whose views must be consulted and whose acquiescence won before curricular change can proceed. And any new curriculum which attempts to circumvent the loosely coupled decision structure of schools will naturally appear illegitimate.

Last, the features of localism, multiple group access, and citizen participation in schooling, along with the loosely coupled structure of authority within schools, assure that curriculum innovation will usually be a tortuously slow process. Empirical studies of curriculum innovation in America bear this prediction out. Keynesian economics provides one example, because although Keynes's ideas had become a staple part of university economics courses by the 1940s, it was another twenty years before even one American high school economics textbook devoted as much as 40 percent of its space to Keynesian ideas.[9] The same story could be told of the widely heralded science curriculum innovations of the 1960s, which never entirely took hold.[10] A loosely bounded school culture and a loosely coupled school structure combine to impede rapid curricular innovation. There is no central educational authority which can mandate curriculum change, and therefore such innovations must be slow, piecemeal, and eventually incomplete. When the school deliberately exposes itself to multiple conflicting pressures, it must expect that reform will be painful and controversial. Eventually, the measured pace of educational innovation itself becomes a cultural norm, the violation of which engenders suspicion and resistance.

At first glance the curriculum known as MACOS appears to defy the norm of slowness. MACOS, a year-long, fifth-grade social studies course, first reached schools on a large scale in 1967, and during that year it was adopted in 367 elementary schools. A scant three years later it had found its way into 1,700 schools, reaching 200,000 children. The growth rate was meteoric, considering that 1970 was only its first year of mass marketing. The high-water mark for MACOS came in 1975, at which time a National Science Foundation (NSF) study found it in use in forty-seven states, among 328,000 students.[11] After 1975, however, its usage declined, and no current estimate is available. Still, during the early days of MACOS the growth rate was indeed impressive.

The National Science Foundation is one of the federal government's major research support arms for both the natural and the social sciences; NSF's contribution to MACOS was substantial, approximating $5 million between 1963 and 1975 toward development and evaluation. In addition, from 1967 to 1975 NSF allocated another $2,166,000 for the distribution of MACOS to elementary schools around the country, as well as for the training of MACOS teachers.[12] In 1975, following severe criticism from congressmen and some groups of parents, NSF ceased supporting MACOS, thereby initiating a process of NSF withdrawal from curriculum development in all the social sciences. And only recently President Reagan proposed that NSF refrain from any curriculum development at all henceforth.

As we can see, the period 1963–75 marked an important departure from previous federal government policy toward education, and toward curriculum development in particular. During this period NSF curriculum development projects permitted government for the first time to directly influence the curriculum culture of the American public school. The new government thrust was a reaction both to Sputnik and to critics of education, such as Hyman Rickover and Arthur Bestor, who proclaimed that American schools were "failing" and that our students could no longer compete with students in the Soviet Union.[13] NSF began its efforts in the hard sciences and mathematics, justifying its actions as helping American education "keep up with the Russians" in defense-related fields. Soon, however, major figures in the burgeoning curriculum development movement, such as Jerrold Zacharias of MIT, broadened their attention to include social studies education. They argued that the same defense-related arguments that justified curriculum reform in the hard sciences applied with equal force to the social sciences. They also claimed that in a world of newly developing, Third World nations the United States could retain its dominance only by "understanding" exotic cultures which traditional social studies invariably overlooked. MACOS became the prototype of a social studies education tailored to those novel circumstances.[14]

At first glance, therefore, MACOS appears to exemplify the sort of cultural expansion on the part of the federal government that fits well the Durkheimian formulation. With MACOS, government appeared to be trying to fill the cultural void that loose boundedness creates. Such a reading would be wrong, however, for, as we shall see, the state proved too weak to accomplish its purpose, and was thereby forced—contrary to Durkheim—to retire from the field. Moreover, MACOS turns out on examination actually to have been a *loosely* bounded curriculum in most respects, and could never, under any conditions, have served the purposes of cultural cohesion. From the standpoint of cultural reorganization or state "hegemony," therefore, MACOS was doomed from the outset. It could not surmount the cultural dilemma that called it forth.

MACOS as a Loosely Bounded Curriculum

MACOS is a fifth-grade social studies program that combines films, booklets of stories, anthropological descriptions, games, and simulations with two instructional purposes: to examine the idea of culture, and to investigate how ecological and economic pressures affect social adaptation. The curriculum offers units on herring gulls, salmon, baboons, and most controversially as it turned out, a small group of Alaskan Eskimos, the Netsiliks, whose yearly cycle of activities the Canadian Film Board recorded extensively for classroom use. Pedagogically as well as substantively, MACOS conforms in most respects to loosely bounded cultural assumptions. Therefore, its developers had every reason to expect the new program to be welcomed warmly by most students, parents, and teachers. It came as a shock when opposition developed.

It is obviously paradoxical that an effort by the state to produce greater cultural cohesion in America should have taken the form of a social studies curriculum embodying loose boundedness. It is also paradoxical that such a program should have engendered resistance. But why a loosely bounded curriculum in the first place?

This question can be answered in three ways. First, no political system can ever function as a monolithic problem-solver. The American political system must respond to many groups and individuals who compete with each other for power and control. When "the state" acts, therefore, one is really speaking only about a temporary coalition of groups and individuals struggling desperately to maintain control over a specific area of public policy. Furthermore, in order to operate at all effectively, every coalition must compromise and conciliate; small wonder, therefore, that policy makers should so often support policies that do not entirely conform to their best interests or even to their original intentions. MACOS was therefore simply a tentative, groping experiment toward cultural cohesion.

It is important to realize that the government was acting in a cultural context where the dominant ideas are loosely bounded. One aspect of loose boundedness is confusion about and resistance to sharp value choices and philosophically grounded positions; the state cannot escape this confusion any more than private groups and individuals can. Therefore, if it proceeds inconsistently in pursuing cultural cohesion, the state only mirrors the culture which creates the need for such cohesion in the first place. Overcoming a loosely bounded culture is like performing an autopsy on an amoeba.

Finally, MACOS must be understood as a vain attempt to discover a moral position that might anchor loose boundedness. The necessity to spell out such premises for elementary schoolers provided a golden opportunity for policy makers to see if loose boundedness could in fact serve as a satisfactory cultural framework. Understandably, the curriculum's proponents could not resist their chance. Needless to say, the fate of MACOS laid their brave hopes to rest.

In both content and form MACOS bears the stamp of Jerome Bruner, one of America's leading cognitive psychologists. Bruner served as head of Educational Development Center, Inc. (EDC), a consortium of Cambridge-based educators who devoted themselves during the 1960s to the design of innovative precollege curricula. It was also Bruner who was the moving force at conferences in the late 1950s which laid the groundwork for MACOS; when he took over as head of EDC in 1964, Bruner initiated the major development and testing phase of MACOS.[15] Most important, it was Bruner, more than anyone else, who helped shape MACOS into a loosely bounded curriculum.

Bruner's main contribution was to propose the three basic questions which MACOS investigated: "What is human about human beings? How did they get that way? How can they be made more so?"[16] These three questions appeared often in guides for teachers of the new course and had considerable influence on teacher practices. What is especially striking about these questions is their underlying assumptions, assumptions that are eminently congruent with loose boundedness. For example, the first question is premised on the assumption that there exists a basic human nature which unites varied cultures and nationalities. Consequently, the question encourages students to focus on what people have in common (a loosely bounded conception), rather than on what might divide people sharply and even durably from each other (a tightly bounded conception).

Or consider the question of how people become human, which is almost certainly predicated on a belief in some form of evolutionary theory. To the developers of MACOS the theory of human evolution could be taken for granted as being scientifically valid and popularly accepted (a mistake, as things turned out). Evolutionary theory is thoroughly in line with a loosely bounded culture's emphasis on continuity—for the idea of "becoming" human assumes that there exist important resemblances between men and animals, an assumption that was reinforced by placing the Eskimo unit immediately after the animal units. There was a struggle within EDC between those favoring the evolutionary organization of MACOS and those favoring a more comparative organization which would highlight differences among groups and cultures. This struggle was symptomatic of a larger struggle within EDC between loosely and tightly bounded conceptions of society, a struggle that, on balance, evolutionists within EDC won for the loosely bounded culture.[17]

Finally, the question of how people become *more* human, though in strictly logical terms nonsensical, also reflects a loosely bounded conception. It is in fact reminiscent of themes we encountered in our earlier investigations of television and advertising, namely, beliefs that people can improve themselves almost instantaneously so as to make themselves attractive to others. This assumption—no doubt derived from Enlightenment ideas of human perfectibility—supposes not only that people have the capacity to expand their boundaries and "grow" quickly, but also that they are somehow morally required to do so. Indeed, Bruner's question—with its boundless conception of human nature—flirts with the idea that what is "essentially" human is nothing other than the capacity for change itself. Thus, the energizing questions in MACOS are incontestably loosely bounded.

Pedagogically, MACOS is equally loosely bounded. Three pedagogical assumptions command our attention: one involving content, one involving the child's learning potential, and one involving course goals. As to content, MACOS aims to cultivate certain general *skills* of reasoning, such as the making of hypotheses, the evaluation of evidence, and the generalization of conclusions. As Dow points out, MACOS specifically avoided teaching traditional disciplines, such as history or geography, opting instead to inculcate aspects of reasoning that would crosscut and unite the social studies.[18] Thus, from the standpoint of pedagogy MACOS saw the child's reasoning capacity as both universal and boundless in application, rather than as naturally divided into discrete substantive compartments.

Although this approach may appear at first to be overly ambitious for fifth graders, the developers of MACOS attempted to justify it by advancing a second pedagogical postulate that was also consistent with loose boundedness, namely, that there is no essential difference between the child's reasoning and the adult's. Bruner enunciated this principle with perhaps undue rhetorical excess in his famous claim that with proper teaching any person can learn any body of ideas at any age.[19] MACOS in fact went even further, for it proceeded on the premise that the child could be trained to think like a miniature social scientist. This premise too became an object of attack to later opponents of MACOS.

Indeed, the pedagogical goal of MACOS exceeded even the learning of supposedly universal reasoning skills. At bottom, the course aimed to instill a particular habit of mind. This Bruner and his associates enunciated in their injunction to students to "go beyond the information given,"[20] that is, to treat information not as fixed, unquestionable, or settled, but rather as fluid, loosely bounded, suggestive, and open to revision. MACOS wished to develop the child's cognitive inventiveness and creativity. Following a line of theory at least as old as John Dewey, the pedagogy of MACOS proposed a "discovery/inquiry" method which would move the child away from being the passive receptacle of established truths to becoming a partner with the teacher in a mutual effort to arrive at conclusions about what it means to be fully human, what social structure enjoins, and what human nature and social structure together might be able to produce in the way of developed human behavior. The pedagogical devices of discovery learning, of hypothesis generation, and of experimentation and simulation thus served as metaphors for the overall loosely bounded goal of the curriculum: to get children *beyond* (my emphasis) the information given, and thus to reshape the child's cognitive world.

The centrality of loose boundedness in MACOS's pedagogy should by now be evident. Amazingly, some people who contributed to the development of MACOS believed that the curriculum actually did not go far enough in the direction of loose boundedness, and in fact took Bruner to task for being too restricted in his assumptions. Richard Jones, a psychologist who was active in the early classroom evaluation of MACOS, charged Bruner with "an over-emphasis on cognitive skills and curricular materials and ... corresponding under-emphasis on emotional skills."[21] Jones argued that "if ever a course was designed to create special opportunities for engaging the softer, more precious reaches of children's minds, it is *"Man:* A Course of Study"* (italics in the original).[22] Yet MACOS had missed its opportunity, because it had artificially separated the cognitive from the emotive aspects of learning. Luckily, with appropriate revisions, MACOS could encourage the same freedom of emotional expression that it had already proved itself capable of producing in the cognitive realm. Given the subsequent lambasting of the cognitive goals of MACOS, Jones's point of view appears almost quaint today. One shudders to think of what might have happened to MACOS had his views been taken seriously. Still, that Jones could have envisaged yet more loose boundedness for MACOS indicates how strong a hold loosely bounded pedagogy had even on MACOS's more conservative developers.

Two additional aspects of MACOS pedagogy exemplify a loosely bounded conception of learning. The first is the emphasis on multimedia learning, and particularly the innovative reliance on films of the Eskimos. With its speed and its sense of immediacy, the film medium is particularly conducive to disseminating an image of loose boundaries. MACOS doubly emphasized this element of film presentation, for the Eskimo filmstrips contained neither narration nor sound. The film thereby forced the student to develop his or her own interpretation of events, a good example of suiting a loosely bounded medium to the loosely bounded purpose of "going beyond the information given."

Lastly, MACOS attempted to shrink the pedagogical distance between teacher and student. As Dow puts it, the student was to see the teacher as a "partner in inquiry," not as an infallible authority.[23] And as we saw in the preceding chapter, equalizing the relationship between student and teacher is one way by which the loosely bounded culture intrudes into the school setting. At the same time, however, MACOS was unique in that it required all teachers of the course to attend special technique workshops in order to learn how to impart the material effectively. Thus, ironically enough, it was apparent that the egalitarianism that MACOS encouraged between teacher and learner could emerge only if teachers were themselves first treated in a tightly bounded fashion, that is as a distinct group in need of special training. Perhaps it was the dominance of loose boundedness in the cultural conceptions of the developers of MACOS that prevented their appreciating the paradox in this uneasy juxtaposition of equality and professionalism; in any case, they later paid a heavy political price for their flawed perception.

So much for the close pedagogical fit between MACOS and loose boundedness. What about course content? The content of MACOS is thoroughly loosely bounded, most vividly so in its depictions of the Netsilik Eskimos, whose customs became the focal point of attack among those opposed to the program. Both in filmstrips and booklets students were exposed to examples of fratricide, multiple marriages, senilicide, gory hunting techniques, exotic tastes in food (Eskimo children eating with relish the eyes of freshly slaughtered seals), cannibalism, a mother's murder of her daughter out of sexual jealousy, and the abduction of one man's wife by another man. One of its critics labeled these depictions "controversial or even shocking,"[24] a judgment that the more severe detractors of MACOS would clearly have found too generous by half.

Why would a fifth-grade social studies program depict scenes so predictably certain to arouse the ire of some children and their parents? Why court such dangers? A partial answer to this question lies in the MACOS evaluational process; Peter Dow claims that only a few of the children who viewed these events actually recoiled from them, a line of argument which other project developers dispute.[25] But even if Dow is correct, why were these particular scenes chosen in the first place? The answer to this question—and the key to the underlying substantive theme of MACOS—is that the course reflected assumptions about the pervasiveness and acceptability of loose boundedness in American culture.

To begin with, the curriculum's developers were hoping to teach "cultural relativism."[26] They wanted to show "that beliefs and values unacceptable in our culture might be acceptable in others."[27] Cultural relativism is a social science version of loose boundedness, for it argues that because what one culture takes to be good may be judged bad in another culture, the line between good and evil is neither invariant nor absolute. All is a matter of individual choice. This unwillingness or inability to make sharp value distinctions is, of course, a key aspect of loosely bounded cultures.

The developers of MACOS intended events among the Eskimos to teach a specific loosely bounded alternative to any rigid distinction between good and evil. This alternative was the lesson of "functional equivalence." Dorothy Nelkin describes it:

> The study of a traditional tribal culture showed how human beings as well as animals adapt to a particular environment; in order for the Netsilik to survive in an environment with limited food resources they practice infanticide and senilicide as means of controlling the population. MACOS suggested that in some societies such practices, disturbing as they would be in our own culture, were functional, and that neither behavior nor beliefs have an absolute value apart from the social and physical context.[28]

In short, MACOS proposed to students that a loosely bounded message of "functional equivalence" and a non-judgmental, accepting frame of mind should take the place of a tightly bounded value position and a harshly judgmental, intemperate frame of mind. After all, where "styles of life" are concerned, one should be "laid back," not "uptight."

Indeed, lest the pupils miss the point, MACOS encouraged each student to apply the lessons learned from the Netsiliks to "comparable" areas of his own life or the lives of his family. As was carefully explained in the course guidelines given to all teachers, MACOS assumed that American children already experience "horrors" in everyday television "entertainment" which are functionally equivalent to the exotic horrors depicted in MACOS.[29] More important, MACOS also posited that the social environment of the American child and of the Eskimo child are functionally similar enough—regardless of their obvious physical differences—that the American child can employ the Eskimos as an intellectual vehicle for reflecting profitably on his or her own life.[30] In other words, is there really any "essential" difference between, say, senilicide and the consigning of grandparents to "senior citizen" communities? Surely both practices are functionally acceptable solutions to the same human problem.

Unfortunately, the developers of MACOS had trouble getting some students to believe that the Eskimos were in fact truly "human." Dow admits that in the early stages of MACOS testing, some students refused to see the Eskimos sympathetically, preferring instead to view them as reacting mechanically, unimaginatively, and "inhumanly" to an admittedly harsh environment.[31] Therefore, MACOS was reworked in order to present the Eskimos more attractively, and teachers were encouraged to avoid the troublesome question of comparative levels of civilization. But even these alterations were not entirely satisfactory. Loose boundedness, at least as sponsored by the state, had met its limits. Some students, apparently, were hopelessly tightly bounded.

The Attack on MACOS

On April 9, 1975, Congressman John Conlan of Arizona rose in the House of Representatives to protest additional NSF funding for the dissemination of MACOS. Because Conlan sat on the subcommittee responsible for authorizing NSF expenditures, his arguments inevitably carried considerable weight. Conlan offered an amendment to the NSF program-authorization bill which, had the amendment been adopted, would have required every future NSF science curriculum project to come before the Congress for approval. After a spirited debate the amendment lost by a scant fourteen votes. Conlan's proposal climaxed a period of anti-MACOS protests in several school districts around the country. Acting in response to these protests, as well as to Conlan's proposed amendment, NSF immediately abandoned further efforts to implement MACOS, and also initiated an internal investigation not just of MACOS but of all its science curriculum projects. Meanwhile, the House Committee on Science and Technology produced its own separate investigation of MACOS, and the General Accounting Office also conducted a third full investigation. As *Science* magazine observed, "Until the storm over MACOS broke NSF had not experienced serious difficulties in two decades of experience with its curriculum improvement projects."[32] But once the storm broke it was intense.

The mystery, of course, is how MACOS, whose pedagogical orientations reflect a loosely bounded culture so faithfully, could have fallen victim to such criticisms at all. If the course so well suited the culture, to what could its detractors possibly object? The answer, I believe, is that those who opposed MACOS spoke for enclaves of tight boundedness in the dominant loose boundedness of American culture. As dissenters from the prevailing creed, they felt with particular sensitivity the vulnerability of the individual in loosely bounded cultures. They found in MACOS symbols of much else that they feared about loose boundedness. However, although they were themselves products of tight boundedness, their own protest suffered from having to be couched in the language of the dominant code. To put it differently, the opponents of MACOS were themselves contaminated by the loose boundedness they abhorred. As a result, paradoxically enough, they insisted on playing up those few aspects of MACOS that were tightly bounded, and confusedly portrayed themselves as defenders of loose boundedness. In so doing, they not only strained logic, but also undercut their own position. Indeed, the entire episode illustrates how effectively a dominant loose boundedness disarms people whose real values would support a more tightly bounded culture. And thus what might have been a useful confrontation between loose and tight boundedness became instead a confused babble of voices.

The Procedural Attack

As we have seen, attempts by the state to directly impose culture in America are inconsistent with our liberal political tradition. Therefore, when government *does* attempt to shape culture it must move indirectly and circuitously. For example, NSF felt that it could not itself develop and disseminate MACOS, for curriculum development in America must remain a private not a public function. Instead, NSF provided grants that supported private development of MACOS. In addition, NSF financed workshops in the teaching of MACOS, and by reducing its normal share of royalties, NSF also attempted to make MACOS financially competitive with curricula available elsewhere in the private market.

Still, despite all its efforts to avoid direct cultural intervention, NSF laid itself open to charges that it had violated the norms of loose boundedness. Essentially, seven arguments emerged to condemn the development and marketing of MACOS as being procedurally incongruent with a loosely bounded culture.

The first procedural issue on which MACOS came under attack involved congressional oversight. As Congressman Ketchum lamented when supporting Conlan in the House debate, "We do not have an opportunity to know what is going on in all the research areas . . . because they are carefully hidden in appropriation and authorization bills which we pass every day on the floor of this House."[33] Ketchum's cry of dismay evokes the image of a tightly bounded world in which proposals for curriculum support escape the light of day in the House of Representatives because "hidden," tightly bounded processes at NSF somehow keep the Congress from pursuing its legitimate function of oversight. And so, while Congress appears as the representative of loose boundedness, NSF is cast in the negative role of tight boundedness.

Ketchum's misgivings about the process of authorizing curriculum development dovetailed nicely with similar anxieties about specific NSF decisions on funding. Here the attack focused on the usual NSF practice of anonymous peer review of curriculum proposals. According to its detractors, anonymous peer review shielded proposals from public scrutiny, and was therefore unjustifiable from the standpoint of the public interest. In addition, anonymous peer reviews virtually invited prejudicial decisions. What Conlan had in mind became clear when he charged that "NSF has given millions to a small group of closely related individuals."[34] As Conlan saw it, peer review was a closed, tightly bounded process by which a small number of educators, all of whom knew each other well, contrived to feather each other's nests. The irony is that Conlan attacked a process that NSF intended to be *open*, not closed. From NSF's standpoint, peer review respects anonymity only for the purpose of encouraging reviewers to speak freely and frankly about proposals. Thus, the purpose of anonymity is an open exchange of ideas where constraints of friendship or reputation do not bias assessments.

At the same time, however, peer review does possess some tightly bounded features. It does single out and empower a small body of "experts" who are unaccountable to the public. It thus removes the public from an important area of educational policy. Conlan could therefore legitimately seize on the tightly bounded elements of peer review and ignore peer review's loosely bounded qualities. The result of his attack was to delegitimize NSF's actions.

As one might expect, given these comments, the most potent procedural objection to MACOS revolved around congressional fears of "elitism" in education. Peter Dow claims that a signal victory of MACOS was its luring of respected academics into precollege curriculum development. Until the 1950s academicians had scrupulously avoided precollege education; now, however, they hastened to incorporate their most recent findings into new elementary and secondary curricula. MACOS became a primary vehicle for their efforts. Dow himself characterizes as "elitist" the movements to reform science education which MACOS spearheaded.[35] Now "elitism" is perhaps an innocent enough term if we use it, as Dow obviously did, with the intention of describing the high quality of ideas in MACOS. But it loses its innocence quickly when it is used to describe a process whereby a small group of "scientists" "takes over" curriculum development from "the people." As Nelkin puts it, "The protests ... reflect the fact that many people are afraid that the structured, meritocratic processes operating within science threaten more egalitarian, pluralist values."[36] Thus, the much heralded importation of a university elite into curriculum development appeared to many people to be a strategy for excluding the "people" with their "diverse values" from the educational process. Or as Conlan put it, "This is the new world society [*sic*] envisioned by an elite group of scholars."[37] In short, MACOS apparently proposed that a tightly bounded coherent culture governed by a tightly bounded elite should replace the loosely bounded "diversity" of an egalitarian democracy.

The opponents of MACOS proposed a loosely bounded cure for "elitism" in the form of "public participation" in the curriculum design process. As we might expect, the absence of any provision for such participation became an additional ground on which MACOS came under attack, for, as Nelkin observes, "Textbook disputes are organized around demands for the increased participation of laymen in decisions about the school curriculum."[38] Again the irony is rich. While its opponents charged that the development of MACOS avoided public participation, its defenders protested that MACOS would teach the child skills that would later contribute to enhanced adult participation in politics. As is usual in a loosely bounded culture, everybody agrees about general, vaguely defined goals, but there remain vast, but predictably obscure, disagreements about the concrete meaning of goals and about the relationship of goals to practice.

Although lay persons played no role in the MACOS development process, they might have exerted some power had the developers at least bothered to assess curricular "needs." But, charged opponents, no one in the process took the trouble to inquire into the need for a new curriculum. For this reason the House subcommittee's investigating team recommended that

NSF set up a "needs assessment program" in order to discover what, if any, curriculum needs actually existed in the social studies area. No longer were developers and scholars to "invent" public needs.[39] Undeterred by the patent unmanageability of the task (a fact NSF admitted),[40] NSF's own report on MACOS solemnly stated that "a needs assessment program should be initiated to develop and establish priorities for curriculum development."[41] In a loosely bounded culture, "need" is a crucial symbol of legitimacy. Therefore, to ignore need is to ignore or impugn loose boundedness.

The financial arrangements among NSF, EDC, and the producer of MACOS, Curriculum Development Associates, also came under attack for being tightly bounded. This time opponents were able to mobilize another potent symbol of loose boundedness: free market competition. Conlan charged in the House debate that "NSF permitted only a 3 percent royalty return to the Government: one-fifth the customary amount—and has in turn received from EDC at last report less than 10 percent of that greatly discounted royalty."[42] George Weber, another critic of MACOS, put his finger on the heart of the issue when he remarked derisively that reduced federal royalties would never have been required in the first place if MACOS had been a good curriculum; market forces could be relied on to disseminate good educational materials. Therefore, MACOS must be defective.[43]

The financial provisions for distributing MACOS are technically complex, but NSF did undeniably subsidize the distribution of MACOS. Federal underwriting could be portrayed as "closing" or "bounding" the market, an illegitimate act from a cultural standpoint. As Congressman Annunzio put it, "The NSF . . . stepped beyond its authority and the authority of the Government when it presumed to influence the free market mechanism which underpins the economy of our Nation."[44] In a loosely bounded culture, stepping "beyond . . . authority" is often encouraged, for authority itself is always culturally suspect. However, when the result is tight market boundaries, government has clearly violated its cultural mandate.

The vulnerability of NSF on the issue of finance proceeded directly from the ambiguous role loose boundedness imposed. In *Science*'s words:

> NSF officials did recognize that they were intervening in the marketplace and tried to develop procedures which were fair and satisfactory to commercial publishers. At the same time, pressure was applied by Congress on NSF to make sure that the extensive and innovative programs did not stay on the shelf. As a consequence, NSF has spent considerable amounts of money on "implementation" programs, designed to provide information and teacher training course materials without crossing the line into subsidizing the adoption of federally sponsored courses. [45]

Thus, loose boundedness forced NSF to enter the curriculum development business through the back door. At most, the government could assist in the development of new curricula; but it could not be seen to impose curricula, for such an imposition would amount to the construction of a more tightly bounded culture. The result of this dilemma was an awkward financial structure vulnerable to attack on the grounds Conlan and his supporters discovered.

The Substantive Attack on MACOS

If the procedure under which MACOS was developed and implemented left it open to arguments that it had violated the norms of a loosely bounded culture, surely the same charge could not be made about the substance of the curriculum. After all, didn't MACOS fall into the long tradition of scientific neutrality and rational planning that had become part of American education, beginning with Franklin Bobbitt and his Tayloresque conceptions of curricula? [46] MACOS was "value-free"; it saw cultures as relative and "functional"; it proclaimed continuity between Eskimos and modern Americans; it saw people as people no matter where they lived. All these conceptions fit comfortably within the confines of a loosely bounded culture, for they imply that everyone should be treated equally, fairly, and individually. What could be more in line with American values?

Surprisingly enough, however, the content of MACOS did come under attack, and precisely for its loosely bounded substance. How can we explain this fact? After all, we have argued that it is tight boundedness that disqualifies ideas in America, not loose boundedness. Still, consider Conlan's charge:

> They are planning to study a subculture group with only 30 or 40 people in it. That is a culture that is so low that even the other Eskimos do not want to associate with this clan.
>
> Yet this is lauded here as a type of cultural pattern for our children to study.
>
> One of the previous speakers said that this is part of the American society and part of our civilization. If we push these materials, we are undermining the family and traditional Judaic-Christian society values.[47]

What could be more tightly bounded than this argument? To Conlan, Eskimos are qualitatively different from Americans, and some Eskimos are clearly better than others. The Netsiliks were "lower"; they engage in revolting, "un-American" practices, such as senilicide and infanticide, which separate them irreparably from Judaeo-Christian values. Furthermore, as if to emphasize the tightly bounded nature of his attack, Conlan asserted that MACOS would undermine the child's traditional religious heritage. On all these counts Conlan appears to reject MACOS because it is incompatible with a *tightly* bounded conception of American culture.

Conlan and the opponents of MACOS were, therefore, defectors from loose boundedness. They preferred that the United States be culturally coherent, respectful of well-defined values, and protective of traditional institutions. But in a dominantly loosely bounded culture even defectors from loose boundedness cannot advance a fully consistent tightly bounded argument, for loose boundedness obscures the sharp distinctions tight boundedness requires. Thus, even in the midst of a tightly bounded argument, Conlan hints at a loosely bounded alternative to MACOS. He envisages close, warm, loving, trusting relationships between parents and children, relationships that practices such as senilicide and infanticide would obviously destroy. Even Conlan, therefore, does not entirely object to loose boundedness; he objects only to the way in which MACOS construes the dominant cultural pattern.

A more important question is how Conlan could have interpreted MACOS as an "attack" on the family and on Judaeo-Christian values. Why did he reject the protestations of value neutrality which proponents of the curriculum advanced? The answer is that Conlan, along with a great many Americans, refuses to distinguish between social "facts" and social "values." Its detractors believed MACOS to be a "religion of secular humanism," which surreptitiously inculcates values under the cover of "science." By rejecting the fact-value distinction, opponents could paint MACOS as *advocating* particular values. This intellectual task completed, the anti-MACOS forces could legitimately resist on the usual, loosely bounded grounds of individual freedom in value choice. And the defenders of MACOS found themselves playing the same cultural game. Thus, Congressman Kreuger, in defending MACOS on the House floor, stated, "Although the values of this particular program . . . may not be mine—and they are not—they are nonetheless values which have the right to be heard."[48] But the damage had already been done. By appearing to metamorphose "science" into "values," MACOS became culturally obnoxious.

In loosely bounded cultures the distinction between facts and values is not strong enough to support a curriculum such as MACOS. But movement may take place in either direction across the fuzzy divide between facts and values. For example, another method of attacking MACOS was to dispute its claim to scientific truth. The trick was accomplished when opponents of MACOS insisted on treating religious fundamentalism—a value-position—as if it were a serious scientific competitor to the evolutionary thrust of the course. Such a position demands that "evolution" and "creationism" be treated as equally plausible scientific hypotheses. In this case, values are made to appear as factual assertions, instead of factual assertions being made to appear as values. Clearly, of the two disqualifying strategies we have examined, this latter is superior from the perspective of loose boundedness. After all, treating science as if it were a religion runs the risk of open value conflict, whereas assimilating religion to science seemingly invites "open," "rational" discussion, compromise, and the possible reconciliation of disjunct views. Not surprisingly, this is the strategy creationists have recently adopted in their attacks on the biology curriculum.

Ultimately, the confusion among both MACOS supporters and MACOS opponents about the line between religion and science became itself an additional source of controversy. And because in a loosely bounded culture real controversy is always a danger and never an opportunity—threatening to pit individual against individual, group against group—even a misleading controversy counts against a curriculum. As William Lowe Boyd notes, any disagreement immediately frightens American educators away from curriculum innovation;[49] ironically, the mere existence of controversy becomes a negative judgment on a curriculum, rather than a useful means of establishing the curriculum's value.

And once more the spectre of elitism emerged. The charge of elitism was applied to the content of MACOS in two basic respects. First, critics like George Weber charged that the apparently egalitarian pedagogy of MACOS was a fraud. According to Weber, "There is an air of indoctrination about the course."[50] Contrary to the claims of its defenders, MACOS did not really encourage children to think for themselves. Instead, teachers mechanically repeated pat answers to any question a child might raise. To Weber the appearance of openness only camouflaged the process of indoctrination into the "value" of "cultural relativism."

Other critics argued that the abstract reasoning skills of social science exceeded the grasp of MACOS students. Most fifth-graders could not really think like social scientists. Inevitably, therefore, only a few students would perform really well, and as a result, MACOS would create an elite among students early in the educational cycle. The metaphor of separation once more raised its ugly head. Not only did MACOS divide educators from society, and teachers from students, but it also set student against student. Worse yet, today's elite of MACOS students might become tomorrow's elite of professional educational reformers, thereby perpetuating damaging divisions within the loosely bounded culture.

The revulsion that attackers of MACOS displayed about the possible resemblance between young Americans and "uncivilized" Eskimos suggests how unsettling loose boundedness can occasionally be. To its tightly bounded opponents, MACOS symbolized in an extreme form the painfully vulnerable status of all people in loosely bounded cultures. Luckily, the tenderness of their age makes it legitimate to protect children even in a loosely bounded culture; indeed, it becomes absolutely vital to protect *children*, precisely because it is so difficult for *adults* to legitimately protect themselves. Ultimately, however, this process is self-defeating, for it helps preserve loose boundedness as the dominant American cultural form. The problem is that successful protection works against a rational reconsideration of loose boundedness in its entirety. Again we see how subtly loosely bounded cultures undercut arguments in favor of tight boundedness. Eventually, many of those who feel themselves particularly victimized by loose boundedness come to believe that what is in fact a general cultural condition is only their own personal "neurosis," or a conspiracy among a small group of "elitists," or an isolated flaw in an otherwise effective cultural fabric.

In summary: MACOS fell victim to an attack launched by defenders of tightly bounded enclaves in a predominantly loosely bounded culture. Rather than speaking forthrightly as advocates of tight boundedness, however, the opponents of MACOS attacked those few elements of the course that were tightly bounded, and obscured discussion of the value relativism and egalitarianism which they found most objectionable. The opponents of MACOS portrayed themselves, rather than MACOS, as defenders of loose boundedness, a position quite at variance with their respect for the family, the nation, and the child. They therefore deprived themselves (and the country) of a useful debate between two visions of culture. And, as a result, no serious challenge to loose boundedness emerged. Rather than being forced to advance any well-defined position of its own, the state simply abandoned its efforts to shape the culture of education.

THE FAMILY HOUR FEUD

The vulnerability of the individual in a loosely bounded culture became an issue more directly in the controversy over television's "family hour." In the case of MACOS the child's vulnerability was used as a means of preventing the government from helping to transmit a loosely bounded social studies course to students. By contrast, in the family hour case, interest groups in the public actually demanded that government institute a tightly bounded cultural code to protect young viewers against "harmful" television programming by networks and their affiliates. Here government was finally able to exercise its interest directly in creating a more cohesive culture. With MACOS government could only promote a curriculum that exaggerated the dominant cultural code. But in the case of the family hour, government—with widespread public support—finally moved positively to assert an alternative, tightly bounded code to the dominant loose boundedness of television.

Two observations should be made at the outset. First, in a loosely bounded culture, government's efforts to influence culture cannot be consistent. Sometimes (as with MACOS) government conforms to a loosely bounded code, sometimes (as with the family hour) it proposes a tightly bounded code. Loose boundedness assures that government as a cultural "center" will vacillate, for government lacks the powerful arguments that tight boundedness alone can provide. Thus, the governmental "center" does not hold. Second, despite their differences in intent, both of these efforts failed. The inescapable conclusion, therefore, is that in a loosely bounded culture the state rarely succeeds in structuring any consistent cultural code, even when—as in the case of the family hour—it can claim to be responding positively to widespread public feelings.

The beginnings of the family hour may be traced to 1972, when the Surgeon General's Report on Television and Social

Behavior appeared. The Report climaxed a long period of debate about the possible "antisocial" effects of sustained television viewing among children. Although the Report addressed a wide range of topics, public attention focused on several studies that reported a modest statistical association between a young child's sustained viewing of televised aggression and the aggressive behavior of the same child some years later.[51] The Report stimulated increased congressional pressure on the networks and on the Federal Communications Commission (FCC) to "do something" about "inappropriate" television programming for the young. "Inappropriate" was generally interpreted to mean programs that depicted sex and violence.

Following a series of congressional hearings on these issues, the House Appropriations Committee ordered the FCC "to submit a report to the committee by December 31, 1974, outlining the specific positive actions taken or planned by the commission to protect children from excessive violence and obscenity."[52] The vagueness of this charge to the commission is entirely understandable, since the commission possesses no legal jurisdiction whatever over the content of television programs. All parties to the controversy agreed that any such jurisdiction would violate the First Amendment's guarantee of free speech. Indeed, commission members have always bent over backwards in this area, stubbornly refusing, for example, to consider program content in license renewal hearings before the commission.

Nevertheless, faced with an apparent ultimatum from Congress, the commission reluctantly acted. It conveyed the impression informally both to the networks and to the National Association of Broadcasters (NAB) that "something had to be done." The FCC chairman, Richard Wiley, then embarked on a course of "jawboning" in an effort to get the networks to voluntarily adopt a policy of "self-regulation" that would reduce televised sex and violence without forcing any specific action by the commission.[53] Wiley's campaign included speeches to network executives, private sessions with the head of each of the three networks, and discussions with the NAB. These efforts bore fruit on April 10, 1975, when the NAB announced a new policy of "family viewing" for its member stations. Briefly stated, the policy set aside the first hour of prime-time evening programming as well as the immediately preceding hour for programming appropriate "for viewing by a general family audience." The new policy went into effect on all three networks in September 1975.

It did not take long for challenges to the new policy to emerge. The Writers Guild of America, which represents television writers and directors, brought suit against all three networks as well as the FCC. The guild contended that the family hour violated the First Amendment to the Constitution, the U.S. Administrative Procedure Act, and section 326 of the Federal Communications Code. The guild won its case in California and was sustained on appeal. Subsequently, the networks—though no longer acting under the family hour formula—continued to monitor violence and obscenity in early evening programs; in essence, however, this renewed "vigilance" merely reinstated the standard process of program screening which the networks had practiced before the family hour. But the government itself—through the FCC—was effectively restrained from any effort to impose standards on television programming. The government had moved—however tentatively—and it had lost.

The Family Hour as a Tightly Bounded Code

The family hour policy was an attempt by government to impose a tightly bounded cultural code on television. Indeed, the term "family hour" itself connotes such a code, for it implies that a conflict existed between the family unit and television programming prior to the family hour. Simply put, before the family hour existed, television programming could be conceived of as first penetrating and then fragmenting the family unit. Erecting a "cordon sanitaire" between the family and television was thus an attempt to prevent the alienation of the old from the young in the family. The family hour reflected a desire to unite the family as a cohesive unit vis à vis television, rather than to permit television unlimited and divisive access to youthful family members.

In fact, however, this conceptual division between the family unit and television programming is itself built on a tightly bounded conception of family structure, in which the division between old and young is absolute. Proponents of the family hour wanted television to treat children and adults differently. Children ought not to see all that adult viewers can see. The family hour concept is diametrically opposed to the assumptions of MACOS about children. Unlike MACOS, the family hour assumes that children cannot understand in a mature fashion such emotionally charged issues as sex and violence. The child is vulnerable to televised depictions of these issues, and therefore deserves protection.

Thus, the family hour concept is doubly tightly bounded: it assumes opposition between the family unit as a whole and much television entertainment, and it assumes a distinction between the capacities of younger and older family members. In addition, the family hour attempted to isolate particular hours of television entertainment from other hours, thereby reducing the homogeneous-flow qualities of the medium. Indeed, if Thomas Meehan is correct in his argument that the family hour allowed the networks to justify the programming of *increased* sex and violence in non-family-hour periods, then the distinction between programs during the family hour and other programs becomes particularly obvious.[54] In fact, research conducted during the first season of the family hour sustains Meehan's argument.[55] Thus, the family hour did divide television programming from within.

But what contributed most to the tightly bounded qualities of the family-hour concept is the nature of the television content—sex and violence—which the policy attempted to regulate. Sex and violence are types of intimate conduct; both render participants vulnerable to each other. Sexual relationships expose people deeply to each other, and in the puritanical vernacular of Western Christianity, sex outside of marriage "despoils" participants and encourages "promiscuity." These are all metaphors of loose boundedness. And violence renders passive those who suffer, thus exposing the sufferer to greater victimization in the future. Sex and violence, therefore, both breach the boundaries of personal space, and each in its own way can thus be said to "weaken the will." Finally, the person who initiates and enacts violence has "lost control" of himself. Sex and violence therefore touch particularly sensitive nerves in a loosely bounded culture, for they exploit the vulnerability of the individual in such a culture. Adults may be able to "handle" sex and violence (i.e., they may not be contaminated by it), but children cannot.

The family hour concept also assumes that the daily cycle of the child's life is neatly segmented into specialized time periods. Thus, children are presumed to go to bed immediately after the family hour, though not before, just as they are assumed to be in school during certain hours. These beliefs are based on the unspoken premise that parents and schools control children's lives, and that children abide by a tightly bounded time code. In fact, however, this view is quite at odds with another aspect of our folklore about children, namely, that children "have all the time in the world." The family hour concept thus assumes that parents can prevent their children from acting out their "natural" inclination to use time as if it were infinite and unbounded. In short, the family hour assumes that parents control their children by programming the child's use of time.

Two additional aspects of the family hour bespeak its tightly bounded quality. It is perhaps significant that only a specific deadline forced the FCC to move on the family hour concept. And, just as Congress imposed a tightly bounded requirement on the FCC, so also did the FCC use the family hour to prescribe a tightly bounded code to the networks, children, and their parents. Can it be true that only a definite set of time expectations embodied in "deadlines" can get a tightly bounded cultural code under way in a predominantly loosely bounded culture? Perhaps deadlines stimulate a kind of cultural chain reaction among cultural agents. "Tightening up" a society's cultural code may therefore be a dynamic, sequential process, in which the model of tight boundedness assumes multiple forms.

Certainly the image of tight boundedness suffused the language of those who debated the family hour. For example, in one congressional hearing Allan Burns, an articulate television writer deeply opposed to the family hour, complained to Congressman Henry Waxman of having been informed by network executives that the standard of acceptable television fare henceforth would be that which would appeal to "the most uptight parent." The colloquy between Waxman and Burns consisted of a potent mixture of tightly bounded personal standards ("of the uptight parent") and tightly bounded cultural standards (a judgment about what Burns himself dubs the "product," i.e., television programs):

> Waxman: And you mentioned the standard that you cannot offend the most uptight parent.
>
> Burns: Yes; that was one thing that was thrown out. It is hard to forget that once you have heard it.
>
> Waxman: Did they hire uptight parents to act as consultants, to advise them of the standards?
>
> Burns: I don't know where they had them; I mean, if they had a roomful of uptight parents and they would show them the product and see if they pushed buttons, that would be one way of telling, I suppose.[56]

"Uptight parents," a "hard" set of standards applied by such parents, and the terminology of "production"—this terminology creates a tightly bounded language for the family hour, shared by proponents and opponents alike.

The Attack on the Family Hour

The family hour, like MACOS, fell victim to procedural attacks. The policy-making process which led to the family hour could easily be portrayed as tightly bounded and therefore at odds with the loosely bounded culture of American politics.

To begin with, the Writers Guild depicted the family hour as a misguided action undertaken by the networks only because of government compulsion. The family hour therefore violated the norm of voluntarism in the culture. The court agreed. In his decision Judge Ferguson wrote, "The plaintiffs have evidenced a successful attempt by the FCC to pressure the networks and the NAB into adopting a programming policy they did not wish to adopt."[57] In a loosely bounded culture ideas and images should emerge from the voluntary actions of free individuals or groups, in this case from the networks and their affiliates. Voluntarism assures that information will flow freely across cultural boundaries, back and forth between audience and culture creator. By contrast, "coercion" not only restricts the flow of information but also draws the networks, the NAB, and the FCC together into a tightly bounded conspiracy to control culture.

The point at issue regarding the question of compulsion was the legal status of FCC chairman Wiley's actions. As we have observed, the FCC possesses no legal right to control programming, for such a right could well lead to a tightly bounded, sharply demarcated cultural system in television presentations. Not surprisingly, therefore, Wiley attempted to portray his policy-making role as the actions of a private citizen, not as the actions of an FCC chief operating under his agency's mandate. Wiley and the networks characterized Wiley's role as "jawboning," a term that suggests intense, intimate, voluntary dialogue among interested and more or less equal parties. This characterization represented Wiley's attempt to locate a middle ground between FCC inaction, on the one hand, and unconstitutional FCC action, on the other.[58]

Jawboning thus straddles the boundary between compulsion, which is tightly bounded, and freedom, which is loosely bounded. It can be thought of as a sort of mythic resolution of the tension Wiley felt. But it was not a mythic resolution the court was prepared to accept. Equally mythical both in form and aspiration was the network's defense of its actions as "voluntary self-regulation"[59]—a logically dubious concept which ignores the question of whether self-regulation can really be voluntary. After all, there must be a *reason* to engage in "voluntary" regulation in the first place, and such a reason can hardly be assumed to issue entirely from the self as opposed to the pressure of others. Like jawboning, the concept of voluntary self-regulation attempts to honor the cultural norm of loose boundedness, even as it masks an underlying tightly bounded reality.

As a general rule, a loosely bounded culture favors the informal actions of "jawboners" like Wiley over the tightly bounded, authoritative decrees of administrative agencies and legislatures. Unfortunately, however, informal actions do not always guarantee access and participation to all interested and affected parties, and access and participation are also components of a loosely bounded culture. On this ground the family hour, like MACOS, was open to criticism. In particular, television writers and directors complained of being excluded from the discussions that led to the family hour. And the court agreed, stating, "If government intervenes . . . it shall do so not in closed-door negotiating sessions but in conformity with legislatively mandated administrative procedures."[60] The court thus argued that standard administrative procedures were necessary to ensure access to all. In a loosely bounded culture openness is even more important than informality, and when the latter prevents the former, the latter must give way. Or, in the angry words of an irate Hollywood producer, "What we are saying is, it is wrong to be legislated. It was wrong to be told. It is wrong not to be consulted. It is wrong not to seek our input. It is wrong to say, here it is, do it."[61]

If the policy-making process that created the family hour could be disqualified as incompatible with a loosely bounded culture, similar arguments could be leveled at the family hour itself, even though at the time the family hour was adopted large majorities of Americans objected to the amount of violence on television.[62] Still, two aspects of the family hour disqualified it culturally. The less important of the two involves the "boundability" of the family hour's key terms. For example, the family hour time-slot clearly did not succeed in demarcating children's television viewing from that of adults. According to congressional testimony in 1976, more than twenty million children viewed television after the family hour;[63] these twenty million were therefore consistent viewers of sex and violence.

In a loosely bounded culture, time cannot accurately demarcate the private realm of individual consumption, although it does effectively demarcate the public realm of production.

More important, the obnoxious targets of the policy—"sex" and "violence"—continue to defy definition. Courts and legislatures have argued for a long time about the meaning of these terms, and about whether sex and violence are so influenced by situational and personality factors as to yield no firm definition at all. Indeed, as one insightful witness in the 1976 committee hearings observed, sex on television is mostly talk about something that is not actually seen.[64] Therefore, to try to restrict sex on television to some tightly bounded formula is actually to engage in the practice of censorship.

This observation points us toward the primary disqualification of the family hour: the issue of censorship. Once it had satisfied itself that the FCC, acting through Chairman Wiley, had exceeded its authority, it was inevitable that the court would construe the family hour as a form of censorship. In our terms, censorship may be understood as government's illegitimate imposition of a tightly bounded cultural code on a loosely bounded cultural context. The court did, however, reserve the right of the networks or their affiliates to adopt a family hour policy for themselves, for in this way they would conform to requirements of loose boundedness. But so great is government's power and so questionable is its cultural role that for it to proceed on its own to produce and implement a cultural innovation is for it to behave unacceptably. Government must never bound the realm of cultural discourse.

LIBERAL DEMOCRACY AND AMERICAN CULTURE

Michael Margolis writes, "The values of liberal democracy, whether justified by social contract or social utility, nonetheless placed the welfare of the individual citizen over and above that of the community."[65] Margolis's observation suggests another, namely, that because the individual is more important than the community, the individual must be more important than any entity—including government—that purports to speak for the community. And if this remains so, it will be impossible for the American polity ever to serve as a cultural center.

Most readers, when asked to choose between democracy in its American version, on the one hand, and a more coherent, tightly bounded, government-supported American culture, on the other, would choose our current version of democracy, despite the cultural costs to which loose boundedness gives rise. Yet it is important to address an additional question before this choice can reasonably be made: When Margolis speaks of the "individual citizen" or the "self," which loose boundedness and liberalism both encourage us to affirm, what precisely does he mean? What does it mean to be loyal to the self?

The answer to this question would be obvious were it not for the fact that loose boundedness so wholly confuses us. The self is a social creation. People define themselves in considerable part by the social identifications their society and their personal history make available to them. Our "selves" are complicated, idiosyncratic amalgams of collective identifications, such as sex, social class, religion, race, and ethnicity. The question, therefore, is whether these collective identifications are legitimate bases for political action in America. The answer is that our particular interpretation of liberalism has eroded the group bases of personal identification, and as a result, an impossibility — "abstract individualism" — rules the American political world.

The most important result of this situation is a decline in the citizen's power over government, an important limitation on American democracy. After all, if the individual is to be truly served by government, he must be in a position to know what he wants, and it is his group identifications which help tell him what he wants. But in the United States it is culturally suspect to behave as a loyal member of, say, a social class. There is always the danger that class conflict will emerge from such identifications, and class conflict is incompatible with American democracy. Remember how class conflict destroyed democracy in Europe during the 1930s. So the combination of an absent socialist party, a modest welfare state, and a myth of ready social mobility delegitimizes class consciousness as a basis for self-definition in America.

If we ought not to employ class to define ourselves politically, what about religion? Surely we can act politically as Protestants, Catholics, or Jews. Not so, however, for the separation of church and state restrains Americans from using religion to define the political self. Our political system is heir to the wisdom of the Enlightenment; we know that we must avoid the potent mixture of politics and religion that fueled centuries of bloody warfare in Europe. So, it is wrong to behave politically as Protestant, Catholic, or Jew, and when we do so act—as we sometimes do—we cannot help feeling a bit uneasy.[66]

As to race, our history is equally persuasive. The Civil War was an object lesson in the calamities of racial politics. Of course, the Civil War, though shaped by the dilemma of black slavery, was not something blacks themselves actively shaped. Blacks were acted upon by both North and South; they were not themselves major actors. In the 1960s blacks did finally become full actors—and cities burned. So, we cannot risk race as an element of the political self.

And so it goes through all the many effective group identifications we might use to define our political selves. All are compromised by the loosely bounded culture, hence few Americans have selves which the polity can readily serve.

Collective identifications are not only sources of individual differences in politics, they are also criteria around which culturally coherent dichotomies might develop. Yet loose boundedness prevents these dichotomies from playing their full cultural role. However, there is a strictly political dichotomy which, if it were developed, might also make the culture more coherent for people. This is the elite-mass dichotomy that the Founding Fathers themselves envisaged as central to our system of politics. As Barry Holden puts it:

An important aspect of the idea of liberal democracy is that of a dichotomy between the government and the governed. In contradiction of the ideas of democracy based on Rousseau's thought, the government is often not really seen as an integral part of the community. . . . Rather, the people are seen as acted upon by a body which is, in an important sense, separate from them, i.e., the government.[67]

But this potential dichotomy no more successfully structures American culture than do the other potential dichotomies we have examined. Instead, modern democratic theory in the form of the elitist theory of democracy has delegitimized this dichotomy. The elitist theory considers mass distrust of government antidemocratic, rather than seeing such distrust as a predictable and healthy sign of democracy in action.[68] No matter that, as Vivien Hart puts it, "Generally, the behavior linked with distrust has been well within the bounds of democratic modes of action. . . . Observers have been right to see the distrustful as a threat to the dominant power-holders in society, but wrong to see them as a threat to the political values of the system."[69] The elitist theory of democracy fears sudden gusts of mass discontent because it cannot distinguish between sharply contrasting perspectives, on the one hand, and deadly conflicts, on the other. To the extent that it is accepted, therefore, the elitist theory of democracy delegitimizes any dichotomy between the government and the governed as a foundation for the restructuring of culture and politics in America.

Thus, over time, loose boundedness has stripped Americans of many lines of connection to a cohesive political community and to a cohesive culture. Particularly striking is the fact that this process has occurred at the very time when government has assumed a major economic role. The cultural and moral role of the state has not begun to keep pace with the state's economic ascent. By contrast, consider the early modern period, during which the state was wholly absent from the economic lives of most people; yet, buttressed by the divine right of kings and the Catholic church, the moral and cultural role of the state greatly exceeded that of the state in our own time.

The costs of this gradual delegitimization process are paid in the coin of popular attitudes toward politics. Declining rates of electoral participation are but one indirect measure of the costs an illusory individualism entails in politics. People who must rely

mainly on themselves politically because they are no logically embedded in groups find few secure guidelin litical action.[70] Declining rates of political efficacy and measures of the same phenomenon.[71] After all, peopl not identify with groups must stand alone against gove No wonder they are distrustful of government and do themselves; it is far easier for government to manipu lated individuals than cohesive groups. Trusting solely t breeds bewilderment and political impotence.

Today abstract individualism erodes popular power political process. As a result real democracy—which above all "rule of the people"[72]—becomes an impossibil conclusion should come as no surprise, for it has bee shadowed by the cultural arguments we have advance the way. A loosely bounded culture inhibits people fro trolling the finely tuned economic structures in which t their productive private lives. So why shouldn't abstra vidualism—as the political form of loose boundedness the same effect on popular control over public institutio

There are democracies which operate successfully more tightly bounded cultural lines. Lijphart's examples sociational democracy are the most conspicuous cases; Li shows conclusively that democracy can thrive in segmen chotomized cultures, so long as these cultures are protec delicate political mechanisms.[73] However, a consociationa tion is impossible in the United States; indeed, our one the cal attempt at consociationalism—Calhoun's idea of a "cc rent majority"—sank from sight almost as soon as it surfac

If I have accomplished nothing else in this book, I h have suggested that a "politics of abstract individualism" i a fully successful democratic alternative, and that democ theory must reconstitute a theory of group action. In United States we have tried to divorce politics from cul but have only succeeded in blinding ourselves to the inevit connection between the two. It is now time to bring politics culture together in a new form, and to recognize at last tha cannot make something of *ourselves* without first making c mon cause with *each other*.

Notes

CHAPTER ONE

1. See the plethora of definitions in Paul Bohanan, "Rethinking Culture: A Project for Current Anthropologists," *Current Anthropology* 14, no. 4 (October 1973), 357–65.

2. Emile Durkheim, *The Division of Labor in Society,* trans. George Simpson (New York: Free Press, 1964), chap. 5.

3. Anthony Giddens, *Capitalism and Modern Social Theory* (Cambridge: Cambridge University Press, 1971), Part 2.

4. David Reisman, Nathan Glazer, and Ruel Denney, *The Lonely Crowd* (Garden City: Anchor Books, 1950).

5. Daniel Bell, *The Cultural Contradictions of Capitalism* (New York: Basic Books, 1976).

6. Jules Henry, *Culture Against Man* (New York: Random House, 1964).

7. Herbert Marcuse, *Counterrevolution and Revolt* (Boston: Beacon Press, 1972).

8. Christopher Lasch, *The Culture of Narcissism* (New York: Norton, 1978).

9. Perry Miller, *Errand into the Wilderness* (Cambridge, Mass.: Belknap Press, 1956), chaps. 1 and 3.

10. Sacvan Bercovitch, *The Puritan Origins of the American Self* (New Haven: Yale University Press, 1975), 10–11.

11. Miller, *Errand into the Wilderness,* 77.

12. Miller, 143.

13. Miller, 145.

14. Larzer Ziff, *Puritanism in America* (New York: Viking, 1973), 144.

15. Perry Miller, *The New England Mind from Colony to Province* (Cambridge, Mass.: Harvard University Press, 1953), 95–104.

16. See Linda Pritchard, "Religious Change in Nineteenth-Century America," in Charles Y. Glock and Robert N. Bellah, eds., *The New Religious Consciousness* (Berkeley: University of California Press, 1976), 297–331.

17. Rodney Stark and Charles Y. Glock, *American Piety* (Berkeley and Los Angeles: University of California Press, 1968).

18. Daniel Yankelovich, *New Rules: Searching for Self-Fulfilment in a World Turned Upside Down* (New York: Random House, 1981).

19. Bernard Bailyn, *The Ideological Origins of the American Revolution* (Cambridge, Mass.: Belknap Press, 1967), 32–33.

20. Robert N. Bellah, "Civil Religion in America," *Daedalus* 96, no. 1 (Winter 1967), 1–22.

21. Bellah, 18.

22. Rush Welter, *The Mind of America, 1820–1860* (New York: Columbia University Press, 1975).

23. Alexis de Tocqueville, *Democracy in America,* vol. 1, ed. Phillips Bradley (New York: Vintage, 1960), 14.

24. For a critique of the idea of tolerance in this vision, see Robert Paul Wolff, "Beyond Tolerance," in Wolff, Barrington Moore, Jr., and Herbert Marcuse, *A Critique of Pure Tolerance* (Boston: Beacon Press, 1965), 3–53.

25. Talcott Parsons, *Sociological Theory and Modern Society* (New York: Free Press, 1967), chaps. 10 – 11.

26. William Gamson, *Power and Discontent* (Homewood, Ill.: Dorsey, 1968), 42.

27. Gamson, 154 – 55.

28. See the argument in Edward Rosenbaum, *Political Culture* (New York: Praeger, 1975), 53 – 54, 120 – 21, 124 – 25.

29. Geraint Parry, "Trust, Distrust, and Consensus," *British Journal of Political Science* 6 (1976), 129 – 42.

30. Yankelovich, *New Rules*, 95; Paul Abramson and Ada Finifter, "On the Meaning of Political Trust: New Evidence from Items Introduced in 1978," *American Journal of Political Science* 24, no. 2 (May 1981): 297 – 308; Paul Sniderman, *A Question of Loyalty* (Berkeley and Los Angeles: University of California Press, 1981).

31. James Prothro and Charles Grigg, "Fundamental Principles of Democracy: Bases of Argument and Disagreement," *Journal of Politics* 22 (May 1960): 276 – 94. For a recent reconsideration of this same problem, see John Sullivan et al., "The Sources of Political Tolerance: A Multivariate Analysis," *American Political Science Review* 75, no. 1 (March 1981): 92 – 106.

32. For relevant studies, see James C. Davis, "Communism, Conformity, Cohorts, and Categories: American Tolerance in 1954 and 1972 – 3," *American Journal of Sociology* 81, no 3 (November 1975): 491 – 513; Christopher Achen, "Mass Political Attitudes and the Survey Response," *American Political Science Review* 64, no 3 (1975): 1218 – 32; Lawrence J. R. Herson and C. Richard Hofstetter, "Tolerance, Consensus, and the Democratic Creed: A Contextual Explanation," *Journal of Politics* 37, no. 4 (November 1975): 1007 – 33; John Sullivan, James Piereson, and George E. Marcus, "An Alternative Conceptualization of Political Tolerance," *American Political Science Review* 73, no. 3 (September 1979): 781 – 95.

33. V. O. Key, *Public Opinion and American Democracy* (New York: Knopf, 1961).

34. Donald J. Devine, *The Political Culture of the United States* (Boston: Little, Brown, 1972), chap. 5.

35. Michael Mann, "The Social Cohesion of Liberal Democracy," *American Sociological Review* 35 (June 1970): 423 – 40.

36. Devine, *Political Culture*; Mann, "Social Cohesion"; and Donald J. Devine, *The Attentive Public: Polyarchical Democracy* (Chicago: Rand McNally, 1970).

37. See, for example, Paul Allen Beck, "Partisan Dealignment in the Postwar South," *American Political Science Review* 71 (1977): 477 – 96.

38. Jack Dennis, "On Being an Independent Partisan Supporter" (Paper presented at the 1981 Annual Meeting of the Midwest Political Science Association, April 15 – 18, Cincinnati, Ohio), 1.

39. An exception to this argument is the issue of race. See Edward Carmines and James A. Stimson, "Issue Evolution, Population Replacement, and Normal Partisan Change," *American Political Science Review* 75, no. 1 (March 1981): 107 – 19.

40. Arthur Marwick, *Class* (New York: Oxford University Press, 1980), 293.

41. For a relevant argument, see William J. Williams, *The Declining Significance of Race* (Chicago: University of Chicago Press, 1979).

42. See the argument in Ralph Miliband, *The State in Capitalist Society* (London: Quartet Books, 1969).

43. R. W. Connell, *Ruling Class, Ruling Culture* (Cambridge: Cambridge University Press, 1977), chap. 8. See also William R. Morgan, Duane Alwin, and Larry J. Griffith, "Social Origins, Parental Values, and the Transmission of Inequality," *American Journal of Sociology* 85, no. 1 (1979): 156 – 67; Robert A. Rothman, *Inequality and Stratification in the United States* (Englewood Cliffs, N.J.: Prentice-Hall, 1978), 196.

44. See the articles in Basil Bernstein, ed., *Class, Codes, and Control*, vol. 2 (London: Routledge and Kegan Paul, 1973).

45. Compare, for example, David Easton and Jack Dennis, "The Child's Acquisition of Regime Norms: Political Efficacy," *American Political Science Review* 61, no. 1 (March 1967): 25–39, with L. Richard Della Fave, "Success Values: Are They Universal or Class Differentiated?" *American Journal of Sociology* 80, no. 1 (1974): 153–70.

46. For a summary of pertinent research, see David Milmer, *Children and Race* (Harmondsworth, Eng.: Penguin Books, 1975), chap. 3.

47. Donald Searing and Allen Stern, "The Stratification Beliefs of English and American Adolescents," *British Journal of Political Science* (April 1976), 177–203.

48. Paul Abramson, *Generational Change in American Politics* (Lexington, Mass.: Heath, 1975). For a further exchange and critique, see Paul Abramson, "Developing Party Identification: A Further Examination of Life-Cycle, Generational, and Period Effects," *American Journal of Political Science* 23, no. 1 (February 1979): 78–79, with rejoinder by Philip E. Converse, 97–101.

49. Morris Janowitz, *The Last Half-Century: Societal Change and Politics in America,* (Chicago: University of Chicago Press, 1978), 153.

50. Richard F. Hamilton, *Class and Politics in the United States* (New York: Wiley, 1972), chap. 5.

51. Richard Coleman and Lee Rainwater, *Social Standing in America: New Dimensions of Class* (New York: Basic Books, 1978).

52. Sidney Verba and Kay Schlozman, "Unemployment, Class Consciousness, and Radical Politics: What Didn't Happen in the Thirties," *Journal of Politics* 39, no. 2 (May 1977): 291–324.

53. D. Garth Taylor, "Subjective Social Class" (Unpublished paper, National Opinion Research Center, April 1975), 1.

54. For an excellent introduction to false-consciousness theory, see David Miller, "Ideology and the Problem of False Consciousness," *Political Studies* 20, no. 4 (1977): 432–47; see also Herbert Marcuse, *One-Dimensional Man* (Boston: Beacon Press, 1964).

55. John Diggins, "Reification and the Cultural Hegemony of Capitalism: The Perspectives of Marx and Veblen," *Social Research* 44 (Summer 1977) 354–83.

56. See Frank Parkin, *Class Inequality and Political Order* (New York: Praeger, 1971) for an interpretation.

57. Ibid.

58. Benjamin O. Singer, "Mass Media and Communication Processes in the Detroit Riot of 1967," *Public Opinion Quarterly* 34, no. 2 (1970): 236–46.

59. Michael Lewis, *The Culture of Inequality* (Amherst: University of Massachusetts Press, 1978).

60. See Miriam Glucksmann, *Structuralist Analysis in Contemporary Social Thought* (London: Routledge and Kegan Paul, 1974); Philip Petit, *The Concept of Structuralism* (Berkeley and Los Angeles: University of California Press, 1975).

61. Glucksmann, *Structuralist Analysis,* 36.

62. J. R. Rayfield, "The Dualism of Lévi-Strauss," *International Journal of Comparative Sociology* 12 (1971): 267–80.

63. Edmund Leach, *Culture and Communication* (Cambridge: Cambridge University Press, 1976), 35.

64. Ibid.

65. Mary Douglas, *Implicit Meanings: Essays in Anthropology* (London: Routledge and Kegan Paul, 1975), 51.

66. Mary Douglas, *Purity and Danger* (London: Routledge and Kegan Paul, 1966), 35.

67. Leach, *Culture and Communication,* 62.

68. Claude Lévi-Strauss, "The Story of Asdiwal," in Edmund Leach, ed., *The Structural Study of Myth and Totemism* (London: Tavistock, 1967), 1–48; Victor Turner, *The Forest of Symbols* (Ithaca, N.Y.: Cornell University Press, 1967), 25ff.

CHAPTER TWO

1. Emile Durkheim and Marcel Mauss, *Primitive Classification*, trans. and ed. Rodney Needham (Chicago: University of Chicago Press, 1963).

2. Needham, "Introduction" to Durkheim and Mauss, xii.

3. Emile Durkheim, *Professional Ethics and Civic Morals* (London: Routledge and Kegan Paul, 1957), makes much the same argument in terms of property.

4. S. J. Tambiah, "Animals Are Good to Eat and Good to Prohibit," *Ethnology* 8 (1969): 423 – 59.

5. Claude Lévi-Strauss, *Totemism* (Boston: Beacon Press, 1963).

6. Lévi-Strauss, 87 – 88.

7. Victor W. Turner, *The Ritual Process* (London: Routledge and Kegan Paul, 1969), 129.

8. Ibid.

9. Robert Hertz, "The Pre-Eminence of the Right Hand: A Study in Religious Polarity," in Rodney Needham, ed., *Right and Left: Essays on Dual Symbolic Classifications* (Chicago: University of Chicago Press, 1973); for extensions, see J. A. Laponce, "Spatial Archetypes and Political Perceptions," *American Political Science Review* 69 (March 1975): 11–21; J. A. Laponce, *Left and Right: The Topography of Political Perceptions* (Toronto: University of Toronto Press, 1981); and Harold D. Lasswell, *The Signature of Power: Buildings, Communication, and Policy* (New Brunswick, N.J.: Transaction Books, 1979).

10. Needham, ed., *Right and Left.*

11. See, for example, Mircea Eliade, *The Sacred and the Profane*, trans. Willard Trask (New York: Harcourt, Brace and World, 1959).

12. See the findings of nonconvergence in Edward O. Laumann, *Bonds of Pluralism* (New York: Wiley, 1973).

13. Daniel Boorstin, *The Americans: The National Experience* (New York: Vintage, 1967), 95.

14. Note the way American railroad cars broke down divisions between passengers, as if in emulation. Boorstin, 109.

15. For a general theory with primary application to economic development, see Conrad M. Kozak, "Economic Systems, Child Rearing Practices, and Personality Development," *American Journal of Economics and Sociology* 37 (1978): 9 – 25; for an example, see Bennett M. Berger and Bruce M. Hackett, "On the Decline of Age Grading in Rural Hippie Communes," *Journal of Social Issues* 30, no. 2 (1974): 163 – 83.

16. Bernard Bailyn, *Education in the Formation of American Society* (New York: Random House, 1960).

17. For evidence, see Ruby Ray Seward, *The American Family: A Demographic History* (Beverly Hills: Sage, 1978).

18. For an interesting extension, see Godfrey Ellis, Gary Lee, and Larry Petersen, "Supervision and Conformity: A Cross-cultural Analysis of Parental Socialization Patterns," *American Journal of Sociology* 84, no. 2(1978): 386 – 404.

19. Edgar Litt, *Ethnic Politics in America* (Glenview, Ill: Scott, Foresman, 1970), chap. 3.

20. Ibid.

21. See, for an interesting theory of community based on this realization, Melvin M. Webber, "Order in Diversity: Community Without Propinquity," in London Wingo, Jr., ed., *Cities and Space: The Future Use of Urban Land* (Baltimore: Johns Hopkins University Press, 1963), 23 – 57.

22. Jack Goody, *The Domestication of the Savage Mind* (Cambridge: Cambridge University Press, 1977), 37.

23. Goody, 81.

24. For a theory of the presidency based in part on this phenomenon, see James

David Barber, *The Pulse of Politics: Electing Presidents in the Media Age* (New York: Norton, 1980).

25. See, for example, Lee Becker, Marshall McCombs, and Jack McLeod, "The Development of Political Cognitions," in Steven H. Chaffee, ed., *Political Communication* (Beverly Hills: Sage, 1975), 21–65.

26. See Raymond Williams, *Television: Technology and Cultural Form* (New York: Schocken Books, 1975), 86.

27. Goody, *Domestication of the Savage Mind*, 112.

28. Goody, 122–23.

29. Paul Petit, *The Concept of Structuralism* (Berkeley: University of California Press, 1975), 7.

30. For an attempt to link these Wittgensteinian analyses of language to politics, see Hannah Pitkin, *Wittgenstein and Justice* (Berkeley: University of California Press, 1972).

31. Raymond Williams, *Keywords* (London: Macmillan, 1976). For an analysis of the intractability of power to a settled form of political analysis, see Stephen Lukes, *Power: A Radical View* (London: Macmillan, 1974).

32. Harold J. Lasswell, *The Signature of Power*.

33. Thus, for example, we see similar tendencies in the slow decay of role specialization in the family. See, for example, Charles A. Thrall, "Who Does What: Role Stereotypes, Children's Work, and Continuity Between Generations in the Household Division of Labor," *Human Relations* 31, no. 3 (1978): 249–65.

34. Walter C. Kidney, *The Architecture of Choice: Eclecticism in America 1880–1930* (New York: George Braziller, 1974), 2.

35. Ibid.

36. Lewis Mumford, *Sticks and Stones* (New York: Dover, 1955), 60–63.

37. Ibid.

38. For a related observation, see Carl W. Condit, *American Building Art: The Twentieth Century* (New York: Oxford University Press, 1961), 298.

39. Ibid.

40. Condit, *American Building Art*, 300.

41. Lewis Mumford, *The Brown Decades: A Study of the Arts in America, 1865–95* (New York: Dover, 1955), 186–87.

42. Mumford, *Sticks and Stones*, 87.

43. Vincent Scully, Jr., *American Architecture and Urbanism* (New York: Praeger, 1969), 60.

44. Scully, 52.

45. Stephen A. Kurtz, *Wasteland: Building the American Dream* (New York: Praeger, 1973), 22–23.

46. Ibid.

47. Mumford, *Sticks and Stones*, 107–8; Scully, *American Architecture and Urbanism*, 12–13.

48. Mumford, *The Brown Decades*, 64–65 and 75.

49. Mumford, *Sticks and Stones*, 97–98.

50. Robert Venturi, Denise Scott Brown, and Steven Izenour, *Learning from Las Vegas* (Cambridge: MIT Press, 1972).

51. Mumford, *The Brown Decades*, 68.

52. Scully, *American Architecture*, 102–3.

53. Ibid.

54. One might contrast this use of space with the old-fashioned "parlor," which was purely an adult room for entertaining visitors formally, and into which children rarely ventured.

55. Mumford, *Sticks and Stones*, 79.

56. Venturi, Brown, and Izenour, *Learning from Las Vegas*, 44.

57. Kurtz, *Wasteland*, 73.

58. Mumford, *The Brown Decades*, 105.

59. Condit, *American Building Art*, esp. 302.

60. Lewis Mumford, *From the Ground Up* (New York: Harvest Books, 1956), 137.

61. See A. D. Edwards, *Language in Culture and Class* (London: Heinemann, 1976), 13 – 14.

62. Richard Lanham, "The Abuse of Usage," *Virginia Quarterly* 53, no. 1 (Winter 1977): 33 – 57.

63. David Gold, "'Frying Pan' versus 'Frypan': A Trend in English Compounds," *American Speech* 44 (1969): 299 – 302.

64. H. L. Mencken, *The American Language* (New York: Knopf, 1919), 140 – 41.

65. Albert H. Marckwardt, *American English* (New York: Oxford University Press, 1958), 95.

66. Mencken, 204.

67. Mencken, 227.

68. Marckwardt, 82.

69. Mencken, 210.

70. Marckwardt, 14 – 15.

71. Mencken, 19.

72. Mencken, 17.

73. J. L. Dillar, *All American English* (New York: Random House,1975), 79 – 80.

74. Dillar, 72 – 73.

75. Ibid.

76. Marckwardt, *American English*, 111.

77. Mencken, *The American Language*, 119.

78. Marckwardt, 98 – 99.

79. Marckwardt, 111.

80. Dillar, *All American English*, 6 – 7.

81. Mencken, *The American Language*, 172.

82. Alexis de Tocqueville, *Democracy in America*, vol. 2, trans. Phillips Bradley, (New York: Vintage, 1960), 58 – 84. These tendencies are sufficiently dominant that they tend to paint writers who defend proper English as unnecessarily priggish. For a good example, see Arthur Schlesinger, Jr., "Politics and the American Language," *American Scholar* 43 (Fall 1974): 553 – 63.

CHAPTER THREE

1. The standard history is Erik Barnouw, *Tube of Plenty: The Evolution of American Television* (New York: Oxford University Press, 1975).

2. Frank Mankiewicz and Joel Swerdlow, *Remote Control: Television and the Manipulation of American Life* (New York: New York Times Books, 1978), 7.

3. Raymond Williams, *The Long Revolution* (Westport, Conn.: Greenwood, 1975 – first published in 1961), 156 – 73.

4. Dwight MacDonald, "A Theory of Mass Culture," in Bernard Rosenberg and David M. White, eds., *Mass Culture* (Glencoe: Free Press, 1957), 59 – 74.

5. Mankiewicz and Swerdlow, *Remote Control*, 7.

6. Jerry Mander, *Four Arguments for the Elimination of Television* (New York: William Morrow, 1978), 67.

7. Robert Lewis Shayon, *The Crowd-Catcher: Introducing Television* (New York: Saturday Review Press, 1973).

8. For a study of interest-group response to televised violence, see William Melody, *Children's TV* (New Haven: Yale University Press, 1973).

9. For an impressive argument against this position, see Harold Wilensky, "Mass Society and Mass Culture: Interdependence or Independence?" in Gaye Tuchman, ed., *The TV Establishment: Programming for Power and Profit* (Englewood Cliffs, N.J.: Prentice-Hall, 1974), 139–61.

10. Gaye Tuchman, "Introduction," *TV Establishment*, 39.

11. Erik Barnouw, *The Sponsor* (New York: Oxford University Press, 1978); see also A. Frank Reel, *The Networks: How They Stole The Show* (New York: Scribners, 1979).

12. Barnouw, *Tube of Plenty*, 263.

13. Richard Bunce, *Television in the Corporate Interest* (New York: Praeger, 1976), 129.

14. Barnouw, *Tube of Plenty*, 231–33. See also Herbert Schiller, *Communication and Cultural Domination* (White Plains, N.Y.: International Arts and Sciences Press, 1976).

15. Oskar Negt, "Mass Media: Tools of Domination or Instruments of Emancipation? Aspects of the Frankfurt School's Communication Analysis," unpublished.

16. Negt, 24.

17. Reel, *The Networks*, x–xi.

18. T. W. Adorno, "Television and the Patterns of Mass Culture," in Horace Newcomb, ed., *Television: The Critical View* (New York: Oxford University Press, 1976), 239–60.

19. Herbert Marcuse, *One-Dimensional Man* (Boston: Beacon Press, 1969).

20. Barnouw, *The Sponsor*, 70–71; Rose Goldsen, *The Show and Tell Machine* (New York: Dial Press, 1974), 154.

21. Goldsen, 158.

22. Anthony Piepe, Miles Emerson, and Judy Lannon, *Television and the Working Class* (Lexington, Mass.: Lexington Books, 1975).

23. David Sallach, "Class Domination and Ideological Hegemony," in Tuchman, *The TV Establishment*, 161–73.

24. Tuchman, "Introduction," *The TV Establishment*, 28.

25. Ben Stein, *The View from Sunset Boulevard: America As Brought to You by the People Who Make Television* (New York: Basic Books, 1979), 134.

26. Muriel Cantor, *The Hollywood TV Producer: His Work and Audience* (New York: Basic Books, 1971), 171–73.

27. John Ravage, *Television: The Director's Viewpoint* (Boulder, Colo.: Westview Press, 1978), 10.

28. Barnouw's work is most helpful on this evolution.

29. Shayon, *The Crowd-Catcher*, 9 (see n. 7 above).

30. Shayon, 12.

31. For a recent evocative description of the making of a commercial, see Michael Arlen, *Thirty Seconds* (New York: Farrar, Straus & Giroux, 1980).

32. Barnouw, *The Sponsor*, 87.

33. Shayon, *The Crowd-Catcher*, 15.

34. Ravage, *The Director's Viewpoint*.

35. Cantor, *Hollywood TV Producer*, 87.

36. Barnouw, *Tube of Plenty*, 44–45.

37. Tuchman, "Introduction," *TV Establishment*, 35.

38. Stein, *View from Sunset Boulevard*, 87.

39. Jonathan Price, *The Best Thing on TV: Commercials* (New York: Viking, 1978), 61.

40. For a synthesis of relevant research indicating just how large (or small) the gap is, see Sidney Kraus and Dennis Davis, *The Effects of Mass Communication on Political Behavior* (University Park: Pennsylvania State University Press, 1976).

41. Herbert Gans, *Deciding What's News* (New York: Vintage, 1980); Philip Schlesinger, *Putting "Reality" Together: BBC News* (London: Constable, 1978), 106–35.

42. Frank Wolf, *Television Programming for News and Public Affairs: A Quantitative Analysis of Networks and Stations* (New York: Praeger, 1972), 33–34.

43. Robert Prisuta, "The Impact of Media Concentration and Economic Factors on Broadcast Public Interest Programming," *Journal of Broadcasting* 21, no. 3 (Summer 1977): 321–33.

44. Bunce, *Television in the Corporate Interest*, 62 (see n. 13 above).

45. In part, this reflects the conventional wisdom that characters who change in essential ways during a series will thereby lose the audience.

46. Edwin Diamond, *The Tin Kazoo: Television, Politics, and the News* (Cambridge: MIT Press, 1975), 63.

47. Schlesinger, *Putting "Reality" Together*, 83–106.

48. Diamond, 64.

49. For a more elaborate discussion, see Raymond Williams, *Television: Technology and Cultural Form* (New York: Schocken Books, 1975).

50. Price, *The Best Thing on TV*, 1.

51. Mander, *Four Arguments*, 304–5 (see n. 6 above).

52. Horace Newcomb, *TV: The Most Popular Art* (Garden City: Anchor, 1974), 134.

53. Goldsen, *Show and Tell Machine*, 8.

54. Mander, *Four Arguments*, 306–7. See also T. R. Fyvel, "Children of the Television Age," *Encounter* 35, no. 4 (October 1970): 46–53.

55. Mander, 128.

56. Newcomb, *Most Popular Art*, 177.

57. Robert Jay Lifton, *Boundaries: Psychological Man in Evolution* (New York: Vintage, 1970), chap. 4.

58. Williams, *Television*, 86.

59. Diamond, *Tin Kazoo*, 91–101.

60. Diamond, 96.

61. Mankiewicz and Swerdlow, *Remote Control*, 69–70 (see n. 2 above).

62. Herbert Krugman, "The Impact of Television Advertising: Learning Without Involvement," *Public Opinion Quarterly* 29 (1965): 349–56.

63. Goldsen, *Show and Tell Machine*, 37.

64. Martha Wolfenstein and Nathan Leites, *Movies: A Psychological Study* (Glencoe: Free Press, 1950).

65. Goldsen, *Show and Tell Machine*, 101–8.

66. Mariya Kisova, "Value Orientations of the Personality and the Mass Media," *Sotsiologicheski Problemi* 4 (1972), 38–46.

67. John M. Phelan, *Mediaworld: Programming the Public* (New York: Seabury Press, 1977), 40–41.

68. Arthur Asa Berger, *The TV Guided American* (New York: Walker, 1976), 30.

69. This observation fits nicely into Kenneth Burke's theory of the "scene-act" ratio. See Kenneth Burke, *A Grammar of Motives* (New York: Knopf, 1945), 6–7.

70. Stein, *View from Sunset Boulevard*, 127 (see no. 25 above).

71. Michael Arlen, *The View from Highway I* (New York: Farrar, Straus & Giroux, 1978), 39.

72. Arlen, 58.

73. Stein, 127.

74. Arlen, 75.

75. Price, *The Best Thing on TV* (see n. 39 above).

76. Barnouw, *The Sponsor*, 82.

77. Berger, *TV Guided American*, 159. For a different view of the same problem, see Newcomb, *Most Popular Art*, chap. 1 (see n. 52 above).

78. Ibid.

79. Berger, *TV Guided American,* 120.

80. Berger, 52.

81. Berger, 147.

82. Hervé Varenne, *Americans Together: Structured Diversity in a Midwestern Town* (New York: Teachers College Press, 1977).

83. Maxwell McCombs and Donald L. Shaw, "The Agenda-Setting Functions of Mass Media," *Public Opinion Quarterly* 36 (1972): 176 – 87. The agenda-setting hypothesis remains an object of considerable contention, however.

84. Diamond, *Tin Kazoo,* 66 (see n. 46 above). M. Margaret Conway, A. Jay Stevens, and Robert G. Smith, "The Relationship Between Media Use and Children's Civic Awareness," *Journalism Quarterly* 52 (1975): 531 – 38.

85. Mankiewicz and Swerdlow, *Remote Control,* 246 (see n. 2 above).

86. Richard Pride and Barbara Richards, "The Denigration of Political Authority in Television News: the Ecology Issue," *Western Political Quarterly* 28 (1975): 635 – 45.

87. Schlesinger, *Putting "Reality" Together,* 163 – 205; Gans, *Deciding What's News* (see n. 41 above).

88. Diamond, *Tin Kazoo.*

89. Arlen, *View from Highway I,* 34. For a similar view, see Marvin Barrett, "Broadcast Journalism Since Watergate," *Columbia Journalism Review* 14 (1976): 73 – 83.

90. Schlesinger, *Putting "Reality" Together,* chap. 8.

91. Tuchman, "Introduction," *TV Establishment,* 33.

92. Robert S. Frank, *Message Dimensions of Television News* (Lexington, Mass.: Lexington Books, 1973); Don Evarts and Guido H. Stempel, III, "Coverage of the 1972 Campaign by TV, News Magazines, and Major Newspapers," *Journalism Quarterly* 51 (1974): 645 – 49.

93. Frank, *Message Dimensions,* 41.

94. Newcomb, *Most Popular Art,* 16.

95. Barnouw, *Tube of Plenty,* 215, (see n. 1 above).

96. Ronald S. Drabman and Margaret Thomas, "Does Media Violence Increase Children's Toleration of Real-Life Aggression?" *Developmental Psychology* 10 (1974), 418 – 21; Robert P. Snow, "How Children Interpret TV Violence in Play Context," *Journalism Quarterly* 51 (1974): 13 – 22.

CHAPTER FOUR

1. Stewart Ewen, *Captains of Consciousness: Advertising and the Social Roots of the Consumer Culture* (New York: McGraw-Hill, 1976), part I.

2. Mary Douglas and Baron Isherwood, *The World of Goods* (New York: Basic Books, 1979), 115 – 16.

3. Ewen, *Captains of Consciousness.*

4. R. W. Connell, *Ruling Class, Ruling Culture* (Cambridge: Cambridge University Press, 1977), 214.

5. Erving Goffman, *Gender Advertisements* (New York: Harper & Row, 1979).

6. Connell, *Ruling Class,* 213.

7. Ralph Miliband, *The State in Capitalist Society* (London: Quartet Books, 1969), 194 – 95.

8. Robert Freedman, "Try American Capitalism Today," *More* 6, no. 5 (May 1976): 12 – 16.

9. Miliband, *State in Capitalist Society,* 195.

10. Ewen, *Captains of Consciousness,* 18.

11. For a relevant study, see F. T. Marquez, "Advertising Content: Persuasion, Information or Intimidation?" *Journalism Quarterly* 54, no. 3 (Autumn 1977): 482–91.

12. See in particular, Jules Henry, *Culture Against Man* (New York: Random House, 1964), 45–100.

13. For an interestingly balanced view of the issue, see Raymond Bauer and Stephen A. Greyser, "The Dialogue That Never Happens," *Harvard Business Review* (November–December 1967) 2–12.

14. Hans Thorelli, Helmut Becker, and Jack Engledow, *The Information Seekers: An International Study of Consumer Information and Advertising Image* (Cambridge, Mass.: Ballinger, 1975).

15. For an account, see Michael Arlen, *Thirty Seconds* (New York: Farrar, Straus & Giroux, 1980).

16. Joseph Bensman, *Dollars and Sense: Ideology, Ethics, and the Meaning of Work in Profit and Nonprofit Organizations* (New York: Macmillan, 1967), 16.

17. Jeremy Tunstall, *The Advertising Man in London Advertising Agencies* (London: Chapman and Hall, 1964), 32–33.

18. Tunstall, 50.

19. Bensman, *Dollars and Sense,* 17–18. See also Martin Mayer, *Madison Avenue, USA* (New York: Harper & Bros, 1958), 27–31.

20. Bensman, 31.

21. Bensman, 36.

22. Ibid.

23. Mayer, *Madison Avenue, USA.*

24. Mayer, 22–23.

25. Jonathan Price, *The Best Thing on TV: Commercials* (New York: Viking, 1978), 8.

26. Ibid.

27. Price, 91.

28. Ibid.

29. Price, 61. See also Bauer and Greyser, "Dialogue That Never Happens."

30. Jean-Jacques Lambin, "What Is the Real Impact of Advertising?" *Harvard Business Review* (May–June 1975), 139–48.

31. Julian Simon, *Issues in the Economics of Advertising* (Urbana: University of Illinois Press, 1970), 222–23.

32. Lambin, 142.

33. Harry Block, "Advertising and Profitability: A Reappraisal," *Journal of Political Economy* 82, no. 2, Part 1 (March/April 1974): 267–87.

34. Simon, *Economics of Advertising,* 196–97.

35. Harold Demsetz, "More on Collusion and Advertising: A Reply," *Journal of Law and Economics* 19, no. 1 (April 1976): 205–9.

36. Price, *Best Thing on TV,* 8.

37. Thorelli, Becker, and Engledow, *Information Seekers,* 226. For a related study, see Scott Ward, Daniel Wackman, and Ellen Wartella, *How Children Learn to Buy: The Development of Consumer Information-Processing Skills* (Beverly Hills: Sage, 1977).

38. Johan Arndt, "What's Wrong with Advertising Research," *Journal of Advertising Research* 16, no. 3 (June 1976): 9–21.

39. For a related argument, see Jurgen Habermas, *Legitimation Crisis* (Boston: Beacon Press, 1976), 48–49.

40. James C. Cary, "Advertising: An Institutional Approach," in C. H. Sandage and Vernon Fryburger, eds., *The Role of Advertising* (Homewood, Ill.: Richard D. Irwin, 1960), 3–16.

41. Marquez, "Advertising Content," 483 (see n. 11 above).

42. Bauer and Greyser, "Dialogue That Never Happens," 4 (see n. 13 above).

43. Marquez, "Advertising Content," 483.

44. See Ivan Preston, "Theories of Rationality and the Concept of Rationality in Advertising," *Journal of Communication* 17 (1967): 211–15; and Preston, *The Great American Blow-Up: Puffery in Advertising and Selling* (Madison: University of Wisconsin Press, 1979).

45. Henry, *Culture Against Man*, 46–47. For related arguments, see Henry K. Skolimowski, "The Semantic Environment in the Age of Advertising," in Raymond Liedlich, ed., *Coming to Terms with Language* (New York: Wiley, 1973), 25–35.

46. Preston, "Theories of Rationality," 213.

47. Ibid., 214.

48. See, for example, H. Martyn, "Symbolism and Advertising," *Frontier* (January 1967), 9–11.

49. Douglas and Isherwood, *World of Goods* (see n. 2 above).

50. Douglas and Isherwood; and see John Diggins, "Reification and the Cultural Hegemony of Capitalism," *Social Research* 44, no. 2 (1977): 354–83.

51. See, for example, Tom E. Sullenberger, "Ajax Meets the Jolly Green Giant: Some Observations on the Use of Folklore and Myth in American Mass Marketing," *Journal of American Folklore* 84 (January–March 1974): 53–66.

52. Mary Douglas, *Purity and Danger* (London: Routledge and Kegan Paul, 1966).

53. Mary Douglas, "Deciphering a Meal," *Daedalus* 101 (1972): 61–83.

54. For an important discussion of the cultural importance of territoriality as a basis of urban order, see Gerald M. Suttles, *The Social Construction of Communities* (Chicago: University of Chicago Press, 1972).

55. Victor Turner, *The Ritual Process* (London: Routledge and Kegan Paul, 1969).

56. Most advertisements, as of the early 1970s, continued to show blacks in lower statuses than whites, however. See J. David Colfax and Susan Steinberg, "The Perpetuation of Racial Stereotypes: Blacks in Mass Circulation Magazine Advertisements," *Public Opinion Quarterly* 36 (Spring 1972): 8–19.

57. Ewen, *Captains of Consciousness*, 154 (see n. 1 above).

58. Henry, *Culture Against Man*, 65.

59. Ibid.

60. James W. Tankard, Jr., "The Effects of Advertising on Language: Making the Sacred Profane," *Journal of Popular Culture* 9, no. 2 (Fall 1975): 325–31.

61. Mary Douglas, *Natural Symbols* (New York: Vintage, 1973).

62. Martyn, "Symbolism and Advertising" (see n. 48 above).

63. Sullenberger, "Ajax Meets the Jolly Green Giant," 54.

64. Ibid.

65. Skolimowski, "Age of Advertising" (see n. 45 above); and F. R. Leavis and Denys Thompson, *Culture and Environment: The Training of Critical Awareness* (London: Chatto and Windus, 1950), 26.

66. *Culture and Environment*, 26.

67. Ibid.

68. *Culture and Environment*, 53.

69. Varda Langholz Leymore, *Hidden Myth: Structure and Symbolism in Advertising* (New York: Basic Books, 1975), 135.

70. Leymore, 154.

71. Leymore, 104ff.

72. Leymore, 84.

73. Leymore, 50.

74. Colfax and Steinberg, "Perpetuation of Racial Stereotypes" (see n. 56 above); Ward, Wackman, and Wartella, *How Children Learn to Buy*, 64 (see n. 37 above); V. Kanti Prasad, T. R. Rao, and Andes A. Sheikh, "Mothers vs. Commercial," *Journal of Communication* 28, no. 1 (Winter 1978): 91–97; Alan Remik and Bruce L. Stern, "Children's Television Advertising and Brand Choice: A Laboratory Experiment," *Journal of Adver-*

tising 6, no. 3 (1977): 11 – 18; Thomas S. Robertson and John R. Rossiter, "Children's Responsiveness to Commercials," *Journal of Communication* 27, no. 1 (Winter 1977): 101 – 7.

75. Douglas and Isherwood, *World of Goods* (see n. 2 above).

76. Leavis and Thompson, *Culture and Environment,* 49 – 50.

77. I have previously placed this argument within the context of the family's effect on political socialization. See Richard M. Merelman, "The Family and Political Socialization: Toward a Theory of Exchange," *Journal of Politics* 42 (June 1980): 461 – 86.

78. Merle Curti, "The Changing Concept of 'Human Nature' in the Literature of American Advertising," *Business History Review* 41, no. 4 (Winter 1967): 335 – 58. For a related study with similar conclusions, see William Stephenson, "The 'Infantile' vs. the 'Sublime' in Advertisements," *Journalism Quarterly* 40, no. 2 (Spring 1963): 181 – 86.

79. Thus, it is possible to have at one and the same time popular psychological tracts advocating individual self-assertion and "winning" over others, on the one hand, and a "laid-back" relaxed emotionalism, on the other.

80. For a book which treats images of personal and public order with special attention to the dramaturgy of dress and images, see Richard Sennett, *The Fall of Public Man* (New York: Vintage, 1978), esp. chap. 8.

81. For an excursus on this dialectic, see Marshall Sahlins, *Culture and Practical Reason* (Chicago: University of Chicago Press, 1976), pp. 190 – 1.

82. See Arlen, *Thirty Seconds* (n. 15 above).

CHAPTER FIVE

1. Herbert Krugman, "The Impact of Televised Advertising," *Public Opinion Quarterly* 29 (1965), 349 – 65.

2. See John Meyer, "The Effects of Education as an Institution," *American Journal of Sociology* (July 1977), 54 – 76.

3. Christopher Jencks et al., *Inequality* (New York: Basic Books, 1972), 256 – 57.

4. For an attack on this position, see Thomas S. Popkiewitz, "Myth of Social Science in Curriculum," *Educational Forum* 40, no. 3 (March 1976): 317 – 29.

5. For a relevant study, see Michael B. Katz, *Class, Bureaucracy, and Schools* (New York: Praeger, 1971), chap. 1.

6. Edward Morgan, *Inequality in Classroom Learning: Schooling and Democratic Citizenship* (New York: Praeger, 1977), 105.

7. George Bereday, "Social Stratification and Education in Industrial Countries," *Comparative Education Review* 21, no. 2 – 3 (June – October 1977): 195 – 211.

8. Ted Tapper and Brian Salter, *Education and the Political Order* (London: Macmillan, 1978), 29.

9. Martin Carnoy, *Education as Cultural Imperialism* (New York: David McKay, 1974); Samuel Bowles and Herbert Gintis, *Schooling in Capitalist America* (New York: Basic Books, 1976).

10. Carnoy, 5.

11. Raymond Callahan, *Education and the Cult of Efficiency* (Chicago: University of Chicago Press, 1962).

12. Maurice Levitas, *Marxist Perspectives in the Sociology of Education* (London: Routledge and Kegan Paul, 1974), 55.

13. David Cohen and Marvin Lazerson, "Education and the Corporate Order," in Jerome Karabel and A. H. Halsey, eds., *Power and Ideology in American Education* (New York: Oxford University Press, 1977), 373 – 86.

14. Frederick Wirt and Michael Kirst, *The Political Web of American Schools* (Berkeley, Calif.: McCutchan, 1972), 79.

15. Ibid.

16. For a useful framework through which to view this issue, see Randall Collins, "Functional and Conflict Theories of Educational Stratification," *American Sociological Review* 36, no. 6 (December 1971): 1002 – 19.

17. Pierre Bourdieu, "Cultural Reproduction and Social Reproduction," in Karabel and Halsey, *Power and Ideology in American Education,* 487 – 511.

18. Pierre Bourdieu, "Systems of Education and Systems of Thought," in Michael F. D. Young, ed., *Knowledge and Control* (London: Collier-Macmillan, 1971), 189 – 208.

19. Basil Bernstein, "On the Classification and Framing of Educational Knowledge," in B. Bernstein, *Class, Codes, and Control,* vol.1 (London: Routledge and Kegan Paul, 1971), 202 – 31.

20. Barry J. Wilson and Donald W. Schmits, "What's New in Ability Grouping," *Phi Delta Kappan* 57 (1978): 535 – 36.

21. J. D. McAulay, "An Evaluation of 120 Recent Elementary School Social Studies Programs," *Educational Horizons* 53 (1975): 171 – 76.

22. Morgan, *Inequality in Classroom Learning,* 72 – 80.

23. Mary Metz, *Classrooms and Corridors: The Crisis of Authority in Desegregated Secondary Schools* (Berkeley: University of California Press, 1978).

24. For a study that suggests how useful disciplined inquiry might be to the learning of political tolerance, see H. Dean Nielsen, *Tolerating Political Dissent* (Stockholm: Almquist and Wiksell International, 1977), 70.

25. Mary Metz, *Classrooms and Corridors,* 243.

26. Nell Keddie, "Classroom Knowledge," in Young, *Knowledge and Control,* 133 – 61.

27. Edgar Friedenberg, *Coming of Age in America: Growth and Acquiescence* (New York: Vintage, 1963).

28. Bowles and Gintis, *Schooling in Capitalist America,* 53 – 125.

29. Philip Jackson, *Life in Classrooms* (Chicago: University of Chicago Press, 1968), chap. 1.

30. For a good restatement, see Michael Apple, "Ideology Reproduction and Educational Reform," *Comparative Education Review* (1978), 367 – 88.

31. Metz, *Classrooms and Corridors,* 57, 125 – 33.

32. Keddie, "Classroom Knowledge."

33. Estelle Fuchs, "How Teachers Learn to Help Children Fail," in Nell Keddie, ed., *Tinker, Tailor . . . The Myth of Cultural Deprivation* (New York: Penguin, 1973), 75 – 86.

34. Aaron Cicourel et al., *Language Use and School Performance* (New York: Academic Press, 1974), 58.

35. Jencks et al., *Inequality,* 181; Christopher Jencks et al., *Who Gets Ahead? The Determinants of Economic Success in America* (New York: Basic Books, 1979), 169.

36. See Samuel H. Barnes et al., *Political Action* (Beverly Hills: Sage, 1979), chaps. 11 – 12.

37. James Coleman, *The Adolescent Society* (Glencoe, Ill.: Free Press, 1961), chaps. 2 – 5 and 10.

38. W. D. Runciman, *Relative Deprivation and Social Justice* (Berkeley: University of California Press, 1966).

39. See Jencks et al., *Inequality,* chap. 6.

40. See also Robert Hauser and David Featherman, *The Process of Stratification* (New York: Academic Press, 1977).

41. Richard Flacks, "The Liberated Generation," *Journal of Social Issues* 23 (1967), no. 1, 52 – 75.

42. Morgan, *Inequality in Classroom Learning,* 96.

43. Paul Willis, *Learning to Labour* (Fansborough, Eng.: Saxon House, 1977).

44. Diane Ravitch, *The Revisionists Revised: A Critique of the Radical Attack on the Schools* (New York: Basic Books, 1978), 41 – 42.

45. See, for example, J. Arch Phillips, Jr., and Richard Hawthorne, "Political Dimensions of Curriculum Decision Making," *Educational Leadership* 35 (1978): 362 – 67; and William Lowe Boyd, "The Changing Politics of Curriculum Policy-Making for American Schools," *Review of Educational Research* 48 (1978): 577 – 628.

46. Paul Peterson, *School Politics: Chicago-Style* (Chicago: University of Chicago Press, 1976).

47. L. Harmon Zeigler and M. Kent Jennings, *Governing American Schools* (North Scituate, Mass.: Duxbury Press, 1974), 4 ff.

48. For a relevant study, see Dean Jaros, "Transmitting the Political Culture: The Teacher and Political Socialization," *Social Science Quarterly* 49 (1968): 284 – 95.

49. Shirley Werdin, "Screening for Teaching," *Improving College and University Teaching* 20 (1972): 124.

50. Study Commission on Undergraduate Education and the Education of Teachers, *Teacher Education in the United States: The Responsibility Gap* (Lincoln: University of Nebraska Press, 1976), 48.

51. Robert Rosenthal and Lenore Jacobson, *Pygmalion in the Classroom* (New York: Holt, Rinehart and Winston, 1968).

52. Metz, *Classrooms and Corridors*, pp. 36 – 38.

53. Dan Lortie, *Schoolteacher* (Chicago: University of Chicago Press, 1975), chap. 6.

54. N. L. Gage, "Theories of Teaching," in Ernest R. Hilgard, ed., *Theories of Learning and Instruction*, 63rd Yearbook of the National Society for the Study of Education, Part 1 (Chicago: University of Chicago Press, 1964), 268 – 86.

55. Jaros, "Transmitting the Political Culture."

56. For an interesting comparative study, see Zev Klein and Yohanan Eshel, "The Open Classroom in Cross-Cultural Perspective: A Research Note," *Sociology of Education* 53 (1980), 114 – 21.

57. Jaros, "Transmitting the Political Culture."

58. Philip A. Cusick, *Inside High School: The Student's World* (New York: Holt, Rinehart and Winston, 1973), 214.

59. Eugene Genovese, *Roll Jordan Roll* (New York: Pantheon, 1973), 285 – 325.

60. Willis, *Learning to Labour* (see n. 43 above).

61. See n. 37 above.

62. See *Phi Delta Kappan*, special issue on "The Problems of Discipline and Violence in American Education," vol. 59 (January 1978).

63. Michael Apple and Nancy R. King, "What Do Schools Teach?" in Alex Molnar and John Zahorik, eds., *Curriculum Theory* (Washington: Association for Supervision and Curriculum Development, 1977).

64. See, for example, Ravitch's argument about the movement toward expansion of education for blacks, in Ravitch, *The Revisionists Revised*, 63 – 64.

65. Robert Dreeben, "The Contribution of Schooling to the Learning of Norms," in Karabel and Halsey, *Power and Ideology*, 544 – 49 (see n. 13 above).

66. Metz, *Classrooms and Corridors*, 73 – 74.

67. Zeigler and Jennings, *Governing American Schools* (see n. 47 above).

68. Paul Peterson, "Politics of Educational Reform in England and the United States," *Comparative Education Review* 17, no. 2 (June 1973): 160 – 80.

69. Michael P. Smith, "Elite Theory and Policy Analysis: The Politics of Education in Suburbia," *Journal of Politics* 36 (November 1974): 1006 – 33; Norman Kerr, "The School Board as an Agency of Legitimation," *Sociology of Education* 38, no. 1 (Fall 1964): 34 – 58; Zeigler and Jennings, *Governing American Schools*.

70. Wirt and Kirst, *Political Web of American Schools* (see n. 14 above); Zeigler and Jennings also discover that where class conflicts are permitted to express themselves electorally, they do impinge on school board politics.

71. On these historical matters, see R. Freeman Butts, "Public Education and Political Community," *History of Education Quarterly* 14, no. 2; 165 – 85; and David W.

Swift, *Ideology and Change in Public Schools: Latent Functions of Progressive Education* (Columbus, Ohio: Merrill, 1971).

72. Metz, *Classrooms and Corridors*, 249.

73. For an exchange on this point, see M. Kent Jennings, "Comment on Richard Merelman's 'Democratic Politics and the Culture of American Education,' " *American Political Science Review* 74 (1980): 333–37, and this author's response, 338–41.

74. Wilson and Schmits, "What's New in Ability Grouping" (see n. 20 above).

75. For a contrast in the area of mathematics teaching, see Ernest Rakow, Peter Airasian, and George Madaus, "Assessing School and Program Effectiveness: Estimating Teacher Level Effects," *Journal of Educational Measurement* 14, no. 1 (Spring 1978): 15–21.

76. Donald Oliver, *Education and Community* (Berkeley, Calif.: Glendessary Press, 1976); Seymour Sarason, *The Culture of the School and the Problem of Change* (Boston: Little, Brown, 1969).

77. Bernice Fisher, "The Reconstruction of Failure: Ideologies of Educational Failure in their Relation to Social Mobility and Social Control," *Social Problems* 19 (1971–72): 322–36.

78. "Contemporary Tests in Basic Skills Cost Few Pupils Their Diplomas," *New York Times*, March 26, 1979.

79. Werdin, "Screening for Teaching" (see n. 49 above).

80. See n. 50 above.

81. Lortie, *Schoolteacher*, 111–13 (see n. 53 above).

82. Stanley Mour, "Do Teachers Read?" *The Reading Teacher* 30 (1977): 397–401.

83. U.S. Office of Education, *The Education Professions: A Report on the People Who Serve Our Schools and Colleges* (Washington, D.C.: U.S. Department of Health, Education, and Welfare, 1969), 41.

84. William Perry, *Forms of Intellectual and Ethical Development in the College Years* (Cambridge, Mass: Harvard University Press, 1968).

85. Klein and Eshel, "The Open Classroom" (see n. 56 above).

86. Frances Fitzgerald, *America Revised: History Schoolbooks in the Twentieth Century* (Boston: Little, Brown, 1979), 73–145.

87. For a description, see William Schonfeld, *Obedience and Revolt: French Behavior Toward Authority* (Beverly Hills: Sage, 1976).

88. This pattern appears particularly strong with regard to educational innovation. See Robert Agger and Marshall N. Goldstein, *Who Will Rule the Schools: A Cultural Class Crisis* (Belmont, Calif.: Wadsworth, 1971).

89. George Male, *The Struggle for Power* (Beverly Hills: Sage, 1974), 167.

90. Oliver, *Education and Community.*

91. Meyer, "The Effects of Education" (see n. 2 above).

92. Rhoda Metraux, "Implicit and Explicit Values in Education and Teaching as Related to Growth and Development," in George D. Spindler, ed., *Education and Culture: Anthropological Approaches* (New York: Holt, Rinehart and Winston, 1963), 121–32.

93. Metz, *Classrooms and Corridors*, 125–26, 244–45.

94. Schonfeld, *Obedience and Revolt*, 25.

95. For a related set of arguments, see Harold Entwistle, *Political Education in a Democracy* (London: Routledge and Kegan Paul, 1971).

96. James P. Shaver, "A Critical View of the Social Studies Profession," *Social Education* 41 (1977): 300–307.

97. Mary Jackman, "General and Applied Tolerance: Does Education Increase Commitment to Racial Integration?" *American Journal of Political Science* 22 (1978): 303–25; for a strong critique, however, see Michael Corbett, "Education and Political Tolerance: Group-Relatedness and Consistency Reconsidered," *American Politics Quarterly* 8 (1980): 345–60.

98. Friedenberg, *Coming of Age in America*, chap. 8 (see n. 27 above).

99. See Arthur Okun, *Equality and Efficiency: The Big Tradeoff* (Washington, D.C.: Brookings, 1975).

100. See Harvard Educational Review, *Equal Educational Opportunity* (Cambridge: Harvard University Press, 1969).

101. For a recent study in the context of public opinion, see W. Lance Bennett, *Public Opinion in American Politics* (New York: Harcourt, Brace, Jovanovitch, 1980).

CHAPTER SIX

1. For an excellent treatment of these images, see James Oliver Robertson, *American Myth, American Reality* (New York: Hill and Wang, 1980), Part 2.

2. Emile Durkheim, *Professional Ethics and Civic Morals*, trans. Cornelia Brookfield (London: Routledge and Kegan Paul, 1957), 92.

3. The definitive treatment is Louis Hartz, *The Liberal Tradition in America* (New York: Harcourt, Brace and World, 1955).

4. For a consideration of an influential set of views about the problem of a connection between government and culture in America, see Peter Steinfels, *The Neoconservatives* (New York: Simon and Schuster, 1979).

5. For a rather different approach to curricula, with special emphasis on its reformist qualities, see Jon Schaffarzick, "Federal Curriculum Reform: A Crucible for Value Conflict," in Jon Schaffarzick and Gary Sykes, eds., *Value Conflicts and Curriculum Issues* (Berkeley: McCutchan, 1979), 1 – 25.

6. William Lowe Boyd, "The Changing Politics of Curriculum Policy-Making for American Schools," *Review of Educational Research* 48, no. 4 (Fall 1978): 577 – 628.

7. For a discussion of the myriad national legal regulations surrounding curricular decisions, see Tyll van Geel, "The New Law of the Curriculum," in Schaffarzick and Sykes, *Value Conflicts*, 25 – 73.

8. Karl Weick, "Educational Organizations as Loosely Coupled Systems," *Administrative Science Quarterly*, March 1976, 1 – 19.

9. Herbert W. Voege, "The Diffusion of Keynesian Macroeconomics through American High School Textbooks, 1936 – 70," in William A. Reid and Decker F. Walker, eds., *Case Studies in Curriculum Change* (London: Routledge and Kegan Paul, 1975), 208 – 40.

10. Larry Cuban, "Determinants of Curriculum Change and Stability, 1870 – 1970," in Schaffarzick and Sykes, *Value Conflicts*, 139 – 97.

11. National Science Foundation, *Curriculum Development and Implementation for Pre-College Science Education*. Report Prepared for the Committee on Science and Technology, U.S. House of Representatives, 94th Congress, First Session (Washington, D.C.: U.S. Government Printing Office, 1975), 231.

12. NSF, *Curriculum Development*, 229 – 30.

13. Peter Dow, "Innovation's Perils: An Account of the Origins, Development, Implementation, and Public Reactions to 'Man: A Course of Study' " (Ph.D. dissertation, Harvard University School of Education, 1979), chap. 1.

14. Dow, "Innovation's Perils," 82, 108.

15. Dow, "Innovation's Perils," chap. 2.

16. See, for example, Peter B. Dow, "Man: A Course of Study: A Continuing Exploration of Man's Humanness," in *Man: A Course of Study: Talks to Teachers* (Cambridge, Mass.: Education Development Center, 1970), 3 – 17.

17. Dow, "Innovation's Perils," 132, 155.

18. Dow, "Innovation's Perils," 176.

19. Jerome Bruner, *The Process of Education* (Cambridge: Belnap Press, 1960), 33.

20. Dow, "Innovation's Perils," 80.

21. Richard M. Jones, *Fantasy and Feeling in Education* (New York: New York University Press, 1968), 97.

22. *Fantasy and Feeling,* 27.

23. Dow, "Innovation's Perils," 122.

24. George Weber, "The Case against *Man: A Course of Study,*" *Phi Delta Kappan* 57, no. 2 (October 1975): 82–83.

25. Dow, "Innovation's Perils," 227 ff.

26. Dorothy Nelkin, "The Science-Textbook Controversies," *Scientific American* 234, no. 4 (April 1976): 33–39.

27. Nelkin, 34.

28. Ibid.

29. Peter Dow, "The Case for *Man: A Course of Study,*" *Phi Delta Kappan* 57, no. 2 (October 1975): 79–81.

30. Ibid.

31. Dow, "Innovation's Perils," 257.

32. "NSF: Congress Takes Hard Look at Behavioral Science Course," *Science* (May 2, 1975), 426.

33. *Congressional Record*, House of Representatives, April 9, 1975 (hereafter *Cong. Rec.*), 9506.

34. *Cong. Rec.,* 9498.

35. Dow, "Innovation's Perils," chap. 1.

36. Nelkin, "Science-Textbook Controversies," 35.

37. *Cong. Rec.,* 9497.

38. Nelkin, "Science-Textbook Controversies," 37.

39. *Report of the Science Curriculum Implementation Review Group to the Chairman, Committee on Science and Technology, U.S. House of Representatives,* October 1, 1975 (Washington: U.S. Government Printing Office, 1975), 9–10.

40. *Pre-College Science Curriculum Activities of the National Science Foundation. Report of the Science Curriculum Review Team.* May 1975. vol. 1 (Washington: U.S. Government Printing Office, 1975), vi.

41. Ibid.

42. *Cong. Rec.,* 9498.

43. Weber, "Case against MACOS," 82 (see n. 24 above).

44. *Cong. Rec.,* 9500.

45. "NSF: How Much Responsibility for Course Content, Implementation," *Science* (November 14, 1975), 646.

46. Herbert M. Kliebard, "Systematic Curriculum Development, 1890–1959," in Schaffarzick and Sykes, *Value Conflicts,* 197–237 (see n. 5 above).

47. *Cong. Rec.,* 9505.

48. *Cong. Rec.,* 9501.

49. William Lowe Boyd, "The Politics of Curriculum Change and Stability," *Educational Researcher* 8, no. 2 (February 1979): 12–19.

50. Weber, "Case against MACOS," 82.

51. For a review, see Leo Bogart, "Warning: The Surgeon General Has Determined that TV Violence Is Moderately Dangerous to Your Child's Mental Health," *Public Opinion Quarterly* 26, no. 4 (Winter 1972–1973): 491–522.

52. House of Representatives Report No. 1139, 93rd Congress, 2nd Sess. 15, 1974.

53. The process is described in Writers Guild of America, West, Inc., v. FCC, 432 F. Supp. 1064 (1976).

54. Thomas Meehan, "The Children's Hour after Hour," *New York Times Magazine* (August 10, 1975), 4.

55. *Congressional Quarterly* (May 5, 1977), 409.

56. *Hearings Before the Subcommittee on Communications of the Committee on Interstate and Foreign Commerce.* House of Representatives, 94th Congress, 2nd Session, on *The Issue of Televised Violence and Obscenity.* Ser. No. 94 – 140 (Washington: U.S. Government Printing Office, 1977), 93.

57. Writers Guild of America, West, Inc., v. FCC, 432 F. Supp. 1064 (1976), 1072.

58. Writers Guild v. FCC, 1106.

59. See, for example, *Hearings*, 40 – 41.

60. Writers Guild v. FCC, 1073.

61. *Hearings*, 83.

62. *Broadcasting Magazine*, August 8, 1977.

63. *Hearings*, 38.

64. *Hearings*, 140.

65. Michael Margolis, *Viable Democracy* (New York: Penguin, 1979), 44.

66. For a case study in uneasiness and uncertainty, see Frances Fitzgerald, "A Reporter at Large (the Reverend Jerry Falwell)," *New Yorker* (May 18, 1981), 53 – 142.

67. Barry Holden, *The Nature of Democracy* (London: Nelson, 1974), 37.

68. For a particularly extreme version of this theory, see Michel Crozier, Samuel P. Huntington, and Joji Watanuki, *The Crisis of Democracy* (New York: Trilateral Commission, 1975), 59 – 119.

69. Vivien Hart, *Distrust and Democracy* (Cambridge: Cambridge University Press, 1978), 186.

70. See, for example, Sidney Verba, Norman Nie, and Jae-On Kim, *Participation and Political Equality* (Cambridge: Cambridge University Press, 1978).

71. Hart, *Distrust and Democracy*, chap. 5.

72. Jack Lively, *Democracy* (Oxford: Basil Blackwell, 1975), chap. 2.

73. Arend Lijphart, *Democracy in Plural Societies* (New Haven: Yale University Press, 1977).

Index

Designer:	Lisa Mirski
Compositor:	Innovative Media, Inc.
Printer:	Vail-Ballou
Binder:	Vail-Ballou
Text:	11/13 Baskerville
Display:	Baskerville